THE
BORZOI
COLLEGE READER

SHORTER EDITION

THE
BORZOI
COLLEGE READER

Edited by

CHARLES MUSCATINE

University of California, Berkeley

and

MARLENE GRIFFITH

Laney College

SHORTER EDITION

Alfred · A · Knopf : New York

Shorter Edition, 1968
Second Printing
© Copyright, 1966, by Charles Muscatine and Marlene Griffith
All rights reserved under International and Pan-American
Copyright Conventions. Distributed by Random House,
Inc. Published simultaneously in Toronto, Canada, by
Random House of Canada Limited.

Library of Congress Catalog Card Number: 68-20893
Manufactured in the United States of America.

ACKNOWLEDGMENTS

From "Party of One—Thinking as a Hobby" by William Golding, first published in *Holiday* © 1961 The Curtis Publishing Company. Reprinted by permission of the author.

"On Various Kinds of Thinking" from *The Mind in the Making* by James H. Robinson. Copyright 1921 by Harper & Brothers; renewed 1949 by Bankers Trust Company. Reprinted by permission of Harper & Row, Publishers.

"Propaganda Under a Dictatorship" from *Brave New World Revisited* by Aldous Huxley. Copyright © 1958 by Aldous Huxley. Reprinted by permission of Harper & Row, Publishers, Chatto and Windus Ltd., and Mrs. Laura Huxley.

"The Disadvantages of Being Educated" from *Free Speech and Plain Language* by Albert Jay Nock. Copyright 1937 by Albert Jay Nock. By permission of William Morrow and Company, Inc.

"since feeling is first" from *Poems 1923-1954* by e. e. cummings. Copyright 1926 by Horace Liveright; copyright 1954 by e. e. cummings. By permission of Harcourt, Brace & World, Inc.

"The Lord of Creation" by Susanne K. Langer from *Fortune* (January, 1944), 127-128, 130, 132, 134, 136, 139-140, 142, 144, 146, 148, 150, 152, 154. Reprinted by permission.

"Politics and the English Language" from *Shooting an Elephant and Other Essays* by George Orwell. Copyright 1945, 1946, 1949, 1950 by Sonia Brownell Orwell. Reprinted by permission of Harcourt, Brace & World, Inc., and Martin Secker & Warburg Ltd.

"Ultimate Terms in Contemporary Rhetoric" from Chapter 9 of *The Ethics of Rhetoric* by Richard M. Weaver. Copyright 1953 by Henry Regnery Company. Reprinted by permission.

"The Arts of Selling" from *Brave New World Revisited* by Aldous Huxley. Copyright © 1958 by Aldous Huxley. Reprinted by permission of Harper & Row, Publishers, Chatto and Windus Ltd., and Mrs. Laura Huxley.

"The Most Cheerful Graveyard in the World" by Paul Jacobs from *The Reporter* (September 18, 1958), 26-30. Copyright 1958 by The Reporter Magazine Company. Reprinted by permission.

"In Favor of Capital Punishment" by Jacques Barzun from *The American Scholar* (Spring, 1962). Copyright © 1962 by the United Chapters of Phi Beta Kappa. By permission of the publishers.

"The Penalty of Death" from *A Mencken Chrestomathy* by H. L. Mencken. Copyright 1926 by Alfred A. Knopf, Inc.; renewed 1954 by H. L. Mencken. Reprinted by permission of the publisher.

"A Hanging" from *Shooting an Elephant and Other Essays* by George Orwell. Copyright 1945, 1946, 1949, 1950 by Sonia Brownell Orwell. Reprinted by permission of Harcourt, Brace & World, Inc., and Martin Secker & Warburg Ltd.

From "Reflections on the Guillotine" by Albert Camus from *Resistance, Rebellion, and Death* trans. Justin O'Brien. Copyright © 1960 by Alfred A. Knopf, Inc. By permission of the publisher.

[The Committee of 100] by Bertrand Russell from *A Matter of Life* ed. Clara Urquhart. Copyright © 1963 by Clara Urquhart Reprinted by permission of Jonathan Cape Ltd.

"Public Statement of Eight Alabama Clergymen" issued April 12, 1963, Pamphlet No. 589A of the American Friends Service Committee. Reprinted by permission of the Protestant Episcopal Church in the Diocese of Alabama, a corporation.

"Letter from Birmingham Jail" from *Why We Can't Wait* by Martin Luther King, Jr. Copyright © 1963 by Martin Luther King, Jr. Reprinted by permission of Harper & Row, Publishers.

"Authority and the Role of Coercion" from *Catholic Viewpoint on Censorship* by Harold C. Gardiner. Copyright © 1958, 1961 by Doubleday & Company, Inc. Reprinted by permission of the publisher.

"The Nature of the Battle Over Censorship" from *Men of Destiny* by Walter Lippmann. Copyright 1927 by The Macmillan Company; renewed 1955 by Walter Lippmann. By permission of the publisher.

"Defense of the Freedom to Read" by Henry Miller from *The Henry Miller Reader* ed. Lawrence Durrell. © 1959 by Henry Miller. Reprinted by permission of the author and New Directions Publishing Company.

"U.S.A. v. One Book *Ulysses*" by John M. Woolsey. Reprinted from James Joyce's *Ulysses*. By permission of Random House, Inc.

From "Racism—The *ism* of the Modern World" by Ruth Benedict from Chapter I of *Race: Science and Politics*, The Viking Press, Inc., and Chapter I of *Race and Racism*, Routledge & Kegan Paul Ltd. Copyright 1940 by Ruth Benedict. Reprinted by permission of the publishers.

"The Respective Characteristics of the Three Great Races" by Joseph Arthur, Comte de Gobineau from Chapter 16 of *The Inequality of Human Races* trans. Adrian Collins. Reprinted by permisison of G. P. Putnam's Sons.

From "Nation and Race" by Adolf Hitler from Vol. I, Chapter 11 of *Mein Kampf* trans. Ralph Manheim. Copyright 1943 by Houghton Mifflin Company. Reprinted by permission.

"Genetics of Race Equality" by Theodosius Dobzhansky from *Eugenics Quarterly* (December, 1963), 151–160. Reprinted by permission.

"Marrakech" from *Such, Such Were the Joys* by George Orwell. Copyright 1945, 1952, 1953 by Sonia Brownell Orwell. Reprinted by permission of Harcourt, Brace & World, Inc., and Martin Secker & Warburg Ltd.

"The Case for the White Southerner" by Perry Morgan from *Esquire* (January, 1962), 41, 43, 45, 134. © 1961 by Esquire, Inc. Reprinted by permission of Esquire, Inc.

"Letter to the North" by William Faulkner. © Copyright 1956 by William Faulkner. Reprinted from *Essays, Speeches & Public Letters* by William Faulkner, ed. James B. Meriwether. By permission of Random House, Inc.

"Faulkner and Desegregation" from *Nobody Knows My Name* by James Baldwin. Copyright © 1954, 1956, 1958, 1960, 1961 by James Baldwin. Reprinted by permission of The Dial Press, Inc.

"My Negro Problem—and Ours" from *Doings and Undoings* by Norman Podhoretz. Copyright © 1963 by Norman Podhoretz. Reprinted by permission of Farrar, Straus & Giroux, Inc.

[The Grand Academy of Lagado] from Part 3 entitled "A Voyage to Laputa, Balnibarbi, Luggnagg, Glubbdubdrib, and Japan" by Jonathan Swift from *Gulliver's Travels* ed. Herbert Davis, Oxford, Basil Blackwell, 1959. Reprinted by permission.

"The Culture of Machine Living" from *America as a Civilization* by Max Lerner. Copyright © 1957 by Max Lerner. Reprinted by permission of Simon and Schuster, Inc.

"Technical Progress Is Always Ambiguous" by Jacques Ellul from *Technology and Culture* (Fall, 1962), trans. John Wilkinson, The Society for the History of Technology. Reprinted by permission of The University of Chicago Press.

"Sawdust, Seaweed, and Synthetics" by Edgar Ansel Mowrer from *Saturday Review* (December 8, 1956), 11–13, 54–56. Reprinted by permission.

"The Morning of the Day They Did It" (February 25, 1950) from *The Second Tree from the Corner* by E. B. White. Copyright 1950 by E. B. White. Originally appeared in *The New Yorker*, and reprinted by permission of Harper & Row, Publishers.

"The Cultural Importance of Art" from *Philosophical Sketches* by Susanne K. Langer, Baltimore, The Johns Hopkins Press, 1962. Reprinted by permission.

"Notes of a Painter" by Henri-Matisse from *Matisse: His Art and His Public* by Alfred H. Barr, Jr. Copyright 1951 by The Museum of Modern Art, New York. Reprinted with its permission. "Notes d'un peintre" was originally published in *La Grande Revue*, Paris, December 25, 1908. The first complete English translation by Margaret Scolari Barr was published in *Henri-Matisse*, The Museum of Modern Art, 1931, and then again in *Matisse: His Art and His Public*, together with paragraph headings which were added by the author for the convenience of the reader.

"The Function of Art" by Ernst Fischer from *The Necessity of Art* trans. Anna Bostock, London, Penguin Books Ltd., 1963. Reprinted by permission.

"Wanted: An American Novel" editorial from *Life* (September 12, 1955). Reprinted by permission.

[What Can the Artist Do in the World of Today?] from "The Artist and His Time" by Albert Camus from *The Myth of Sisyphus and Other Essays* trans. Justin O'Brien. Copyright © 1955 by Alfred A. Knopf, Inc. By permission of the publisher.

"Why I Write" from *Such, Such Were the Joys* by George Orwell. Copyright 1945, 1952, 1953 by Sonia Brownell Orwell. Reprinted by permission of Harcourt, Brace & World, Inc., and Martin Secker & Warburg Ltd.

WE WISH to thank the many colleagues and friends who have given us their advice during the preparation of this book, especially Mary Arnold, Margaret Barrier, Irving Berg, Robert Bloom, Gaylord Chambers II, Ann Connor, Bernard L. Diamond, David Dushkin, Laurence Hartmann, T. J. Kent, Jr., I. Michael Lerner, Allan Metcalf, Henry Morgan, and J. William Ward. We are grateful, too, to Sondra Shair and Martha Platt for bibliographical assistance; to Arlyn Diamond, Susan Scarff Webster, and Estelle Fine for help with the manuscript; and most of all to Joan Glassel, whose support has at every step made the improbable seem possible.

C. M.
M. G.

Berkeley, California
1967

CONTENTS

Contents

INTRODUCTION

The generous response to *The Borzoi College Reader* has encouraged us to prepare the present volume for those whose purposes would be better served by a shorter book. We present here about half of the original text and, we hope, most of the original design: to teach the art of critical thinking.

We agree with Aldous Huxley that the survival of our democratic civilization depends on the effort of all concerned to impart rationality, and we can think of no better means to this end than honest reading and honest writing and no better time and place than a beginning college course. Using "critical" and "honest" as synonyms, we wish also to suggest that there is deep personal value in the kind of reading or writing which tests the idea and leads to discovery or confirmation of what we mean or believe. Critical thinking, reading, and writing are closely interwoven, but all three depend on a sensibility and a mind which are active, not passive. Although each individual will pick up the thread to his own self at a different place, all three can and ultimately do lead him back to a discovery of what he really is and lead him forward to a discovery of what he really wants, both personally and socially. As Emerson suggests, Man Thinking is also Man Being.

Because we believe that critical reading and writing are best taught in an atmosphere of live ideas, we have chosen our reading material from what we consider important areas of intellectual, social, and moral concern, topical, but not soon to become dated. The book gives the reader plenty of choice, plenty of variety, and, of course, the option to read in whatever order he may find most stimulating. But our focus is on expository prose, the prose of thought, and our arrangement is by subject matter rather than by rhetorical genre or device.

We have done much of our own teaching in a course whose readings are supposed to help the student "to follow critically the argument of a text, to perceive its structure, and to appreciate its style," and we teach that argument, structure, and style work together. But in both reading and composition we prefer to *begin* with argument, with the main idea, and to consider how structure and style help to express or support it. We believe that the expository essay that makes a point is the heart and soul of the course in composition, and we feel that the other rhetorical categories—

description, narration, definition, comparison, and the like—had best be taught as adjuncts to the presentation of a well-buttressed main idea.

The book is organized in eight sections by topic. From among many respectable topics we have tried to choose some on which meaningful current debate is possible. We have, thus, been able to collect under each topic pieces representing a variety of arguments, often in direct conflict with each other. The reading presents, then, a wide range of subjects, ideas, and assumptions, and at the same time a continuous dialogue or debate among them. We hope that presenting ideas in the form of issues will help the reader to see that he has something to think about. Suggesting comparison at every point, giving ready occasion to take sides and to criticize, the material is directly suited to generating discussion and writing.

Before each section we have placed an introduction, briefly indicating the main issues raised by the pieces in the section. The sections differ from each other in organization, depending on the nature of the issue and on the availability of writings. In our first two sections, on "The Necessity for Thinking" and "The Right Use of Language," we have not labored to find a compensating number of spokesmen for bad thinking and dishonest use of language, feeling that the reader's own observation will provide material aplenty. Under "Technology and Human Values" we have not supplied an essay that praises technology uncritically. The reader cannot help but know that attitude already. All other sections, however, contain overt debate within themselves, and some of the individual essays address themselves specifically to others in the collection.

While the essays have thus been arranged for the play of their ideas, most of them have also been chosen as rhetorical models, with an eye to their usefulness as guides to the reader's own writing. We have included a few selections from classical sources and some translations of more modern continental authors. But most of the selections are original English essays, both traditional and modern, in a great range of styles and techniques. Of these, all but two or three are either complete works in themselves or are coherent, unabridged sections (usually chapters) of longer works and can be studied as compositional wholes. We have not followed the common practice of making silent changes and omissions, preferring to present the essays as they were written, with the occasional peculiarities and defects of their time and place. In this spirit, we preface each selection with a headnote on its author and with facts on its original publication.

We hope that this small insistence on realism will help the reader to feel the excitement of genuine moral commitment that many of the essays transmit. Good writing, we mean to suggest, comes from a person who not only commands some verbal skill but has something he wants to say. Our ideal essay is a rational statement—propelled by conviction. We agree with Brock Brower: "It is so easy to quote, generalize, qualify, extrapolate *neutrally* around a subject—*Let the reader draw his own conclusions—*

instead of facing it directly as something that must be plumbed by a drop-line of pure thought." We are hopeful that in reading writers like Orwell, Camus, Langer, and many of the others, the reader will also be moved to drop plumblines of his own.

THE
BORZOI
COLLEGE READER

SHORTER EDITION

The Necessity for Thinking

So many of the selections in this book are records of hard thinking, that —in the spirit that nothing should be urged on the reader for which we cannot make a good case—we present here a group of essays about thinking itself. This group and the one that follows, on the right use of language, thus serve as preface and justification to the whole collection.

Perhaps only a few readers nowadays will need to read about thinking in order to be convinced of the necessity for thought. The eminent biochemist Albert Szent-Györgyi, thinking of the possibility of atomic war, has put our dilemma plainly: "If it is our intelligence which led us into trouble it may be our intelligence which can lead us out of it." The essay by Aldous Huxley printed in this section similarly suggests forcible, topical, practical arguments—in this case for thought as necessary protection against political annihilation.

But what we accept rationally we often find hard to put into practice, and for some readers the real controversy over the necessity for thinking is more likely to go on among their own inner impulses than in public debate. It is precisely the recognition of this idea that adds to the persuasiveness of most of these writers and makes of thinking itself a topic of complex interest. Golding's essay is surrounded by his awareness of the problem of distinguishing thought and feeling, and developed within by a witty account of three different kinds of thinking. Robinson's fuller and more philosophical treatment of kinds of thinking is similarly based on his recognition of the unconscious and his wish to distinguish real thinking from emotional prejudice. Emerson's famous essay is the pivotal piece in the group. It relates to the first two with its challenging distinction between "Man Thinking" and man as a "mere thinker" or parroter or bookworm; and its insistence on action and experience—"Only so much do I know, as I have lived"—relates it to the essays of Newman and Nock and to the issues of practical and "liberal" thought, active and contemplative life, and the kinds of education these involve.

In the general spirit of debate, the section ends with a piquantly anti-intellectual poem. Given the absolute necessity of thinking, is thinking all? And if not, does it necessarily come first?

WILLIAM GOLDING

William Gerald Golding, a British author, was born in 1911 and educated at Marlborough grammar school and at Oxford. At first destined for a scientific career, he shifted his attention to literature after two years in the University and published a volume of poems. During World War II he served in the Royal Navy, rising to the command of a rocket-launching ship. Since the war he has devoted himself to teaching and writing, and to his hobbies, which he once described as "thinking, classical Greek, sailing, and archaeology." He is widely known for his strikingly original novels, especially Pincher Martin *(1956), describing the feelings of a shipwrecked sailor on an isolated rock in mid-ocean, and* Lord of the Flies *(1954), a deeply symbolic account of a group of schoolboys who revert to savagery when marooned on an island. The present essay first appeared in the August, 1961, issue of* Holiday.

THINKING AS A HOBBY

While I was still a boy, I came to the conclusion that there were three grades of thinking; and since I was later to claim thinking as my hobby, I came to an even stranger conclusion—namely, that I myself could not think at all.

I must have been an unsatisfactory child for grownups to deal with. I remember how incomprehensible they appeared to me at first, but not, of course, how I appeared to them. It was the headmaster of my grammar school who first brought the subject of thinking before me—though neither in the way, nor with the result he intended. He had some statuettes in his study. They stood on a high cupboard behind his desk. One was a lady wearing nothing but a bath towel. She seemed frozen in an eternal panic lest the bath towel slip down any farther; and since she had no arms, she was in an unfortunate position to pull the towel up again. Next to her, crouched the statuette of a leopard, ready to spring down at the top drawer of a filing cabinet labeled A-AH. My innocence interpreted this as the victim's last, despairing cry. Beyond the leopard was a naked, muscular gentleman, who sat, looking down, with his chin on his fist and his elbow on his knee. He seemed utterly miserable.

Some time later, I learned about these statuettes. The headmaster had placed them where they would face delinquent children, because they symbolized to him the whole of life. The naked lady was the Venus of Milo. She was Love. She was not worried about the towel. She was just busy being beautiful. The leopard was Nature, and he was being natural. The naked, muscular gentleman was not miserable. He was Rodin's Thinker, an image of pure thought. It is easy to buy small plaster models of what you think life is like.

I had better explain that I was a frequent visitor to the headmaster's study, because of the latest thing I had done or left undone. As we now say, I was not integrated. I was, if anything, disintegrated; and I was puzzled. Grownups never made sense. Whenever I found myself in a penal position before the headmaster's desk, with the statuettes glimmering whitely above him, I would sink my head, clasp my hands behind my back and writhe one shoe over the other.

The headmaster would look opaquely at me through flashing spectacles.

"What are we going to do with you?"

Well, what *were* they going to do with me? I would writhe my shoe some more and stare down at the worn rug.

"Look up, boy! Can't you look up?"

Then I would look up at the cupboard, where the naked lady was frozen in her panic and the muscular gentleman contemplated the hind-quarters of the leopard in endless gloom. I had nothing to say to the headmaster. His spectacles caught the light so that you could see nothing human behind them. There was no possibility of communication.

"Don't you ever think at all?"

No, I didn't think, wasn't thinking, couldn't think—I was simply waiting in anguish for the interview to stop.

"Then you'd better learn—hadn't you?"

On one occasion the headmaster leaped to his feet, reached up and plonked Rodin's masterpiece on the desk before me.

"That's what a man looks like when he's really thinking."

I surveyed the gentleman without interest or comprehension.

"Go back to your class."

Clearly there was something missing in me. Nature had endowed the rest of the human race with a sixth sense and left me out. This must be so, I mused, on my way back to the class, since whether I had broken a window, or failed to remember Boyle's Law, or been late for school, my teachers produced me one, adult answer: "Why can't you think?"

As I saw the case, I had broken the window because I had tried to hit Jack Arney with a cricket ball and missed him; I could not remember Boyle's Law because I had never bothered to learn it; and I was late for school because I preferred looking over the bridge into the river. In fact, I was wicked. Were my teachers, perhaps, so good that they could not understand the depths of my depravity? Were they clear, untormented people who could direct their every action by this mysterious business of thinking? The whole thing was incomprehensible. In my earlier years, I found even the statuette of the Thinker confusing. I did not believe any of my teachers were naked, ever. Like someone born deaf, but bitterly determined to find out about sound, I watched my teachers to find out about thought.

There was Mr. Houghton. He was always telling me to think. With a modest satisfaction, he would tell me that he had thought a bit himself. Then why did he spend so much time drinking? Or was there more sense in drinking than there appeared to be? But if not, and if drinking were in fact ruinous to health—and Mr. Houghton was ruined, there was no doubt about that—why was he always talking about the clean life and the virtues of fresh air? He would spread his arms wide with the action of a man who habitually spent his time striding along mountain ridges.

"Open air does me good, boys—I know it!"

Sometimes, exalted by his own oratory, he would leap from his desk and hustle us outside into a hideous wind.

"Now, boys! Deep breaths! Feel it right down inside you—huge draughts of God's good air!"

He would stand before us, rejoicing in his perfect health, an open-air man. He would put his hands on his waist and take a tremendous breath. You could hear the wind, trapped in the cavern of his chest and struggling with all the unnatural impediments. His body would reel with shock and his ruined face go white at the unaccustomed visitation. He would stagger back to his desk and collapse there, useless for the rest of the morning.

Mr. Houghton was given to high-minded monologues about the good life, sexless and full of duty. Yet in the middle of one of these monologues, if a girl passed the window, tapping along on her neat little feet, he would interrupt his discourse, his neck would turn of itself and he would watch her out of sight. In this instance, he seemed to me ruled not by thought but by an invisible and irresistible spring in his nape.

His neck was an object of great interest to me. Normally it bulged a bit over his collar. But Mr. Houghton had fought in the First World War alongside both Americans and French, and had come—by who knows what illogic?—to a settled detestation of both countries. If either country happened to be prominent in current affairs, no argument could make Mr.

Houghton think well of it. He would bang the desk, his neck would bulge still further and go red. "You can say what you like," he would cry, "but I've thought about this—and I know what I think!"

Mr. Houghton thought with his neck.

There was Miss Parsons. She assured us that her dearest wish was our welfare, but I knew even then, with the mysterious clairvoyance of childhood, that what she wanted most was the husband she never got. There was Mr. Hands—and so on.

I have dealt at length with my teachers because this was my introduction to the nature of what is commonly called thought. Through them I discovered that thought is often full of unconscious prejudice, ignorance and hypocrisy. It will lecture on disinterested purity while its neck is being remorselessly twisted toward a skirt. Technically, it is about as proficient as most businessmen's golf, as honest as most politicians' intentions, or—to come near my own preoccupation—as coherent as most books that get written. It is what I came to call grade-three thinking, though more properly, it is feeling, rather than thought.

True, often there is a kind of innocence in prejudices, but in those days I viewed grade-three thinking with an intolerant contempt and an incautious mockery. I delighted to confront a pious lady who hated the Germans with the proposition that we should love our enemies. She taught me a great truth in dealing with grade-three thinkers; because of her, I no longer dismiss lightly a mental process which for nine-tenths of the population is the nearest they will ever get to thought. They have immense solidarity. We had better respect them, for we are outnumbered and surrounded. A crowd of grade-three thinkers, all shouting the same thing, all warming their hands at the fire of their own prejudices, will not thank you for pointing out the contradictions in their beliefs. Man is a gregarious animal, and enjoys agreement as cows will graze all the same way on the side of a hill.

Grade-two thinking is the detection of contradictions. I reached grade two when I trapped the poor, pious lady. Grade-two thinkers do not stampede easily, though often they fall into the other fault and lag behind. Grade-two thinking is a withdrawal, with eyes and ears open. It became my hobby and brought satisfaction and loneliness in either hand. For grade-two thinking destroys without having the power to create. It set me watching the crowds cheering His Majesty the King and asking myself what all the fuss was about, without giving me anything positive to put in the place of that heady patriotism. But there were compensations. To hear people justify their habit of hunting foxes and tearing them to pieces by claiming that the foxes liked it. To hear our Prime Minister talk about the great benefit we conferred on India by jailing people like Pandit Nehru and Gandhi. To hear American politicians talk about peace in one sentence and refuse to join the League of Nations in the next. Yes, there were moments of delight.

But I was growing toward adolescence and had to admit that Mr. Houghton was not the only one with an irresistible spring in his neck. I, too, felt the compulsive hand of nature and began to find that pointing out contradiction could be costly as well as fun. There was Ruth, for example, a serious and attractive girl. I was an atheist at the time. Grade-two thinking is a menace to religion and knocks down sects like skittles. I put myself in a position to be converted by her with an hypocrisy worthy of grade three. She was a Methodist—or at least, her parents were, and Ruth had to follow suit. But, alas, instead of relying on the Holy Spirit to convert me, Ruth was foolish enough to open her pretty mouth in argument. She claimed that the Bible (King James Version) was literally inspired. I countered by saying that the Catholics believed in the literal inspiration of Saint Jerome's *Vulgate,* and the two books were different. Argument flagged.

At last she remarked that there were an awful lot of Methodists, and they couldn't be wrong, could they—not all those millions? That was too easy, said I restively (for the nearer you were to Ruth, the nicer she was to be near to) since there were more Roman Catholics than Methodists anyway; and they couldn't be wrong, could they—not all those hundreds of millions? An awful flicker of doubt appeared in her eyes. I slid my arm round her waist and murmured breathlessly that if we were counting heads, the Buddhists were the boys for my money. But Ruth had *really* wanted to do me good, because I was so nice. She fled. The combination of my arm and those countless Buddhists was too much for her.

That night her father visited my father and left, red-cheeked and indignant. I was given the third degree to find out what had happened. It was lucky we were both of us only fourteen. I lost Ruth and gained an undeserved reputation as a potential libertine.

So grade-two thinking could be dangerous. It was in this knowledge, at the age of fifteen, that I remember making a comment from the heights of grade two, on the limitations of grade three. One evening I found myself alone in the school hall, preparing it for a party. The door of the headmaster's study was open. I went in. The headmaster had ceased to thump Rodin's Thinker down on the desk as an example to the young. Perhaps he had not found any more candidates, but the statuettes were still there, glimmering and gathering dust on top of the cupboard. I stood on a chair and rearranged them. I stood Venus in her bath towel on the filing cabinet, so that now the top drawer caught its breath in a gasp of sexy excitement. "A-ah!" The portentous Thinker I placed on the edge of the cupboard so that he looked down at the bath towel and waited for it to slip.

Grade-two thinking, though it filled life with fun and excitement, did not make for content. To find out the deficiencies of our elders bolsters the young ego but does not make for personal security. I found that grade two was not only the power to point out contradictions. It took the swimmer some distance from the shore and left him there, out of his depth. I decided that Pontius Pilate was a typical grade-two thinker. "What is truth?" he said, a very common grade-two thought, but one that is used always as the end of an argument instead of the beginning. There is a still higher grade of thought which says, "What is truth?" and sets out to find it.

But these grade-one thinkers were few and far between. They did not visit my grammar school in the flesh though they were there in books. I aspired to them, partly because I was ambitious and partly because I now saw my hobby as an unsatisfactory thing if it went no further. If you set out to climb a mountain, however high you climb, you have failed if you cannot reach the top.

I *did* meet an undeniably grade-one thinker in my first year at Oxford. I was looking over a small bridge in Magdalen Deer Park, and a tiny mustached and hatted figure came and stood by my side. He was a German who had just fled from the Nazis to Oxford as a temporary refuge. His name was Einstein.

But Professor Einstein knew no English at that time and I knew only two words of German. I beamed at him, trying wordlessly to convey by my bearing all the affection and respect that the English felt for him. It is possible—and I have to make the admission—that I felt here were two grade-one thinkers standing side by side; yet I doubt if my face conveyed more than a formless awe. I would have given my Greek and Latin and French and a good slice of my English for enough German to communicate. But we were divided; he was as inscrutable as my headmaster. For perhaps five minutes we stood together on the bridge, undeniable grade-one thinker and breathless aspirant. With true greatness, Professor Einstein realized that any contact was better than none. He pointed to a trout wavering in midstream.

He spoke: *"Fisch."*

My brain reeled. Here I was, mingling with the great, and yet helpless as the veriest grade-three thinker. Desperately I sought for some sign by which I might convey that I, too, revered pure reason. I nodded vehemently. In a brilliant flash I used up half of my German vocabulary. *"Fisch. Ja. Ja."*

For perhaps another five minutes we stood side by side. Then Professor Einstein, his whole figure still conveying good will and amiability, drifted away out of sight.

I, too, would be a grade-one thinker. I was irreverent at the best of times. Political and religious systems, social customs, loyalties and traditions, they all came tumbling down like so many rotten apples off a tree. This was a fine hobby and a sensible substitute for cricket, since you could play it all the year round. I came up in the end with what must always remain the justification for grade-one thinking, its sign, seal and charter. I devised a coherent system for living. It was a moral system, which was wholly logical. Of course, as I readily admitted, conversion of the world to my way of thinking might be difficult, since my system did away with a number of trifles, such as big business, centralized government, armies, marriage. . . .

It was Ruth all over again. I had some very good friends who stood by me, and still do. But my acquaintances vanished, taking the girls with them. Young women seemed oddly contented with the world as it was. They valued the meaningless ceremony with a ring. Young men, while willing to concede the chaining sordidness of marriage, were hesitant about abandoning the organizations which they hoped would give them a career. A young man on the first rung of the Royal Navy, while perfectly agreeable to doing away with big business and marriage, got as red-necked as Mr. Houghton when I proposed a world without any battleships in it.

Had the game gone too far? Was it a game any longer? In those prewar days, I stood to lose a great deal, for the sake of a hobby.

Now you are expecting me to describe how I saw the folly of my ways and came back to the warm nest, where prejudices are so often called loyalties, where pointless actions are hallowed into custom by repetition, where we are content to say we think when all we do is feel.

But you would be wrong. I dropped my hobby and turned professional.

If I were to go back to the headmaster's study and find the dusty statuettes still there, I would arrange them differently. I would dust Venus and put her aside, for I have come to love her and know her for the fair thing she is. But I would put the Thinker, sunk in his desperate thought, where there were shadows before him—and at his back, I would put the leopard, crouched and ready to spring.

JAMES HARVEY ROBINSON

James Harvey Robinson (1863–1936), American historian and university professor, was educated at Harvard and Freiburg. He taught history at the University of Pennsylvania, and from 1895 to 1919 at Columbia. Resigning in 1919 in protest against the expulsion of a group of professors for their opposition to World War I, he attacked Columbia president Nicholas Murray Butler for his alleged attempts to suppress freedom of expression at the University. Robinson then helped to found the New School for Social Research in New York City where he taught until 1921, when he retired to devote the rest of his life to writing. Among his dozen volumes of historical and philosophical writing, perhaps the best known to the general public is The Mind in the Making *(1921), subtitled* The Relation of Intelligence to Social Reform. *Chapter II of this book has been excerpted and reprinted so often that it has itself been the subject of an amusing article by Professor David Novarr ("OVKOT," AAUP Bulletin, 1951, Vol. 37). But familiarity has not reduced its value. We reprint the chapter here in full, using the heading of the first section as title for the whole.*

ON VARIOUS KINDS OF THINKING

Good sense is, of all things among men, the most equally distributed; for everyone thinks himself so abundantly provided with it that those even who are the most difficult to satisfy in everything else do not usually desire a larger measure of this quality than they already possess.—DESCARTES.

We see man to-day, instead of the frank and courageous recognition of his status, the docile attention to his biological history, the determination to let nothing stand in the way of the security and permanence of his future, which alone can establish the safety and happiness of the race, substituting blind confidence in his destiny, unclouded faith in the essentially respectful attitude of the universe toward his moral code, and a belief no less firm that his traditions and laws and institutions necessarily contain permanent qualities of reality.

—WILLIAM TROTTER.

1. ON VARIOUS KINDS OF THINKING

The truest and most profound observations on Intelligence have in the past been made by the poets and, in recent times, by story-writers. They have been keen observers and recorders and reckoned freely with the emotions and sentiments. Most philosophers, on the other hand, have exhibited a grotesque ignorance of man's life and have built up systems that are elaborate and imposing, but quite unrelated to actual human affairs. They have almost consistently neglected the actual process of thought and have set the mind off as something apart to be studied by itself. *But no such mind, exempt from bodily processes, animal impulses, savage traditions, infantile impressions, conventional reactions, and traditional knowledge, ever existed,* even in the case of the most abstract of metaphysicians. Kant entitled his great work *A Critique of Pure Reason.* But to the modern student of mind pure reason seems as mythical as the pure gold, transparent as glass, with which the celestial city is paved.

Formerly philosophers thought of mind as having to do exclusively with conscious thought. It was that within man which perceived, remembered, judged, reasoned, understood, believed, willed. But of late it has been shown that we are unaware of a great part of what we perceive, remember, will, and infer; and that a great part of the thinking of which we are aware is determined by that of which we are not conscious. It has indeed been demonstrated that our unconscious psychic life far outruns our conscious. This seems perfectly natural to anyone who considers the following facts:

The sharp distinction between the mind and the body is, as we shall find, a very ancient and spontaneous uncritical savage prepossession. What we think of as "mind" is so intimately associated with what we call "body" that we are coming to realize that the one cannot be understood without the other. Every thought reverberates through the body, and, on the other hand, alterations in our physical condition affect our whole attitude of mind. The insufficient elimination of the foul and decaying products of digestion may plunge us into deep melancholy, whereas a few whiffs of nitrous monoxide may exalt us to the seventh heaven of supernal knowledge and godlike complacency. And *vice versa,* a sudden word or thought may cause our heart to jump, check our breathing, or make our knees as water. There is a whole new literature growing up which studies the effects of our bodily secretions and our muscular tensions and their relation to our emotions and our thinking.

Then there are hidden impulses and desires and secret longings of which we can only with the greatest difficulty take account. They influence our conscious thought in the most bewildering fashion. Many of these unconscious influences appear to originate in our very early years. The older philosophers seem to have forgotten that even they were infants and children at their most impressionable age and never could by any possibility get over it.

The term "unconscious," now so familiar to all readers of modern works on psychology, gives offense to some adherents of the past. There should, however, be no special mystery about it. It is not a new animistic abstraction, but simply a collective word to include all the physiological changes which escape our notice, all the forgotten experiences and impressions of the past which continue to influence our desires and reflections and conduct, even if we cannot remember them. What we can remember at any time is indeed an infinitesimal part of what has happened to us. We could not remember anything unless we forgot almost everything. As

Bergson says, the brain is the organ of forgetfulness as well as of memory. Moreover, we tend, of course, to become oblivious to things to which we are thoroughly accustomed, for habit blinds us to their existence. So the forgotten and the habitual make up a great part of the so-called "unconscious."

If we are ever to understand man, his conduct and reasoning, and if we aspire to learn to guide his life and his relations with his fellows more happily than heretofore, we cannot neglect the great discoveries briefly noted above. We must reconcile ourselves to novel and revolutionary conceptions of the mind, for it is clear that the older philosophers, whose works still determine our current views, had a very superficial notion of the subject with which they dealt. But for our purposes, with due regard to what has just been said and to much that has necessarily been left unsaid (and with the indulgence of those who will at first be inclined to dissent), *we shall consider mind chiefly as conscious knowledge and intelligence, as what we know and our attitude toward it—our disposition to increase our information, classify it, criticize it, and apply it.*

We do not think enough about thinking, and much of our confusion is the result of current illusions in regard to it. Let us forget for the moment any impressions we may have derived from the philosophers, and see what seems to happen in ourselves. The first thing that we notice is that our thought moves with such incredible rapidity that it is almost impossible to arrest any specimen of it long enough to have a look at it. When we are offered a penny for our thoughts we always find that we have recently had so many things in mind that we can easily make a selection which will not compromise us too nakedly. On inspection we shall find that even if we are not downright ashamed of a great part of our spontaneous thinking it is far too intimate, personal, ignoble or trivial to permit us to reveal more than a small part of it. I believe this must be true of everyone. We do not, of course, know what goes on in other people's heads. They tell us very little and we tell them very little. The spigot of speech, rarely fully opened, could never emit more than driblets of the ever renewed hogshead of thought—*noch grösser wie's Heidelberger Fass.* We find it hard to believe that other people's thoughts are as silly as our own, but they probably are.

We all appear to ourselves to be thinking all the time during our waking hours, and most of us are aware that we go on thinking while we are asleep, even more foolishly than when awake. When uninterrupted by some practical issue we are engaged in what is now known as a *reverie*. This is our spontaneous and favorite kind of thinking. We allow our ideas to take their own course and this course is determined by our hopes and fears, our spontaneous desires, their fulfillment or frustration; by our likes and dislikes, our loves and hates and resentments. There is nothing else anything like so interesting to ourselves as ourselves. All thought that is not more or less laboriously controlled and directed will inevitably circle about the beloved Ego. It is amusing and pathetic to observe this tendency in ourselves and in others. We learn politely and generously to overlook this truth, but if we dare to think of it, it blazes forth like the noontide sun.

The reverie or "free association of ideas" has of late become the subject of scientific research. While investigators are not yet agreed on the results, or at least on the proper interpretation to be given to them, there can be no doubt that our reveries form the chief index to our fundamental character. They are a reflection of our nature as modified by often hidden and forgotten experiences. We need not go into the matter further here, for it is only necessary to observe that the reverie is at all times a potent and in many cases an omnipotent rival to every other kind of thinking. It doubtless influences all our speculations in its persistent tendency to self-magnification and self-justification, which are its chief preoccupations, but it is the last thing to make directly or indirectly for honest increase of knowledge.[1] Philosophers usually talk as if such thinking did not exist or were in some way negligible. This is what makes their speculations so unreal and often worthless.

The reverie, as any of us can see for himself, is frequently broken and interrupted by the necessity of a second kind of thinking. We have to make practical decisions. Shall we write a letter or no? Shall we take the subway or a bus? Shall we have dinner at seven or half past? Shall we buy U. S. Rubber or a Liberty Bond? Decisions are easily distinguishable from the free flow of the reverie. Sometimes they demand a good deal of careful pondering and the recollection of pertinent facts; often, however, they are made impulsively. They are a more difficult and laborious thing than the reverie, and we resent having to "make up our mind" when we are tired, or absorbed in a congenial reverie. Weighing a decision, it should be noted, does not necessarily add anything to our knowledge, although we may, of course, seek further information before making it.

2. RATIONALIZING

A third kind of thinking is stimulated when anyone questions our belief and opinions. We sometimes find ourselves changing our minds without any resistance or heavy emotion, but if we are told that we are

---

[1] The poet-clergyman, John Donne, who lived in the time of James I, has given a beautifully honest picture of the doings of a saint's mind: "I throw myself down in my chamber and call in and invite God and His angels thither, and when they are there I neglect God and His angels for the noise of a fly, for the rattling of a coach, for the whining of a door. I talk on in the same posture of praying, eyes lifted up, knees bowed down, as though I prayed to God, and if God or His angels should ask me when I thought last of God in that prayer I cannot tell. Sometimes I find that I had forgot what I was about, but when I began to forget it I cannot tell. A memory of yesterday's pleasures, a fear of to-morrow's dangers, a straw under my knee, a noise in mine ear, a light in mine eye, an anything, a nothing, a fancy, a chimera in my brain troubles me in my prayer."—Quoted by ROBERT LYND, *The Art of Letters*, pp. 46-47.

wrong we resent the imputation and harden our hearts. We are incredibly heedless in the formation of our beliefs, but find ourselves filled with an illicit passion for them when anyone proposes to rob us of their companionship. It is obviously not the ideas themselves that are dear to us, but our self-esteem, which is threatened. We are by nature stubbornly pledged to defend our own from attack, whether it be our person, our family, our property, or our opinion. A United States Senator once remarked to a friend of mine that God Almighty could not make him change his mind on our Latin-America policy. We may surrender, but rarely confess ourselves vanquished. In the intellectual world at least peace is without victory.

Few of us take the pains to study the origin of our cherished convictions; indeed, we have a natural repugnance to so doing. We like to continue to believe what we have been accustomed to accept as true, and the resentment aroused when doubt is cast upon any of our assumptions leads us to seek every manner of excuse for clinging to them. *The result is that most of our so-called reasoning consists in finding arguments for going on believing as we already do.*

I remember years ago attending a public dinner to which the Governor of the state was bidden. The chairman explained that His Excellency could not be present for certain "good" reasons; what the "real" reasons were the presiding officer said he would leave us to conjecture. This distinction between "good" and "real" reasons is one of the most clarifying and essential in the whole realm of thought. We can readily give what seem to us "good" reasons for being a Catholic or a Mason, a Republican or a Democrat, an adherent or opponent of the League of Nations. But the "real" reasons are usually on quite a different plane. Of course the importance of this distinction is popularly, if somewhat obscurely, recognized. The Baptist missionary is ready enough to see that the Buddhist is not such because his doctrines would bear careful inspection, but because he happened to be born in a Buddhist family in Tokio. But it would be treason to his faith to acknowledge that his own partiality for certain doctrines is due to the fact that his mother was a member of the First Baptist church of Oak Ridge. A savage can give all sorts of reasons for his belief that it is dangerous to step on a man's shadow, and a newspaper editor can advance plenty of arguments against the Bolsheviki. But neither of them may realize why he happens to be defending his particular opinion.

The "real" reasons for our beliefs are concealed from ourselves as well as from others. As we grow up we simply adopt the ideas presented to us in regard to such matters as religion, family relations, property, business, our country, and the state. We unconsciously absorb them from our environment. They are persistently whispered in our ear by the group in which we happen to live. Moreover, as Mr. Trotter has pointed out, these judgments, being the product of suggestion and not of reasoning, have the quality of perfect obviousness, so that to question them

... is to the believer to carry skepticism to an insane degree, and will be met by contempt, disapproval, or condemnation, according to the nature of the belief in question. When, therefore, we find ourselves entertaining an opinion about the basis of which there is a quality of feeling which tells us that to inquire into it would be absurd, obviously unnecessary, unprofitable, undesirable, bad form, or wicked, we may know that that opinion is a nonrational one, and probably, therefore, founded upon inadequate evidence.[2]

Opinions, on the other hand, which are the result of experience or of honest reasoning do not have this quality of "primary certitude." I remember when as a youth I heard a group of business men discussing the question of the immortality of the soul, I was outraged by the sentiment of doubt expressed by one of the party. As I look back now I see that I had at the time no interest in the matter, and certainly no least argument to urge in favor of the belief in which I had been reared. But neither my personal indifference to the issue, nor the fact that I had previously given it no attention, served to prevent an angry resentment when I heard *my* ideas questioned.

This spontaneous and loyal support of our preconceptions—this process of finding "good" reasons to justify our routine beliefs—is known to modern psychologists as "rationalizing"—clearly only a new name for a very ancient thing. Our "good" reasons ordinarily have no value in promoting honest enlightenment, because, no matter how solemnly they may be marshaled, they are at bottom the result of personal preference or prejudice, and not of an honest desire to seek or accept new knowledge.

In our reveries we are frequently engaged in self-justification, for we cannot bear to think ourselves wrong, and yet have constant illustrations of our weaknesses and mistakes. So we spend much time finding fault with circumstances and the conduct of others, and shifting on to them with great ingenuity the onus of our own failures and disappointments. *Rationalizing is the self-exculpation which occurs when we feel ourselves, or our group, accused of misapprehension or error.*

The little word *my* is the most important one in all human affairs, and properly to reckon with it is the beginning of wisdom. It has the same force whether it is *my* dinner, *my* dog, and *my* house, or *my* faith, *my* country, and *my* God. We not only resent the imputation that our watch is wrong, or our car shabby, but that our conception of the canals of Mars, of the pronunciation of "Epictetus," of the medicinal value of salicine, or the date of Sargon I, are subject to revision.

Philosophers, scholars, and men of science exhibit a common sensitiveness in all decisions in which their *amour propre* is involved. Thousands of argumentative works have been written to vent a grudge. However stately their reasoning, it may be nothing but rationalizing, stimulated by

---

[2] *Instincts of the Herd*, p. 44.

the most commonplace of all motives. A history of philosophy and
theology could be written in terms of grouches, wounded pride, and
aversions, and it would be far more instructive than the usual treatments
of these themes. Sometimes, under Providence, the lowly impulse of resentment leads to great achievements. Milton wrote his treatise on divorce as
a result of his troubles with his seventeen-year-old wife, and when he
was accused of being the leading spirit in a new sect, the Divorcers, he
wrote his noble *Areopagitica* to prove his right to say what he thought
fit, and incidentally to establish the advantage of a free press in the
promotion of Truth.

All mankind, high and low, thinks in all the ways which have been
described. The reverie goes on all the time not only in the mind of the
mill hand and the Broadway flapper, but equally in weighty judges and
godly bishops. It has gone on in all the philosophers, scientists, poets, and
theologians that have ever lived. Aristotle's most abstruse speculations were
doubtless tempered by highly irrelevant reflections. He is reported to
have had very thin legs and small eyes, for which he doubtless had to
find excuses, and he was wont to indulge in very conspicuous dress and
rings and was accustomed to arrange his hair carefully.[3] Diogenes the
Cynic exhibited the impudence of a touchy soul. His tub was his distinction. Tennyson in beginning his "Maud" could not forget his chagrin over
losing his patrimony years before as the result of an unhappy investment in
the Patent Decorative Carving Company. These facts are not recalled here
as a gratuitous disparagement of the truly great, but to insure a full
realization of the tremendous competition which all really exacting
thought has to face, even in the minds of the most highly endowed mortals.

And now the astonishing and perturbing suspicion emerges that perhaps
almost all that had passed for social science, political economy, politics, and
ethics in the past may be brushed aside by future generations as mainly
rationalizing. John Dewey has already reached this conclusion in regard to
philosophy.[4] Veblen[5] and other writers have revealed the various un-
perceived presuppositions of the traditional political economy, and now
comes an Italian sociologist, Vilfredo Pareto, who, in his huge treatise on
general sociology, devotes hundreds of pages to substantiating a similar
thesis affecting all the social sciences.[6] This conclusion may be ranked by
students of a hundred years hence as one of the several great discoveries of

---

[3] Diogenes Lærtius, book v.
[4] *Reconstruction in Philosophy.*
[5] *The Place of Science in Modern Civilization.*
[6] *Traité de Sociologie Générale, passim.* The author's term *"derivations"* seems to
be his precise way of expressing what we have called the "good" reasons, and his
"residus" correspond to the "real" reasons. He well says, *"L'homme éprouve le besoin
de raisonner, et en outre d'étendre un voile sur ses instincts et sur ses sentiments"*—
hence, rationalization. (P. 788.) His aim is to reduce sociology to the "real" reasons.
(P. 791.)

our age. It is by no means fully worked out, and it is so opposed to nature that it will be very slowly accepted by the great mass of those who consider themselves thoughtful. As a historical student I am personally fully reconciled to this newer view. Indeed, it seems to me inevitable that just as the various sciences of nature were, before the opening of the seventeenth century, largely masses of rationalizations to suit the religious sentiments of the period, so the social sciences have continued even to our own day to be rationalizations of uncritically accepted beliefs and customs.

It will become apparent as we proceed that the fact that an idea is ancient and that it has been widely received is no argument in its favor, but should immediately suggest the necessity of carefully testing it as a probable instance of rationalization.

3. HOW CREATIVE THOUGHT TRANSFORMS THE WORLD

This brings us to another kind of thought which can fairly easily be distinguished from the three kinds described above. It has not the usual qualities of the reverie, for it does not hover about our personal complacencies and humiliations. It is not made up of the homely decisions forced upon us by everyday needs, when we review our little stock of existing information, consult our conventional preferences and obligations, and make a choice of action. It is not the defense of our own cherished beliefs and prejudices just because they are our own—mere plausible excuses for remaining of the same mind. On the contrary, it is that peculiar species of thought which leads us to *change* our mind.

It is this kind of thought that has raised man from his pristine, subsavage ignorance and squalor to the degree of knowledge and comfort which he now possesses. On his capacity to continue and greatly extend this kind of thinking depends his chance of groping his way out of the plight in which the most highly civilized peoples of the world now find themselves. In the past this type of thinking has been called Reason. But so many misapprehensions have grown up around the word that some of us have become very suspicious of it. I suggest, therefore, that we substitute a recent name and speak of "creative thought" rather than of Reason. *For this kind of meditation begets knowledge, and knowledge is really creative inasmuch as it makes things look different from what they seemed before and may indeed work for their reconstruction.*

In certain moods some of us realize that we are observing things or making reflections with a seeming disregard of our personal preoccupations. We are not preening or defending ourselves; we are not faced by the necessity of any practical decision, nor are we apologizing for believing this or that. We are just wondering and looking and mayhap seeing what we never perceived before.

Curiosity is as clear and definite as any of our urges. We wonder what is in a sealed telegram or in a letter in which some one else is absorbed, or what is being said in the telephone booth or in low conversation. This inquisitiveness is vastly stimulated by jealousy, suspicion, or any hint that we ourselves are directly or indirectly involved. But there appears to be a fair amount of personal interest in other people's affairs even when they do not concern us except as a mystery to be unraveled or a tale to be told. The reports of a divorce suit will have "news value" for many weeks. They constitute a story, like a novel or play or moving picture. This is not an example of pure curiosity, however, since we readily identify ourselves with others, and their joys and despair then become our own.

We also take note of, or "observe," as Sherlock Holmes says, things which have nothing to do with our personal interests and make no personal appeal either direct or by way of sympathy. This is what Veblen so well calls "idle curiosity." And it is usually idle enough. Some of us when we face the line of people opposite us in a subway train impulsively consider them in detail and engage in rapid inferences and form theories in regard to them. On entering a room there are those who will perceive at a glance the degree of preciousness of the rugs, the character of the pictures, and the personality revealed by the books. But there are many, it would seem, who are so absorbed in their personal reverie or in some definite purpose that they have no bright-eyed energy for idle curiosity. The tendency to miscellaneous observation we come by honestly enough, for we note it in many of our animal relatives.

Veblen, however, uses the term "idle curiosity" somewhat ironically, as is his wont. It is idle only to those who fail to realize that it may be a very rare and indispensable thing from which almost all distinguished human achievement proceeds. Since it may lead to systematic examination and seeking for things hitherto undiscovered. For research is but diligent search which enjoys the high flavor of primitive hunting. Occasionally and fitfully idle curiosity thus leads to creative thought, which alters and broadens our own views and aspirations and may in turn, under highly favorable circumstances, affect the views and lives of others, even for generations to follow. An example or two will make this unique human process clear.

Galileo was a thoughtful youth and doubtless carried on a rich and varied reverie. He had artistic ability and might have turned out to be a musician or painter. When he had dwelt among the monks at Valambrosa he had been tempted to lead the life of a religious. As a boy he busied himself with toy machines and he inherited a fondness for mathematics. All these facts are of record. We may safely assume also that, along with many other subjects of contemplation, the Pisan maidens found a vivid place in his thoughts.

One day when seventeen years old he wandered into the cathedral of his native town. In the midst of his reverie he looked up at the lamps hanging by long chains from the high ceiling of the church. Then something very difficult to explain occurred. He found himself no longer thinking of the building, worshipers, or the services; of his artistic or religious interests; of his reluctance to become a physician as his father wished. He forgot the question of a career and even the *graziosissime donne*. As he watched the swinging lamps he was suddenly wondering if mayhap their oscillations, whether long or short, did not occupy the same time. Then he tested this hypothesis by counting his pulse, for that was the only timepiece he had with him.

This observation, however remarkable in itself, was not enough to produce a really creative thought. Others may have noticed the same thing and yet nothing came of it. Most of our observations have no assignable results. Galileo may have seen that the warts on a peasant's face formed a perfect isosceles triangle, or he may have noticed with boyish glee that just as the officiating priest was uttering the solemn words, *ecce agnus Dei*, a fly lit on the end of his nose. To be really creative, ideas have to be worked up and then "put over," so that they become a part of man's social heritage. The highly accurate pendulum clock was one of the later results of Galileo's discovery. He himself was led to reconsider and successfully to refute the old notions of falling bodies. It remained for Newton to prove that the moon was falling, and presumably all the heavenly bodies. This quite upset all the consecrated views of the heavens as managed by angelic engineers. The universality of the laws of gravitation stimulated the attempt to seek other and equally important natural laws and cast grave doubts on the miracles in which mankind had hitherto believed. In short, those who dared to include in their thought the discoveries of Galileo and his successors found themselves in a new earth surrounded by new heavens.

On the 28th of October, 1831, two hundred and fifty years after Galileo had noticed the isochronous vibrations of the lamps, creative thought and its currency had so far increased that Faraday was wondering what would happen if he mounted a disk of copper between the poles of a horseshoe magnet. As the disk revolved an electric current was produced. This would doubtless have seemed the idlest kind of an experiment to the stanch business men of the time, who, it happened, were just then denouncing the child-labor bills in their anxiety to avail themselves to the full of the results of earlier idle curiosity. But should the dynamos and motors which have come into being as the outcome of Faraday's experiment be stopped this evening, the business man of to-day, agitated over labor troubles, might, as he trudged home past lines of "dead" cars, through dark streets to an unlighted house, engage in a little creative thought of his own and perceive that he and his laborers would have no modern factories and mines to quarrel about had it not been for the strange practical effects of the idle curiosity of scientists, inventors, and engineers.

The examples of creative intelligence given above belong to the realm of modern scientific achievement, which furnishes the most striking instances of the effects of scrupulous, objective thinking. But there are, of course, other great realms in which the recording and embodiment of acute observation and insight have wrought themselves into the higher life of man. The great poets and dramatists and our modern story-tellers have found themselves engaged in productive reveries, noting and artistically presenting their discoveries for the delight and instruction of those who have the ability to appreciate them.

The process by which a fresh and original poem or drama comes into being is doubtless analogous to that which originates and elaborates so-called scientific discoveries; but there is clearly a temperamental difference. The genesis and advance of painting, sculpture, and music offer still other problems. We really as yet know shockingly little about these matters, and indeed very few people have the least curiosity about them.[7] Nevertheless, creative intelligence in its various forms and activities is what makes man. Were it not for its slow, painful, and constantly discouraged operations through the ages man would be no more than a species of primate living on seeds, fruit, roots, and uncooked flesh, and wandering naked through the woods and over the plains like a chimpanzee.

The origin and progress and future promotion of civilization are ill understood and misconceived. These should be made the chief theme of education, but much hard work is necessary before we can reconstruct our ideas of man and his capacities and free ourselves from innumerable persistent misapprehensions. There have been obstructionists in all times, not merely the lethargic masses, but the moralists, the rationalizing theologians, and most of the philosophers, all busily if unconsciously engaged in ratifying existing ignorance and mistakes and discouraging creative thought. Naturally, those who reassure us seem worthy of honor and respect. Equally naturally those who puzzle us with disturbing criticisms and invite us to change our ways are objects of suspicion and readily discredited. Our personal discontent does not ordinarily extend to any critical questioning of the general situation in which we find ourselves. In every age the prevailing conditions of civilization have appeared quite natural and inevitable to those who grew up in them. The cow asks no questions as to how it happens to have a dry stall and a supply of hay. The kitten laps its warm milk from a china saucer, without knowing anything about porcelain; the dog nestles in the corner of a divan with no sense of obligation to the inventors of upholstery and the manufacturers of down pillows. So we humans accept our breakfasts, our trains and telephones and orchestras and movies, our national Constitution, our moral code and standards of manners, with the simplicity and innocence of a pet rabbit. We have absolutely inexhaustible capacities for appropriating what others do

[7] Recently a re-examination of creative thought has begun as a result of new knowledge which discredits many of the notions formerly held about "reason." See, for example, *Creative Intelligence,* by a group of American philosophic thinkers; John Dewey, *Essays in Experimental Logic* (both pretty hard books); and Veblen, *The Place of Science in Modern Civilization.* Easier than these and very stimulating are Dewey, *Reconstruction in Philosophy,* and Woodworth, *Dynamic Psychology.*

for us with no thought of a "thank you." We do not feel called upon to make any least contribution to the merry game ourselves. Indeed, we are usually quite unaware that a game is being played at all.

We have now examined the various classes of thinking which we can readily observe in ourselves and which we have plenty of reasons to believe go on, and always have been going on, in our fellow-men. We can sometimes get quite pure and sparkling examples of all four kinds, but commonly they are so confused and intermingled in our reverie as not to be readily distinguishable. The reverie is a reflection of our longings, exultations, and complacencies, our fears, suspicions, and disappointments. We are chiefly engaged in struggling to maintain our self-respect and in asserting that supremacy which we all crave and which seems to us our natural prerogative. It is not strange, but rather quite inevitable, that our beliefs about what is true and false, good and bad, right and wrong, should be mixed up with the reverie and be influenced by the same considerations which determine its character and course. We resent criticisms of our views exactly as we do of anything else connected with ourselves. Our notions of life and its ideals seem to us to be *our own* and as such necessarily true and right, to be defended at all costs.

We very rarely consider, however, the process by which we gained our convictions. If we did so, we could hardly fail to see that there was usually little ground for our confidence in them. Here and there, in this department of knowledge or that, some one of us might make a fair claim to have taken some trouble to get correct ideas of, let us say, the situation in Russia, the sources of our food supply, the origin of the Constitution, the revision of the tariff, the policy of the Holy Roman Apostolic Church, modern business organization, trade unions, birth control, socialism, the League of Nations, the excess-profits tax, preparedness, advertising in its social bearings; but only a very exceptional person would be entitled to opinions on all of even these few matters. And yet most of us have opinions on all these, and on many other questions of equal importance, of which we may know even less. We feel compelled, as self-respecting persons, to take sides when they come up for discussion. We even surprise ourselves by our omniscience. Without taking thought we see in a flash that it is most righteous and expedient to discourage birth control by legislative enactment, or that one who decries intervention in Mexico is clearly wrong, or that big advertising is essential to big business and that big business is the pride of the land. As godlike beings why should we not rejoice in our omniscience?

It is clear, in any case, that our convictions on important matters are not the result of knowledge or critical thought, nor, it may be added, are they often dictated by supposed self-interest. Most of them are *pure prejudices* in the proper sense of that word. We do not form them ourselves. They are the whisperings of "the voice of the herd." We have in the last analysis no responsibility for them and need assume none. They are not really our own ideas, but those of others no more well informed or inspired than ourselves, who have got them in the same careless and humiliating manner as we. It should be our pride to revise our ideas and not to adhere to what passes for respectable opinion, for such opinion can frequently be shown to be not respectable at all. We should, in view of the considerations that have been mentioned, resent our supine credulity. As an English writer has remarked:

"If we feared the entertaining of an unverifiable opinion with the warmth with which we fear using the wrong implement at the dinner table, if the thought of holding a prejudice disgusted us as does a foul disease, then the dangers of man's suggestibility would be turned into advantages."[8]

The purpose of this essay is to set forth briefly the way in which the notions of the herd have been accumulated. This seems to me the best, easiest, and least invidious educational device for cultivating a proper distrust for the older notions on which we still continue to rely.

The "real" reasons, which explain how it is we happen to hold a particular belief, are chiefly historical. Our most important opinions—those, for example, having to do with traditional, religious, and moral convictions, property rights, patriotism, national honor, the state, and indeed all the assumed foundations of society—are, as I have already suggested, rarely the result of reasoned consideration, but of unthinking absorption from the social environment in which we live. Consequently, they have about them a quality of "elemental certitude," and we especially resent doubt or criticism cast upon them. So long, however, as we revere the whisperings of the herd, we are obviously unable to examine them dispassionately and to consider to what extent they are suited to the novel conditions and social exigencies in which we find ourselves to-day.

The "real" reasons for our beliefs, by making clear their origins and history, can do much to dissipate this emotional blockade and rid us of our prejudices and preconceptions. Once this is done and we come critically to examine our traditional beliefs, we may well find some of them sustained by experience and honest reasoning, while others must be revised to meet new conditions and our more extended knowledge. But only after we have undertaken such a critical examination in the light of experience and modern knowledge, freed from any feeling of "primary certitude," can we claim that the "good" are also the "real" reasons for our opinions.

I do not flatter myself that this general show-up of man's thought through the ages will cure myself or others of carelessness in adopting ideas, or of unseemly heat in defending them just because we have adopted them. But if the considerations which I propose to recall are really in-

---

[8] Trotter, *op. cit.*, p. 45. The first part of this little volume is excellent.

corporated into our thinking and are permitted to establish our general outlook on human affairs, they will do much to relieve the imaginary obligation we feel in regard to traditional sentiments and ideals. Few of us are capable of engaging in creative thought, but some of us can at least come to distinguish it from other and inferior kinds of thought and accord to it the esteem that it merits as the greatest treasure of the past and the only hope of the future.

ALDOUS HUXLEY

Aldous Leonard Huxley (1894–1963), one of the most well-known of modern English novelists and essayists, came from a family celebrated for intellectual achievement. He was the son of Leonard Huxley, author and editor; grandson of the naturalist Thomas Huxley; and grandnephew of Matthew Arnold. His brother Sir Julian is a distinguished biologist and his half-brother David won the 1963 Nobel Prize in physiology. Huxley studied at Eton and Oxford, despite a serious eye disease which made him almost totally blind for three years. Reading with the aid of a magnifying glass, he graduated from Oxford in 1915 with honors in English literature. In 1919 he joined the staff of Athenaeum, *a London literary magazine, and then followed a steady production of writings in all genres.*

The success of his early novels allowed Huxley to move to Italy in 1923 and thence to France; in 1934 he traveled in the United States, and finally settled in southern California, near Los Angeles. Here he continued to write books, articles, and an occasional movie scenario. He studied Vedanta and other eastern religions, and became interested in the effect of drugs on the mind.

Huxley wrote eleven novels, the best-known being Antic Hay *(1923),* Point Counter Point *(1928),* Brave New World *(1932), and* After Many a Summer Dies the Swan *(1940). Huxley's reputation rests equally on his over twenty volumes of essays and belles lettres, including* On the Margin *(1923),* Jesting Pilate *(1926),* Vulgarity in Literature *(1930),* Ends and

Means *(1937)*, The Perennial Philosophy *(1946)*, Science, Liberty, and Peace *(1946)*, *and* Literature and Science *(1963)*.

Huxley's Brave New World *(1932) has turned out to be devastatingly accurate both as a piece of futuristic science fiction and as a satire on modern technological mass-produced civilization. It has become so widely known that in 1958 Huxley could safely give the title* Brave New World Revisited *to a study of the progress of dehumanization and mental tyranny in the intervening quarter century. The two Huxley essays in the present volume are taken from* Brave New World Revisited. *The following is Chapter 5.*

PROPAGANDA UNDER A DICTATORSHIP

At his trial after the Second World War, Hitler's Minister for Armaments, Albert Speer, delivered a long speech in which, with remarkable acuteness, he described the Nazi tyranny and analyzed its methods. "Hitler's dictatorship," he said, "differed in one fundamental point from all its predecessors in history. It was the first dictatorship in the present period of modern technical development, a dictatorship which made complete use of all technical means for the domination of its own country. Through technical devices like the radio and the loud-speaker, eighty million people were deprived of independent thought. It was thereby possible to subject them to the will of one man. . . . Earlier dictators needed highly qualified assistants even at the lowest level—men who could think and act independently. The totalitarian system in the period of modern technical development can dispense with such men; thanks to modern methods of communication, it is possible to mechanize the lower leadership. As a result of this there has arisen the new type of the uncritical recipient of orders."

In the Brave New World of my prophetic fable technology had advanced far beyond the point it had reached in Hitler's day; consequently the recipients of orders were far less critical than their Nazi counterparts, far more obedient to the order-giving elite. Moreover, they had been genetically standardized and postnatally conditioned to perform their subordinate functions, and could therefore be depended upon to behave almost as predictably as machines. As we shall see in a later chapter, this conditioning of "the lower leadership" is already going on under the Communist dictatorships. The Chinese and the Russians are not relying merely on the indirect effects of advancing technology; they are working directly on the psychophysical organisms of their lower leaders, subjecting minds and bodies to a system of ruthless and, from all accounts, highly effective conditioning. "Many a man," said Speer, "has been haunted by the nightmare that one day nations might be dominated by technical means. That nightmare was almost realized in Hitler's totalitarian system." Almost, but not quite. The Nazis did not have time—and perhaps did not have the intelligence and the necessary knowledge—to brainwash and condition their lower leadership. This, it may be, is one of the reasons why they failed.

Since Hitler's day the armory of technical devices at the disposal of the would-be dictator has been considerably enlarged. As well as the radio, the loud-speaker, the moving picture camera and the rotary press, the contemporary propagandist can make use of television to broadcast the image as well as the voice of his client, and can record both image and voice on spools of magnetic tape. Thanks to technological progress, Big Brother can now be almost as omnipresent as God. Nor is it only on the technical front that the hand of the would-be dictator has been strengthened. Since Hitler's day a great deal of work has been carried out in those fields of applied psychology and neurology which are the special province of the propagandist, the indoctrinator and the brainwasher. In the past these specialists in the art of changing people's minds were empiricists. By a method of trial and error they had worked out a number of techniques and procedures, which they used very effectively without, however, knowing precisely why they were effective. Today the art of mind-control is in process of becoming a science. The practitioners of this science know what they are doing and why. They are guided in their work by theories and hypotheses solidly established on a massive foundation of experimental evidence. Thanks to the new insights and the new techniques made possible by these insights, the nightmare that was "all but realized in Hitler's totalitarian system" may soon be completely realizable.

But before we discuss these new insights and techniques let us take a look at the nightmare that so nearly came true in Nazi Germany. What were the methods used by Hitler and Goebbels for "depriving eighty million people of independent thought and subjecting them to the will of one man"? And what was the theory of human nature upon which those terrifyingly successful methods were based? These questions can be answered, for the most part, in Hitler's own words. And what remarkably clear and astute words they are! When he writes about such vast abstractions as Race and History and Providence, Hitler is strictly unreadable. But when he writes about the German masses and the methods he used for dominating and directing them, his style changes. Nonsense gives place to sense, bombast to a hard-boiled and cynical lucidity. In his philosophical lucubrations Hitler was either cloudily daydreaming or reproducing other people's half-baked notions. In his comments on crowds and propaganda he was writing of things he knew by firsthand experience. In the words of his ablest biographer, Mr. Alan Bullock, "Hitler was the

greatest demagogue in history." Those who add, "only a demagogue," fail
to appreciate the nature of political power in an age of mass politics. As
he himself said, "To be a leader means to be able to move the masses."
Hitler's aim was first to move the masses and then, having pried them
loose from their traditional loyalties and moralities, to impose upon them
(with the hypnotized consent of the majority) a new authoritarian order
of his own devising. "Hitler," wrote Hermann Rauschning in 1939, "has
a deep respect for the Catholic church and the Jesuit order; not because
of their Christian doctrine, but because of the 'machinery' they have
elaborated and controlled, their hierarchical system, their extremely clever
tactics, their knowledge of human nature and their wise use of human
weaknesses in ruling over believers." Ecclesiasticism without Christianity,
the discipline of a monastic rule, not for God's sake or in order to achieve
personal salvation, but for the sake of the State and for the greater glory
and power of the demagogue turned Leader—this was the goal toward
which the systematic moving of the masses was to lead.

Let us see what Hitler thought of the masses he moved and how he did
the moving. The first principle from which he started was a value
judgment: the masses are utterly contemptible. They are incapable of
abstract thinking and uninterested in any fact outside the circle of
their immediate experience. Their behavior is determined, not by
knowledge and reason, but by feelings and unconscious drives. It is in
these drives and feelings that "the roots of their positive as well as their
negative attitudes are implanted." To be successful a propagandist must
learn how to manipulate these instincts and emotions. "The driving force
which has brought about the most tremendous revolutions on this earth
has never been a body of scientific teaching which has gained power over
the masses, but always a devotion which has inspired them, and often a
kind of hysteria which has urged them into action. Whoever wishes to
win over the masses must know the key that will open the door of their
hearts." . . . In post-Freudian jargon, of their unconscious.

Hitler made his strongest appeal to those members of the lower middle
classes who had been ruined by the inflation of 1923, and then ruined all
over again by the depression of 1929 and the following years. "The
masses" of whom he speaks were these bewildered, frustrated and chronically anxious millions. To make them more masslike, more homogeneously
subhuman, he assembled them, by the thousands and the tens of thousands,
in vast halls and arenas, where individuals could lose their personal identity,
even their elementary humanity, and be merged with the crowd. A man
or woman makes direct contact with society in two ways: as a member
of some familial, professional or religious group, or as a member of a
crowd. Groups are capable of being as moral and intelligent as the individuals who form them; a crowd is chaotic, has no purpose of its own
and is capable of anything except intelligent action and realistic thinking.
Assembled in a crowd, people lose their powers of reasoning and their

capacity for moral choice. Their suggestibility is increased to the point where they cease to have any judgment or will of their own. They become very excitable, they lose all sense of individual or collective responsibility, they are subject to sudden accesses of rage, enthusiasm and panic. In a word, a man in a crowd behaves as though he had swallowed a large dose of some powerful intoxicant. He is a victim of what I have called "herd-poisoning." Like alcohol, herd-poison is an active, extraverted drug. The crowd-intoxicated individual escapes from responsibility, intelligence and morality into a kind of frantic, animal mindlessness.

During his long career as an agitator, Hitler had studied the effects of herd-poison and had learned how to exploit them for his own purposes. He had discovered that the orator can appeal to those "hidden forces" which motivate men's actions, much more effectively than can the writer. Reading is a private, not a collective activity. The writer speaks only to individuals, sitting by themselves in a state of normal sobriety. The orator speaks to masses of individuals, already well primed with herd-poison. They are at his mercy and, if he knows his business, he can do what he likes with them. As an orator, Hitler knew his business supremely well. He was able, in his own words, "to follow the lead of the great mass in such a way that from the living emotion of his hearers the apt word which he needed would be suggested to him and in its turn this would go straight to the heart of his hearers." Otto Strasser called him "a loud-speaker, proclaiming the most secret desires, the least admissible instincts, the sufferings and personal revolts of a whole nation." Twenty years before Madison Avenue embarked upon "Motivational Research," Hitler was systematically exploring and exploiting the secret fears and hopes, the cravings, anxieties and frustrations of the German masses. It is by manipulating "hidden forces" that the advertising experts induce us to buy their wares— a toothpaste, a brand of cigarettes, a political candidate. And it is by appealing to the same hidden forces—and to others too dangerous for Madison Avenue to meddle with—that Hitler induced the German masses to buy themselves a Fuehrer, an insane philosophy and the Second World War.

Unlike the masses, intellectuals have a taste for rationality and an interest in facts. Their critical habit of mind makes them resistant to the kind of propaganda that works so well on the majority. Among the masses "instinct is supreme, and from instinct comes faith. . . . While the healthy common folk instinctively close their ranks to form a community of the people" (under a Leader, it goes without saying) "intellectuals run this way and that, like hens in a poultry yard. With them one cannot make history; they cannot be used as elements composing a community." Intellectuals are the kind of people who demand evidence and are shocked by logical inconsistencies and fallacies. They regard over-simplification as the original sin of the mind and have no use for the slogans, the unqualified assertions and sweeping generalizations which are the propagandist's stock in trade. "All effective propaganda," Hitler wrote, "must be confined to a few bare necessities and then must be expressed in a few stereotyped formulas." These stereotyped formulas must be constantly repeated, for "only constant repetition will finally succeed in imprinting an idea upon the memory of a crowd." Philosophy teaches us to feel uncertain about the things that seem to us self-evident. Propaganda, on the other hand, teaches us to accept as self-evident matters about which it would be reasonable to suspend our judgment or to feel doubt. The aim of the demagogue is to create social coherence under his own leadership. But, as Bertrand Russell has pointed out, "systems of dogma without empirical foundations, such as scholasticism, Marxism and fascism, have the advantage of producing a great deal of social coherence among their disciples." The demagogic propagandist must therefore be consistently dogmatic. All his statements are made without qualification. There are no grays in his picture of the world; everything is either diabolically black or celestially white. In Hitler's words, the propagandist should adopt "a systematically one-sided attitude towards every problem that has to be dealt with." He must never admit that he might be wrong or that people with a different point of view might be even partially right. Opponents should not be argued with; they should be attacked, shouted down, or, if they become too much of a nuisance, liquidated. The morally squeamish intellectual may be shocked by this kind of thing. But the masses are always convinced that "right is on the side of the active aggressor."

Such, then, was Hitler's opinion of humanity in the mass. It was a very low opinion. Was it also an incorrect opinion? The tree is known by its fruits, and a theory of human nature which inspired the kind of techniques that proved so horribly effective must contain at least an element of truth. Virtue and intelligence belong to human beings as individuals freely associating with other individuals in small groups. So do sin and stupidity. But the subhuman mindlessness to which the demagogue makes his appeal, the moral imbecility on which he relies when he goads his victims into action, are characteristic not of men and women as individuals, but of men and women in masses. Mindlessness and moral idiocy are not characteristically human attributes; they are symptoms of herd-poisoning. In all the world's higher religions, salvation and enlightenment are for individuals. The kingdom of heaven is within the mind of a person, not within the collective mindlessness of a crowd. Christ promised to be present where two or three are gathered together. He did not say anything about being present where thousands are intoxicating one another with herd-poison. Under the Nazis enormous numbers of people were compelled to spend an enormous amount of time marching in serried ranks from point A to point B and back again to point A. "This keeping of the whole population on the march seemed to be a senseless waste of time and energy. Only much later," adds Hermann Rauschning, "was there revealed in it a subtle intention based on a well-judged adjustment of ends and means. Marching diverts men's thoughts. Marching kills thought. Marching makes an end of individuality. Marching is the indispensable magic stroke performed in order to accustom the people to a mechanical, quasi-ritualistic activity until it becomes second nature."

From his point of view and at the level where he had chosen to do his dreadful work, Hitler was perfectly correct in his estimate of human nature. To those of us who look at men and women as individuals rather than as members of crowds, or of regimented collectives, he seems hideously wrong. In an age of accelerating over-population, of accelerating over-organization and ever more efficient means of mass communication, how can we preserve the integrity and reassert the value of the human individual? This is a question that can still be asked and perhaps effectively answered. A generation from now it may be too late to find an answer and perhaps impossible, in the stifling collective climate of that future time, even to ask the question.

RALPH WALDO EMERSON

ᡶᡶᡶ

Emerson (1803–1882) is one of the greatest figures in American thought and letters. He spent his childhood in Boston and was trained at Harvard to be a Unitarian minister in the family tradition. Beset by doubts, he resigned from the ministry in 1832 and took up a career of writing and lecturing, during which he continued to work out his transcendentalist philosophy and his ethical doctrine of self-reliance. The present essay was an address delivered to the Phi Beta Kappa chapter at Harvard on August 31, 1837. Its vehement oratorical quality, the memorableness of single phrases, are typical of Emerson, whose style inherits much from the tradition of the New England sermon. Oliver Wendell Holmes called this essay "our intellectual Declaration of Independence." Its appeal to "literary nationalism" (here somewhat muffled by our omission of the final fifth of the essay) is perhaps less important than its recording of a stage in the struggle of a first-class man and thinker to find a way of life that could be pursued with self-reliance and integrity.

THE AMERICAN SCHOLAR

MR. PRESIDENT AND GENTLEMEN:

I greet you on the recommencement of our literary year. Our anniversary is one of hope, and, perhaps, not enough of labor. We do not meet for games of strength or skill, for the recitation of histories, tragedies, and odes, like the ancient Greeks; for parliaments of love and poesy, like the Troubadours; nor for the advancement of science, like our contemporaries in the British and European capitals. Thus far, our holiday has been simply a friendly sign of the survival of the love of letters amongst a people too busy to give to letters any more. As such it is precious as the sign of an indestructible instinct. Perhaps the time is already come when it ought to be, and will be, something else; when the sluggard intellect of this continent will look from under its iron lids and fill the postponed expectation of the world with something better than the exertions of mechanical skill. Our day of dependence, our long apprenticeship to the learning of other lands, draws to a close. The millions that around us are rushing into life, cannot always be fed on the sere remains of foreign harvests. Events, actions arise, that must be sung, that will sing themselves. Who can doubt that poetry will revive and lead in a new age, as the star in the constellation Harp, which now flames in our zenith, astronomers announce, shall one day be the pole-star for a thousand years?

In this hope I accept the topic which not only usage but the nature of our association seem to prescribe to this day,—the AMERICAN SCHOLAR. Year by year we come up hither to read one more chapter of his biography. Let us inquire what light new days and events have thrown on his character and his hopes.

It is one of those fables which out of an unknown antiquity convey an unlooked-for wisdom, that the gods, in the beginning, divided Man into men, that he might be more helpful to himself; just as the hand was divided into fingers, the better to answer its end.

The old fable covers a doctrine ever new and sublime; that there is One Man,—present to all particular men only partially, or through one faculty; and that you must take the whole society to find the whole man. Man is not a farmer, or a professor, or an engineer, but he is all. Man is priest, and scholar, and statesman, and producer, and soldier. In the *divided* or social state these functions are parcelled out to individuals, each of whom aims to do his stint of the joint work, whilst each other performs his. The fable implies that the individual, to possess himself, must sometimes return from his own labor to embrace all the other laborers. But, unfortunately, this original unit, this fountain of power, has been so distributed to multitudes, has been so minutely subdivided and peddled out, that it is spilled into drops, and cannot be gathered. The state of society is one in which the members have suffered amputation from the trunk, and strut about so many walking monsters,—a good finger, a neck, a stomach, an elbow, but never a man.

Man is thus metamorphosed into a thing, into many things. The planter, who is Man sent out into the field to gather food, is seldom cheered by any idea of the true dignity of his ministry. He sees his bushel and his cart, and nothing beyond, and sinks into the farmer, instead of Man on the farm. The tradesman scarcely ever gives an ideal worth to his work, but is ridden by the routine of his craft, and the soul is subject to dollars. The priest becomes a form; the attorney a statute-book; the mechanic a machine; the sailor a rope of the ship.

In this distribution of functions the scholar is the delegated intellect. In the right state he is *Man Thinking*. In the degenerate state, when the victim of society, he tends to become a mere thinker, or still worse, the parrot of other men's thinking.

In this view of him, as Man Thinking, the theory of his office is contained. Him Nature solicits with all her placid, all her monitory pictures; him the past instructs; him the future invites. Is not indeed every man a student, and do not all things exist for the student's behoof? And, finally, is not the true scholar the only true master? But the old oracle said, "All things have two handles: beware of the wrong one." In life, too often, the scholar errs with mankind and forfeits his privilege. Let us see him in his school, and consider him in reference to the main influences he receives.

I. The first in time and the first in importance of the influences upon the mind is that of nature. Every day, the sun; and, after sunset, Night and her stars. Ever the winds blow, ever the grass grows. Every day, men and women, conversing—beholding and beholden. The scholar is he of all men whom this spectacle most engages. He must settle its value in his mind. What is nature to him? There is never a beginning, there is never an end, to the inexplicable continuity of this web of God, but always circular power returning into itself. Therein it resembles his own spirit, whose beginning, whose ending, he never can find,—so entire, so boundless. Far too as her splendors shine, system on system shooting like rays, upward, downward, without centre, without circumference,—in the mass and in the particle, Nature hastens to render account of herself to the mind. Classification begins. To the young mind every thing is individual, stands by itself. By and by, it finds how to join two things and see in them one nature; then three, then three thousand; and so, tyrannized over by its own unifying instinct, it goes on tying things together, diminishing anomalies, discovering roots running under ground whereby contrary and remote things cohere and flower out from one stem. It presently learns that since the dawn of history there has been a constant accumulation and classifying of facts. But what is classification but the perceiving that these objects are not chaotic, and are not foreign, but have a law which is also a law of the human mind? The astronomer discovers that geometry, a pure abstraction of the human mind, is the measure of planetary motion. The chemist finds proportions and intelligible method throughout matter; and science is nothing but the finding of analogy, identity, in the most remote parts. The ambitious soul sits down before each refractory fact; one after another reduces all strange constitutions, all new powers, to their class and their law, and goes on forever to animate the last fibre of organization, the outskirts of nature, by insight.

Thus to him, to this schoolboy under the bending dome of day, is suggested that he and it proceed from one root; one is leaf and one is flower; relation, sympathy, stirring in every vein. And what is that root? Is not that the soul of his soul? A thought too bold; a dream too wild. Yet when this spiritual light shall have revealed the law of more earthly natures,—when he has learned to worship the soul, and to see that the natural philosophy that now is, is only the first gropings of its gigantic hand, he shall look forward to an ever expanding knowledge as to a becoming creator. He shall see that nature is the opposite of the soul, answering to it part for part. One is seal and one is print. Its beauty is the beauty of his own mind. Its laws are the laws of his own mind. Nature then becomes to him the measure of his attainments. So much of nature as he is ignorant of, so much of his own mind does he not yet possess. And, in fine, the ancient precept, "Know thyself," and the modern precept, "Study nature," become at last one maxim.

II. The next great influence into the spirit of the scholar is the mind of the Past,—in whatever form, whether of literature, of art, of institutions, that mind is inscribed. Books are the best type of the influence of the past, and perhaps we shall get at the truth,—learn the amount of this influence more conveniently,—by considering their value alone.

The theory of books is noble. The scholar of the first age received into him the world around; brooded thereon; gave it the new arrangement of his own mind, and uttered it again. It came into him life; it went out from him truth. It came to him short-lived actions; it went out from him immortal thoughts. It came to him business; it went from him poetry. It was dead fact; now, it is quick thought. It can stand, and it can go. It now endures, it now flies, it now inspires. Precisely in proportion to the depth of mind from which it issued, so high does it soar, so long does it sing.

Or, I might say, it depends on how far the process had gone, of transmuting life into truth. In proportion to the completeness of the distillation, so will the purity and imperishableness of the product be. But none is quite perfect. As no air-pump can by any means make a perfect vacuum, so neither can any artist entirely exclude the conventional, the local, the perishable from his book, or write a book of pure thought, that shall be as efficient, in all respects, to a remote posterity, as to contemporaries, or rather to the second age. Each age, it is found, must write its own books;

or rather, each generation for the next succeeding. The books of an older period will not fit this.

Yet hence arises a grave mischief. The sacredness which attaches to the act of creation, the act of thought, is transferred to the record. The poet chanting was felt to be a divine man: henceforth the chant is divine also. The writer was a just and wise spirit: henceforward it is settled the book is perfect; as love of the hero corrupts into worship of his statue. Instantly the book becomes noxious: the guide is a tyrant. The sluggish and perverted mind of the multitude, slow to open to the incursions of Reason, having once so opened, having once received this book, stands upon it, and makes an outcry if it is disparaged. Colleges are built on it. Books are written on it by thinkers, not by Man Thinking; by men of talent, that is, who start wrong, who set out from accepted dogmas, not from their own sight of principles. Meek young men grow up in libraries, believing it their duty to accept the views which Cicero, which Locke, which Bacon, have given; forgetful that Cicero, Locke, and Bacon were only young men in libraries when they wrote these books.

Hence, instead of Man Thinking, we have the bookworm. Hence the book-learned class, who value books, as such; not as related to nature and the human constitution, but as making a sort of Third Estate with the world and the soul. Hence the restorers of readings, the emendators, the bibliomaniacs of all degrees.

Books are the best of things, well used; abused, among the worst. What is the right use? What is the one end which all means go to effect? They are for nothing but to inspire. I had better never see a book than to be warped by its attraction clean out of my own orbit, and made a satellite instead of a system. The one thing in the world, of value, is the active soul. This every man is entitled to; this every man contains within him, although in almost all men obstructed and as yet unborn. The soul active sees absolute truth and utters truth, or creates. In this action it is genius; not the privilege of here and there a favorite, but the sound estate of every man. In its essence it is progressive. The book, the college, the school of art, the institution of any kind, stop with some past utterance of genius. This is good, say they,—let us hold by this. They pin me down. They look backward and not forward. But genius looks forward: the eyes of man are set in his forehead, not in his hindhead: man hopes: genius creates. Whatever talents may be, if the man create not, the pure efflux of the Deity is not his;—cinders and smoke there may be, but not yet flame. There are creative manners, there are creative actions, and creative words; manners, actions, words, that is, indicative of no custom or authority, but springing spontaneous from the mind's own sense of good and fair.

On the other part, instead of being its own seer, let it receive from another mind its truth, though it were in torrents of light, without periods of solitude, inquest, and self-recovery, and a fatal disservice is done. Genius is always sufficiently the enemy of genius by over-influence. The literature of every nation bears me witness. The English dramatic poets have Shakspearized now for two hundred years.

Undoubtedly there is a right way of reading, so it be sternly subordinated. Man Thinking must not be subdued by his instruments. Books are for the scholar's idle times. When he can read God directly, the hour is too precious to be wasted in other men's transcripts of their readings. But when the intervals of darkness come, as come they must,—when the sun is hid and the stars withdraw their shining,—we repair to the lamps which were kindled by their ray, to guide our steps to the East again, where the dawn is. We hear, that we may speak. The Arabian proverb says, "A fig tree, looking on a fig tree, becometh fruitful."

It is remarkable, the character of the pleasure we derive from the best books. They impress us with the conviction that one nature wrote and the same reads. We read the verses of one of the great English poets, of Chaucer, of Marvell, of Dryden, with the most modern joy,—with a pleasure, I mean, which is in great part caused by the abstraction of all *time* from their verses. There is some awe mixed with the joy of our surprise, when this poet, who lived in some past world, two or three hundred years ago, says that which lies close to my own soul, that which I also had well-nigh thought and said. But for the evidence thence afforded to the philosophical doctrine of the identity of all minds, we should suppose some preëstablished harmony, some foresight of souls that were to be, and some preparation of stores for their future wants, like the fact observed in insects, who lay up food before death for the young grub they shall never see.

I would not be hurried by any love of system, by any exaggeration of instincts, to underrate the Book. We all know, that as the human body can be nourished on any food, though it were boiled grass and the broth of shoes, so the human mind can be fed by any knowledge. And great and heroic men have existed who had almost no other information than by the printed page. I only would say that it needs a strong head to bear that diet. One must be an inventor to read well. As the proverb says, "He that would bring home the wealth of the Indies, must carry out the wealth of the Indies." There is then creative reading as well as creative writing. When the mind is braced by labor and invention, the page of whatever book we read becomes luminous with manifold allusion. Every sentence is doubly significant, and the sense of our author is as broad as the world. We then see, what is always true, that as the seer's hour of vision is short and rare among heavy days and months, so is its record, perchance, the least part of his volume. The discerning will read, in his Plato or Shakspeare, only that least part,—only the authentic utterances of the oracle;—all the rest he rejects, were it never so many times Plato's and Shakspeare's.

Of course there is a portion of reading quite indispensable to a wise man. History and exact science he must learn by laborious reading. Colleges, in like manner, have their indispensable office,—to teach elements. But they can only highly serve us when they aim not to drill, but to create; when they gather from far every ray of various genius to their hospitable halls, and by the concentrated fires, set the hearts of their youth on flame. Thought and knowledge are natures in which apparatus and pretension avail nothing. Gowns and pecuniary foundations, though of towns of gold, can never countervail the least sentence or syllable of wit. Forget this, and our American colleges will recede in their public importance, whilst they grow richer every year.

III. There goes in the world a notion that the scholar should be a recluse, a valetudinarian,—as unfit for any handiwork or public labor as a penknife for an axe. The so-called "practical men" sneer at speculative men, as if, because they speculate or *see*, they could do nothing. I have heard it said that the clergy,—who are always, more universally than any other class, the scholars of their day,—are addressed as women; that the rough, spontaneous conversation of men they do not hear, but only a mincing and diluted speech. They are often virtually disfranchised; and indeed there are advocates for their celibacy. As far as this is true of the studious classes, it is not just and wise. Action is with the scholar subordinate, but it is essential. Without it he is not yet man. Without it thought can never ripen into truth. Whilst the world hangs before the eye as a cloud of beauty, we cannot even see its beauty. Inaction is cowardice, but there can be no scholar without the heroic mind. The preamble of thought, the transition through which it passes from the unconscious to the conscious, is action. Only so much do I know, as I have lived. Instantly we know whose words are loaded with life, and whose not.

The world,—this shadow of the soul, or *other me*,—lies wide around. Its attractions are the keys which unlock my thoughts and make me acquainted with myself. I run eagerly into this resounding tumult. I grasp the hands of those next me, and take my place in the ring to suffer and to work, taught by an instinct that so shall the dumb abyss be vocal with speech. I pierce its order; I dissipate its fear; I dispose of it within the circuit of my expanding life. So much only of life as I know by experience, so much of the wilderness have I vanquished and planted, or so far have I extended my being, my dominion. I do not see how any man can afford, for the sake of his nerves and his nap, to spare any action in which he can partake. It is pearls and rubies to his discourse. Drudgery, calamity, exasperation, want, are instructors in eloquence and wisdom. The true scholar grudges every opportunity of action past by, as a loss of power. It is the raw material out of which the intellect moulds her splendid products. A strange process too, this by which experience is converted into thought, as a mulberry leaf is converted into satin. The manufacture goes forward at all hours.

The actions and events of our childhood and youth are now matters of calmest observation. They lie like fair pictures in the air. Not so with our recent actions,—with the business which we now have in hand. On this we are quite unable to speculate. Our affections as yet circulate through it. We no more feel or know it than we feel the feet, or the hand, or the brain of our body. The new deed is yet a part of life,—remains for a time immersed in our unconscious life. In some contemplative hour it detaches itself from the life like a ripe fruit, to become a thought of the mind. Instantly it is raised, transfigured; the corruptible has put on incorruption. Henceforth it is an object of beauty, however base its origin and neighborhood. Observe too the impossibility of antedating this act. In its grub state, it cannot fly, it cannot shine, it is a dull grub. But suddenly, without observation, the selfsame thing unfurls beautiful wings, and is an angel of wisdom. So is there no fact, no event, in our private history, which shall not, sooner or later, lose its adhesive, inert form, and astonish us by soaring from our body into the empyrean. Cradle and infancy, school and playground, the fear of boys, and dogs, and ferules, the love of little maids and berries, and many another fact that once filled the whole sky, are gone already; friend and relative, profession and party, town and country, nation and world, must also soar and sing.

Of course, he who has put forth his total strength in fit actions has the richest return of wisdom. I will not shut myself out of this globe of action, and transplant an oak into a flowerpot, there to hunger and pine; nor trust the revenue of some single faculty, and exhaust one vein of thought, much like those Savoyards, who, getting their livelihood by carving shepherds, shepherdesses, and smoking Dutchmen, for all Europe, went out one day to the mountain to find stock, and discovered that they had whittled up the last of their pine trees. Authors we have, in numbers, who have written out their vein, and who, moved by a commendable prudence, sail for Greece or Palestine, follow the trapper into the prairie, or ramble round Algiers, to replenish their merchantable stock.

If it were only for a vocabulary, the scholar would be covetous of action. Life is our dictionary. Years are well spent in country labors; in town; in the insight into trades and manufactures; in frank intercourse with many men and women; in science; in art; to the one end of mastering in all their facts a language by which to illustrate and embody our perceptions. I learn immediately from any speaker how much he has already lived, through the poverty or the splendor of his speech. Life lies behind us as the quarry from whence we get tiles and copestones for the masonry of to-day. This is the way to learn grammar. Colleges and books only copy the language which the field and the work-yard made.

But the final value of action, like that of books, and better than books, is that it is a resource. That great principle of Undulation in nature, that shows itself in the inspiring and expiring of the breath; in desire and satiety; in the ebb and flow of the sea; in day and night; in heat and cold; and, as yet more deeply ingrained in every atom and every fluid, is known to us under the name of Polarity,—these "fits of easy transmission and reflection," as Newton called them, are the law of nature because they are the law of spirit.

The mind now thinks, now acts, and each fit reproduces the other. When the artist has exhausted his materials, when the fancy no longer paints, when thoughts are no longer apprehended and books are a weariness,—he has always the resource *to live*. Character is higher than intellect. Thinking is the function. Living is the functionary. The stream retreats to its source. A great soul will be strong to live, as well as strong to think. Does he lack organ or medium to impart his truths? He can still fall back on this elemental force of living them. This is a total act. Thinking is a partial act. Let the grandeur of justice shine in his affairs. Let the beauty of affection cheer his lowly roof. Those "far from fame," who dwell and act with him, will feel the force of his constitution in the doings and passages of the day better than it can be measured by any public and designed display. Time shall teach him that the scholar loses no hour which the man lives. Herein he unfolds the sacred germ of his instinct, screened from influence. What is lost in seemliness is gained in strength. Not out of those on whom systems of education have exhausted their culture, comes the helpful giant to destroy the old or to build the new, but out of unhandselled savage nature; out of terrible Druids and Berserkers come at last Alfred and Shakspeare.

I hear therefore with joy whatever is beginning to be said of the dignity and necessity of labor to every citizen. There is virtue yet in the hoe and the spade, for learned as well as for unlearned hands. And labor is everywhere welcome; always we are invited to work; only be this limitation observed, that a man shall not for the sake of wider activity sacrifice any opinion to the popular judgments and modes of action.

I have now spoken of the education of the scholar by nature, by books, and by action. It remains to say somewhat of his duties.

They are such as become Man Thinking. They may all be comprised in self-trust. The office of the scholar is to cheer, to raise, and to guide men by showing them facts amidst appearances. He plies the slow, unhonored, and unpaid task of observation. Flamsteed and Herschel, in their glazed observatories, may catalogue the stars with the praise of all men, and the results being splendid and useful, honor is sure. But he, in his private observatory, cataloguing obscure and nebulous stars of the human mind, which as yet no man has thought of as such,—watching days and months sometimes for a few facts; correcting still his old records;—must relinquish display and immediate fame. In the long period of his preparation he must betray often an ignorance and shiftlessness in popular arts, incurring the disdain of the able who shoulder him aside. Long he must stammer in his speech; often forego the living for the dead. Worse yet, he must accept—how often!—poverty and solitude. For the ease and pleasure of treading the old road, accepting the fashions, the education, the religion of society, he takes the cross of making his own, and, of course, the self-accusation, the faint heart, the frequent uncertainty and loss of time, which are the nettles and tangling vines in the way of the self-relying and self-directed; and the state of virtual hostility in which he seems to stand to society, and especially to educated society. For all this loss and scorn, what offset? He is to find consolation in exercising the highest functions of human nature. He is one who raises himself from private considerations and breathes and lives on public and illustrious thoughts. He is the world's eye. He is the world's heart. He is to resist the vulgar prosperity that retrogrades ever to barbarism, by preserving and communicating heroic sentiments, noble biographies, melodious verse, and the conclusions of history. Whatsoever oracles the human heart, in all emergencies, in all solemn hours, has uttered as its commentary on the world of actions,—these he shall receive and impart. And whatsoever new verdict Reason from her inviolable seat pronounces on the passing men and events of to-day,—this he shall hear and promulgate.

These being his functions, it becomes him to feel all confidence in himself, and to defer never to the popular cry. He and he only knows the world. The world of any moment is the merest appearance. Some great decorum, some fetish of a government, some ephemeral trade, or war, or man, is cried up by half mankind and cried down by the other half, as if all depended on this particular up or down. The odds are that the whole question is not worth the poorest thought which the scholar has lost in listening to the controversy. Let him not quit his belief that a popgun is a popgun, though the ancient and honorable of the earth affirm it to be the crack of doom. In silence, in steadiness, in severe abstraction, let him hold by himself; add observation to observation, patient of neglect, patient of reproach, and bide his own time,—happy enough if he can satisfy himself alone that this day he has seen something truly. Success treads on every right step. For the instinct is sure, that prompts him to tell his brother what he thinks. He then learns that in going down into the secrets of his own mind he has descended into the secrets of all minds. He learns that he who has mastered any law in his private thoughts, is master to that extent of all men whose language he speaks, and of all into whose language his own can be translated. The poet, in utter solitude remembering his spontaneous thoughts and recording them, is found to have recorded that which men in crowded cities find true for them also. The orator distrusts at first the fitness of his frank confessions, his want of knowledge of the persons he addresses, until he finds that he is the complement of his hearers; —that they drink his words because he fulfils for them their own nature; the deeper he dives into his privatest, secretest presentiment, to his wonder he finds this is the most acceptable, most public, and universally true. The people delight in it; the better part of every man feels, This is my music; this is myself.

In self-trust all the virtues are comprehended. Free should the scholar be,—free and brave. Free even to the definition of freedom, "without any hindrance that does not arise out of his own constitution." Brave; for fear is a thing which a scholar by his very function puts behind him. Fear always springs from ignorance. It is a shame to him if his tranquillity, amid dangerous times, arise from the presumption that like children and women his is a protected class; or if he seek a temporary peace by the diversion of his thoughts from politics or vexed questions, hiding his head like an ostrich in the flowering bushes, peeping into microscopes, and turning rhymes, as a boy whistles to keep his courage up. So is the danger a danger still; so is the fear worse. Manlike let him turn and face it. Let him look into its eye and search its nature, inspect its origin,—see the whelping of this lion,—which lies no great way back; he will then find in himself a perfect comprehension of its nature and extent; he will have made his hands meet on the other side, and can henceforth defy it and pass on superior. The world is his who can see through its pretension. What deafness, what stone-blind custom, what overgrown error you behold is there only by sufferance,—by your sufferance. See it to be a lie, and you have already dealt it its mortal blow.

Yes, we are the cowed,—we the trustless. It is a mischievous notion that we are come late into nature; that the world was finished a long time ago. As the world was plastic and fluid in the hands of God, so it is ever to so much of his attributes as we bring to it. To ignorance and sin, it is flint. They adapt themselves to it as they may; but in proportion as a man has any thing in him divine, the firmament flows before him and takes his signet and form. Not he is great who can alter matter, but he who can alter my state of mind. They are the kings of the world who give the color of their present thought to all nature and all art, and persuade men by the cheerful serenity of their carrying the matter, that this thing which they do is the apple which the ages have desired to pluck, now at last ripe, and inviting nations to the harvest. The great man makes the great thing. Wherever Macdonald sits, there is the head of the table. Linnæus makes botany the most alluring of studies, and wins it from the farmer and the herb-woman; Davy, chemistry; and Cuvier, fossils. The day is always his who works in it with serenity and great aims. The unstable estimates of men crowd to him whose mind is filled with a truth, as the heaped waves of the Atlantic follow the moon.

For this self-trust, the reason is deeper than can be fathomed,—darker than can be enlightened. I might not carry with me the feeling of my audience in stating my own belief. But I have already shown the ground of my hope, in adverting to the doctrine that man is one. I believe man has been wronged; he has wronged himself. He has almost lost the light that can lead him back to his prerogatives. Men are become of no account. Men in history, men in the world of to-day, are bugs, are spawn, and are called "the mass" and "the herd." In a century, in a millennium, one or two men; that is to say, one or two approximations to the right state of every man. All the rest behold in the hero or the poet their own green and crude being,—ripened; yes, and are content to be less, so *that* may attain to its full stature. What a testimony, full of grandeur, full of pity, is borne to the demands of his own nature, by the poor clansman, the poor partisan, who rejoices in the glory of his chief. The poor and the low find some amends to their immense moral capacity, for their acquiescence in a political and social inferiority. They are content to be brushed like flies from the path of a great person, so that justice shall be done by him to that common nature which it is the dearest desire of all to see enlarged and glorified. They sun themselves in the great man's light, and feel it to be their own element. They cast the dignity of man from their downtrod selves upon the shoulders of a hero, and will perish to add one drop of blood to make that great heart beat, those giant sinews combat and conquer. He lives for us, and we live in him.

Men, such as they are, very naturally seek money or power; and power because it is as good as money,—the "spoils," so called, "of office." And why not? for they aspire to the highest, and this, in their sleep-walking, they dream is highest. Wake them and they shall quit the false good and leap to the true, and leave governments to clerks and desks. This revolution is to be wrought by the gradual domestication of the idea of Culture. The main enterprise of the world for splendor, for extent, is the up-building of a man. Here are the materials strewn along the ground. The private life of one man shall be a more illustrious monarchy, more formidable to its enemy, more sweet and serene in its influence to its friend, than any kingdom in history. For a man, rightly viewed, comprehendeth the particular natures of all men. Each philosopher, each bard, each actor has only done for me, as by a delegate, what one day I can do for myself. The books which once we valued more than the apple of the eye, we have quite exhausted. What is that but saying that we have come up with the point of view which the universal mind took through the eyes of one scribe; we have been that man, and have passed on. First, one, then another, we drain all cisterns, and waxing greater by all these supplies, we crave a better and more abundant food. The man has never lived that can feed us ever. The human mind cannot be enshrined in a person who shall set a barrier on any one side to this unbounded, unboundable empire. It is one central fire, which, flaming now out of the lips of Etna, lightens the capes of Sicily, and now out of the throat of Vesuvius, illuminates the towers and vineyards of Naples. It is one light which beams out of a thousand stars. It is one soul which animates all men.

. . .

JOHN HENRY NEWMAN

Newman (1801–1890) was born in London, educated at Oxford, and became an Oxford don. A profoundly religious man, he took Holy Orders in the Anglican Church in 1824. His friendship with such thinkers as Hurrell Froude, John Keble, and Edward Pusey led to the founding of the Oxford Movement, which attempted to combat the rationalistic and "liberal" tendencies in the English church and to establish a firmer basis for its latent tradition of Catholicism. His controversial views led to his withdrawal from Oxford, and in 1845 he became a Roman Catholic. He soon joined the Oratorians, a semi-monastic order, and was Head of the order's house at Egbaston for almost forty years. An attack by Charles Kingsley in 1864 became the occasion for a series of pamphlets, revised and published later as Apologia pro vita sua, *in which Newman gave an account of his religious life and opinions. Its argument, style, and temper did much to restore his standing in British public opinion. The last part of his life was spent amidst universal reverence. He was made Honorary Fellow of Trinity College, Oxford, in 1878 and was created Cardinal in the next year.*

In 1852 Newman was made rector-elect of a projected Catholic University in Dublin. Sensing that the community needed a clear explanation of what a University should be, he delivered a series of nine lectures in Dublin from May 10 to June 7, 1852. They were published that year as Discourses on the Scope and Nature of a University Education *and in his collected works as* The Idea of a University. *His plan for the University fell through, but the lectures have survived as the classical statement of the aims of a liberal education. The present selection (title supplied by us) is the sixth part of the fifth lecture, "Knowledge Its Own End."*

ON LIBERAL KNOWLEDGE

Now bear with me, Gentlemen, if what I am about to say, has at first sight a fanciful appearance. Philosophy, then, or Science, is related to Knowledge in this way:—Knowledge is called by the name of Science or Philosophy, when it is acted upon, informed, or if I may use a strong figure, impregnated by Reason. Reason is the principle of that intrinsic fecundity of Knowledge, which, to those who possess it, is its especial value, and which dispenses with the necessity of their looking abroad for any end to rest upon external to itself. Knowledge, indeed, when thus exalted into a scientific form, is also power; not only is it excellent in itself, but whatever such excellence may be, it is something more, it has a result beyond itself. Doubtless; but that is a further consideration, with which I am not concerned. I only say that, prior to its being a power, it is a good; that it is, not only an instrument, but an end. I know well it may resolve itself into an art, and terminate in a mechanical process, and in tangible fruit; but it also may fall back upon that Reason which informs it, and resolve itself into Philosophy. In one case it is called Useful Knowledge, in the other Liberal. The same person may cultivate it in both ways at once; but this again is a matter foreign to my subject; here I do but say that there are two ways of using Knowledge, and in matter of fact those who use it in one way are not likely to use it in the other, or at least in a very limited measure. You see, then, here are two methods of Education; the end of the one is to be philosophical, of the other to be mechanical; the one rises towards general ideas, the other is exhausted upon what is particular and external. Let me not be thought to deny the necessity, or to decry the benefit, of such attention to what is particular and practical, as belongs to the useful or mechanical arts; life could not go on without them; we owe our daily welfare to them; their exercise is the duty of the many, and we owe to the many a debt of gratitude for fulfilling that duty. I only say that Knowledge, in proportion as it tends more and more to be particular, ceases to be Knowledge. It is a question whether Knowledge can in any proper sense be predicated of the brute creation; without pretending to metaphysical exactness of phraseology, which would be unsuitable to an occasion like this, I say, it seems to me improper to call that passive sensation, or perception of things, which brutes seem to possess, by the name of Knowledge. When I speak of Knowledge, I mean something intellectual, something which grasps what it perceives through the senses; something which takes a view of things; which sees more than the senses convey; which reasons upon what it sees, and while it sees; which invests it with an idea. It expresses itself, not in a mere enunciation, but by an enthymeme: it is of the nature of science from the first, and in this consists its dignity. The principle of real dignity in Knowledge, its worth, its desirableness, considered irrespectively of its results, is this germ within it of a scientific or a philosophical process. This is how it comes to be an end in itself; this is why it admits of being called Liberal. Not to know the relative disposition of things is the state of slaves or children; to have mapped out the Universe is the boast, or at least the ambition, of Philosophy.

Moreover, such knowledge is not a mere extrinsic or accidental advantage, which is ours to-day and another's to-morrow, which may be got up from a book, and easily forgotten again, which we can command or communicate at our pleasure, which we can borrow for the occasion, carry about in our hand, and take into the market; it is an acquired illumination, it is a habit, a personal possession, and an inward endowment. And this is the reason, why it is more correct, as well as more usual, to speak of a University as a place of education, than of instruction, though, when knowledge is concerned, instruction would at first sight have seemed the more appropriate word. We are instructed, for instance, in manual exercises, in the fine and useful arts, in trades, and in ways of business; for these are methods, which have little or no effect upon the mind itself, are contained in rules committed to memory, to tradition, or to use, and bear upon an end external to themselves. But education is a higher word; it implies an action upon our mental nature, and the formation of a character; it is something individual and permanent, and is commonly spoken of in connexion with religion and virtue. When, then, we speak of the communication of Knowledge as being Education, we thereby really imply that that Knowledge is a state or condition of mind; and since cultivation of mind is surely worth seeking for its own sake, we are thus brought once more to the conclusion, which the word "Liberal" and the word "Philosophy" have already suggested, that there is a Knowledge, which is desirable, though nothing come of it, as being of itself a treasure, and a sufficient remuneration of years of labour.

ALBERT JAY NOCK

By the time of his death in 1945 at the age of 72, Albert Jay Nock had achieved a considerable reputation for his "distinguished, humorous, and incisive" style of writing and his intensely iconoclastic views. After a strictly classical education at St. Stephen's College (now part of Columbia University), he spent some years as a clergyman, then turned to journalism and to critical studies of American involvement in war and diplomacy. He was a great admirer of Henry George, Thomas Jefferson, and François Rabelais, and in his last years a devoted enemy of the New Deal and of Franklin D. Roosevelt. A prolific writer of articles for magazines, he published several collections, including On Doing the Right Thing, and Other Essays *(1928),* The Book of the Journeyman *(1930), and* Free Speech and Plain Language *(1937), from which we take the present essay, first published in* Harper's *in 1932. A more elaborate statement of his views on education will be found in his* The Theory of Education in the United States *(1932).*

THE DISADVANTAGES OF BEING EDUCATED

My interest in education had been comfortably asleep since my late youth, when circumstances waked it up again about six years ago. I then discovered that in the meantime our educational system had changed its aim. It was no longer driving at the same thing as formerly, and no longer contemplated the same kind of product. When I examined it I was as far "out" on what I expected to find as if I had gone back to one of the sawmills familiar to my boyhood in Michigan, and found it turning out boots and shoes.

The difference seemed to be that while education was still spoken of as a "preparation for life," the preparation was of a kind which bore less directly on intellect and character than in former times, and more directly on proficiency. It aimed at what we used to call training rather than education; and it not only did very little with education, but seemed to assume that training *was* education, thus overriding a distinction that formerly was quite clear. Forty years ago a man trained to proficiency in anything was respected accordingly, but was not regarded as an educated man, or "just as good," on the strength of it. A trained mechanic, banker, dentist or man of business got all due credit for his proficiency, but his education, if he had any, lay behind that and was not confused with it. His training, in a word, bore directly upon what he could do or get, while his education bore directly on neither; it bore upon what he could become and be.

Curiosity led me to look into the matter a little more closely, and my observations confirmed the impression that the distinction between training and education was practically wiped out. I noticed, too, that

there was a good deal of complaint about this: even professional educators, many of them, were dissatisfied with it. Their complaints, when
boiled down, seemed to be that education is too little regarded as an
end in itself, and that most of the country's student-population take a
too strictly vocational view of what they are doing, while the remainder
look at it as a social experience, encouraged largely in order to keep the
cubs from being underfoot at home, and reciprocally appreciated mostly
because it puts off the evil day when they must go to work; and that
our institutions show too much complacency in accommodating themselves to these views.

These complaints, I observed, were not confined to educators; one
heard them from laymen as well, and the laymen seemed to be as clear
in their minds about the difference between education and training as the
professional educators were. For example, one of America's most distinguished artists (whom I am not authorized to quote, and I, therefore,
call him Richard Roe) told a friend of mine that when his ship came
in he proposed to give magnificent endowments to Columbia, Harvard,
Princeton and Yale on the sole condition that they should shut up shop
and go out of business forever. Then he proposed to put up a bronze
plate over the main entrance to each of these institutions, bearing this
legend:

CLOSED

THROUGH THE BENEFACTION

OF

RICHARD ROE

AN HUMBLE PAINTER

IN BEHALF OF EDUCATION

As I saw the situation at the moment, these complaints seemed reasonable. Training is excellent, it can not be too well done, and opportunity
for it can not be too cheap and abundant. Probably a glorified crèche for
delayed adolescents here and there is a good thing, too; no great harm in it
anyway. Yet it struck me as apparently it struck others, that there should
also be a little education going on. Something should be done to mature
the national resources of intellect and character as well as the resources
of proficiency; and, moreover, something should be done to rehabilitate
a respect for these resources as a social asset. Full of this idea, I rushed
into print with the suggestion that in addition to our present system of
schools, colleges and universities which are doing first-class work as
training-schools, we ought to have a few educational institutions. My
notion was that the educable person ought to have something like an
even chance with the ineducable, because he is socially useful. I thought
that even a society composed of well-trained ineducables might be improved by having a handful of educated persons sifted around in it

every now and then. I, therefore, offered the suggestion, which did not seem exorbitant, that in a population of a hundred and twenty-odd million there should be at least one set of institutions, consisting of a grade-school, a secondary school and an undergraduate college, which should be strictly and rigorously educational, kept in perpetual quarantine against the contagion of training.

II

This was five years ago, and about eighteen months ago I repeated the suggestion. My modest proposal was hardly in print before I received a letter from a friend in the University of Oxford, propounding a point which—believe it or not—had never occurred to me.

But think of the poor devils who shall have gone through your mill! It seems a cold-blooded thing . . . to turn out a lot of people who simply can't live at home. Vivisection is nothing to it. As I understand your scheme, you are planning to breed a batch of cultivated, sensitive beings who would all die six months after they were exposed to your actual civilization. This is not Oxford's superciliousness, I assure you, for things nowadays are precious little better with us. I agree that such people are the salt of the earth, and England used to make some kind of place for them. . . . But now—well, I hardly know. It seems as though some parts of the earth were jolly well salt-proof. The salt melts and disappears, and nothing comes of it.

As I say, I had never thought of that. It had never occurred to me that there might be disadvantages in being educated. I saw at once where my mistake lay. I had been looking at the matter from the point of view of an elderly person to whom such education as he had was just so much clear gain, not from the point of view of a youth who is about to make his start in the world. I saw at once that circumstances, which had been more or less in favour of my educated contemporaries, were all dead against the educated youngster of to-day. Therefore, last year, when I was appointed to deal again with the subject in a public way, I went back on all I had said, and ate my ration of humble-pie with the best grace I could muster.

Every shift in the social order, however slight, puts certain classes irrevocably out of luck, as our vulgarism goes. At the beginning of the sixteenth century the French feudal nobility were out of luck. They could do nothing about it, nobody could do anything about it, they were simply out of luck. Since the middle of the last century, monarchs and a hereditary aristocracy are out of luck. The *Zeitgeist* seems always arbitrarily to be picking out one or another social institution, breathing on it with the devouring breath of a dragon; it decays and dissolves, and those who represent it are out of luck. Up to a few years ago an educated person, even in the United States, was not wholly out of luck; since then, however, an educated young man's chance, or an educated young woman's, is slim. I do not here refer exclusively to the mere matter of picking up a living, although, as I shall show, education is a good bit of hindrance even to that; but also to conditions which make any sort of living enjoyable and worth while.

So in regard to my championship of education it turned out again that everybody is wiser than anybody, at least from the short-time point of view, which is the one that human society invariably takes. Some philosophers think that society is an organism, moving instinctively always towards the immediate good thing, as certain blind worms of a very low order of sensibility move towards food. From the long-time point of view, this may often be a bad thing for the worm; it may get itself stepped on or run over or picked up by a boy looking for fish-bait. Nothing can be done about it, however, for the worm's instinct works that way and, according to these philosophers, so does society's, and the individual member of society has little practical choice but to go along.

Hence our institutions which profess and call themselves educational, have probably done the right thing—the immediate right thing, at any rate—in converting themselves, as our drugstores have done, into something that corresponds only very loosely to their profession. No doubt the lay and professional complaint against this tendency is wrong; no doubt the artist Richard Roe's proposal to close up our four great training-schools is wrong. No doubt, too, our young people are right in instinctively going at education, in the traditional sense of the term, with very long teeth. If I were in their place, I now think I should do as they do; and since I am in the way of recantation, as an old offender who has at last seen the light of grace, I may be allowed to say why I should do so—to show what I now plainly see to be the disadvantages of being educated.

III

Education deprives a young person of one of his most precious possessions, the sense of co-operation with his fellows. He is like a pacifist in 1917, alone in spirit—a depressing situation, and especially, almost unbearably, depressing to youth. "After all," says Dumas's hero, "man is man's brother," and youth especially needs a free play of the fraternal sense; it needs the stimulus and support of association in common endeavour. The survivor of an older generation in America has had these benefits in some degree; he is more or less established and matured and can rub along fairly comfortably on his spiritual accumulations; and besides, as age comes on, emotions weaken and sensitiveness is dulled. In his day, from the spiritual and social point of view, one could afford to be educated—barely and with difficulty afford it perhaps, but education was not a flat liability. It netted enough to be worth its price. At present one can afford only to be trained. The young person's fellows are turning all their energy into a single narrow channel of interest; they have set the whole current of their being in one direction. Education is all against his doing that, while training is all for it; hence training puts him in step with his fellows, while education tends to leave him a solitary figure, spiritually disqualified.

For these reasons: education, in the first place, discloses other channels of interest and makes them look inviting. In the second place, it gives rise to the view that the interest which absorbs his fellows is not worth mortgaging one's whole self, body, mind and spirit, to carry on. In the third place, it shows what sort of people one's fellows inevitably become, through their exclusive absorption in this one interest, and makes it hard to reconcile oneself to the thought of becoming like them. Training, on the other hand, raises no such disturbances; it lets one go on one's chosen way, with no uncertainty, no loss of confidence, as a man of the crowd. Education is divisive, separatist; training induces the exhilarating sense that one is doing with others what others do and thinking the thoughts that others think.

Education, in a word, leads a person on to ask a great deal more from life than life, as at present organized, is willing to give him; and it begets dissatisfaction with the rewards that life holds out. Training tends to satisfy him with very moderate and simple returns. A good income, a home and family, the usual run of comforts and conveniences, diversions addressed only to the competitive or sporting spirit or else to raw sensation—training not only makes directly for getting these, but also for an inert and comfortable contentment with them. Well, these are all that our present society has to offer, so it is undeniably the best thing all round to keep people satisfied with them, which training does, and not to inject a subversive influence, like education, into this easy complacency. Politicians understand this—it is their business to understand it—and hence they hold up "a chicken in every pot and two cars in every garage" as a satisfying social ideal. But the mischief of education is its exorbitance. The educated lad may like stewed chicken and motor-cars as well as anybody, but his education has bred a liking for other things too, things that the society around him does not care for and will not countenance. It has bred tastes which society resents as culpably luxurious, and will not connive at gratifying. Paraphrasing the old saying, education sends him out to shift for himself with a champagne appetite amidst a gin-guzzling society.

Training, on the other hand, breeds no such tastes; it keeps him so well content with synthetic gin that a mention of champagne merely causes him to make a wry face. Not long ago I met a young acquaintance from the Middle West who has done well by himself in a business way and is fairly rich. He looked jaded and seedy, evidently from overwork, and as I was headed for Munich at the moment, I suggested he should take a holiday and go along. He replied, "Why, I couldn't sell anything in

Munich—I'm a business man." For a moment or two I was rather taken aback by his attitude, but I presently recognized it as the characteristic attitude of trained proficiency, and I saw that as things are it was right. Training had kept his demands on life down to a strictly rudimentary order and never tended to muddle up their clear simplicity or shift their direction. Education would have done both; he was lucky to have had none.

It may be plainly seen, I think, that in speaking as he did, my friend enjoyed the sustaining sense of co-operation with his fellows. In his intense concentration, his singleness of purpose, and in the extremely primitive simplicity of his desires and satisfactions, he was completely in the essential movement of the society surrounding him; indeed, if his health and strength hold out, he may yet become one of those representative men like Mr. Ford, the late Mr. Eastman or Mr. Hoover, who take their tone from society in the first instance and in turn give back that tone with interest. Ever since the first westward emigration from the Atlantic seaboard, American civilization may be summed up as a free-for-all scuffle to get rich quickly and by any means. In so far as a person was prepared to accept the terms of this free-for-all and engage in it, so far he was sustained by the exhilaration of what Mr. Dooley called "th' common impulse f'r th' same money." In so far as he was not so prepared, he was deprived of this encouragement.

To mark the tendency of education in these circumstances, we need consider but one piece of testimony. The late Charles Francis Adams was an educated man who overlived the very fag-end of the period when an American youth could afford, more or less hardly, to be educated. He was a man of large affairs, in close relations with those whom the clear consenting voice of American society acclaimed as its representative men, and whose ideals of life were acclaimed as adequate and satisfying; they were the Fords, Eastmans, Owen Youngs, Hoovers, of the period. At the close of his career he wrote this:

> As I approach the end, I am more than a little puzzled to account for the instances I have seen of business success—money-getting. It comes from rather a low instinct. Certainly, as far as my observation goes, it is rarely met in combination with the finer or more interesting traits of character. I have known, and known tolerably well, a good many "successful" men—"big" financially—men famous during the last half-century; and a less interesting crowd I do not care to encounter. Not one that I have ever known would I care to meet again, either in this world or in the next; nor is one of them associated in my mind with the idea of humour, thought or refinement. A set of mere money-getters and traders, they were essentially unattractive and uninteresting. The fact is that money-getting, like everything else, calls for a special aptitude and great concentration; and for it I did not

have the first to any marked degree, and to it I never gave the last. So, in now summing up, I may account myself fortunate in having got out of my ventures as well as I did.

This is by no means the language of a man who, like my acquaintance from the Middle West, is sustained and emboldened by the consciousness of being in co-operation with his fellows—far from it. It will be enough, I think, to intimate pretty clearly the divisive and separatist tendency of education, and to show the serious risk that a young person of the present day incurs in acquiring an education. As matters now stand, I believe that he should not take that risk, and that any one advising or tempting him to take it is doing him a great disservice.

IV

An educated young man likes to think; he likes ideas for their own sake and likes to deal with them disinterestedly and objectively. He will find this taste an expensive one, much beyond his means, because the society around him is thoroughly indisposed towards anything of the kind. It is pre-eminently a society, as John Stuart Mill said, in which the test of a great mind is agreeing in the opinions of small minds. In any department of American life this is indeed the only final test; and this fact is in turn a fair measure of the extent to which our society is inimical to thought. The president of Columbia University is reported in the press as having said the other day that "thinking is one of the most unpopular amusements of the human race. Men hate it largely because they can not do it. They hate it because if they enter upon it as a vocation or avocation it is likely to interfere with what they are doing." This is an interesting admission for the president of Columbia to make—interesting and striking. Circumstances have enabled our society to get along rather prosperously, though by no means creditably, without thought and without regard for thought, proceeding merely by a series of improvisations; hence it has always instinctively resented thought, as likely to interfere with what it was doing. Therefore, the young person who has cultivated the ability to think and the taste for thinking is at a decided disadvantage, for this resentment is now stronger and more heavily concentrated than it ever was. Any doubt on this point may be easily resolved by an examination of our current literature, especially our journalistic and periodical literature.

The educated lad also likes to cultivate a sense of history. He likes to know how the human mind has worked in the past, and upon this knowledge he instinctively bases his expectations of its present and future workings. This tends automatically to withdraw him from many popular movements and associations because he knows their like of old, and knows to a certainty how they will turn out. In the realm of public affairs, for instance, it shapes his judgment of this-or-that humbugging political nostrum that the crowd is running eagerly to swallow; he can match it all

the way back to the politics of Rome and Athens, and knows it for precisely what it is. He can not get into a ferment over this-or-that exposure
of the almost incredible degradation of our political, social and cultural
character; over an investigation of Tammany's misdoings; over the Federal
Government's flagitious employment of the income-tax law to establish
a sleeping-partnership in the enterprises of gamblers, gangsters, assassins
and racketeers; over the wholesale looting of public property through
official connivance; over the crushing burden which an ever-increasing
bureaucratic rapacity puts upon production. He knows too much about
the origin and nature of government not to know that all these matters
are representative, and that nothing significant can be done about them
except by a self-sprung change of character in the people represented.
He is aware, with Edmund Burke, that "there never was for any long
time a corrupt representation of a virtuous people, or a mean, sluggish,
careless people that ever had a good government of any form." He perceives, with Ibsen, that "men still call for special revolutions, for revolutions in politics, in externals. But all that sort of thing is trumpery. It
is the soul of man that must revolt."

Thus in these important directions, and in others more or less like
them, the educated youth starts under disadvantages from which the
trained youth is free. The trained youth has no incentive to regard these
matters except as one or another of them may bear upon his immediate
personal interest. Again, while education does not make a gentleman, it
tends to inculcate certain partialities and repugnances which training does
not tend to inculcate, and which are often embarrassing and retarding.
They set up a sense of self-respect and dignity as an arbiter of conduct,
with a jurisdiction far outreaching that of law and morals; and this is most
disadvantageous. Formerly this disadvantage was not so pressing, but now
it is of grave weight. At the close of Mr. Jefferson's first term, some of
his political advisers thought it would be a good move for him to make
a little tour in the North and let the people see him. He replied, with
what now seems an incomprehensible austerity, that he was "not reconciled
to the idea of a chief magistrate parading himself through the several
States as an object of public gaze, and in quest of an applause which, to
be valuable, should be purely voluntary." In his day a chief magistrate
could say that and not lose by it; Mr. Jefferson carried every northern
State except Connecticut and every southern State except Maryland.
At the present time, as we have lately been reminded, the exigencies of
politics have converted candidacy for public office into an exact synonym
for an obscene and repulsive exhibitionism.

Again, education tends towards a certain reluctance about pushing
oneself forward; and in a society so notoriously based on the principle of
each man for himself, this is a disadvantage. Charles Francis Adams's
younger brother Henry, in his remarkable book called *The Education of
Henry Adams*, makes some striking observations on this point. Henry

Adams was no doubt the most accomplished man in America, probably the ablest member of the family which as a whole has been the most notable in American public service since 1776. His youth was spent in acquiring an uncommonly large experience of men and affairs. Yet he says that his native land never offered him but one opportunity in the whole course of his life, and that was an assistant-professorship of history at Harvard, at four dollars a day; and he says further that he "could have wept on President Eliot's shoulder in hysterics, so grateful was he for the rare good-will that inspired the compliment." He recalls that at the age of thirty:

> No young man had a larger acquaintance and relationship than Henry Adams, yet he knew no one who could help him. He was for sale, in the open market. So were many of his friends. All the world knew it, and knew too that they were cheap; to be bought at the price of a mechanic. There was no concealment, no delicacy and no illusion about it. Neither he nor his friends complained; but he felt sometimes a little surprised that, as far as he knew, no one seeking in the labour-market even so much as inquired about their fitness. . . . The young man was required to impose himself, by the usual business methods, as a necessity on his elders, in order to compel them to buy him as an investment. As Adams felt it, he was in a manner expected to black-mail.

Such were the disabilities imposed upon the educated person fifty years ago, when as Adams says, "the American character showed singular limitations which sometimes drove the student of civilized man to despair." Owing to increased tension of the economic system, they are now much heavier. Even more than then, the educated youth emerges, as Adams and his friends did, to find himself "jostled of a sudden by a crowd of men who seem to him ignorant that there is a thing called ignorance; who have forgotten how to amuse themselves; who can not even understand that they are bored."

One might add a few more items to the foregoing, chiefly in the way of spiritual wear and tear—specific discouragements, irritations, disappointments—which in these days fall to the lot of the educated youth, and which the trained youth escapes; but I have mentioned enough for the purpose. Now, it is quite proper to say that the joys and satisfactions of being educated should be brought out as an offset. One can not get something for nothing, nor can one "have it going and coming." If an education is in itself as rewarding a thing as it is supposed to be, it is worth some sacrifice. It is unreasonable to court the joy of making oneself at home in the world's culture, and at the same time expect to get Standard Oil dividends out of it. Granted that your educated lad is out of step, lonesome, short on business acumen and concentration, and all the rest of it—well, he has his education; nobody can get it away from him; his treasure is of the sort that moth and rust do not corrupt, and stock-market operators can not break through and mark down quotations on it. Agreed that if Charles Francis Adams had not been an educated gentleman he might have become another Gould, Fisk, Harriman, Rockefeller, Huntington, Morgan; but given his choice, would he have swapped off his education and its satisfactions for the chance to change places with any of them? Certainly not.

Certainly not; but times have changed. If economic opportunity were now what it was even in Henry Adams's day, a young person just starting out might think twice about balancing the advantages of an education against its disadvantages. In that day, by a little stretching and with a little luck, a young person might come to some sort of compromise with society, but the chance of this is now so remote that no one should take it. Since the closing of the frontier, in or about 1890, economic exploitation has tightened up at such a rate that compromise is hardly possible. It takes every jot of a young person's attention and energy merely to catch on and hang on; and as we have been noticing these last two years, he does not keep going any too well, even at that. The question is not one of being willing to make reasonable sacrifices; it is one of accepting every reasonable prospect of utter destitution. The joys and satisfactions of an education are all that Commencement orators say they are, and more; yet there is force in the Irishman's question, "What's the world to a man when his wife's a widdy?"

v

Things may change for the better, in time; no doubt they will. Economic opportunity may, by some means unforeseen at present, be released from the hold of its present close monopoly. The social value of intellect and character may some day be rediscovered, and the means of their development may be rehabilitated. Were I to be alive when all this happens, I should take up my parable of five years ago, and speak as strongly for education as I did then. But I shall not be alive, and I suspect also that none of the young persons now going out into the world from our training-schools will be alive; so there is no practical point to considering this prospect at present. Hence I can only raise my voice in recantation from the mourner's bench, a convert by force of expediency if not precisely in principle—rice-Christian style, perhaps, and yet, what is one to say? I belong to an earlier time, and for one reason or another the matter of rice does not present itself as an over-importunate problem, but nevertheless I see that the Christians have now "cornered" all the rice, so I can not advise young persons to do as I and my contemporaries did. No, they are right, their training-schools are right; Richard Roe and I are wrong. Let them be honest Christians if they can possibly manage the will-to-believe—one can make astonishing successes with that sometimes by hard trying—but if not, let them be rice-Christians, they can do no better.

Gastein, June, 1932.

---

e. e. cummings (1894-1962)

since feeling is first

since feeling is first
who pays any attention
to the syntax of things
will never wholly kiss you;

wholly to be a fool
while Spring is in the world

my blood approves,
and kisses are a better fate
than wisdom
lady i swear by all flowers. Don't cry
—the best gesture of my brain is less than
your eyelids' flutter which says

we are for each other: then
laugh, leaning back in my arms
for life's not a paragraph

And death i think is no parenthesis

(1926)

The Right Use of Language

"Language" has become a particularly lively subject in recent years. The relatively new science of Linguistics is growing rapidly and noisily, and among the immediate results have been continuing controversies over the proper description of English grammar and over usage versus the rules, in dictionary-making and in speaking generally. Overshadowing the structural and scientific issues, however, still stand the moral ones, at least as venerable as the Greek rhetoricians and sophists—Plato and Aristotle among them— who debated the question of the right use of language and distinguished between eloquence devoted to good persuasion and eloquence devoted to bad. It is the same question, in its modern setting, that is taken up in this group of essays.

We present Mrs. Langer's essay first for a number of reasons. While it touches only peripherally on language itself, it powerfully and clearly describes the mechanism in which language and thought are related— symbolism—and thus provides a link between this and the preceding section. Mrs. Langer's stress on man's unique capacity to manipulate symbols leads directly to a consideration of the political significance of the use of language, a subject taken up in detail by Orwell. Both of these essays, written with World War II vividly in mind, take a special urgency from their setting. Weaver's study, focussing carefully on a few key terms, shows that in postwar America the subject has lost none of its interest. Huxley and Jacobs, respectively, analyze and illustrate, in varying tones, the problem of language in commercial life.

SUSANNE K. LANGER

Mrs. Langer (born 1895) was educated at Radcliffe College where she received the Ph.D. in 1926. She has taught philosophy at Radcliffe, Wellesley, Smith, and Columbia, and in 1954 became chairman of the Philosophy Department at Connecticut College. She is now Professor Emeritus and research scholar, pursuing investigations in the philosophy of art, expression, and meaning. One of the few notable women in a field traditionally dominated by men, Mrs. Langer has reached a large audience and has had great influence on recent thinking, especially about the arts. Her best-known book is Philosophy in a New Key *(1942), in which, taking her cue from the researches of Ernst Cassirer, she investigates "the symbolism of reason, rite, and art." A collection of her essays and talks was published as* Philosophical Sketches *in 1962. She has also written* An Introduction to Symbolic Logic *(1937),* Feeling and Form *(1953), and* The Problem of Art *(1957). The present essay, clearly deriving from her interest in symbolism, appeared in* Fortune *in January, 1944, at the height of World War II.*

THE LORD OF CREATION

The world is aflame with man-made public disasters, artificial rains of brimstone and fire, planned earthquakes, cleverly staged famines and floods. The Lord of Creation is destroying himself. He is throwing down the cities he has built, the works of his own hand, the wealth of many thousand years in his frenzy of destruction, as a child knocks down its own handiwork, the whole day's achievement, in a tantrum of tears and rage.

What has displeased the royal child? What has incurred his world-shattering tantrum?

The bafflement of the magnificent game he is playing. Its rules and its symbols, his divine toys, have taken possession of the player. For this global war is not the old, hard, personal fight for the means of life, *bellum omnium contra omnes*, which animals perpetually wage; this is a war of monsters. Not mere men but great superpersonal giants, the national states, are met in combat. They do not hate and attack and wrestle as injured physical creatures do; they move heavily, inexorably, by strategy and necessity, to each other's destruction. The game of national states has come to this pass, and the desperate players ride their careening animated toys to a furious suicide.

These moloch gods, these monstrous states, are not natural beings; they are man's own work, products of the power that makes him lord over all other living things—his mind. They are not of the earth, earthy, as families and herds, hives and colonies are, whose members move and fight as one by instinct and habit until a physical disturbance splits them and the severed parts reconstitute themselves as new organized groups. The national states are not physical groups; they are social symbols, profound and terrible.

They are symbols of the new way of life, which the past two centuries have given us. For thousands of years, the pattern of daily life—working, praying, building, fighting, and raising new generations—repeated itself with only slow or unessential changes. The social symbols expressive of this life were ancient and familiar. Tribal gods or local saints, patriarchs, squires, or feudal lords, princes and bishops, raised to the highest power in the persons of emperors and popes—they were all expressions of needs and duties and opinions grounded in an immemorial way of life. The average man's horizon was not much greater than his valley, his town, or whatever geographical ramparts bounded his community. Economic areas were small, and economic problems essentially local. Naturally in his conception the powers governing the world were local, patriarchal, and reverently familiar.

Then suddenly, within some two hundred years, and for many places far less than that, the whole world has been transformed. Communities of different tongues and faiths and physiognomies have mingled; not as of old in wars of conquest, invading lords and conquered population gradually mixing their two stocks, but by a new process of foot-loose travel and trade, dominated by great centers of activity that bring individuals from near and far promiscuously together as a magnet draws filings from many heaps into close but quite accidental contact. Technology has made old horizons meaningless and localities indefinite. For goods and their destinies determine the structure of human societies. This is a new world, a world of persons, not of families and clans, or parishes and manors. The proletarian order is not founded on a hearth and its history. It does not express itself in a dialect, a local costume, a rite, a patron saint. All such traditions by mingling have canceled each other, and disappeared.

Most of us feel that since the old controlling ideas of faith and custom are gone, mankind is left without anchorage of any sort. None of the old social symbols fit this modern reality, this shrunken and undifferentiated world in which we lead a purely economic, secular, essentially homeless life.

But mankind is never without its social symbols; when old ones die, new ones are already in process of birth; and the new gods that have superseded all faiths are the great national states. The conception of them is mystical and moral, personal and devotional; they conjure with names and emblems, and demand our constant profession and practice of the new orthodoxy called "Patriotism."

Of all born creatures, man is the only one that cannot live by bread alone. He lives as much by symbols as by sense report, in a realm compounded of tangible things and virtual images, of actual events and ominous portents, always between fact and fiction. For he sees not only actualities but meanings. He has, indeed, all the impulses and interests of animal nature; he eats, sleeps, mates, seeks comfort and safety, flees pain, falls sick and dies, just as cats and bears and fishes and butterflies do. But he has something more in his repertoire, too—he has laws and religions, theories and dogmas, because he lives not only through sense but through symbols. That is the special asset of his mind, which makes him the master of earth and all its progeny.

By the agency of symbols—marks, words, mental images, and icons of all sorts—he can hold his ideas for contemplation long after their original causes have passed away. Therefore, he can think of things that are not presented or even suggested by his actual environment. By associating symbols in his mind, he combines things and events that were never together in the real world. This gives him the power we call imagination. Further, he can symbolize only part of an idea and let the rest go out of consciousness; this gives him the faculty that has been his pride throughout the ages—the power of abstraction. The combined effect of these two powers is inestimable. They are the roots of his supreme talent, the gift of reason.

In the war of each against all, which is the course of nature, man has an unfair advantage over his animal brethren; for he can see what is not yet there to be seen, know events that happened before his birth, and take possession of more than he actually eats; he can kill at a distance; and by rational design he can enslave other creatures to live and act for him instead of for themselves.

Yet this mastermind has strange aberrations. For in the whole animal kingdom there is no such unreason, no such folly and impracticality as man displays. He alone is hounded by imaginary fears, beset by ghosts and devils, frightened by mere images of things. No other creature wastes time in unprofitable ritual or builds nests for dead specimens of its race. Animals are always realists. They have intelligence in varying degrees—chickens are stupid, elephants are said to be very clever—but, bright or foolish, animals react only to reality. They may be fooled by appearance, by pictures or reflections, but once they know them as such, they promptly lose interest. Distance and darkness and silence are not fearful to them, filled with voices or forms, or invisible presences. Sheep in the pasture do not seem to fear phantom sheep beyond the fence, mice don't look for mouse goblins in the clock, birds do not worship a divine thunderbird.

But oddly enough, men do. They think of all these things and guard against them, worshiping animals and monsters even before they conceive of divinities in their own image. Men are essentially unrealistic. With all their extraordinary intelligence, they alone go in for patently impractical actions—magic and exorcism and holocausts—rites that have no connection with common-sense methods of self-preservation, such as a highly intelligent animal might use. In fact, the rites and sacrifices by which primitive man claims to control nature are sometimes fatal to the performers. Indian puberty rites are almost always intensely painful, and African natives have sometimes died during initiations into honorary societies.

We usually assume that very primitive tribes of men are closer to animal estate than highly civilized races; but in respect of practical attitudes, this is not true. The more primitive man's mind, the more fantastic it seems to be; only with high intellectual discipline do we gradually approach the realistic outlook of intelligent animals.

Yet this human mind, so beclouded by phantoms and superstitions, is probably the only mind on earth that can reach out to an awareness of things beyond its practical environment and can also conceive of such notions as truth, beauty, justice, majesty, space and time and creation.

There is another paradox in man's relationship with other creatures: namely, that those very qualities he calls animalian—"brutal," "bestial," "inhuman"—are peculiarly his own. No other animal is so deliberately cruel as man. No other creature intentionally imprisons its own kind, or invents special instruments of torture such as racks and thumbscrews for the sole purpose of punishment. No other animal keeps its own brethren in slavery; so far as we know, the lower animals do not commit anything like the acts of pure sadism that figure rather largely in our newspapers. There is no torment, spite, or cruelty for its own sake among beasts, as there is among men. A cat plays with its prey, but does not conquer and torture smaller cats. But man, who knows good and evil, is cruel for cruelty's sake; he who has a moral law is more brutal than the brutes, who have none; he alone inflicts suffering on his fellows with malice aforethought.

If man's mind is really a higher form of the animal mind, his morality a specialized form of herd instinct, then where in the course of evolution did he lose the realism of a clever animal and fall prey to subjective fears? And why should he take pleasure in torturing helpless members of his own race?

The answer is, I think, that man's mind is *not* a direct evolution from the beast's mind, but is a unique variant and therefore has had a meteoric and startling career very different from any other animal history. The trait that sets human mentality apart from every other is its preoccupation with symbols, with images and names that *mean* things, rather than with things themselves. This trait may have been a mere sport of nature once upon a time. Certain creatures do develop tricks and interests that seem biologically unimportant. Pack rats, for instance, and some birds of the crow family take a capricious pleasure in bright objects and carry away such things for which they have, presumably, no earthly use. Perhaps man's tendency to see certain forms as *images*, to hear certain sounds not only as signals but as expressive tones, and to be excited by sunset colors or starlight, was originally just a peculiar sensitivity in a rather highly developed brain. But whatever its cause, the ultimate destiny of this trait was momentous; for all human activity is based on the appreciation and use of symbols. Language, religion, mathematics, all learning, all science and superstition, even right and wrong, are products of symbolic expression rather than direct experience. Our commonest words, such as "house" and "red" and "walking," are symbols; the pyramids of Egypt and the mysterious circles of Stonehenge are symbols; so are dominions and empires and astronomical universes. We live in a mind-made world, where the things of prime importance are images or words that embody ideas and feelings and attitudes.

The animal mind is like a telephone exchange; it receives stimuli from outside through the sense organs and sends out appropriate responses through the nerves that govern muscles, glands, and other parts of the body. The organism is constantly interacting with its surroundings, receiving messages and acting on the new state of affairs that the messages signify.

But the human mind is not a simple transmitter like a telephone exchange. It is more like a great projector; for instead of merely mediating between an event in the outer world and a creature's responsive action, it transforms or, if you will, distorts the event into an image to be looked at, retained, and contemplated. For the images of things that we remember are not exact and faithful transcriptions even of our actual sense impressions. They are made as much by what we think as by what we see. It is a well-known fact that if you ask several people the size of the moon's disk as they look at it, their estimates will vary from the area of a dime to that of a barrel top. Like a magic lantern, the mind projects its ideas of things on the screen of what we call "memory"; but like all projections, these ideas are transformations of actual things. They are, in fact, *symbols* of reality, not pieces of it.

A symbol is not the same thing as a sign; that is a fact that psychologists and philosophers often overlook. All intelligent animals use signs; so do we. To them as well as to us sounds and smells and motions are signs of food, danger, the presence of other beings, or of rain or storm. Furthermore, some animals not only attend to signs but produce them for the benefit of others. Dogs bark at the door to be let in; rabbits thump to call each other; the cooing of doves and the growl of a wolf defending his kill are unequivocal signs of feelings and intentions to be reckoned with by other creatures.

We use signs just as animals do, though with considerably more elaboration. We stop at red lights and go on green; we answer calls and bells, watch the sky for coming storms, read trouble or promise or anger in each other's eyes. That is animal intelligence raised to the human level. Those of us who are dog lovers can probably all tell wonderful stories of how high our dogs have sometimes risen in the scale of clever sign interpretation and sign using.

A sign is anything that announces the existence or the imminence of some event, the presence of a thing or a person, or a change in a state of affairs. There are signs of the weather, signs of danger, signs of future good or evil, signs of what the past has been. In every case a sign is closely bound up with something to be noted or expected in experience. It is always a part of the situation to which it refers, though the reference may be remote in space and time. In so far as we are led to note or expect the signified event we are making correct use of a sign. This is the essence of rational behavior, which animals show in varying degrees. It is entirely realistic, being closely bound up with the actual objective course of history—learned by experience, and cashed in or voided by further experience.

If man had kept to the straight and narrow path of sign using, he would be like the other animals, though perhaps a little brighter. He would not talk, but grunt and gesticulate and point. He would make his wishes known, give warnings, perhaps develop a social system like that of bees and ants, with such a wonderful efficiency of communal enterprise that all men would have plenty to eat, warm apartments—all exactly alike and perfectly convenient—to live in, and everybody could and would sit in the sun or by the fire, as the climate demanded, not talking but just basking, with every want satisfied, most of his life. The young would romp and make love, the old would sleep, the middle-aged would do the routine work almost unconsciously and eat a great deal. But that would be the life of a social, superintelligent, purely sign-using animal.

To us who are human, it does not sound very glorious. We want to go places and do things, own all sorts of gadgets that we do not absolutely need, and when we sit down to take it easy we want to talk. Rights and property, social position, special talents and virtues, and above all our ideas, are what we live for. We have gone off on a tangent that takes us far away from the mere biological cycle that animal generations accomplish; and that is because we can use not only signs but symbols.

A symbol differs from a sign in that it does not announce the presence of the object, the being, condition, or whatnot, which is its meaning, but merely *brings this thing to mind*. It is not a mere "substitute sign" to which we react as though it were the object itself. The fact is that our reaction to hearing a person's name is quite different from our reaction to the person himself. There are certain rare cases where a symbol stands directly for its meaning: in religious experience, for instance, the Host is not only a symbol but a Presence. But symbols in the ordinary sense are not mystic. They are the same sort of thing that ordinary signs are; only they do not call our attention to something necessarily present or to be physically dealt with—they call up merely a conception of the thing they "mean."

The difference between a sign and a symbol is, in brief, that a sign causes us to think or act *in face of* the thing signified, whereas a symbol causes us to think *about* the thing symbolized. Therein lies the great importance of symbolism for human life, its power to make this life so different from any other animal biography that generations of men have found it incredible to suppose that they were of purely zoological origin. A sign is always embedded in reality, in a present that emerges from the actual past and stretches to the future; but a symbol may be divorced from reality altogether. It may refer to what is *not* the case, to a mere idea, a figment, a dream. It serves, therefore, to liberate thought from the immediate stimuli of a physically present world; and that liberation marks the essential difference between human and nonhuman mentality. Animals think, but they think *of* and *at* things; men think primarily *about* things. Words, pictures, and memory images are symbols that may be combined and varied in a thousand ways. The result is a symbolic structure whose meaning is a complex of all their respective meanings, and this kaleidoscope of *ideas* is the typical product of the human brain that we call the "stream of thought."

The process of transforming all direct experience into imagery or into that supreme mode of symbolic expression, language, has so completely taken possession of the human mind that it is not only a special talent but a dominant, organic need. All our sense impressions leave their traces in our memory not only as signs disposing our practical reactions in the future but also as symbols, images representing our *ideas* of things; and the tendency to manipulate ideas, to combine and abstract, mix and extend them by playing with symbols, is man's outstanding characteristic. It seems to be what his brain most naturally and spontaneously does. Therefore his primitive mental function is not judging reality, but *dreaming his desires*.

Dreaming is apparently a basic function of human brains, for it is free and unexhausting like our metabolism, heartbeat, and breath. It is easier to dream than not to dream, as it is easier to breathe than to refrain from breathing. The symbolic character of dreams is fairly well established. Symbol mongering, on this ineffectual, uncritical level, seems to be instinctive, the fulfillment of an elementary need rather than the purposeful exercise of a high and difficult talent.

The special power of man's mind rests on the evolution of this special activity, not on any transcendently high development of animal intelligence. We are not immeasurably higher than other animals; we are different. We have a biological need and with it a biological gift that they do not share.

Because man has not only the ability but the constant need of *conceiving* what has happened to him, what surrounds him, what is demanded of him —in short, of symbolizing nature, himself, and his hopes and fears—he has a constant and crying need of *expression*. What he cannot express, he cannot conceive; what he cannot conceive is chaos, and fills him with terror.

If we bear in mind this all-important craving for expression we get a new picture of man's behavior; for from this trait spring his powers and his weaknesses. The process of symbolic transformation that all our experiences undergo is nothing more nor less than the process of *conception*, which underlies the human faculties of abstraction and imagination.

When we are faced with a strange or difficult situation, we cannot react directly, as other creatures do, with flight, aggression, or any such simple instinctive pattern. Our whole reaction depends on how we manage to conceive the situation—whether we cast it in a definite dramatic form, whether we see it as a disaster, a challenge, a fulfillment of doom, or a fiat of the Divine Will. In words or dreamlike images, in artistic or religious or even in cynical form, we must *construe* the events of life. There is great virtue in the figure of speech, "I can *make* nothing of it," to express a failure to understand something. Thought and memory are processes of *making* the thought content and the memory image; the pattern of our ideas is given by the symbols through which we express them. And in the course of manipulating those symbols we inevitably distort the original experience, as we abstract certain features of it, embroider and reinforce those features with other ideas, until the conception we project on the screen of memory is quite different from anything in our real history.

Conception is a necessary and elementary process; what we do with our conceptions is another story. That is the entire history of human culture— of intelligence and morality, folly and superstition, ritual, language, and the arts—all the phenomena that set man apart from, and above, the rest of the animal kingdom. As the religious mind has to make all human history a drama of sin and salvation in order to define its own moral attitudes, so a scientist wrestles with the mere presentation of "the facts" before he can reason about them. The process of *envisaging* facts, values, hopes, and fears underlies our whole behavior pattern; and this process is reflected in the evolution of an extraordinary phenomenon found always, and only, in human societies—the phenomenon of language.

Language is the highest and most amazing achievement of the symbolistic human mind. The power it bestows is almost inestimable, for without it anything properly called "thought" is impossible. The birth of language is the dawn of humanity. The line between man and beast—between the highest ape and the lowest savage—is the language line. Whether the primitive Neanderthal man was anthropoid or human depends less on his cranial capacity, his upright posture, or even his use of tools and fire, than on one issue we shall probably never be able to settle—whether or not he spoke.

In all physical traits and practical responses, such as skills and visual judgments, we can find a certain continuity between animal and human mentality. Sign using is an ever evolving, ever improving function throughout the whole animal kingdom, from the lowly worm that shrinks into his hole at the sound of an approaching foot, to the dog obeying his master's command, and even to the learned scientist who watches the movements of an index needle.

This continuity of the sign-using talent has led psychologists to the belief that language is evolved from the vocal expressions, grunts and coos and cries, whereby animals vent their feelings or signal their fellows; that man has elaborated this sort of communion to the point where it makes a perfect exchange of ideas possible.

I do not believe that this doctrine of the origin of language is correct. The essence of language is symbolic, not signific; we use it first and most vitally to formulate and hold ideas in our own minds. Conception, not social control, is its first and foremost benefit.

Watch a young child that is just learning to speak play with a toy; he says the name of the object, e.g.: "Horsey! horsey! horsey!" over and over again, looks at the object, moves it, always saying the name to himself or to the world at large. It is quite a time before he talks to anyone in particular; he talks first of all to himself. This is his way of forming and fixing the *conception* of the object in his mind, and around this conception all his knowledge of it grows. *Names* are the essence of language; for the *name* is what abstracts the conception of the horse from the horse itself, and lets the mere idea recur at the speaking of the name. This permits the conception gathered from one horse experience to be exemplified again by another instance of a horse, so that the notion embodied in the name is a general notion.

To this end, the baby uses a word long before he *asks for* the object; when he wants his horsey he is likely to cry and fret, because he is reacting to an actual environment, not forming ideas. He uses the animal language of *signs* for his wants; talking is still a purely symbolic process—its practical value has not really impressed him yet.

Language need not be vocal; it may be purely visual, like written language, or even tactual, like the deaf-mute system of speech; but it *must be denotative*. The sounds, intended or unintended, whereby animals communicate do not constitute a language, because they are signs, not names. They never fall into an organic pattern, a meaningful syntax of even the most rudimentary sort, as all language seems to do with a sort of driving necessity. That is because signs refer to actual situations, in which things have obvious relations to each other that require only to be noted; but symbols refer to ideas, which are not physically there for inspection, so their connections and features have to be represented. This gives all true language a natural tendency toward growth and development, which seems almost like a life of its own. Languages are not invented; they grow with our need for expression.

In contrast, animal "speech" never has a structure. It is merely an emotional response. Apes may greet their ration of yams with a shout of "Nga!" But they do not say "Nga" between meals. If they could *talk about* their yams instead of just saluting them, they would be the most primitive men instead of the most anthropoid of beasts. They would have ideas, and tell each other things true or false, rational or irrational; they would make plans and invent laws and sing their own praises, as men do.

The history of speech is the history of our human descent. Yet the habit of transforming reality into symbols, of contemplating and combining and distorting symbols, goes beyond the confines of language. All *images* are symbols, which make us think about the things they mean.

This is the source of man's great interest in "graven images," and in *mere appearances* like the face of the moon or the human profiles he sees in rocks and trees. There is no limit to the meanings he can read into natural phenomena. As long as this power is undisciplined, the sheer enjoyment of finding meanings in everything, the elaboration of concepts without any regard to truth and usefulness, seems to run riot; superstition and ritual in their pristine strength go through what some anthropologists have called a "vegetative" stage, when dreamlike symbols, gods and ghouls and rites, multiply like the overgrown masses of life in a jungle. From this welter of symbolic forms emerge the images that finally govern a civilization; the great symbols of religion, society, and selfhood.

What does an image "mean?" Anything it is thought to resemble. It is only because we can abstract quite unobvious forms from the actual appearance of things that we see line drawings in two dimensions as images of colored, three-dimensional objects, find the likeness of a dipper in a constellation of seven stars, or see a face on a pansy. Any circle may represent the sun or moon; an upright monolith may be a man.

Wherever we can fancy a similarity we tend to see something represented. The first thing we do, upon seeing a new shape, is to assimilate it to our own idea of something that it resembles, something that is known and important to us. Our most elementary concepts are of our own actions, and the limbs or organs that perform them; other things are named by comparison with them. The opening of a cave is its mouth, the divisions of a river its arms. Language, and with it all articulate thought, grows by this process of unconscious metaphor. Every new idea urgently demands a word; if we lack a name for it, we call it after the first namable thing seen to bear even a remote analogy to it. Thus all the subtle and variegated vocabulary of a living language grows up from a few roots of very general application; words as various in meaning as "gentle" and "ingenious" and "general" spring from the one root "ge" meaning "to give life."

Yet there are conceptions that language is constitutionally unfit to express. The reason for this limitation of our verbal powers is a subject for logicians and need not concern us here. The point of interest to us is that, just as rational, discursive thought is bound up with language, so the life of feeling, of direct personal and social consciousness, the emotional stability of man and his sense of orientation in the world are bound up with images directly given to his senses: fire and water, noise and silence, high mountains and deep caverns, the brief beauty of flowers, the persistent grin of a skull. There seem to be irresistible parallels between the expressive forms we find in nature and the forms of our inner life; thus the use of light to represent all things good, joyful, comforting, and of darkness to express all sorts of sorrow, despair, or horror, is so primitive as to be well-nigh unconscious.

A flame is a soul; a star is a hope; the silence of winter is death. All such images, which serve the purpose of metaphorical thinking, are *natural symbols*. They have not conventionally assigned meanings, like words, but recommend themselves even to a perfectly untutored mind, a child's or a savage's, because they are definitely articulated *forms*, and to see something expressed in such forms is a universal human talent. We do not have to learn to use natural symbols; it is one of our primitive activities.

The fact that sensuous forms of natural processes have a significance beyond themselves makes the range of our symbolism, and with it the horizon of our consciousness, much wider and deeper than language. This is the source of ritual, mythology, and art. Ritual is a symbolic rendering of certain emotional *attitudes*, which have become articulate and fixed by being constantly expressed. Mythology is man's image of his world, and of himself in the world. Art is the exposition of his own subjective history, the life of feeling, the human spirit in all its adventures.

Yet this power of envisagement, which natural symbolism bestows, is a dangerous one; for human beings can envisage things that do not exist, and create horrible worlds, insupportable duties, monstrous gods and ancestors. The mind that can see past and future, the poles and the antipodes, and guess at obscure mechanisms of nature, is ever in danger of seeing what is not there, imagining false and fantastic causes, and courting death instead of life. Because man can play with ideas, he is unrealistic; he is inclined to neglect the all-important interpretation of signs for a rapt contemplation of symbols.

Some twenty years ago, Ernst Cassirer set forth a theory of human mentality that goes far toward explaining the vagaries of savage religions and the ineradicable presence of superstition even in civilized societies: a symbol, he observed, is the embodiment of an idea; it is at once an abstract and a physical fact. Now its great emotive value lies in the concept it conveys; this inspires our reverent attitude, the attention and awe with which we view it. But man's untutored thought always tends to lose its way between the symbol and the fact. A skull represents death; but to a primitive mind the skull *is* death. To have it in the house is not unpleasant but dangerous. Even in civilized societies, symbolic objects—figures of saints, relics, crucifixes—are revered for their supposed efficacy. Their actual power is a power of *expression*, of embodying and thus revealing the greatest concepts humanity has reached; these concepts are the commanding forces that change our estate from a brute existence to the transcendent life of the spirit. But the symbol-loving mind of man reveres the meaning not *through* the articulating form but *in* the form so that the image appears to be the actual object of love and fear, supplication and praise.

Because of this constant identification of concepts with their expressions, our world is crowded with unreal beings. Some societies have actually realized that these beings do not belong to nature, and have postulated a so-called "other world" where they have their normal existence and from which they are said to descend, or arise, into our physical realm. For savages it is chiefly a nether world that sends up spooks; for more advanced cults it is from the heavens that supernatural beings, the embodiments of human ideas—of virtue, triumph, immortality—descend to the mundane realm. But from this source emanates also a terrible world government, with heavy commands and sanctions. Strange worship and terrible sacrifices may be the tithes exacted by the beings that embody our knowledge of nonanimalian human nature.

So the gift of symbolism, which is the gift of reason, is at the same time the seat of man's peculiar weakness—the danger of lunacy. Animals go mad with hydrophobia or head injuries, but purely mental aberrations are rare; beasts are not generally subject to insanity except through a confusion of signs, such as the experimentally produced "nervous breakdown" in rats. It is man who hears voices and sees ghosts in the dark, feels irrational compulsions and holds fixed ideas. All these phantasms are symbolic forms that have acquired a false factual status. It has been truly said that everybody has some streak of insanity; i.e., the threat of madness is the price of reason.

Because we can think of things potential as well as actual, we can be held in nonphysical bondage by laws and prohibitions and commands and by images of a governing power. This makes men tyrants over their own kind. Animals control each other's actions by immediate threats, growls and snarls and passes; but when the bully is roving elsewhere, his former domain is free of him. We control our inferiors by setting up symbols of our power, and the mere idea that words or images convey stands there to hold our fellows in subjection even when we cannot lay our hands on them. There is no flag over the country where a wolf is king; he is king where he happens to prowl, so long as he is there. But men, who can embody ideas and set them up to view, oppress each other by symbols of might.

The envisagements of good and evil, which make man a moral agent, make him also a conscript, a prisoner, and a slave. His constant problem is to escape the tyrannies he has created. Primitive societies are almost entirely tyrannical, symbol-bound, coercive organizations; civilized governments are so many conscious schemes to justify or else to disguise man's inevitable bondage to law and conscience.

Slowly, through ages and centuries, we have evolved a picture of the world we live in; we have made a drama of the earth's history and enhanced it with a backdrop of divinely ordered, star-filled space. And all this structure of infinity and eternity against which we watch the pageant of life and death, and all the moral melodrama itself, we have wrought by a gradual articulation of such vast ideas in symbols—symbols of good and evil, triumph and failure, birth and maturity and death. Long before the beginning of any known history, people saw in the heavenly bodies, in the changes of day and night or of the seasons, and in great beasts, symbolic forms to express those ultimate concepts that are the very frame of human existence. So gods, fates, the cohorts of good and evil were conceived. Their myths were the first formulations of cosmic ideas. Gradually the figures and traditions of religion emerged; ritual, the overt expression of our mental attitudes, became more and more intimately bound to definite and elaborate concepts of the creative and destructive powers that seem to control our lives.

Such beings and stories and rites are sacred because they are the great symbols by which the human mind orients itself in the world. To a creature that lives by reason, nothing is more terrible than what is formless and meaningless; one of our primary fears is fear of chaos. And it is the fight against chaos that has produced our most profound and indispensable images—the myths of light and darkness, of creation and passion, the symbols of the altar flame, the daystar, and the cross.

For thousands of years people lived by the symbols that nature presented to them. Close contact with earth and its seasons, intimate knowledge of stars and tides, made them feel the significance of natural phenomena and gave them a poetic, unquestioning sense of orientation. Generations of erudite and pious men elaborated the picture of the temporal and spiritual realms in which each individual was a pilgrim soul.

Then came the unprecedented change, the almost instantaneous leap of history from the immemorial tradition of the plow and the anvil to the new age of the machine, the factory, and the ticker tape. Often in no more than the length of a life-time the shift from handwork to mass production, and with it from poetry to science and from faith to nihilism, has taken place. The old nature symbols have become remote and have lost their meanings; in the clatter of gears and the confusion of gadgets that fill the new world, there will not be any obvious and rich and sacred meanings for centuries to come. All the accumulated creeds and rites of men are suddenly in the melting pot. There is no fixed community, no dynasty, no family inheritance—only the one huge world of men, vast millions of men, still looking on each other in hostile amazement.

A sane, intelligent animal should have invented, in the course of ten thousand years or more, some sure and obvious way of accommodating indefinite numbers of its own kind on the face of a fairly spacious earth. Modern civilization has achieved the highest triumphs of knowledge, skill, ingenuity, theory; yet all around its citadels, engulfing and demolishing them, rages the maddest war and confusion, inspired by symbols and slogans as riotous and irrational as anything the "vegetative" stage of savage phantasy could provide. How shall we reconcile this primitive nightmare excitement with the achievements of our high, rational, scientific culture?

The answer is, I think, that we are no longer in possession of a definite, established culture; we live in a period between an exhausted age—the European civilization of the white race—and an age still unborn, of which we can say nothing as yet. We do not know what races shall inherit the earth. We do not know what even the next few centuries may bring. But it is quite evident, I think, that we live in an age of transition, and that before many more generations have passed, mankind will make a new beginning and build itself a different world. Whether it will be a "brave, new world," or whether it will start all over with an unchronicled "state of nature" such as Thomas Hobbes described, wherein the individual's life is "nasty, brutish, and short," we simply cannot tell. All we know is that every tradition, every institution, every tribe is gradually becoming uprooted and upset, and we are waiting in a sort of theatrical darkness between the acts.

Because we are at a new beginning, our imaginations tend to a wild, "vegetative" overgrowth. The political upheavals of our time are marked, therefore, by a veritable devil dance of mystical ideologies, vaguely conceived, passionately declared, holding out fanatic hopes of mass redemption and mass beatitudes. Governments vie with each other in proclaiming social plans, social aims, social enterprises, and demanding bloody sacrifices in the name of social achievements.

New conceptions are always clothed in an extravagant metaphorical form, for there is no language to express genuinely new ideas. And in their pristine strength they imbue the symbols that express them with their own mystery and power and holiness. It is impossible to disengage the welter of ideas embodied in a swastika, a secret sign, or a conjuring word from the physical presence of the symbol itself; hence the apparently nonsensical symbol worship and mysticism that go with new movements and visions. This identification of symbolic form and half-articulate meaning is the essence of all mythmaking. Of course the emotive value is incomprehensible to anyone who does not see such figments as expressive forms. So an age of vigorous new conception and incomplete formulation always has a certain air of madness about it. But it is really a fecund and exciting period in the life of reason. Such is our present age. Its apparent unreason is a tremendous unbalance and headiness of the human spirit, a conflict not only of selfish wills but of vast ideas in the metaphorical state of emergence.

The change from fixed community life and ancient local custom to the mass of unpedigreed human specimens that actually constitutes the world in our industrial and commercial age has been too sudden for the mind of man to negotiate. Some transitional form of life had to mediate between those extremes. And so the idol of nationality arose from the wreckage of tribal organization. The concept of the national state is really the old tribe concept applied to millions of persons, unrelated and different creatures gathered under the banner of a government. Neither birth nor language nor even religion holds such masses together, but a mystic bond is postulated even where no actual bond of race, creed, or color may ever have existed.

At first glance it seems odd that the concept of nationality should reach its highest development just as all actual marks of national origins—language, dress, physiognomy, and religion—are becoming mixed and obliterated by our new mobility and cosmopolitan traffic. But it is just the loss of these things that inspires this hungry seeking for something like the old egocentric pattern in the vast and formless brotherhood of the whole earth. While mass production and universal communication clearly portend a culture of world citizenship, we cling desperately to our nationalism, a more and more attenuated version of the old clan civilization. We fight passionate and horrible wars for the symbols of our nations, we make a virtue of self-glorification and exclusiveness and invent strange anthropologies to keep us at least theoretically set apart from other men.

Nationalism is a transition between an old and a new human order. But even now we are not really fighting a war of nations; we are fighting a war of fictions, from which a new vision of the order of nature will someday emerge. The future, just now, lies wide open—open and dark, like interstellar space; but in that emptiness there is room for new gods, new cultures, mysterious now and nameless as an unborn child.

GEORGE ORWELL

Orwell's reputation has shown no sign of decline since his death at 46 in 1950. He is likely to be ranked permanently among the great English essayists. On presenting him an award in 1949, the editors of Partisan Review *commented that his writing "has been marked by a singular directness and honesty, a scrupulous fidelity to his experience that has placed him in that valuable class of the writer who is a witness to his time."*

His real name was Eric Arthur Blair, and he was born in 1903 in Bengal, a province of British India. He attended Eton on a King's Scholarship from 1917 to 1921, then served for five years in the Imperial Police in Burma. Returning to Europe, he spent some poverty-stricken years doing odd jobs, from teaching to dishwashing, while he wrote novels and short stories that did not sell. His Down and Out in Paris and London *(1933) is a vivid record of those years. In 1936 Orwell went to Spain to take part in the Civil War and reported his experiences in* Homage to Catalonia *(1938). Among his other books are the celebrated* Nineteen Eighty-Four *(1949), a terrifying novel picturing the complete victory of totalitarianism,* Animal Farm, a Fairy Story *(1945), and the essay collections* Shooting an Elephant and Other Essays *(1950), and* Such, Such Were the Joys *(1953). The present essay first appeared in the London monthly* Horizon *in 1946 and was reprinted in the 1950 collection.*

POLITICS AND THE ENGLISH
LANGUAGE

Most people who bother with the matter at all would admit that the English language is in a bad way, but it is generally assumed that we cannot by conscious action do anything about it. Our civilization is decadent and our language—so the argument runs—must inevitably share in the general collapse. It follows that any struggle against the abuse of language is a sentimental archaism, like preferring candles to electric light or hansom cabs to aeroplanes. Underneath this lies the half-conscious belief that language is a natural growth and not an instrument which we shape for our own purposes.

Now, it is clear that the decline of a language must ultimately have political and economic causes: it is not due simply to the bad influence of this or that individual writer. But an effect can become a cause, reinforcing the original cause and producing the same effect in an intensified form, and so on indefinitely. A man may take to drink because he feels himself to be a failure, and then fail all the more completely because he drinks. It is rather the same thing that is happening to the English language. It becomes ugly and inaccurate because our thoughts are foolish, but the slovenliness of our language makes it easier for us to have foolish thoughts. The point is that the process is reversible. Modern English, especially written English, is full of bad habits which spread by imitation and which can be avoided if one is willing to take the necessary trouble. If one gets rid of these habits one can think more clearly, and to think clearly is a necessary first step towards political regeneration: so that the fight against bad English is not frivolous and is not the exclusive concern of professional writers. I will come back to this presently, and I hope that by that time the meaning of what I have said here will have become clearer. Meanwhile, here are five specimens of the English language as it is now habitually written.

These five passages have not been picked out because they are especially bad—I could have quoted far worse if I had chosen—but because they illustrate various of the mental vices from which we now suffer. They are a little below the average, but are fairly representative samples. I number them so that I can refer back to them when necessary:

(1) I am not, indeed, sure whether it is not true to say that the Milton who once seemed not unlike a seventeenth-century Shelley had not become, out of an experience ever more bitter in each year, more alien [*sic*] to the founder of that Jesuit sect which nothing could induce him to tolerate.

Professor Harold Laski
(Essay in Freedom of Expression).

(2) Above all, we cannot play ducks and drakes with a native battery of idioms which prescribes such egregious collocations of vocables as the Basic *put up with* for *tolerate* or *put at a loss* for *bewilder*.

Professor Lancelot Hogben (Interglossa).

(3) On the one side we have the free personality: by definition it is not neurotic, for it has neither conflict nor dream. Its desires,

such as they are, are transparent, for they are just what institutional approval keeps in the forefront of consciousness; another institutional pattern would alter their number and intensity; there is little in them that is natural, irreducible, or culturally dangerous. But *on the other side*, the social bond itself is nothing but the mutual reflection of these self-secure integrities. Recall the definition of love. Is not this the very picture of a small academic? Where is there a place in this hall of mirrors for either personality or fraternity?

Essay on psychology in *Politics* (New York).

(4) All the "best people" from the gentlemen's clubs, and all the frantic fascist captains, united in common hatred of Socialism and bestial horror of the rising tide of the mass revolutionary movement, have turned to acts of provocation, to foul incendiarism, to medieval legends of poisoned wells, to legalize their own destruction of proletarian organizations, and rouse the agitated petty-bourgeoisie to chauvinistic fervor on behalf of the fight against the revolutionary way out of the crisis.

Communist pamphlet.

(5) If a new spirit *is* to be infused into this old country, there is one thorny and contentious reform which must be tackled, and that is the humanization and galvanization of the B.B.C. Timidity here will bespeak canker and atrophy of the soul. The heart of Britain may be sound and of strong beat, for instance, but the British lion's roar at present is like that of Bottom in Shakespeare's *Midsummer Night's Dream*—as gentle as any sucking dove. A virile new Britain cannot continue indefinitely to be traduced in the eyes or rather ears, of the world by the effete languors of Langham Place, brazenly masquerading as "standard English." When the voice of Britain is heard at nine o'clock, better far and infinitely less ludicrous to hear aitches honestly dropped than the present priggish, inflated, inhibited, school-ma'amish arch braying of blameless bashful mewing maidens!

Letter in *Tribune*.

Each of these passages has faults of its own, but, quite apart from avoidable ugliness, two qualities are common to all of them. The first is staleness of imagery; the other is lack of precision. The writer either has a meaning and cannot express it, or he inadvertently says something else, or he is almost indifferent as to whether his words mean anything or not. This mixture of vagueness and sheer incompetence is the most marked characteristic of modern English prose, and especially of any kind of political writing. As soon as certain topics are raised, the concrete melts into the abstract and no one seems able to think of turns of speech that are not hackneyed: prose consists less and less of *words* chosen for the sake of their meaning, and more and more of *phrases* tacked together like the sections of a prefabricated hen-house. I list below, with notes and examples, various of the tricks by means of which the work of prose-construction is habitually dodged:

Dying metaphors. A newly invented metaphor assists thought by evoking a visual image, while on the other hand a metaphor which is technically "dead" (e.g. *iron resolution*) has in effect reverted to being an ordinary word and can generally be used without loss of vividness. But in between these two classes there is a huge dump of worn-out metaphors which have lost all evocative power and are merely used because they save people the trouble of inventing phrases for themselves. Examples are: *Ring the changes on, take up the cudgels for, toe the line, ride roughshod over, stand shoulder to shoulder with, play into the hands of, no axe to grind, grist to the mill, fishing in troubled waters, on the order of the day, Achilles' heel, swan song, hotbed.* Many of these are used without knowledge of their meaning (what is a "rift," for instance?), and incompatible metaphors are frequently mixed, a sure sign that the writer is not interested in what he is saying. Some metaphors now current have been twisted out of their original meaning without those who use them even being aware of the fact. For example, *toe the line* is sometimes written *tow the line.* Another example is *the hammer and the anvil*, now always used with the implication that the anvil gets the worst of it. In real life it is always the anvil that breaks the hammer, never the other way about: a writer who stopped to think what he was saying would be aware of this, and would avoid perverting the original phrase.

Operators or *verbal false limbs.* These save the trouble of picking out appropriate verbs and nouns, and at the same time pad each sentence with extra syllables which give it an appearance of symmetry. Characteristic phrases are *render inoperative, militate against, make contact with, be subjected to, give rise to, give grounds for, have the effect of, play a leading part (role) in, make itself felt, take effect, exhibit a tendency to, serve the purpose of, etc., etc.* The keynote is the elimination of simple verbs. Instead of being a single word, such as *break, stop, spoil, mend, kill*, a verb becomes a *phrase*, made up of a noun or adjective tacked on to some general-purposes verb such as *prove, serve, form, play, render.* In addition, the passive voice is wherever possible used in preference to the active, and noun constructions are used instead of gerunds (*by examination of* instead of *by examining*). The range of verbs is further cut down by means of the *-ize* and *de-* formations, and the banal statements are given an appearance of profundity by means of the *not un-* formation. Simple conjunctions and prepositions are replaced by such phrases as *with respect to, having regard to, the fact that, by dint of, in view of, in the interests of, on the hypothesis that;* and the ends of sentences are saved from anticlimax by such resounding common-places as *greatly to be desired, cannot be left out of account, a development to be expected in the near future, deserving* *of serious consideration, brought to a satisfactory conclusion,* and so on and so forth.

Pretentious diction. Words like *phenomenon, element, individual* (as noun), *objective, categorical, effective, virtual, basic, primary, promote, constitute, exhibit, exploit, utilize, eliminate, liquidate,* are used to dress up simple statement and give an air of scientific impartiality to biased judgments. Adjectives like *epoch-making, epic, historic, unforgettable, triumphant, age-old, inevitable, inexorable, veritable,* are used to dignify the sordid processes of international politics, while writing that aims at glorifying war usually takes on an archaic color, its characteristic words being: *realm, throne, chariot, mailed fist, trident, sword, shield, buckler, banner, jackboot, clarion.* Foreign words and expressions such as *cul de sac, ancien régime, deus ex machina, mutatis mutandis, status quo, gleichschaltung, weltanschauung,* are used to give an air of culture and elegance. Except for the useful abbreviations *i.e., e.g.,* and *etc.,* there is no real need for any of the hundreds of foreign phrases now current in English. Bad writers, and especially scientific, political and sociological writers, are nearly always haunted by the notion that Latin or Greek words are grander than Saxon ones, and unnecessary words like *expedite, ameliorate, predict, extraneous, deracinated, clandestine, subaqueous* and hundreds of others constantly gain ground from their Anglo-Saxon opposite numbers.[1] The jargon peculiar to Marxist writing (*hyena, hangman, cannibal, petty bourgeois, these gentry, lacquey, flunkey, mad dog, White Guard,* etc.) consists largely of words and phrases translated from Russian, German or French; but the normal way of coining a new word is to use a Latin or Greek root with the appropriate affix and, where necessary, the *-ize* formation. It is often easier to make up words of this kind (*deregionalize, impermissible, extramarital, non-fragmentary* and so forth) than to think up the English words that will cover one's meaning. The result, in general, is an increase in slovenliness and vagueness.

Meaningless words. In certain kinds of writing, particularly in art criticism and literary criticism, it is normal to come across long passages which are almost completely lacking in meaning.[2] Words like *romantic, plastic, values, human, dead, sentimental, natural, vitality,* as used in art criticism, are strictly meaningless, in the sense that they not only do not point to

[1] An interesting illustration of this is the way in which the English flower names which were in use till very recently are being ousted by Greek ones, *snapdragon* becoming *antirrhinum, forget-me-not* becoming *myosotis,* etc. It is hard to see any practical reason for this change of fashion: it is probably due to an instinctive turning-away from the more homely word and a vague feeling that the Greek word is scientific.

[2] Example: "Comfort's catholicity of perception and image, strangely Whitmanesque in range, almost the exact opposite in aesthetic compulsion, continues to evoke that trembling atmospheric accumulative hinting at a cruel, an inexorably serene timelessness. . . . Wrey Gardiner scores by aiming at simple bull's-eyes with precision. Only they are not so simple, and through this contented sadness runs more than the surface bitter-sweet of resignation." (*Poetry Quarterly.*)

any discoverable object, but are hardly ever expected to do so by the reader. When one critic writes, "The outstanding feature of Mr. X's work is its living quality," while another writes, "The immediately striking thing about Mr. X's work is its peculiar deadness," the reader accepts this as a simple difference of opinion. If words like *black* and *white* were involved, instead of the jargon words *dead* and *living*, he would see at once that language was being used in an improper way. Many political words are similarly abused. The word *Fascism* has now no meaning except in so far as it signifies "something not desirable." The words *democracy, socialism, freedom, patriotic, realistic, justice*, have each of them several different meanings which cannot be reconciled with one another. In the case of a word like *democracy*, not only is there no agreed definition, but the attempt to make one is resisted from all sides. It is almost universally felt that when we call a country democratic we are praising it: consequently the defenders of every kind of régime claim that it is a democracy, and fear that they might have to stop using the word if it were tied down to any one meaning. Words of this kind are often used in a consciously dishonest way. That is, the person who uses them has his own private definition, but allows his hearer to think he means something quite different. Statements like *Marshal Pétain was a true patriot, The Soviet Press is the freest in the world, The Catholic Church is opposed to persecution*, are almost always made with intent to deceive. Other words used in variable meanings, in most cases more or less dishonestly, are: *class, totalitarian, science, progressive, reactionary, bourgeois, equality*.

Now that I have made this catalogue of swindles and perversions, let me give another example of the kind of writing that they lead to. This time it must of its nature be an imaginary one. I am going to translate a passage of good English into modern English of the worst sort. Here is a well-known verse from *Ecclesiastes:*

"I returned and saw under the sun, that the race is not to the swift, nor the battle to the strong, neither yet bread to the wise, nor yet riches to men of understanding, nor yet favour to men of skill; but time and chance happeneth to them all."

Here it is in modern English:

"Objective consideration of contemporary phenomena compels the conclusion that success or failure in competitive activities exhibits no tendency to be commensurate with innate capacity, but that a considerable element of the unpredictable must invariably be taken into account."

This is a parody, but not a very gross one. Exhibit (3), above, for instance, contains several patches of the same kind of English. It will be seen that I have not made a full translation. The beginning and ending of the sentence follow the original meaning fairly closely, but in the middle the concrete illustrations—race, battle, bread—dissolve into the vague phrase "success or failure in competitive activities." This had to be so, because no modern writer of the kind I am discussing—no one capable of using

phrases like "objective consideration of contemporary phenomena"—
would ever tabulate his thoughts in that precise and detailed way. The
whole tendency of modern prose is away from concreteness. Now analyse
these two sentences a little more closely. The first contains forty-nine
words but only sixty syllables, and all its words are those of everyday life.
The second contains thirty-eight words of ninety syllables: eighteen of its
words are from Latin roots, and one from Greek. The first sentence contains six vivid images, and only one phrase ("time and chance") that could
be called vague. The second contains not a single fresh, arresting phrase,
and in spite of its ninety syllables it gives only a shortened version of the
meaning contained in the first. Yet without a doubt it is the second kind of
sentence that is gaining ground in modern English. I do not want to ex-
aggerate. This kind of writing is not yet universal, and outcrops of simplicity will occur here and there in the worst-written page. Still, if you or
I were told to write a few lines on the uncertainty of human fortunes,
we should probably come much nearer to my imaginary sentence than to
the one from *Ecclesiastes*.

As I have tried to show, modern writing at its worst does not consist
in picking out words for the sake of their meaning and inventing images
in order to make the meaning clearer. It consists in gumming together long
strips of words which have already been set in order by someone else, and
making the results presentable by sheer humbug. The attraction of this
way of writing is that it is easy. It is easier—even quicker, once you have
the habit—to say *In my opinion it is not an unjustifiable assumption that*
than to say *I think*. If you use ready-made phrases, you not only don't
have to hunt about for words; you also don't have to bother with the
rhythms of your sentences, since these phrases are generally so arranged
as to be more or less euphonious. When you are composing in a hurry—
when you are dictating to a stenographer, for instance, or making a public
speech—it is natural to fall into a pretentious, Latinized style. Tags like
a consideration which we should do well to bear in mind or *a conclusion
to which all of us would readily assent* will save many a sentence from
coming down with a bump. By using stale metaphors, similes and idioms,
you save much mental effort, at the cost of leaving your meaning vague,
not only for your reader but for yourself. This is the significance of mixed
metaphors. The sole aim of a metaphor is to call up a visual image. When
these images clash—as in *The Fascist octopus has sung its swan song, the
jackboot is thrown into the melting pot*—it can be taken as certain that
the writer is not seeing a mental image of the objects he is naming; in other
words he is not really thinking. Look again at the examples I gave at the
beginning of this essay. Professor Laski (1) uses five negatives in fifty-
three words. One of these is superfluous, making nonsense of the whole
passage, and in addition there is the slip *alien* for akin, making further
nonsense, and several avoidable pieces of clumsiness which increase the

general vagueness. Professor Hogben (2) plays ducks and drakes with a battery which is able to write prescriptions, and, while disapproving of the everyday phrase *put up with*, is unwilling to look *egregious* up in the dictionary and see what it means; (3), if one takes an uncharitable attitude towards it, is simply meaningless: probably one could work out its intended meaning by reading the whole of the article in which it occurs. In (4), the writer knows more or less what he wants to say, but an accumulation of stale phrases chokes him like tea leaves blocking a sink. In (5), words and meaning have almost parted company. People who write in this manner usually have a general emotional meaning—they dislike one thing and want to express solidarity with another—but they are not interested in the detail of what they are saying. A scrupulous writer, in every sentence that he writes, will ask himself at least four questions, thus: What am I trying to say? What words will express it? What image or idiom will make it clearer? Is this image fresh enough to have an effect? And he will probably ask himself two more: Could I put it more shortly? Have I said anything that is avoidably ugly? But you are not obliged to go to all this trouble. You can shirk it by simply throwing your mind open and letting the ready-made phrases come crowding in. They will construct your sentences for you—even think your thoughts for you, to a certain extent—and at need they will perform the important service of partially concealing your meaning even from yourself. It is at this point that the special connection between politics and the debasement of language becomes clear.

In our time it is broadly true that political writing is bad writing. Where it is not true, it will generally be found that the writer is some kind of rebel, expressing his private opinions and not a "party line." Orthodoxy, of whatever color, seems to demand a lifeless, imitative style. The political dialects to be found in pamphlets, leading articles, manifestos, White Papers and the speeches of under-secretaries do, of course, vary from party to party, but they are all alike in that one almost never finds in them a fresh, vivid, home-made turn of speech. When one watches some tired hack on the platform mechanically repeating the familiar phrases—*bestial atrocities, iron heel, bloodstained tyranny, free peoples of the world, stand shoulder to shoulder*—one often has a curious feeling that one is not watching a live human being but some kind of dummy: a feeling which suddenly becomes stronger at moments when the light catches the speaker's spectacles and turns them into blank discs which seem to have no eyes behind them. And this is not altogether fanciful. A speaker who uses that kind of phraseology has gone some distance towards turning himself into a machine. The appropriate noises are coming out of his larynx, but his brain is not involved as it would be if he were choosing his words for himself. If the speech he is making is one that he is accustomed to make over and over again, he may be almost unconscious of what he is saying, as one is when one utters the responses in church. And this reduced state of consciousness, if not indispensable, is at any rate favorable to political conformity.

In our time, political speech and writing are largely the defence of the indefensible. Things like the continuance of British rule in India, the Russian purges and deportations, the dropping of the atom bombs on Japan, can indeed be defended, but only by arguments which are too brutal for most people to face, and which do not square with the professed aims of political parties. Thus political language has to consist largely of euphemism, question-begging and sheer cloudy vagueness. Defenceless villages are bombarded from the air, the inhabitants driven out into the countryside, the cattle machine-gunned, the huts set on fire with incendiary bullets: this is called *pacification*. Millions of peasants are robbed of their farms and sent trudging along the roads with no more than they can carry: this is called *transfer of population* or *rectification of frontiers*. People are imprisoned for years without trial, or shot in the back of the neck or sent to die of scurvy in Arctic lumber camps: this is called *elimination of unreliable elements*. Such phraseology is needed if one wants to name things without calling up mental pictures of them. Consider for instance some comfortable English professor defending Russian totalitarianism. He cannot say outright, "I believe in killing off your opponents when you can get good results by doing so." Probably, therefore, he will say something like this:

"While freely conceding that the Soviet régime exhibits certain features which the humanitarian may be inclined to deplore, we must, I think, agree that a certain curtailment of the right to political opposition is an unavoidable concomitant of transitional periods, and that the rigors which the Russian people have been called upon to undergo have been amply justified in the sphere of concrete achievement."

The inflated style is itself a kind of euphemism. A mass of Latin words falls upon the facts like soft snow, blurring the outlines and covering up all the details. The great enemy of clear language is insincerity. When there is a gap between one's real and one's declared aims, one turns as it were instinctively to long words and exhausted idioms, like a cuttlefish squirting out ink. In our age there is no such thing as "keeping out of politics." All issues are political issues, and politics itself is a mass of lies, evasions, folly, hatred and schizophrenia. When the general atmosphere is bad, language must suffer. I should expect to find—this is a guess which I have not sufficient knowledge to verify—that the German, Russian and Italian languages have all deteriorated in the last ten or fifteen years, as a result of dictatorship.

But if thought corrupts language, language can also corrupt thought. A bad usage can spread by tradition and imitation, even among people who should and do know better. The debased language that I have been discussing is in some ways very convenient. Phrases like *a not unjustifiable as-*

*sumption, leaves much to be desired, would serve no good purpose, a con-
sideration which we should do well to bear in mind,* are a continuous
temptation, a packet of aspirins always at one's elbow. Look back through
this essay, and for certain you will find that I have again and again committed the very faults I am protesting against. By this morning's post I have
received a pamphlet dealing with conditions in Germany. The author
tells me that he "felt impelled" to write it. I open it at random, and here
is almost the first sentence that I see: "[The Allies] have an opportunity
not only of achieving a radical transformation of Germany's social and
political structure in such a way as to avoid a nationalistic reaction in
Germany itself, but at the same time of laying the foundations of a co-
operative and unified Europe." You see, he "feels impelled" to write—
feels, presumably, that he has something new to say—and yet his words,
like cavalry horses answering the bugle, group themselves automatically
into the familiar dreary pattern. This invasion of one's mind by ready-
made phrases (*lay the foundations, achieve a radical transformation*) can
only be prevented if one is constantly on guard against them, and every
such phrase anaesthetizes a portion of one's brain.

I said earlier that the decadence of our language is probably curable.
Those who deny this would argue, if they produced an argument at all,
that language merely reflects existing social conditions, and that we cannot
influence its development by any direct tinkering with words and constructions. So far as the general tone or spirit of a language goes, this
may be true, but it is not true in detail. Silly words and expressions have
often disappeared, not through any evolutionary process but owing to the
conscious action of a minority. Two recent examples were *explore every
avenue* and *leave no stone unturned,* which were killed by the jeers of a
few journalists. There is a long list of flyblown metaphors which could
similarly be got rid of if enough people would interest themselves in the
job; and it should also be possible to laugh the *not un-* formation out of
existence,[3] to reduce the amount of Latin and Greek in the average sentence, to drive out foreign phrases and strayed scientific words, and, in
general, to make pretentiousness unfashionable. But all these are minor
points. The defence of the English language implies more than this, and
perhaps it is best to start by saying what it does *not* imply.

To begin with it has nothing to do with archaism, with the salvaging of
obsolete words and turns of speech, or with the setting up of a "standard
English" which must never be departed from. On the contrary, it is especially concerned with the scrapping of every word or idiom which has
outworn its usefulness. It has nothing to do with correct grammar and
syntax, which are of no importance so long as one makes one's meaning
clear, or with the avoidance of Americanisms, or with having what is called
a "good prose style." On the other hand it is not concerned with fake

---

[3] One can cure oneself of the *not un-* formation by memorizing this sentence: *A
not unblack dog was chasing a not unsmall rabbit across a not ungreen field.*

simplicity and the attempt to make written English colloquial. Nor does it even imply in every case preferring the Saxon word to the Latin one, though it does imply using the fewest and shortest words that will cover one's meaning. What is above all needed is to let the meaning choose the word, and not the other way about. In prose, the worst thing one can do with words is to surrender to them. When you think of a concrete object, you think wordlessly, and then, if you want to describe the thing you have been visualizing you probably hunt about till you find the exact words that seem to fit it. When you think of something abstract you are more inclined to use words from the start, and unless you make a conscious effort to prevent it, the existing dialect will come rushing in and do the job for you, at the expense of blurring or even changing your meaning. Probably it is better to put off using words as long as possible and get one's meaning as clear as one can through pictures or sensations. Afterwards one can choose—not simply *accept*—the phrases that will best cover the meaning, and then switch round and decide what impression one's words are likely to make on another person. This last effort of the mind cuts out all stale or mixed images, all prefabricated phrases, needless repetitions, and humbug and vagueness generally. But one can often be in doubt about the effect of a word or a phrase, and one needs rules that one can rely on when instinct fails. I think the following rules will cover most cases:

(i) Never use a metaphor, simile or other figure of speech which you are used to seeing in print.

(ii) Never use a long word where a short one will do.

(iii) If it is possible to cut a word out, always cut it out.

(iv) Never use the passive where you can use the active.

(v) Never use a foreign phrase, a scientific word or a jargon word if you can think of an everyday English equivalent.

(vi) Break any of these rules sooner than say anything outright barbarous.

These rules sound elementary, and so they are, but they demand a deep change of attitude in anyone who has grown used to writing in the style now fashionable. One could keep all of them and still write bad English, but one could not write the kind of stuff that I quoted in those five specimens at the beginning of this article.

I have not here been considering the literary use of language, but merely language as an instrument for expressing and not for concealing or preventing thought. Stuart Chase and others have come near to claiming that all abstract words are meaningless, and have used this as a pretext for advocating a kind of political quietism. Since you don't know what Fascism is, how can you struggle against Fascism? One need not swallow such absurdities as this, but one ought to recognize that the present political chaos is connected with the decay of language, and that one can probably bring about some improvement by starting at the verbal end. If you simplify your English, you are freed from the worst follies of orthodoxy. You cannot speak any of the necessary dialects, and when you make a stupid remark its stupidity will be obvious, even to yourself. Political language—and with variations this is true of all political parties, from Conservatives to Anarchists—is designed to make lies sound truthful and murder respectable, and to give an appearance of solidity to pure wind. One cannot change this all in a moment, but one can at least change one's own habits, and from time to time one can even, if one jeers loudly enough, send some worn-out and useless phrase—some *jackboot, Achilles' heel, hotbed, melting pot, acid test, veritable inferno* or other lump of verbal refuse—into the dustbin where it belongs.

RICHARD M. WEAVER

Professor Weaver was born in Asheville, North Carolina, in 1910 and educated at Kentucky, Vanderbilt, and Louisiana State, where he received the doctorate in 1943. He soon joined the Department of English in the College of the University of Chicago and remained there until his death in 1963. An intense, tough-minded man, he was profoundly displeased with the "pseudoscientific" direction of modern thought. In three of his books he attempts to redirect our attention to the ideas of form, order, and human worth that he feels we have lost in the course of our "progress." *These books are* Ideas Have Consequences *(1948)*, Visions of Order; the Cultural Crisis of Our Time *(1964)*, and The Ethics of Rhetoric *(1957)*, *from which we print here the final chapter. The reader should not allow himself to be put off by the rather technical first two paragraphs; a full understanding of them depends on a knowledge of earlier chapters and is not essential to an appreciation of the rest of the essay.*

ULTIMATE TERMS IN
CONTEMPORARY RHETORIC

We have shown that rhetorical force must be conceived as a power transmitted through the links of a chain that extends upward toward some
ultimate source. The higher links of that chain must always be of unique
interest to the student of rhetoric, pointing, as they do, to some prime
mover of human impulse. Here I propose to turn away from general
considerations and to make an empirical study of the terms on these
higher levels of force which are seen to be operating in our age.

We shall define term simply here as a name capable of entering into a
proposition. In our treatment of rhetorical sources, we have regarded the
full predication consisting of a proposition as the true validator. But a
single term is an incipient proposition, awaiting only the necessary coupling with another term; and it cannot be denied that single names set up
expectancies of propositional embodiment. This causes everyone to realize the critical nature of the process of naming. Given the name "patriot,"
for example, we might expect to see coupled with it "Brutus," or "Washington," or "Parnell"; given the term "hot," we might expect to see "sun,"
"stove," and so on. In sum, single terms have their potencies, this being
part of the phenomenon of names, and we shall here present a few of the
most noteworthy in our time, with some remarks upon their etiology.

Naturally this survey will include the "bad" terms as well as the "good"
terms, since we are interested to record historically those expressions to
which the populace, in its actual usage and response, appears to attribute
the greatest sanction. A prescriptive rhetoric may specify those terms
which, in all seasons, ought to carry the greatest potency, but since the
affections of one age are frequently a source of wonder to another, the
most we can do under the caption "contemporary rhetoric" is to give a
descriptive account and withhold the moral until the end. For despite the
variations of fashion, an age which is not simply distraught manages to
achieve some system of relationship among the attractive and among the
repulsive terms, so that we can work out an order of weight and preced-
ence in the prevailing rhetoric once we have discerned the "rhetorical ab-
solutes"—the terms to which the very highest respect is paid.

It is best to begin boldly by asking ourselves, what is the "god term"
of the present age? By "god term" we mean that expression about which
all other expressions are ranked as subordinate and serving dominations
and powers. Its force imparts to the others their lesser degree of force, and
fixes the scale by which degrees of comparison are understood. In the
absence of a strong and evenly diffused religion, there may be several
terms competing for this primacy, so that the question is not always

capable of definite answer. Yet if one has to select the one term which in our day carries the greatest blessing, and—to apply a useful test— whose antonym carries the greatest rebuke, one will not go far wrong in naming "progress." This seems to be the ultimate generator of force flowing down through many links of ancillary terms. If one can "make it stick," it will validate almost anything. It would be difficult to think of any type of person or of any institution which could not be recommended to the public through the enhancing power of this word. A politician is urged upon the voters as a "progressive leader"; a community is proud to style itself "progressive"; technologies and methodologies claim to the "progressive"; a peculiar kind of emphasis in modern education calls itself "progressive," and so on without limit. There is no word whose power to move is more implicitly trusted than "progressive." But unlike some other words we shall examine in the course of this chapter, its rise to supreme position is not obscure, and it possesses some intelligible referents.

Before going into the story of its elevation, we must prepare ground by noting that it is the nature of the conscious life of man to revolve around some concept of value. So true is this that when the concept is withdrawn, or when it is forced into competition with another concept, the human being suffers an almost intolerable sense of being lost. He has to know where he is in the ideological cosmos in order to coordinate his activities. Probably the greatest cruelty which can be inflicted upon the psychic man is this deprivation of a sense of tendency. Accordingly every age, including those of rudest cultivation, sets up some kind of sign post. In highly cultivated ages, with individuals of exceptional intellectual strength, this may take the form of a metaphysic. But with the ordinary man, even in such advanced ages, it is likely to be some idea abstracted from religion or historical speculation, and made to inhere in a few sensible and immediate examples.

Since the sixteenth century we have tended to accept as inevitable an historical development that takes the form of a changing relationship between ourselves and nature, in which we pass increasingly into the role of master of nature. When I say that this seems inevitable to us, I mean that it seems something so close to what our more religious forebears considered the working of providence that we regard as impiety any disposition to challenge or even suspect it. By a transposition of terms, "progress" becomes the salvation man is placed on earth to work out; and just as there can be no achievement more important than salvation, so there can be no activity more justified in enlisting our sympathy and support than "progress." As our historical sketch would imply, the term began to be used in the sixteenth century in the sense of continuous development or improvement; it reached an apogee in the nineteenth century, amid noisy demonstrations of man's mastery of nature, and now in the twentieth century it keeps its place as one of the least assailable of the "uncontested terms," despite critical doubts in certain philosophic quarters. It is probably the only term which gives to the average American or West European of today a concept of something bigger than himself, which he is socially impelled to accept and even to sacrifice for. This capacity to demand sacrifice is probably the surest indicator of the "god term," for when a term is so sacrosanct that the material goods of this life must be mysteriously rendered up for it, then we feel justified in saying that it is in some sense ultimate. Today no one is startled to hear of a man's sacrificing health or wealth for the "progress" of the community, whereas such sacrifices for other ends may be regarded as self-indulgent or even treasonable. And this is just because "progress" is the coordinator of all socially respectable effort.

Perhaps these observations will help the speaker who would speak against the stream of "progress," or who, on the other hand, would parry some blow aimed at him through the potency of the word, to realize what a momentum he is opposing.

Another word of great rhetorical force which owes its origin to the same historical transformation is "fact." Today's speaker says "It is a fact" with all the gravity and air of finality with which his less secular-minded ancestor would have said "It is the truth."[1] "These are facts"; "Facts tend to show"; and "He knows the facts" will be recognized as common locutions drawing upon the rhetorical resource of this word. The word "fact" went into the ascendent when our system of verification changed during the Renaissance. Prior to that time, the type of conclusion that men felt obligated to accept came either through divine revelation, or through dialectic, which obeys logical law. But these were displaced by the system of verification through correspondence with physical reality. Since then things have been true only when measurably true, or when susceptible to some kind of quantification. Quite simply, "fact" came to be the touchstone after the truth of speculative inquiry had been replaced by the truth of empirical investigation. Today when the average citizen says "It is a fact" or says that he "knows the facts in the case," he means that he has the kind of knowledge to which all other knowledges must defer. Possibly it should be pointed out that his "facts" are frequently not facts at all in the etymological sense; often they will be deductions several steps removed from simply factual data. Yet the "facts" of his case carry with them this aura of scientific irrefragability, and he will likely regard any questioning of them as sophistry. In his vocabulary a fact is a fact, and all evidence so denominated has the prestige of science.

These last remarks will remind us at once of the strongly rhetorical character of the word "science" itself. If there is good reason for placing "progress" rather than "science" at the top of our series, it is only that the former has more scope, "science" being the methodological tool of "progress." It seems clear, moreover, that "science" owes its present status to

---

[1] It is surely worth observing that nowhere in the King James Version of the Bible does the word "fact" occur.

an hypostatization. The hypostatized term is one which treats as a substance or a concrete reality that which has only conceptual existence; and every reader will be able to supply numberless illustrations of how "science" is used without any specific referent. Any utterance beginning "Science says" provides one: "Science says there is no difference in brain capacity between the races"; "Science now knows the cause of encephalitis"; "Science says that smoking does not harm the throat." Science is not, as here it would seem to be, a single concrete entity speaking with one authoritative voice. Behind these large abstractions (and this is not an argument against abstractions as such) there are many scientists holding many different theories and employing many different methods of investigation. The whole force of the word nevertheless depends upon a bland assumption that all scientists meet periodically in synod and there decide and publish what science believes. Yet anyone with the slightest scientific training knows that this is very far from a possibility. Let us consider therefore the changed quality of the utterance when it is amended to read "A majority of scientists say"; or "Many scientists believe"; or "Some scientific experiments have indicated." The change will not do. There has to be a creature called "science"; and its creation has as a matter of practice been easy, because modern man has been conditioned to believe that the powers and processes which have transformed his material world represent a very sure form of knowledge, and that there must be a way of identifying that knowledge. Obviously the rhetorical aggrandizement of "science" here parallels that of "fact," the one representing generally and the other specifically the whole subject matter of trustworthy perception.

Furthermore, the term "science" like "progress" seems to satisfy a primal need. Man feels lost without a touchstone of knowledge just as he feels lost without the direction-finder provided by progress. It is curious to note that actually the word is only another name for knowledge (L. *scientia*), so that if we should go by strict etymology, we should insist that the expression "science knows" (*i.e.*, "knowledge knows") is pure tautology. But our rhetoric seems to get around this by implying that science is *the* knowledge. Other knowledges may contain elements of quackery, and may reflect the selfish aims of the knower; but "science," once we have given the word its incorporation, is the undiluted essence of knowledge. The word as it comes to us then is a little pathetic in its appeal, inasmuch as it reflects the deeply human feeling that somewhere somehow there must be people who know things "as they are." Once God or his ministry was the depository of such knowledge, but now, with the general decay of religious faith, it is the scientists who must speak *ex cathedra*, whether they wish to or not.

The term "modern" shares in the rhetorical forces of the others thus far discussed, and stands not far below the top. Its place in the general ordering is intelligible through the same history. Where progress is real, there is a natural presumption that the latest will be the best. Hence it is generally thought that to describe anything as "modern" is to credit it with all the improvements which have been made up to now. Then by a transference the term is applied to realms where valuation is, or ought to be, of a different source. In consequence, we have "modern living" urged upon us as an ideal; "the modern mind" is mentioned as something superior to previous minds; sometimes the modifier stands alone as an epithet of approval: "to become modern" or "to sound modern" are expressions that carry valuation. It is of course idle not to expect an age to feel that some of its ways and habits of mind are the best; but the extensive transformations of the past hundred years seem to have given "modern" a much more decisive meaning. It is as if a difference of degree had changed into a difference of kind. But the very fact that a word is not used very analytically may increase its rhetorical potency, as we shall see later in connection with a special group of terms.

Another word definitely high up in the hierarchy we have outlined is "efficient." It seems to have acquired its force through a kind of nononsense connotation. If a thing is efficient, it is a good adaptation of means to ends, with small loss through friction. Thus as a word expressing a good understanding and management of cause and effect, it may have a fairly definite referent; but when it is lifted above this and made to serve as a term of general endorsement, we have to be on our guard against the stratagems of evil rhetoric. When we find, to cite a familiar example, the phrase "efficiency apartments" used to give an attractive aspect to inadequate dwellings, we may suspect the motive behind such juxtaposition. In many similar cases, "efficient," which is a term above reproach in engineering and physics, is made to hold our attention where ethical and aesthetic considerations are entitled to priority. Certain notorious forms of government and certain brutal forms of warfare are undeniably efficient; but here the featuring of efficiency unfairly narrows the question.

Another term which might seem to have a different provenance but which participates in the impulse we have been studying is "American." One must first recognize the element of national egotism which makes this a word of approval with us, but there are reasons for saying that the force of "American" is much more broadly based than this. "This is the American way" or "It is the American thing to do" are expressions whose intent will not seem at all curious to the average American. Now the peculiar effect that is intended here comes from the circumstance that "American" and "progressive" have an area of synonymity. The Western World has long stood as a symbol for the future; and accordingly there has been a very wide tendency in this country, and also I believe among many people in Europe, to identify that which is American with that which is destined to be. And this is much the same as identifying it with the achievements of "progress." The typical American is quite fatuous in this regard: to him America is the goal toward which all creation moves; and he judges a country's civilization by its resemblance to the American model. The matter of changing nationalities brings out this point very well. For a citizen of a European country to become a citizen of the United States is considered natural and right, and I have known those so transferring their nationality to be congratulated upon their good sense and their anticipated good fortune. On the contrary, when an American takes out British citizenship (French or German would be worse), this transference is felt to be a little scandalous. It is regarded as somehow perverse, or as going against the stream of things. Even some of our intellectuals grow uneasy over the action of Henry James and T. S. Eliot, and the masses cannot comprehend it at all. Their adoption of British citizenship is not mere defection from a country; it is treason to history. If Americans wish to become Europeans, what has happened to the hope of the world? is, I imagine, the question at the back of their minds. The tremendous spread of American fashions in behavior and entertainment must add something to the impetus, but I believe the original source to be this prior idea that America, typifying "progress," is what the remainder of the world is trying to be like.

It follows naturally that in the popular consciousness of this country, "un-American" is the ultimate in negation. An anecdote will serve to illustrate this. Several years ago a leading cigarette manufacturer in this country had reason to believe that very damaging reports were being circulated about his product. The reports were such that had they not been stopped, the sale of this brand of cigarettes might have been reduced. The company thereupon inaugurated an extensive advertising campaign, the object of which was to halt these rumors in the most effective way possible. The concocters of the advertising copy evidently concluded after due deliberation that the strongest term of condemnation which could be conceived was "un-American," for this was the term employed in the campaign. Soon the newspapers were filled with advertising rebuking this "un-American" type of depreciation which had injured their sales. From examples such as this we may infer that "American" stands not only for what is forward in history, but also for what is ethically superior, or at least for a standard of fairness not matched by other nations.

And as long as the popular mind carries this impression, it will be futile to protest against such titles as "The Committee on un-American activities." While "American" and "un-American" continue to stand for these polar distinctions, the average citizen is not going to find much wrong with a group set up to investigate what is "un-American" and therefore reprehensible. At the same time, however, it would strike him as most droll if the British were to set up a "Committee on un-British Activities" or the French a "Committee on un-French Activities." The American, like other nationals, is not apt to be much better than he has been taught, and he has been taught systematically that his country is a special creation. That is why some of his ultimate terms seem to the general view provincial, and why he may be moved to polarities which represent only local poles.

If we look within the area covered by "American," however, we find significant changes in the position of terms which are reflections of cultural and ideological changes. Among the once powerful but now waning terms are those expressive of the pioneer ideal of ruggedness and self-sufficiency. In the space of fifty years or less we have seen the phrase "two-fisted American" pass from the category of highly effective images to that of comic anachronisms. Generally, whoever talks the older language of strenuosity is regarded as a reactionary, it being assumed by social democrats that a socially organized world is one in which cooperation removes the necessity for struggle. Even the rhetorical trump cards of the 1920's, which Sinclair Lewis treated with such satire, are comparatively impotent today, as the new social consciousness causes terms of centrally planned living to move toward the head of the series.

Other terms not necessarily connected with the American story have passed a zenith of influence and are in decline; of these perhaps the once effective "history" is the most interesting example. It is still to be met in such expressions as "History proves" and "History teaches"; yet one feels that it has lost the force it possessed in the previous century. Then it was easy for Byron—"the orator in poetry"—to write, "History with all her volumes vast has but one page"; or for the commemorative speaker to deduce profound lessons from history. But people today seem not to find history so eloquent. A likely explanation is that history, taken as whole, is conceptual rather than factual, and therefore a skepticism has developed as to what it teaches. Moreover, since the teachings of history are principally moral, ethical, or religious, they must encounter today that threshold resentment of anything which savors of the prescriptive. Since "history" is inseparable from judgment of historical fact, there has to be a considerable community of mind before history can be allowed to have a voice. Did the overthrow of Napoleon represent "progress" in history or the reverse? I should say that the most common rhetorical uses of "history" at the present are by intellectuals, whose personal philosophy can provide it with some kind of definition, and by journalists, who seem to use it unreflectively. For the contemporary masses it is substantially true that "history is bunk."

An instructive example of how a coveted term can be monopolized may be seen in "allies." Three times within the memory of those still young, "allies" (often capitalized) has been used to distinguish those fighting on our side from the enemy. During the First World War it was a supreme term; during the Second World War it was again used with effect; and at the time of the present writing it is being used to designate that nondescript combination fighting in the name of the United Nations in Korea. The curious fact about the use of this term is that in each case the enemy also has been constituted of "allies." In the First World War Germany, Austria-Hungary, and Turkey were "allies"; in the Second, Germany and Italy; and in the present conflict the North Koreans and the Chinese and perhaps the Russians are "allies." But in the rhetorical situation it is not possible to refer to them as "allies," since we reserve that term for the alliance representing our side. The reason for such restriction is that when men or nations are "allied," it is implied that they are united on some sound principle or for some good cause. Lying at the source of this feeling is the principle discussed by Plato, that friendship can exist only among the good, since good is an integrating force and evil a disintegrating one. We do not, for example, refer to a band of thieves as "the allies" because that term would impute laudable motives. By confining the term to our side we make an evaluation in our favor. We thus style ourselves the group joined for purposes of good. If we should allow it to be felt for a moment that the opposed combination is also made up of allies, we should concede that they are united by a principle, which in war is never done. So as the usage goes, we are always allies in war and the enemy is just the enemy, regardless of how many nations he has been able to confederate. Here is clearly another instance of how tendencies may exist in even the most innocent-seeming language.

Now let us turn to the terms of repulsion. Some terms of repulsion are also ultimate in the sense of standing at the end of the series, and no survey of the vocabulary can ignore these prime repellants. The counterpart of the "god term" is the "devil term," and it has already been suggested that with us "un-American" comes nearest to filling that role. Sometimes, however, currents of politics and popular feeling cause something more specific to be placed in that position. There seems indeed to be some obscure psychic law which compels every nation to have in its national imagination an enemy. Perhaps this is but a version of the tribal need for a scapegoat, or for something which will personify "the adversary." If a nation did not have an enemy, an enemy would have to be invented to take care of those expressions of scorn and hatred to which peoples must give vent. When another political state is not available to receive the discharge of such emotions, then a class will be chosen, or a race, or a type, or a political faction, and this will be held up to a practically standardized form of repudiation. Perhaps the truth is that we need the enemy in order to define ourselves, but I will not here venture further into psychological complexities. In this type of study it will be enough to recall that during the first half century of our nation's existence, "Tory" was such a devil term. In the period following our Civil War, "rebel" took its place in the Northern section and "Yankee" in the Southern, although in the previous epoch both of these had been terms of esteem. Most readers will remember that during the First World War "pro-German" was a term of destructive force. During the Second World War "Nazi" and "Fascist" carried about equal power to condemn, and then, following the breach with Russia, "Communist" displaced them both. Now "Communist" is beyond any rival the devil term, and as such it is employed even by the American president when he feels the need of a strong rhetorical point.

A singular truth about these terms is that, unlike several which were examined in our favorable list, they defy any real analysis. That is to say, one cannot explain how they generate their peculiar force of repudiation. One only recognizes them as publicly-agreed-upon devil terms. It is the same with all. "Tory" persists in use, though it has long lost any connection with redcoats and British domination. Analysis of "rebel" and "Yankee" only turns up embarrassing contradictions of position. Similarly we have all seen "Nazi" and "Fascist" used without rational perception; and we see this now, in even greater degree, with "Communist." However one might like to reject such usage as mere ignorance, to do so would only evade a very important problem. Most likely these are instances of the "charismatic term," which will be discussed in detail presently.

No student of contemporary usage can be unmindful of the curious reprobative force which has been acquired by the term "prejudice." Etymologically it signifies nothing more than a prejudgment, or a judgment before all the facts are in; and since all of us have to proceed to a great extent on judgments of that kind, the word should not be any more exciting than "hypothesis." But in its rhetorical applications "prejudice" presumes far beyond that. It is used, as a matter of fact, to characterize unfavorably any value judgment whatever. If "blue" is said to be a better color than "red," that is prejudice. If people of outstanding cultural achievement are praised through contrast with another people, that is prejudice. If one mode of life is presented as superior to another, that is prejudice. And behind all is the implication, if not the declaration, that it is un-American to be prejudiced.

I suspect that what the users of this term are attempting, whether consciously or not, is to sneak "prejudiced" forward as an uncontested term, and in this way to disarm the opposition by making all positional judgments reprehensible. It must be observed in passing that no people are so prejudiced in the sense of being committed to valuations as those who are engaged in castigating others for prejudice. What they expect is that they can nullify the prejudices of those who oppose them, and then get their own installed in the guise of the *sensus communis*. Mark Twain's statement, "I know that I am prejudiced in this matter, but I would be ashamed of myself if I weren't" is a therapeutic insight into the process; but it will take more than a witticism to make headway against the repulsive force gathered behind "prejudice."

If the rhetorical use of the term has any rational content, this probably comes through a chain of deductions from the nature of democracy; and we know that in controversies centered about the meaning of democracy, the air is usually filled with cries of "prejudice." If democracy is taken crudely to mean equality, as it very frequently is, it is then a contradiction of democracy to assign inferiority and superiority on whatever grounds. But since the whole process of evaluation is a process of such assignment, the various inequalities which are left when it has done its work are contradictions of this root notion and hence are "prejudice"— the assumption of course being that when all the facts are in, these inequalities will be found illusory. The man who dislikes a certain class or race or style has merely not taken pains to learn that it is just as good as any other. If all inequality is deception, then superiorities must be accounted the products of immature judgment. This affords plausible ground, as we have suggested, for the coupling of "prejudice" and "ignorance."

Before leaving the subject of the ordered series of good and bad terms, one feels obliged to say something about the way in which hierarchies can be inverted. Under the impulse of strong frustration there is a natural tendency to institute a pretense that the best is the worst and the worst is the best—an inversion sometimes encountered in literature and in social deportment. The best illustration for purpose of study here comes from a department of speech which I shall call "GI rhetoric." The average American youth, put into uniform, translated to a new and usually barren environment, and imbued from many sources with a mission of killing, has undergone a pretty severe dislocation. All of this runs counter to the benevolent platitudes on which he was brought up, and there is little ground for wonder if he adopts the inverted pose. This is made doubly likely by the facts that he is at a passionate age and that he is thrust into an atmosphere of superinduced excitement. It would be unnatural for him not to acquire a rhetoric of strong impulse and of contumacious tendency.

What he does is to make an almost complete inversion. In this special world of his he recoils from those terms used by politicians and other civilians and by the "top brass" when they are enunciating public sentiments. Dropping the conventional terms of attraction, this uprooted and specially focussed young man puts in their place terms of repulsion. To be more specific, where the others use terms reflecting love, hope, and charity, he uses almost exclusively terms connected with excretory and reproductive functions. Such terms comprise what Kenneth Burke has ingeniously called "the imagery of killing." By an apparently universal psychological law, faeces and the act of defecation are linked with the idea of killing, of destruction, of total repudiation—perhaps the word "elimination" would comprise the whole body of notions. The reproductive act is associated especially with the idea of aggressive exploitation. Consequently when the GI feels that he must give his speech a proper show of spirit, he places the symbols for these things in places which would normally be filled by prestige terms from the "regular" list. For specimens of such language presented in literature, the reader is referred to the fiction of Ernest Hemingway and Norman Mailer.

Anyone who has been compelled to listen to such rhetoric will recall the monotony of the vocabulary and the vehemence of the delivery. From these two characteristics we may infer a great need and a narrow means of satisfaction, together with the tension which must result from maintaining so arduous an inversion. Whereas previously the aim had been to love (in the broad sense) it is now to kill; whereas it had been freedom and individuality, it is now restriction and brutalization. In taking revenge for a change which so contradicts his upbringing he is quite capable, as the evidence has already proved, of defiantly placing the lower level above the higher. Sometimes a clever GI will invent combinations and will effect metaphorical departures, but the ordinary ones are limited to a reiteration of the stock terms—to a reiteration, with emphasis of intonation, upon "the imagery of killing."[2] Taken as a whole, this rhetoric is a clear if limited example of how the machine may be put in reverse— of how, consequently, a sort of devil worship may get into language.

A similar inversion of hierarchy is to be seen in the world of competitive sports, although to a lesser extent. The great majority of us in the Western world have been brought up under the influence, direct or indirect, of Christianity, which is a religion of extreme altruism. Its terms of value all derive from a law of self-effacement and of consideration for others, and these terms tend to appear whenever we try to rationalize or vindicate our conduct. But in the world of competitive sports, the direction is opposite: there one is applauded for egotistic display and for success at the expense of others—should one mention in particular American professional baseball? Thus the terms with which an athlete is commended will generally point away from the direction of Christian passivity, although when an athlete's character is described for the benefit of the general public, some way is usually found to place him in the other ethos, as by calling attention to his natural kindness, his interest in children, or his readiness to share his money.

Certainly many of the contradictions of our conduct may be explained through the presence of these small inverted hierarchies. When, to cite one familiar example, the acquisitive, hard-driving local capitalist is made the chief lay official of a Christian church, one knows that in a definite area there has been a transvaluation of values.

---

[2] Compare Sherwood Anderson's analysis of the same phenomenon in *A Story Teller's Story* (New York, 1928), p. 198: "There was in the factories where I worked and where the efficient Ford type of man was just beginning his dull reign this strange and futile outpouring of men's lives in vileness through their lips. Ennui was at work. The talk of the men about me was not Rabelaisian. In old Rabelais there was the salt of infinite wit and I have no doubt that the Rabelaisian flashes that came from our own Lincoln, Washington, and others had point and a flare to them.
But in the factories and in army camps!"

Earlier in the chapter we referred to terms of considerable potency whose referents it is virtually impossiole to discover or to construct through imagination. I shall approach this group by calling them "charismatic terms." It is the nature of the charismatic term to have a power which is not derived, but which is in some mysterious way given. By this I mean to say that we cannot explain their compulsiveness through referents of objectively known character and tendency. We normally "understand" a rhetorical term's appeal through its connection with something we apprehend, even when we object morally to the source of the impulse. Now "progress" is an understandable term in this sense, since it rests upon certain observable if not always commendable aspects of our world. Likewise the referential support of "fact" needs no demonstrating. These derive their force from a reading of palpable circumstance. But in charismatic terms we are confronted with a different creation: these terms seem to have broken loose somehow and to operate independently of referential connections (although in some instances an earlier history of referential connection may be made out). Their meaning seems inexplicable unless we accept the hypothesis that their content proceeds out of a popular will that they *shall* mean something. In effect, they are rhetorical by common consent, or by "charisma." As is the case with charismatic authority, where the populace gives the leader a power which can by no means be explained through his personal attributes, and permits him to use it effectively and even arrogantly, the charismatic term is given its load of impulsion without reference, and it functions by convention. The number of such terms is small in any one period, but they are perhaps the most efficacious terms of all.

Such rhetorical sensibility as I have leads me to believe that one of the principal charismatic terms of our age is "freedom." The greatest sacrifices that contemporary man is called upon to make are demanded in the name of "freedom"; yet the referent which the average man attaches to this word is most obscure. Burke's dictum that "freedom inheres in something sensible" has not prevented its breaking loose from all anchorages. And the evident truth that the average man, given a choice between exemption from responsibility and responsibility, will choose the latter, makes no impression against its power. The fact, moreover, that the most extensive use of the term is made by modern politicians and statesmen in an effort to get men to assume more responsibility (in the form of military service, increased taxes, abridgement of rights, etc.) seems to carry no weight either.[3] The fact that what the American pioneer considered freedom has become wholly impossible to the modern apartment-dwelling metropolitan seems not to have damaged its potency. Unless we accept some philosophical interpretation, such as the proposition that freedom consists only in the discharge of responsibility, there

---

[3] One is inevitably reminded of the slogan of Oceania in Orwell's *Nineteen Eighty-four:* "Freedom is Slavery."

seems no possibility of a correlation between the use of the word and circumstantial reality. Yet "freedom" remains an ultimate term, for which people are asked to yield up their first-born.

There is plenty of evidence that "democracy" is becoming the same kind of term. The variety of things it is used to symbolize is too weird and too contradictory for one to find even a core meaning in present-day usages. More important than this for us is the fact, noted by George Orwell, that people resist any attempt to define democracy, as if to connect it with a clear and fixed referent were to vitiate it. It may well be that such resistance to definition of democracy arises from a subconscious fear that a term defined in the usual manner has its charisma taken away. The situation then is that "democracy" means "be democratic," and that means exhibit a certain attitude which you can learn by imitating your fellows.

If rationality is measured by correlations and by analyzable content, then these terms are irrational; and there is one further modern development in the creation of such terms which is strongly suggestive of irrational impulse. This is the increasing tendency to employ in the place of the term itself an abbreviated or telescoped form—which form is nearly always used with even more reckless assumption of authority. I seldom read the abbreviation "U S" in the newspapers without wincing at the complete arrogance of its rhetorical tone. Daily we see "U S Cracks Down on Communists"; "U S Gives OK to Atomic Weapons"; "U S Shocked by Death of Official." Who or what is this "U S"? It is clear that "U S" does not suggest a union of forty-eight states having republican forms of government and held together by a constitution of expressly delimited authority. It suggests rather an abstract force out of a new world of forces, whose will is law and whom the individual citizen has no way to placate. Consider the individual citizen confronted by "U S" or "FBI." As long as terms stand for identifiable organs of government, the citizen feels that he knows the world he moves around in, but when the forces of government are referred to by these bloodless abstractions, he cannot avoid feeling that they are one thing and he another. Let us note while dealing with this subject the enormous proliferation of such forms during the past twenty years or so. If "U S" is the most powerful and prepossessing of the group, it drags behind it in train the previously mentioned "FBI," and "NPA," "ERP," "FDIC," "WPA," "HOLC," and "OSS," to take a few at random. It is a fact of ominous significance that this use of foreshortened forms is preferred by totalitarians, both the professed and the disguised. Americans were hearing the terms "OGPU," "AMTORG" and "NEP" before their own government turned to large-scale state planning. Since then we have spawned them ourselves, and, it is to be feared, out of similar impulse. George Orwell, one of the truest humanists of our age, has described the phenomenon thus: "Even in the early decades of the twentieth century, telescoped words and phrases had been one of the characteristic features of political language; and it had been noticed that the tendency to use abbreviations of this kind was most marked in totalitarian countries and totalitarian organizations. Examples were such words as Nazi, Gestapo, Comintern, Inprecor, Agitprop."[4]

I venture to suggest that what this whole trend indicates is an attempt by the government, as distinguished from the people, to confer charismatic authority. In the earlier specimens of charismatic terms we were examining, we beheld something like the creation of a spontaneous general will. But these later ones of truncated form are handed down from above, and their potency is by fiat of whatever group is administering in the name of democracy. Actually the process is no more anomalous than the issuing of pamphlets to soldiers telling them whom they shall hate and whom they shall like (or try to like), but the whole business of switching impulse on and off from a central headquarters has very much the meaning of *Gleichschaltung* as that word has been interpreted for me by a native German. Yet it is a disturbing fact that such process should increase in times of peace, because the persistent use of such abbreviations can only mean a serious divorce between rhetorical impulse and rational thought. When the ultimate terms become a series of bare abstractions, the understanding of power is supplanted by a worship of power, and in our condition this can mean only state worship.

It is easy to see, however, that a group determined upon control will have as one of its first objectives the appropriation of sources of charismatic authority. Probably the surest way to detect the fabricated charismatic term is to identify those terms ordinarily of limited power which are being moved up to the front line. That is to say, we may suspect the act of fabrication when terms of secondary or even tertiary rhetorical rank are pushed forward by unnatural pressure into ultimate positions. This process can nearly always be observed in times of crisis. During the last war, for example, "defense" and "war effort" were certainly regarded as culminative terms. We may say this because almost no one thinks of these terms as the natural sanctions of his mode of life. He may think thus of "progress" or "happiness" or even "freedom"; but "defense" and "war effort" are ultimate sanctions only when measured against an emergency situation. When the United States was preparing for entry into that conflict, every departure from our normal way of life could be justified as a "defense" measure. Plants making bombs to be dropped on other continents were called "defense" plants. Correspondingly, once the conflict had been entered, everything that was done in military or civilian areas was judged by its contribution to the "war effort." This last became for a period of years the supreme term: not God or Heaven or happiness, but successful effort in the war. It was a term to end all other

---

4 "Principles of Newspeak," *Nineteen Eighty-four* (New York, 1949), p. 310.

terms or a rhetoric to silence all other rhetoric. No one was able to make his claim heard against "the war effort."

It is most important to realize, therefore, that under the stress of feeling or preoccupation, quite secondary terms can be moved up to the position of ultimate terms, where they will remain until reflection is allowed to resume sway. There are many signs to show that the term "aggressor" is now undergoing such manipulation. Despite the fact that almost no term is more difficult to correlate with objective phenomena, it is being rapidly promoted to ultimate "bad" term. The likelihood is that "aggressor" will soon become a depository for all the resentments and fears which naturally arise in a people. As such, it will function as did "infidel" in the mediaeval period and as "reactionary" has functioned in the recent past. Manifestly it is of great advantage to a nation bent upon organizing its power to be able to stigmatize some neighbor as "aggressor," so that the term's capacity for irrational assumption is a great temptation for those who are not moral in their use of rhetoric. This passage from natural or popular to state-engendered charisma produces one of the most dangerous lesions of modern society.

An ethics of rhetoric requires that ultimate terms be ultimate in some rational sense. The only way to achieve that objective is through an ordering of our own minds and our own passions. Every one of psychological sophistication knows that there is a pleasure in willed perversity, and the setting up of perverse shibboleths is a fairly common source of that pleasure. War cries, school slogans, coterie passwords, and all similar expressions are examples of such creation. There may be areas of play in which these are nothing more than a diversion; but there are other areas in which such expressions lure us down the roads of hatred and tragedy. That is the tendency of all words of false or "engineered" charisma. They often sound like the very gospel of one's society, but in fact they betray us; they get us to do what the adversary of the human being wants us to do. It is worth considering whether the real civil disobedience must not begin with our language.

Lastly, the student of rhetoric must realize that in the contemporary world he is confronted not only by evil practitioners, but also, and probably to an unprecedented degree, by men who are conditioned by the evil created by others. The machinery of propagation and inculcation is today so immense that no one avoids entirely the assimilation and use of some terms which have a downward tendency. It is especially easy to pick up a tone without realizing its trend. Perhaps the best that any of us can do is to hold a dialectic with himself to see what the wider circumferences of his terms of persuasion are. This process will not only improve the consistency of one's thinking but it will also, if the foregoing analysis is sound, prevent his becoming a creature of evil public forces and a victim of his own thoughtless rhetoric.

ALDOUS HUXLEY

THE ARTS OF SELLING

This is Chapter 6 of Huxley's Brave New World Revisited *(1958). For information on the author and his writings, see page 25.*

•

The survival of democracy depends on the ability of large numbers of people to make realistic choices in the light of adequate information. A dictatorship, on the other hand, maintains itself by censoring or distorting the facts, and by appealing, not to reason, not to enlightened self-interest, but to passion and prejudice, to the powerful "hidden forces," as Hitler called them, present in the unconscious depths of every human mind.

In the West, democratic principles are proclaimed and many able and conscientious publicists do their best to supply electors with adequate information and to persuade them, by rational argument, to make realistic choices in the light of that information. All this is greatly to the good. But unfortunately propaganda in the Western democracies, above all in America, has two faces and a divided personality. In charge of the editorial department there is often a democratic Dr. Jekyll—a propagandist who would be very happy to prove that John Dewey had been right about the ability of human nature to respond to truth and reason. But this worthy man controls only a part of the machinery of mass communication. In charge of advertising we find an anti-democratic, because anti-rational, Mr. Hyde—or rather a Dr. Hyde, for Hyde is now a Ph.D. in psychology and has a master's degree as well in the social sciences. This Dr. Hyde would be very unhappy indeed if everybody always lived up to John Dewey's faith in human nature. Truth and reason are Jekyll's affair, not his. Hyde is a motivation analyst, and his business is to study human weaknesses and failings, to investigate those unconscious desires and fears by which so much of men's conscious thinking and overt doing is determined. And he does this, not in the spirit of the moralist who would like to make people better, or of the physician who would like to improve their health, but simply in order to find out the best way to take advantage of their ignorance and to exploit their irrationality for the pecuniary benefit of his employers. But after all, it may be argued, "capitalism is dead, consumerism is king"—and consumerism requires the services of expert salesmen versed in all the arts (including the more insidious arts) of persuasion. Under a free enterprise system commercial propaganda by any and every means is absolutely indispensable. But the indispensable is not necessarily the desirable. What is demonstrably good in the sphere of economics may be far from good for men and women as voters or even as human beings. An earlier, more moralistic generation would have been profoundly shocked by the bland cynicism of the motivation analysts. Today we read a book like Mr. Vance Packard's *The Hidden Persuaders*, and are more amused than horrified, more resigned than indignant. Given Freud, given Behaviorism, given the mass producer's chronically desperate need for mass consumption, this is the sort of thing that is only to be expected. But what, we may ask, is the sort of thing that is to be expected in the future? Are Hyde's activities compatible in the long run with Jekyll's? Can a campaign in favor of rationality be successful in the teeth of another and even more vigorous campaign in favor of irrationality? These are questions which, for the moment, I shall not attempt to answer, but shall leave hanging, so to speak, as a backdrop to our discussion of the methods of mass persuasion in a technologically advanced democratic society.

The task of the commercial propagandist in a democracy is in some ways easier and in some ways more difficult than that of a political propagandist employed by an established dictator or a dictator in the making. It is easier inasmuch as almost everyone starts out with a prejudice in favor of beer, cigarettes and iceboxes, whereas almost nobody starts out with a prejudice in favor of tyrants. It is more difficult inasmuch as the commercial propagandist is not permitted, by the rules of his particular game, to appeal to the more savage instincts of his public. The advertiser of dairy products would dearly love to tell his readers and listeners that all their troubles are caused by the machinations of a gang of godless international margarine manufacturers, and that it is their patriotic duty to march out and burn the oppressors' factories. This sort of thing, however, is ruled out, and he must be content with a milder approach. But the mild approach is less exciting than the approach through verbal or physical violence. In the long run, anger and hatred are self-defeating emotions. But in the short run they pay high dividends in the form of psychological and even (since they release large quantities of adrenalin and noradrenalin) physiological satisfaction. People may start out with an initial prejudice against tyrants; but when tyrants or would-be tyrants treat them to adrenalin-releasing propaganda about the wickedness of their enemies—particularly of enemies weak enough to be persecuted—they are ready to follow him with enthusiasm. In his speeches

Hitler kept repeating such words as "hatred," "force," "ruthless," "crush," "smash"; and he would accompany these violent words with even more violent gestures. He would yell, he would scream, his veins would swell, his face would turn purple. Strong emotion (as every actor and dramatist knows) is in the highest degree contagious. Infected by the malignant frenzy of the orator, the audience would groan and sob and scream in an orgy of uninhibited passion. And these orgies were so enjoyable that most of those who had experienced them eagerly came back for more. Almost all of us long for peace and freedom; but very few of us have much enthusiasm for the thoughts, feelings and actions that make for peace and freedom. Conversely almost nobody wants war or tyranny; but a great many people find an intense pleasure in the thoughts, feelings and actions that make for war and tyranny. These thoughts, feelings and actions are too dangerous to be exploited for commercial purposes. Accepting this handicap, the advertising man must do the best he can with the less intoxicating emotions, the quieter forms of irrationality.

Effective rational propaganda becomes possible only when there is a clear understanding, on the part of all concerned, of the nature of symbols and of their relations to the things and events symbolized. Irrational propaganda depends for its effectiveness on a general failure to understand the nature of symbols. Simple-minded people tend to equate the symbol with what it stands for, to attribute to things and events some of the qualities expressed by the words in terms of which the propagandist has chosen, for his own purposes, to talk about them. Consider a simple example. Most cosmetics are made of lanolin, which is a mixture of purified wool fat and water beaten up into an emulsion. This emulsion has many valuable properties: it penetrates the skin, it does not become rancid, it is mildly antiseptic and so forth. But the commercial propagandists do not speak about the genuine virtues of the emulsion. They give it some picturesquely voluptuous name, talk ecstatically and misleadingly about feminine beauty and show pictures of gorgeous blondes nourishing their tissues with skin food. "The cosmetic manufacturers," one of their number has written, "are not selling lanolin, they are selling hope." For this hope, this fraudulent implication of a promise that they will be transfigured, women will pay ten or twenty times the value of the emulsion which the propagandists have so skilfully related, by means of misleading symbols, to a deep-seated and almost universal feminine wish—the wish to be more attractive to members of the opposite sex. The principles underlying this kind of propaganda are extremely simple. Find some common desire, some widespread unconscious fear or anxiety; think out some way to relate this wish or fear to the product you have to sell; then build a bridge of verbal or pictorial symbols over which your customer can pass from fact to compensatory dream, and from the dream to the illusion that your product, when purchased, will make the dream come true. "We no longer buy oranges, we buy vitality. We do not buy just an auto, we buy prestige." And so with all the rest. In toothpaste, for example, we buy, not a mere cleanser and antiseptic, but release from the fear of being sexually repulsive. In vodka and whisky we are not buying a protoplasmic poison which, in small doses, may depress the nervous system in a psychologically valuable way; we are buying friendliness and good fellowship, the warmth of Dingley Dell and the brilliance of the Mermaid Tavern. With our laxatives we buy the health of a Greek god, the radiance of one of Diana's nymphs. With the monthly best seller we acquire culture, the envy of our less literate neighbors and the respect of the sophisticated. In every case the motivation analyst has found some deep-seated wish or fear, whose energy can be used to move the consumer to part with cash and so, indirectly, to turn the wheels of industry. Stored in the minds and bodies of countless individuals, this potential energy is released by, and transmitted along, a line of symbols carefully laid out so as to bypass rationality and obscure the real issue.

Sometimes the symbols take effect by being disproportionately impressive, haunting and fascinating in their own right. Of this kind are the rites and pomps of religion. These "beauties of holiness" strengthen faith where it already exists and, where there is no faith, contribute to conversion. Appealing, as they do, only to the aesthetic sense, they guarantee neither the truth nor the ethical value of the doctrines with which they have been, quite arbitrarily, associated. As a matter of plain historical fact, the beauties of holiness have often been matched and indeed surpassed by the beauties of unholiness. Under Hitler, for example, the yearly Nuremberg rallies were masterpieces of ritual and theatrical art. "I had spent six years in St. Petersburg before the war in the best days of the old Russian ballet," writes Sir Nevile Henderson, the British ambassador to Hitler's Germany, "but for grandiose beauty I have never seen any ballet to compare with the Nuremberg rally." One thinks of Keats—"beauty is truth, truth beauty." Alas, the identity exists only on some ultimate, supramundane level. On the levels of politics and theology, beauty is perfectly compatible with nonsense and tyranny. Which is very fortunate; for if beauty were incompatible with nonsense and tyranny, there would be precious little art in the world. The masterpieces of painting, sculpture and architecture were produced as religious or political propaganda, for the greater glory of a god, a government or a priesthood. But most kings and priests have been despotic and all religions have been riddled with superstition. Genius has been the servant of tyranny and art has advertised the merits of the local cult. Time, as it passes, separates the good art from the bad metaphysics. Can we learn to make this separation, not after the event, but while it is actually taking place? That is the question.

In commercial propaganda the principle of the disproportionately fascinating symbol is clearly understood. Every propagandist has his Art Department, and attempts are constantly being made to beautify the billboards with striking posters, the advertising pages of magazines with lively drawings and photographs. There are no masterpieces; for masterpieces appeal only to a limited audience, and the commercial propagandist is out to captivate the majority. For him, the ideal is a moderate excellence. Those who like this not too good, but sufficiently striking, art may be expected to like the products with which it has been associated and for which it symbolically stands.

Another disproportionately fascinating symbol is the Singing Commercial. Singing Commercials are a recent invention; but the Singing Theological and the Singing Devotional—the hymn and the psalm—are as old as religion itself. Singing Militaries, or marching songs, are coeval with war, and Singing Patriotics, the precursors of our national anthems, were doubtless used to promote group solidarity, to emphasize the distinction between "us" and "them," by the wandering bands of paleolithic hunters and food gatherers. To most people music is intrinsically attractive. Moreover, melodies tend to ingrain themselves in the listener's mind. A tune will haunt the memory during the whole of a lifetime. Here, for example, is a quite uninteresting statement or value judgment. As it stands nobody will pay attention to it. But now set the words to a catchy and easily remembered tune. Immediately they become words of power. Moreover, the words will tend automatically to repeat themselves every time the melody is heard or spontaneously remembered. Orpheus has entered into an alliance with Pavlov—the power of sound with the conditioned reflex. For the commercial propagandist, as for his colleagues in the fields of politics and religion, music possesses yet another advantage. Nonsense which it would be shameful for a reasonable being to write, speak or hear spoken can be sung or listened to by that same rational being with pleasure and even with a kind of intellectual conviction. Can we learn to separate the pleasure of singing or of listening to song from the all too human tendency to believe in the propaganda which the song is putting over? That again is the question.

Thanks to compulsory education and the rotary press, the propagandist has been able, for many years past, to convey his messages to virtually every adult in every civilized country. Today, thanks to radio and television, he is in the happy position of being able to communicate even with unschooled adults and not yet literate children.

Children, as might be expected, are highly susceptible to propaganda. They are ignorant of the world and its ways, and therefore completely unsuspecting. Their critical faculties are undeveloped. The youngest of them have not yet reached the age of reason and the older ones lack the experience on which their new-found rationality can effectively work. In Europe, conscripts used to be playfully referred to as "cannon fodder." Their little brothers and sisters have now become radio fodder and television fodder. In my childhood we were taught to sing nursery rhymes and, in pious households, hymns. Today the little ones warble the Singing

Commercials. Which is better—"Rheingold is my beer, the dry beer," or "Hey diddle-diddle, the cat and the fiddle"? "Abide with me" or "You'll wonder where the yellow went, when you brush your teeth with Pepsodent"? Who knows?

"I don't say that children should be forced to harass their parents into buying products they've seen advertised on television, but at the same time I cannot close my eyes to the fact that it's being done every day." So writes the star of one of the many programs beamed to a juvenile audience. "Children," he adds, "are living, talking records of what we tell them every day." And in due course these living, talking records of television commercials will grow up, earn money and buy the products of industry. "Think," writes Mr. Clyde Miller ecstatically, "think of what it can mean to your firm in profits if you can condition a million or ten million children, who will grow up into adults trained to buy your product, as soldiers are trained in advance when they hear the trigger words, Forward March!" Yes, just think of it! And at the same time remember that the dictators and the would-be dictators have been thinking about this sort of thing for years, and that millions, tens of millions, hundreds of millions of children are in process of growing up to buy the local despot's ideological product and, like well-trained soldiers, to respond with appropriate behavior to the trigger words implanted in those young minds by the despot's propagandists.

Self-government is in inverse ratio to numbers. The larger the constituency, the less the value of any particular vote. When he is merely one of millions, the individual elector feels himself to be impotent, a negligible quantity. The candidates he has voted into office are far away, at the top of the pyramid of power. Theoretically they are the servants of the people; but in fact it is the servants who give orders and the people, far off at the base of the great pyramid, who must obey. Increasing population and advancing technology have resulted in an increase in the number and complexity of organizations, an increase in the amount of power concentrated in the hands of officials and a corresponding decrease in the amount of control exercised by electors, coupled with a decrease in the public's regard for democratic procedures. Already weakened by the vast impersonal forces at work in the modern world, democratic institutions are now being undermined from within by the politicians and their propagandists.

Human beings act in a great variety of irrational ways, but all of them seem to be capable, if given a fair chance, of making a reasonable choice in the light of available evidence. Democratic institutions can be made to work only if all concerned do their best to impart knowledge and to encourage rationality. But today, in the world's most powerful democracy, the politicians and their propagandists prefer to make nonsense of democratic procedures by appealing almost exclusively to the ignorance and irrationality of the electors. "Both parties," we were told in 1956 by the editor of a leading business journal, "will merchandize their candidates and issues by the same methods that business has developed to sell goods. These include scientific selection of appeals and planned repetition. . . . Radio spot announcements and ads will repeat phrases with a planned intensity. Billboards will push slogans of proven power. . . . Candidates need, in addition to rich voices and good diction, to be able to look 'sincerely' at the TV camera."

The political merchandisers appeal only to the weaknesses of voters, never to their potential strength. They make no attempt to educate the masses into becoming fit for self-government; they are content merely to manipulate and exploit them. For this purpose all the resources of psychology and the social sciences are mobilized and set to work. Carefully selected samples of the electorate are given "interviews in depth." These interviews in depth reveal the unconscious fears and wishes most prevalent in a given society at the time of an election. Phrases and images aimed at allaying or, if necessary, enhancing these fears, at satisfying these wishes, at least symbolically, are then chosen by the experts, tried out on readers and audiences, changed or improved in the light of the information thus obtained. After which the political campaign is ready for the mass communicators. All that is now needed is money and a candidate who can be coached to look "sincere." Under the new dispensation, political principles and plans for specific action have come to lose most of their importance. The personality of the candidate and the way he is projected by the advertising experts are the things that really matter.

In one way or another, as vigorous he-man or kindly father, the candidate must be glamorous. He must also be an entertainer who never bores his audience. Inured to television and radio, that audience is accustomed to being distracted and does not like to be asked to concentrate or make a prolonged intellectual effort. All speeches by the entertainer-candidate must therefore be short and snappy. The great issues of the day must be dealt with in five minutes at the most—and preferably (since the audience will be eager to pass on to something a little livelier than inflation or the H-bomb) in sixty seconds flat. The nature of oratory is such that there has always been a tendency among politicians and clergymen to over-simplify complex issues. From a pulpit or a platform even the most conscientious of speakers finds it very difficult to tell the whole truth. The methods now being used to merchandise the political candidate as though he were a deodorant positively guarantee the electorate against ever hearing the truth about anything.

PAUL JACOBS

≪≪

Paul Jacobs, social scientist and writer, was born in New York City in 1918 and attended C.C.N.Y. and the University of Minnesota. He first became active in the union movement as an organizer and later became a labor consultant and co-publisher of a labor paper. He is a member of the staff of the Fund for the Republic's Center for the Study of Democratic Institutions, and has conducted research projects with various institutes at the University of California. He contributes regularly to the Economist *of London and has written for* The Reporter, Commentary, Commonweal, Atlantic, *and* Harper's. *He is joint editor of* Labor in a Free Society *(1959) and author of* The State of the Unions *(1963), and* Is Curley Jewish? *(1965). The present essay first appeared in* The Reporter, *September 18, 1958.*

THE MOST CHEERFUL
GRAVEYARD IN THE WORLD

Along with amassing a comfortable fortune by convincing Los Angelenos that the only fitting way to begin a "happy Eternal Life" is by being laid to rest, in one way or another, at Forest Lawn Memorial Park, the cemetery he founded in 1917, Dr. Hubert Eaton, or "Digger" as he is known in the trade, has also succeeded in almost completely revising the dying industry.

The Digger, whose official title of "Doctor" is purely honorary, accomplished this revision by the simple but profound device of converting the hitherto prosaic act of dying into a gloriously exciting, well-advertised event, somehow intimately and patriotically connected with the American way of life.

❧ Today, thanks to Eaton, dying in Los Angeles is something to be eagerly anticipated, because it is only after death that one can gain permanent tenure at Forest Lawn. Eaton, in one of his earlier roles—that of "the Builder"—described Forest Lawn as "a place where lovers new and old shall love to stroll and watch the sunset's glow, planning for the future or reminiscing of the past; a place where artists study and sketch; where school teachers bring happy children to see the things they read of in books; where little churches invite, triumphant in the knowledge that from their pulpits only words of Love can be spoken; where memorialization of loved ones in sculptured marble and pictorial glass shall be encouraged but controlled by acknowledged artists; a place where the sorrowing will be soothed and strengthened because it will be God's garden. A place that shall be protected by an immense Endowment Care Fund, the principal of which can never be expended—only the income therefrom used to care for and perpetuate this Garden of Memory.

"This is the Builder's Dream; this is the Builder's Creed."

The Builder's Creed is chiseled into a huge, upright stone slab on Forest Lawn's Cathedral Drive, just outside the Great Mausoleum and hard by the Shrine of Love. Viewed, usually in reverent awe, by more than a million visitors each year, Forest Lawn is, along with Disneyland, a favorite tourist attraction in Southern California, far outdrawing the concrete footprints in front of Grauman's Chinese Theatre.

A smaller inscription underneath the Creed points out that on New Year's Day, 1917, Eaton stood on a hilltop overlooking the small country cemetery which had just been placed in his charge. An unemployed mining engineer, Eaton had gone into the cemetery business after a vein of gold in his mine had suddenly vanished.

"A vision came to the man of what this tiny 'God's Acre' might become; and standing there, he made a promise to The Infinite. When he reached home, he put this promise into words and called it 'The Builder's Creed.' Today, Forest Lawn's almost three hundred acres are eloquent witness that The Builder kept faith with his soul."

Indeed, yes. The "almost three hundred acres" also bear eloquent witness to the fact that Eaton, still digging holes in the ground, worked a vein of gold infinitely more reliable than the one that vanished from his mine—the "Science and Art," as he describes it, "of Persuasion." So strongly does Eaton believe the "profession of salesmanship is the greatest of all professions" that he has established The Foundation for the Science and Art of Persuasion at his alma mater, William Jewell College, Liberty, Missouri.

Forest Lawn reflects Eaton's skill in the "Science." The "country cemetery" with only a "scant dozen acres of developed ground" has grown into Forest Lawn Memorial Park, with a permanent "population" of more than 170,000, increasing at the rate of approximately 6,500 a year.

In fact, business has been so good that there are now two additional Forest Lawn "Memorial Parks" in Los Angeles: Forest Lawn-Hollywood Hills, the focus of a bitter political struggle in the city, and adjacent to it Mount Sinai, designed to attract the growing Jewish population of Los Angeles

Forest Lawn offers the largest religious painting in the United States,
displayed in a building, the Hall of the Crucifixion, specially designed for
it. There, for a voluntary contribution of twenty-five cents, the visitor
sits comfortably in a large theatre, in one of a "broad sweep of seats,
richly upholstered in burgundy, rising tier above tier, matching the
splendor of the architecture," and watches the three-thousand-pound
curtain open on Jesus at Calvary, forty-five feet high and 195 feet long.
A lecture about the painting, supplemented with a moving arrow, is delivered by a tape recording in the special kind of rich, organ-tone voice
used throughout Forest Lawn.

There are also hundreds of statues, both originals and reproductions,
scattered throughout the three hundred acres. Typical of these is an
eighteen-figure group depicting Forest Lawn's solution to the "Mystery
of Life." Interpretations of the eighteen figures are supplied: "(17) the
atheist, the fool, who grinningly cares not at all; while (18) the stoic
sits in silent awe and contemplation of that which he believes he knows
but cannot explain with any satisfaction."

At the Court of David there is a huge reproduction of Michelangelo's
"David"—with a large fig leaf added by Forest Lawn. An exact copy of
the sculptor's "Moses" is displayed at the entrance to the Cathedral
Corridor in Memorial Terrace, "the only one," according to Forest Lawn,
"cast from clay masks placed directly on the original statue in the Church
of Saint Peter in Chains at Rome, Italy."

So that the masks could be made, the Church of Saint Peter had to be
closed for a day, something that had not happened before. "I gave
a lot of dinners and I bought a lot of wine and I sent a lot of cables and
St. Peter's was closed," Eaton modestly explains.

Color photos and post cards of the "Moses" statue can be purchased,
along with thousands of other items, at Forest Lawn's souvenir shop.
There, browsing visitors can choose from showcases displaying money
clips, cocktail napkins, book matches, jigsaw puzzles, and charm bracelets
—all decorated with Forest Lawn motifs. Prices range from a modest
twenty-nine cents for a key chain to $125 for a glass vase etched with a
Forest Lawn scene.

There are brown plastic nutshells containing little photos of Forest
Lawn, ladies' compacts, cigarette lighters, cufflinks, salt and pepper shakers,
picture frames, demitasse spoons, bookmarks, cups and saucers, pen and
pencil sets, glass bells, wooden plaques, ashtrays, place mats and doilies,
perfume and powder sets, jackknives, and a great variety of other goodies,
all with an appropriate Forest Lawn theme. Books like *The Loved One*,
Evelyn Waugh's satire of Forest Lawn, are not on sale in the souvenir
shop. (Eaton occasionally expresses resentment over the treatment given
the cemetery by novelists—especially by one writer to whom he extended
free run of the park only to be parodied later. But Eaton also understands that such novels have brought world-wide publicity to Forest

Lawn and have not adversely affected his sales, which come not from England but from Los Angeles.)

Among the most popular items at the souvenir shop are those showing reproductions of Forest Lawn's three churches, the Church of the Recessional, the Little Church of the Flowers, and the Wee Kirk o' the Heather.

"Providing a dignified setting for final tribute," the three churches "serve also for the joyous and memorable ceremonies of christening and the exchange of marriage vows." Since the churches have opened, more than 43,000 persons have had "memorable" marriages in them. But Forest Lawn makes no money directly from marrying people, and the profits from the souvenir shop are used for the upkeep of the Hall of the Crucifixion. Forest Lawn's real business is burying people.

"The hardest thing in the world to sell," states one of the organization's top officials, "are 'spaces.' " ("Space" is the euphemism used at Forest Lawn for "grave plot.") The reason for the difficulty is that Forest Lawn's sales organization, which comprises about 175 people, concentrates on sales made "Before Need," another phrase in Forest Lawn's own peculiar language of the flowers. Selling cemetery plots "Before Need" rather than "At Time of Need" or "Post Need," although difficult, is very profitable, since under California law a cemetery pays taxes only on its unsold plots. Once a "space" has been sold, it is removed from the tax rolls. Thus it is to the obvious advantage of Forest Lawn to sell off its land as quickly as possible, without waiting for "Need."

There are approximately fifteen hundred individual "spaces" to the acre in Forest Lawn. Prices average $300 per space. There are also rather more elegant neighborhoods at Forest Lawn which are less crowded and therefore more expensive. In the Gardens of Memory, entered only with a special key, there are "memorial sanctuaries designed for families who desire the privacy and protection of crypt interment, but who at the same time long for the open skies and the natural beauty of a verdant garden bathed in sunlight. Under the lawns in the Gardens of Memory have been created a number of monolithically constructed crypts of steel-reinforced concrete."

In the area of ground burial, Forest Lawn has contributed a pleasant innovation. No tombstones are permitted, only markers, set flush with the ground so that there is in fact the pleasant appearance of a park with sweeping green lawns.

But one does not have to be interred to take up permanent residence at Forest Lawn. A number of other arrangements can be made, including being inurned after cremation in the columbarium for as little as $145 or entombed in a mausoleum crypt—which can cost as much as $800,000, as in the case of the Irving Thalberg mausoleum. One can also be placed in a large wall out in the open air. Families may be interred, inurned, or entombed as a unit to maintain "togetherness." Should one feel the need for fresh air while spending the "happy Eternal Life" in a crypt, it is possible, at added cost naturally, to have a ventilating system installed. In the mausoleum, tape-recorded music is played as well.

Inurnment is not restricted to a single form of urn. The law in California, which has a strong undertakers' lobby, provides that after cremation ashes must be buried or placed in a columbarium. A wide variety of urn designs can be seen, ranging from books and loving cups to miniature coffins.

The price for the casket or urn sets the approximate amount paid for the funeral itself, but here the range is far greater than for the "space." The least expensive casket, with the metal screw heads showing, is $115; the most expensive goes for $17,500.

Forest Lawn's rich, creamy advertising presentations combine the hard and the soft sell. On radio and television, the same institutional approach is as manifest as at the cemetery itself. Programs of church services and organ music are announced in deep, sonorous tones, and practically no mention is made of the company's product. The institutional approach is also used on billboards picturing stained-glass windows or the "Moses" statue. However, many of Forest Lawn's billboards are given over to the hard, competitive sell, featuring what is Hubert Eaton's original contribution to the American way of death: the concept of combining in one place mortuary functions, such as embalming, with funeral services and burial, thus obviating the necessity for outside undertakers, florists, funeral chapels, and long processions to the cemetery. Forest Lawn successfully undertook the elimination of the undertaking middleman.

Today, Forest Lawn's hard-sell slogans of "Everything In One Beautiful Place" and "Just One Phone Call" are widely copied, as are the ads which usually feature back or side views, sometimes in color, of two dry-eyed, well-groomed people talking to a distinguished-looking, gray-mustached bank-president or diplomat-type man, identified by a discreet sign on his desk as a "Funeral Counselor." Sometimes only the "Counselor" is shown, answering the "Just One Phone Call" with the dedicated air of a statesman. It is clear from the ads that at Forest Lawn, where the concept of death has been abolished, the standards of accepted behavior demand no vulgar signs of outward grief.

But even though its competitors copy Forest Lawn today, Eaton faced a bitter battle when he first attempted to bring a mortuary into the cemetery. Forest Lawn's permit to operate a mortuary was given only after a determined struggle waged against him by some of the undertakers who foresaw disaster for themselves in the new trend of combined services. It was during this period that Forest Lawn began to build up its own political operations, which today make it the most powerful spokesman for the industry in the state.

There have been a number of occasions when, in its self-interest, Forest Lawn has had to do battle, sometimes in ways that might have been frowned on by the dignified gentlemen in their ads. From the 1930's to the early 1950's, Forest Lawn was in a running argument with the county assessor's office over the tax assessments made on its property, with Forest Lawn always claiming that the assessments were too high and almost always getting them reduced, even as much as fifty per cent, by the county board of supervisors. Some supervisors did consistently oppose Forest Lawn's plea for tax reduction and supported the assessor, but when the votes were taken a majority always supported Forest Lawn.

In 1938, in one of its early appearances before the board of supervisors, Forest Lawn requested a tax reduction, claiming that the vacant property in the land it then owned would remain unsold until 1973. At the time, the county assessor pointed out that Forest Lawn had "acquired additional property when they said it was going to take thirty-five years to sell out what they now have, yet they go to work and buy seventy-five acres adjoining at a big price."

Ten years later, in 1948, the issue of how long it would take to fill Forest Lawn's vacant "spaces" became one of the central points in a bitter political hassle within the Los Angeles City Council, and the cemetery completely reversed its argument of ten years earlier. At issue was Forest Lawn's request for a zoning change to permit the use, as a cemetery, of 480 acres of land adjoining Griffith Park, a public park and playground in the Hollywood area.

Forest Lawn's first request to develop this new cemetery was submitted to and rejected by the city planning commission in 1946. When the request was again rejected in 1948, Forest Lawn appealed, claiming, in contrast to its 1938 plea of unsold land, that "by the year 1965 all of the available grave spaces in existing cemeteries will have been exhausted."

The odds against Forest Lawn's gaining approval for its plan to open a new cemetery seemed formidable. The planning commission opposed it, the park department opposed it, the board of health commissioners opposed it, the water and power commission opposed it, the board of public works opposed it, the Hollywood chamber of commerce opposed it, and a variety of community groups opposed it. But the "Builder's Dream" triumphed, and on March 9, 1948, the city council voted 11-3 to permit the opening of the cemetery.

Never an organization to leave stones unturned, within a few hours Forest Lawn had hastily dug six holes in the ground and buried six bodies in them; a move which, under state law, immediately qualified the area as a commercial graveyard that could not then be disturbed or moved except under very specific circumstances.

"We got the bodies we buried through the county hospital or from their next of kin in advance," states Ugene Blalock, vice-president and general counsel of Forest Lawn, "and we made no charge for our services. If the vote in the council had gone against us, we would have given them a free burial elsewhere."

In fact, however, the council vote has rarely gone against Forest Lawn, even when the city fathers were voting on whether to give Beverly Hills the street where Eaton lives, thus providing the Digger with a more distinguished address. Although he hasn't moved, Eaton now lives in Beverly Hills.

No one is quite sure about the exact basis for Eaton's influence; or if they are, they're not willing to talk about it for the record. Blalock states that Forest Lawn as an institution has not made, as far as he knows, any campaign contribution in eighteen years, although he adds, "Individuals may make political contributions." But politics aside, it is Hubert Eaton, master salesman, who is chiefly responsible for Forest Lawn's success.

It is from Eaton's mind that has come the creation of the Council of Regents of Memorial Court of Honor, twenty-two "outstanding business and professional men" who advise "on all matters concerning the growth of the Memorial Park as a cultural center of religion and fine arts."

Its members, who include the president of Occidental College and the chancellor of the University of Southern California, wear a handsome, flowing red robe, trimmed with velvet, and an elegant round red hat, also trimmed daintily with velvet, while around their necks hangs a kind of Maltese Cross decoration, perhaps the Order of Forest Lawn.

Such touches as these distinguish the imaginative Eaton from his colleagues. Eaton's devotion to salesmanship, as evidenced by his creating special heart-shaped children's sections at Forest Lawn, named Babyland and Lullabyland, began early in life, according to "The Forest Lawn Story," his biography sold at the souvenir shop.

The son of a college professor, Eaton, states the biography, "sat in his little cubbyhole behind his father's bookshelves ostensibly studying but actually eavesdropping on his father's conversations with callers. Invariably they came for advice on one thing or another but more often than not, it was advice on matters affecting money. From these conversations he learned the word salesmanship and what it meant."

It was Eaton, too, who initiated many Forest Lawn public-service activities—the inspirational speaker made available to service clubs, the thirteen half-hour Bible films, and the giving of the Forest Lawn Awards for Persuasive Writing as a "practical service to students and Christian liberal arts colleges."

Long interested in "small, independent, liberal arts colleges" as being "America's last bulwark against the march of Socialism . . ." Eaton believes that "most" college professors are "semi-socialists at heart" who teach young people that salesmanship "smacks of chicanery, demagoguery, of influencing people against their wills . . ."

But Eaton isn't always so serious. Even when he was at college himself, he always had a "good sense of humor." His biography relates that one of his favorite tricks was to persuade a visitor to allow a funnel to be inserted into the top of his trousers and then to make him balance a penny on his chin and try to drop it into the funnel. While the visitor was in this position, young Hubert "or one of his cronies would pour a cup of cold water into the funnel."

Eaton's "good sense of humor changed little in succeeding years," states his biographer, and it certainly hadn't changed much the night when Eaton gave one of his usual huge, lavish parties for a group of friends and guests. It was called "An Enchanted Evening in the South Pacific," of which "Trader" Hubert Eaton was the master of ceremonies. Elaborate Hawaiian acts were presented, and guests received a large, beautifully printed eight-page souvenir program in color, in which Eaton had himself depicted as "Your Happy Planter," jumping from page to page on a golden-shovel pogo stick.

On the cultural level, the printed program carried a large reproduction of the "David" statue, with a fig leaf, a Hawaiian lei, and a girl curled around its neck, all illustrating a poem, "The Secret of Hubie's David," which described just how it was decided to add a fig leaf to Forest Lawn's copy of Michelangelo's "David" in order not to shock "the ladies of L.A."

But surely the greatest of all the improvements that Eaton has made on the past is Forest Lawn itself. Here, what might have been just an ordinary "country cemetery" has been parlayed into a solemn institution, profitable and widely imitated, looking like Edgar Guest's idea of Heaven brought to earth, while representing a social level to which all people can aspire after death. And in the future, says Hubert Eaton, "When the place is all filled up, my idea, from a financial standpoint, has always been to make Forest Lawn into a museum and charge admission."

Crime and Punishment

Conflicting theories of how to deal with crime are deeply rooted in Western culture. The Mosaic Code is unequivocal: An eye for an eye; a tooth for a tooth. The Sixth Commandment is equally clear: Thou shalt not kill. And the classic statement of forgiveness is found in the Sermon on the Mount: Whosoever shall smite thee on thy right cheek, turn to him the other also. To the concepts of retribution and forgiveness the modern age has added that of correction and rehabilitation, and all are invoked to defend or attack capital punishment in our society.

In the last decades an increasing number of countries and states have passed laws abolishing the death penalty. But at this writing forty-three states in America still allow it. The four essays in this section present both the practical and the moral issues which continue to be debated. Two of the authors—Barzun and Mencken—offer the case for capital punishment. Although they begin with an apparently similar argument, they differ widely in tone and purpose. Barzun, pragmatic and direct, concerns himself with the fate of the victim and thus with the necessary protection of society, while Mencken's irony also glances at the society that metes out the punishment. It is the moral welfare of this society that deeply concerns Camus, who concludes that "there will be no lasting peace either in the heart of individuals or in social customs until death is outlawed." Orwell's brief narrative effectively dramatizes this philosophy.

JACQUES BARZUN

Born in France in 1907, Jacques Barzun came to this country when he was twelve years old and later became an American citizen. Admitted to Columbia University shortly before his sixteenth birthday, he became lecturer and researcher in history there and by 1945 rose to full professor. He has been Dean of Faculties and Provost at Columbia since 1958 and Seth Low Professor of History since 1960. A tireless critic of education and society, Professor Barzun is also considered an authority on art and music and an articulate spokesman for the humanist tradition. His many books include Darwin, Marx, Wagner: Critique of a Heritage *(1941)*, The Teacher in America *(1945)*, Berlioz and the Romantic Century *(1950)*, The Modern Researcher *(1957)*, and* The House of Intellect *(1959). He is also a frequent contributor to periodicals. The essay we present below first appeared in* The American Scholar, *Spring, 1962.*

IN FAVOR OF CAPITAL
PUNISHMENT

A passing remark of mine in the *Mid-Century* magazine has brought me a number of letters and a sheaf of pamphlets against capital punishment. The letters, sad and reproachful, offer me the choice of pleading ignorance or being proved insensitive. I am asked whether I know that there exists a worldwide movement for the abolition of capital punishment which has everywhere enlisted able men of every profession, including the law. I am told that the death penalty is not only inhuman but also unscientific, for rapists and murderers are really sick people who should be cured, not killed. I am invited to use my imagination and acknowledge the unbearable horror of every form of execution.

I am indeed aware that the movement for abolition is widespread and articulate, especially in England. It is headed there by my old friend and publisher, Mr. Victor Gollancz, and it numbers such well-known writers as Arthur Koestler, C. H. Rolph, James Avery Joyce and Sir John Barry. Abroad as at home the profession of psychiatry tends to support the cure principle, and many liberal newspapers, such as the *Observer*, are committed to abolition. In the United States there are at least twenty-five state leagues working to the same end, plus a national league and several church councils, notably the Quaker and the Episcopal.

The assemblage of so much talent and enlightened goodwill behind a single proposal must give pause to anyone who supports the other side, and in the attempt to make clear my views, which are now close to unpopular, I start out by granting that my conclusion is arguable; that is, I am still open to conviction, *provided* some fallacies and frivolities in the abolitionist argument are first disposed of and the difficulties not ignored but overcome. I should be glad to see this happen, not only because there is pleasure in the spectacle of an airtight case, but also because I am not more sanguinary than my neighbor and I should welcome the discovery of safeguards—for society *and* the criminal—other than killing. But I say it again, these safeguards must really meet, not evade or postpone, the difficulties I am about to describe. Let me add before I begin that I shall probably not answer any more letters on this arousing subject. If this printed exposition does not do justice to my cause, it is not likely that I can do better in the hurry of private correspondence.

I readily concede at the outset that present ways of dealing out capital punishment are as revolting as Mr. Koestler says in his harrowing volume, *Hanged by the Neck*. Like many of our prisons, our modes of execution should change. But this objection to barbarity does not mean that capital punishment—or rather, judicial homicide—should not go on. The illicit jump we find here, on the threshold of the inquiry, is characteristic of the abolitionist and must be disallowed at every point. Let us bear in mind the possibility of devising a painless, sudden and dignified death, and see whether its administration is justifiable.

The four main arguments advanced against the death penalty are: *1.* punishment for crime is a primitive idea rooted in revenge; *2.* capital punishment does not deter; *3.* judicial error being possible, taking life is an appalling risk; *4.* a civilized state, to deserve its name, must uphold, not violate, the sanctity of human life.

I entirely agree with the first pair of propositions, which is why, a moment ago, I replaced the term capital punishment with "judicial homicide." The uncontrollable brute whom I want put out of the way is not to be punished for his misdeeds, nor used as an example or a warning; he is to be killed for the protection of others, like the wolf that escaped not long ago in a Connecticut suburb. No anger, vindictiveness or moral conceit need preside over the removal of such dangers. But a man's inability to control his violent impulses or to imagine the fatal consequences of his acts should be a presumptive reason for his elimination from society. This generality covers drunken driving and teen-age racing on public highways, as well as incurable obsessive violence; it might be extended (as I shall suggest later) to other acts that destroy, precisely, the moral basis of civilization.

But why kill? I am ready to believe the statistics tending to show that the prospect of his own death does not stop the murderer. For one thing he is often a blind egotist, who cannot conceive the possibility of his own death. For another, detection would have to be infallible to deter the more imaginative who, although afraid, think they can escape discovery. Lastly, as Shaw long ago pointed out, hanging the wrong man will deter as effectively as hanging the right one. So, once again, why kill? If I agree that moral progress means an increasing respect for human life, how can I oppose abolition?

I do so because on this subject of human life, which is to me the heart of the controversy, I find the abolitionist inconsistent, narrow or blind. The propaganda for abolition speaks in hushed tones of the sanctity of human life, as if the mere statement of it as an absolute should silence all opponents who have any moral sense. But most of the abolitionists belong to nations that spend half their annual income on weapons of war and that honor research to perfect means of killing. These good people vote without a qualm for the political parties that quite sensibly arm their country to the teeth. The West today does not seem to be the time or place to invoke the absolute sanctity of human life. As for the clergymen in the movement, we may be sure from the experience of two previous world wars that they will bless our arms and pray for victory when called upon, the sixth commandment notwithstanding.

"Oh, but we mean the sanctity of life *within* the nation!" Very well: is the movement then campaigning also against the principle of self-defense? Absolute sanctity means letting the cutthroat have his sweet will of you, even if you have a poker handy to bash him with, for you might kill. And again, do we hear any protest against the police firing at criminals on the street—mere bank robbers usually—and doing this, often enough, with an excited marksmanship that misses the artist and hits the bystander? The absolute sanctity of human life is, for the abolitionist, a slogan rather than a considered proposition.

Yet it deserves examination, for upon our acceptance or rejection of it depend such other highly civilized possibilities as euthanasia and seemly suicide. The inquiring mind also wants to know, why the sanctity of *human* life alone? My tastes do not run to household pets, but I find

something less than admirable in the uses to which we put animals—
in zoos, laboratories and space machines—without the excuse of the
ancient law, "Eat or be eaten."

It should moreover be borne in mind that this argument about sanctity
applies—or would apply—to about ten persons a year in Great Britain
and to between fifty and seventy-five in the United States. These are the
average numbers of those executed in recent years. The count by itself
should not, of course, affect our judgment of the principle: one life
spared or forfeited is as important, morally, as a hundred thousand. But
it should inspire a comparative judgment: there are hundreds and indeed
thousands whom, in our concern with the horrors of execution, we forget: on the one hand, the victims of violence; on the other, the prisoners
in our jails.

The victims are easy to forget. Social science tends steadily to mark
a preference for the troubled, the abnormal, the problem case. Whether
it is poverty, mental disorder, delinquency or crime, the "patient material" monopolizes the interest of increasing groups of people among the
most generous and learned. Psychiatry and moral liberalism go together;
the application of law as we have known it is thus coming to be regarded
as an historic prelude to social work, which may replace it entirely. Modern literature makes the most of this same outlook, caring only for the
disturbed spirit, scorning as bourgeois those who pay their way and do
not stab their friends. All the while the determinism of natural science
reinforces the assumption that society causes its own evils. A French
jurist, for example, says that in order to understand crime we must first
brush aside all ideas of Responsibility. He means the criminal's and takes
for granted that of society. The murderer kills because reared in a broken
home or, conversely, because at an early age he witnessed his parents
making love. Out of such cases, which make pathetic reading in the
literature of modern criminology, is born the abolitionist's state of
mind: we dare not kill those we are beginning to understand so well.

If, moreover, we turn to the accounts of the crimes committed by
these unfortunates, who are the victims? Only dull ordinary people going
about their business. We are sorry, of course, but they do not interest
science on its march. Balancing, for example, the sixty to seventy criminals
executed annually in the United States, there were the seventy to eighty
housewives whom George Cvek robbed, raped and usually killed during
the months of a career devoted to proving his virility. "It is too bad."
Cvek alone seems instructive, even though one of the law officers who
helped track him down quietly remarks: "As to the extent that his villain-
ies disturbed family relationships, or how many women are still haunted
by the specter of an experience they have never disclosed to another
living soul, these questions can only lend themselves to sterile conjecture."

The remote results are beyond our ken, but it is not idle to speculate about those whose death by violence fills the daily two inches at the back of respectable newspapers—the old man sunning himself on a park bench and beaten to death by four hoodlums, the small children abused and strangled, the middle-aged ladies on a hike assaulted and killed, the family terrorized by a released or escaped lunatic, the half-dozen working people massacred by the sudden maniac, the boatload of persons dispatched by the skipper, the mindless assaults upon schoolteachers and shopkeepers by the increasing horde of dedicated killers in our great cities. Where does the sanctity of life begin?

It is all very well to say that many of these killers are themselves "children," that is, minors. Doubtless a nine-year-old mind is housed in that 150 pounds of unguided muscle. Grant, for argument's sake, that the misdeed is "the fault of society," trot out the broken home and the slum environment. The question then is, What shall we do, not in the Utopian city of tomorrow, but here and now? The "scientific" means of cure are more than uncertain. The apparatus of detention only increases the killer's antisocial animus. Reformatories and mental hospitals are full and have an understandable bias toward discharging their inmates. Some of these are indeed "cured"—so long as they stay under a rule. The stress of the social free-for-all throws them back on their violent modes of self-expression. At that point I agree that society has failed—twice: it has twice failed the victims, whatever may be its guilt toward the killer.

As in all great questions, the moralist must choose, and choosing has a price. I happen to think that if a person of adult body has not been endowed with adequate controls against irrationally taking the life of another, that person must be judicially, painlessly, regretfully killed before that mindless body's horrible automation repeats.

I say "irrationally" taking life, because it is often possible to feel great sympathy with a murderer. Certain *crimes passionnels* can be forgiven without being condoned. Blackmailers invite direct retribution. Long provocation can be an excuse, as in that engaging case of some years ago, in which a respectable carpenter of seventy found he could no longer stand the incessant nagging of his wife. While she excoriated him from her throne in the kitchen—a daily exercise for fifty years—the husband went to his bench and came back with a hammer in each hand to settle the score. The testimony to his character, coupled with the sincerity implied by the two hammers, was enough to have him sent into quiet and brief seclusion.

But what are we to say of the type of motive disclosed in a journal published by the inmates of one of our Federal penitentiaries? The author is a bank robber who confesses that money is not his object:

My mania for power, socially, sexually, and otherwise can feel no degree of satisfaction until I feel sure I have struck the ultimate of submission and terror in the minds and bodies of my victims. . . . It's very difficult to explain all the queer fascinating sensations pounding and surging through me while I'm holding a gun on a victim, watching his body tremble and sweat. . . . This is the moment when all the rationalized hypocrisies of civilization are suddenly swept away and two men stand there facing each other morally and ethically naked, and right and wrong are the absolute commands of the man behind the gun.

This confused echo of modern literature and modern science defines the choice before us. Anything deserving the name of cure for such a man presupposes not only a laborious individual psychoanalysis, with the means to conduct and to sustain it, socially and economically, but also a re-education of the mind, so as to throw into correct perspective the garbled ideas of Freud and Nietzsche, Gide and Dostoevski, which this power-seeker and his fellows have derived from the culture and temper of our times. Ideas are tenacious and give continuity to emotion. Failing a second birth of heart and mind, we must ask: How soon will this sufferer sacrifice a bank clerk in the interests of making civilization less hypocritical? And we must certainly question the wisdom of affording him more than one chance. The abolitionists' advocacy of an unconditional "let live" is in truth part of the same cultural tendency that animates the killer. The Western peoples' revulsion from power in domestic and foreign policy has made of the state a sort of counterpart of the bank robber: both having power and neither knowing how to use it. Both waste lives because hypnotized by irrelevant ideas and crippled by contradictory emotions. If psychiatry were sure of its ground in diagnosing the individual case, a philosopher might consider whether such dangerous obsessions should not be guarded against by judicial homicide *before* the shooting starts.

I raise the question not indeed to recommend the prophylactic execution of potential murderers, but to introduce the last two perplexities that the abolitionists dwarf or obscure by their concentration on changing an isolated penalty. One of these is the scale by which to judge the offenses society wants to repress. I can for example imagine a truly democratic state in which it would be deemed a form of treason punishable by death to create a disturbance in any court or deliberative assembly. The aim would be to recognize the sanctity of orderly discourse in arriving at justice, assessing criticism and defining policy. Under such a law, a natural selection would operate to remove permanently from the scene persons who, let us say, neglect argument in favor of banging on the desk with their shoe. Similarly, a bullying minority in a diet, parliament or skupshtina would be prosecuted for treason to the most sacred institutions when fists or flying inkwells replace rhetoric. That the mere suggestion of such a law sounds ludicrous shows how remote we are from civilized institutions, and hence how gradual should be our departure from the severity of judicial homicide.

I say gradual and I do not mean standing still. For there is one form of barbarity in our law that I want to see mitigated before any other. I mean imprisonment. The enemies of capital punishment—and liberals generally—seem to be satisfied with any legal outcome so long as they themselves avoid the vicarious guilt of shedding blood. They speak of the sanctity of life, but have no concern with its quality. They give no impression of ever having read what it is certain they have read, from Wilde's *De Profundis* to the latest account of prison life by a convicted homosexual. Despite the infamy of concentration camps, despite Mr. Charles Burney's remarkable work, *Solitary Confinement*, despite riots in prisons, despite the round of escape, recapture and return in chains, the abolitionists' imagination tells them nothing about the reality of being caged. They read without a qualm, indeed they read with rejoicing, the hideous irony of "Killer Gets Life"; they sigh with relief instead of horror. They do not see and suffer the cell, the drill, the clothes, the stench, the food; they do not feel the sexual racking of young and old bodies, the hateful promiscuity, the insane monotony, the mass degradation, the impotent hatred. They do not remember from Silvio Pellico that only a strong political faith, with a hope of final victory, can steel a man to endure long detention. They forget that Joan of Arc, when offered "life," preferred burning at the stake. Quite of another mind, the abolitionists point with pride to the "model prisoners" that murderers often turn out to be. As if a model prisoner were not, first, a contradiction in terms, and second, an exemplar of what a free society should not want.

I said a moment ago that the happy advocates of the life sentence appear not to have understood what we know they have read. No more do they appear to read what they themselves write. In the preface to his useful volume of cases, *Hanged in Error*, Mr. Leslie Hale, M.P., refers to the tardy recognition of a minor miscarriage of justice—one year in jail: "The prisoner emerged to find that his wife had died and that his children and his aged parents had been removed to the workhouse. By the time a small payment had been assessed as 'compensation' the victim was incurably insane." So far we are as indignant with the law as Mr. Hale. But what comes next? He cites the famous Evans case, in which it is very probable that the wrong man was hanged, and he exclaims: "While such mistakes are possible, should society impose an irrevocable sentence?" Does Mr. Hale really ask us to believe that the sentence passed on the first man, whose wife died and who went insane, was in any sense *revocable?* Would not any man rather be Evans dead than that other wretch "emerging" with his small compensation and his reasons for living gone?

Nothing is revocable here below, imprisonment least of all. The agony of a trial itself is punishment, and acquittal wipes out nothing. Read the heart-rending diary of William Wallace, accused quite implausibly of having murdered his wife and "saved" by the Court of Criminal Appeals

—but saved for what? Brutish ostracism by everyone and a few years of solitary despair. The cases of Adolf Beck, of Oscar Slater, of the unhappy Brooklyn bank teller who vaguely resembled a forger and spent eight years in Sing Sing only to "emerge" a broken, friendless, useless, "compensated" man—all these, if the dignity of the individual has any meaning, had better have been dead before the prison door ever opened for them. This is what counsel always says to the jury in the course of a murder trial and counsel is right: far better hang this man than "give him life." For my part, I would choose death without hesitation. If that option is abolished, a demand will one day be heard to claim it as a privilege in the name of human dignity. I shall believe in the abolitionist's present views only after he has emerged from twelve months in a convict cell.

The detached observer may want to interrupt here and say that the argument has now passed from reasoning to emotional preference. Whereas the objector to capital punishment *feels* that death is the greatest of evils, I *feel* that imprisonment is worse than death. A moment's thought will show that feeling is the appropriate arbiter. All reasoning about what is right, civilized and moral rests upon sentiment, like mathematics. Only, in trying to persuade others, it is important to single out the fundamental feeling, the prime intuition, and from it to reason justly. In my view, to profess respect for human life and be willing to see it spent in a penitentiary is to entertain liberal feelings frivolously. To oppose the death penalty because, unlike a prison term, it is irrevocable is to argue fallaciously.

In the propaganda for abolishing the death sentence the recital of numerous miscarriages of justice commits the same error and implies the same callousness: what is at fault in our present system is not the sentence but the fallible procedure. Capital cases being one in a thousand or more, who can be cheerful at the thought of all the "revocable" errors? What the miscarriages point to is the need for reforming the jury system, the rules of evidence, the customs of prosecution, the machinery of appeal. The failure to see that this is the great task reflects the sentimentality I spoke of earlier, that which responds chiefly to the excitement of the unusual. A writer on Death and the Supreme Court is at pains to point out that when that tribunal reviews a capital case, the judges are particularly anxious and careful. What a left-handed compliment to the highest judicial conscience of the country! Fortunately, some of the champions of the misjudged see the issue more clearly. Many of those who are thought wrongly convicted now languish in jail because the jury was uncertain or because a doubting governor commuted the death sentence. Thus Dr. Samuel H. Sheppard, Jr., convicted of his wife's murder in the second degree is serving a sentence that is supposed to run for the term of his natural life. The story of his numerous trials, as told by Mr. Paul Holmes, suggests that police incompetence, newspaper demagogy, public envy of affluence and the mischances of legal procedure fashioned the result. But Dr. Sheppard's vindicator is under no illusion as to the conditions that this "lucky" evader of the electric chair will face if he is granted parole after ten years: "It will carry with it no right to resume his life as a physician. His privilege to practice medicine was blotted out with his conviction. He must all his life bear the stigma of a parolee, subject to unceremonious return to confinement for life for the slightest misstep. More than this, he must live out his life as a convicted murderer."

What does the moral conscience of today think it is doing? If such a man is a dangerous repeater of violent acts, what right has the state to let him loose after ten years? What is, in fact, the meaning of a "life sentence" that peters out long before life? Paroling looks suspiciously like an expression of social remorse for the pain of incarceration, coupled with a wish to avoid "unfavorable publicity" by freeing a suspect. The man is let out when the fuss has died down; which would mean that he was not under lock and key for our protection at all. He *was* being punished, just a little—for so prison seems in the abolitionist's distorted view, and in the jury's and the prosecutor's, whose "second-degree" murder suggests killing someone "just a little."[1]

If, on the other hand, execution and life imprisonment are judged too severe and the accused is expected to be harmless hereafter—punishment being ruled out as illiberal—what has society gained by wrecking his life and damaging that of his family?

What we accept, and what the abolitionist will clamp upon us all the more firmly if he succeeds, is an incoherence which is not remedied by the belief that second-degree murder merits a kind of second-degree death; that a doubt as to the identity of a killer is resolved by commuting real death into intolerable life; and that our ignorance whether a maniac will strike again can be hedged against by measuring "good behavior" within the gates and then releasing the subject upon the public in the true spirit of experimentation.

These are some of the thoughts I find I cannot escape when I read and reflect upon this grave subject. If, as I think, they are relevant to any discussion of change and reform, resting as they do on the direct and concrete perception of what happens, then the simple meliorists who expect to breathe a purer air by abolishing the death penalty are deceiving themselves and us. The issue is for the public to judge; but I for one shall not sleep easier for knowing that in England and America and the West generally a hundred more human beings are kept alive in degrading conditions to face a hopeless future; while others—possibly less

---

[1] The British Homicide Act of 1957, Section 2, implies the same reasoning in its definition of "diminished responsibility" for certain forms of mental abnormality. The whole question of irrationality and crime is in utter confusion, on both sides of the Atlantic.

conscious, certainly less controlled—benefit from a premature freedom dangerous alike to themselves and society. In short, I derive no comfort from the illusion that in giving up one manifest protection of the law-abiding, we who might well be in any of these three roles—victim, prisoner, licensed killer—have struck a blow for the sanctity of human life.

H. L. MENCKEN

H. L. Mencken (1880–1956) was perhaps America's most witty, ornery, and controversial newspaperman. Regarded by some as an admirable and fearless critic, he was heartily and openly disliked by others, and received a generous share of criticism which he collected and published as Menckeniana, a Schimpflexicon, *in 1928.*

Born and educated in Baltimore, he worked in his family's tobacco business until his father's death in 1899, when he first became a reporter on the Baltimore Herald Tribune. *He soon rose to editor, and, when the paper stopped publication in 1906, moved to the* Baltimore Sun. *Leaving Baltimore for New York, he became editor of the* Smart Set *(1914–1923), and later, in association with George Jean Nathan, he founded and edited* The American Mercury *(1924–1933). He continued as a prolific writer until suffering a cerebral thrombosis in 1948. He died in Baltimore in 1956.*

The American—as opposed to the English—language was of vital interest to Mencken, and perhaps his best known book is The American Language, *first published in 1919. Four editions and two supplements followed. His many other writings include the three autobiographical volumes* Happy Days *(1940),* Newspaper Days *(1941), and* Heathen Days *(1943); and* Prejudices *(1917–1927), a six-volume collection of his newspaper pieces. The essay printed below, typical of Mencken's outspokenness, is taken from* A Mencken Chrestomathy *(1949).*

THE PENALTY OF DEATH

Of the arguments against capital punishment that issue from uplifters, two are commonly heard most often, to wit:

1. That hanging a man (or frying him or gassing him) is a dreadful business, degrading to those who have to do it and revolting to those who have to witness it.

2. That it is useless, for it does not deter others from the same crime.

The first of these arguments, it seems to me, is plainly too weak to need serious refutation. All it says, in brief, is that the work of the hangman is unpleasant. Granted. But suppose it is? It may be quite necessary to society for all that. There are, indeed, many other jobs that are unpleasant, and yet no one thinks of abolishing them—that of the plumber, that of the soldier, that of the garbage-man, that of the priest hearing confessions, that of the sand-hog, and so on. Moreover, what evidence is there that any actual hangman complains of his work? I have heard none. On the contrary, I have known many who delighted in their ancient art, and practised it proudly.

In the second argument of the abolitionists there is rather more force, but even here, I believe, the ground under them is shaky. Their fundamental error consists in assuming that the whole aim of punishing criminals is to deter other (potential) criminals—that we hang or electrocute A simply in order to so alarm B that he will not kill C. This, I believe, is an assumption which confuses a part with the whole. Deterrence, obviously, is *one* of the aims of punishment, but it is surely not the only one. On the contrary, there are at least half a dozen, and some are probably quite as important. At least one of them, practically considered, is *more* important. Commonly, it is described as revenge, but revenge is really not the word for it. I borrow a better term from the late Aristotle: *katharsis.* *Katharsis,* so used, means a salubrious discharge of emotions, a healthy letting off of steam. A school-boy, disliking his teacher, deposits a tack upon the pedagogical chair; the teacher jumps and the boy laughs. This is *katharsis.* What I contend is that one of the prime objects of all judicial punishments is to afford the same grateful relief (*a*) to the immediate victims of the criminal punished, and (*b*) to the general body of moral and timorous men.

These persons, and particularly the first group, are concerned only indirectly with deterring other criminals. The thing they crave primarily is the satisfaction of seeing the criminal actually before them suffer as he made them suffer. What they want is the peace of mind that goes with the feeling that accounts are squared. Until they get that satisfaction they are in a state of emotional tension, and hence unhappy. The instant they get it they are comfortable. I do not argue that this yearning is noble; I simply argue that it is almost universal among human beings. In the face of injuries that are unimportant and can be borne without damage it may yield to higher impulses; that is to say, it may yield to what is called Christian charity. But when the injury is serious Christianity is adjourned, and even saints reach for their sidearms. It is plainly asking too much of human nature to expect it to conquer so natural an impulse. A keeps a store and has a bookkeeper, B. B steals $700, employs it in playing at dice or bingo, and is cleaned out. What is A to do? Let B go? If he does so he will be unable to sleep at night. The sense of injury, of injustice, of frustration will haunt him like pruritus. So he turns B over to the police, and they hustle B to prison. Thereafter A can sleep. More, he has pleasant dreams. He pictures B chained to the wall of a dungeon a hundred feet underground, devoured by rats and scorpions. It is so agreeable that it makes him forget his $700. He has got his *katharsis*.

The same thing precisely takes place on a larger scale when there is a crime which destroys a whole community's sense of security. Every lawabiding citizen feels menaced and frustrated until the criminals have been struck down—until the communal capacity to get even with them, and more than even, has been dramatically demonstrated. Here, manifestly, the business of deterring others is no more than an afterthought. The main thing is to destroy the concrete scoundrels whose act has alarmed everyone, and thus made everyone unhappy. Until they are brought to book that unhappiness continues; when the law has been executed upon them there is a sigh of relief. In other words, there is *katharsis*.

I know of no public demand for the death penalty for ordinary crimes, even for ordinary homicides. Its infliction would shock all men of normal decency of feeling. But for crimes involving the deliberate and inexcusable taking of human life, by men openly defiant of all civilized order—for such crimes it seems, to nine men out of ten, a just and proper punishment. Any lesser penalty leaves them feeling that the criminal has got the better of society—that he is free to add insult to injury by laughing. That feeling can be dissipated only by a recourse to *katharsis*, the invention of the aforesaid Aristotle. It is more effectively and economically achieved, as human nature now is, by wafting the criminal to realms of bliss.

The real objection to capital punishment doesn't lie against the actual extermination of the condemned, but against our brutal American habit of putting it off so long. After all, every one of us must die soon or late, and a murderer, it must be assumed, is one who makes that sad fact the cornerstone of his metaphysic. But it is one thing to die, and quite another thing to lie for long months and even years under the shadow of death. No sane man would choose such a finish. All of us, despite the Prayer Book, long for a swift and unexpected end. Unhappily, a murderer, under the irrational American system, is tortured for what, to him, must seem a whole series of eternities. For months on end he sits in prison while his lawyers carry on their idiotic buffoonery with writs, injunctions, mandamuses, and appeals. In order to get his money (or that of his friends) they have to feed him with hope. Now and then, by the imbecility of a judge or some trick of juridic science, they actually justify it. But let us say that, his money all gone, they finally throw up their hands. Their client is now ready for the rope or the chair. But he must still wait for months before it fetches him.

That wait, I believe, is horribly cruel. I have seen more than one man sitting in the death-house, and I don't want to see any more. Worse, it is wholly useless. Why should he wait at all? Why not hang him the day after the last court dissipates his last hope? Why torture him as not even cannibals would torture their victims? The common answer is that he must have time to make his peace with God. But how long does that take? It may be accomplished, I believe, in two hours quite as comfortably as in two years. There are, indeed, no temporal limitations upon God. He could forgive a whole herd of murderers in a millionth of a second. More, it has been done.

GEORGE ORWELL

⋘⋘

A HANGING

This essay is taken from Orwell's collection Shooting an Elephant and Other Essays *(1950). For information on the author and his writings, see page 74.*

•

It was in Burma, a sodden morning of the rains. A sickly light, like yellow tinfoil, was slanting over the high walls into the jail yard. We were waiting outside the condemned cells, a row of sheds fronted with double bars, like small animal cages. Each cell measured about ten feet by ten and was quite bare within except for a plank bed and a pot for drinking water. In some of them brown silent men were squatting at the inner bars, with their blankets draped round them. These were the condemned men, due to be hanged within the next week or two.

One prisoner had been brought out of his cell. He was a Hindu, a puny wisp of a man, with a shaven head and vague liquid eyes. He had a thick, sprouting moustache, absurdly too big for his body, rather like the moustache of a comic man on the films. Six tall Indian warders were guarding him and getting him ready for the gallows. Two of them stood by with rifles and fixed bayonets, while the others handcuffed him, passed a chain through his handcuffs and fixed it to their belts, and lashed his arms tight to his sides. They crowded very close about him, with their hands always on him in a careful, caressing grip, as though all the while feeling him to make sure he was there. It was like men handling a fish which is still alive and may jump back into the water. But he stood quite unresisting, yielding his arms limply to the ropes, as though he hardly noticed what was happening.

Eight o'clock struck and a bugle call, desolately thin in the wet air, floated from the distant barracks. The superintendent of the jail, who was standing apart from the rest of us, moodily prodding the gravel with his stick, raised his head at the sound. He was an army doctor, with a grey toothbrush moustache and a gruff voice. "For God's sake hurry up, Francis," he said irritably. "The man ought to have been dead by this time. Aren't you ready yet?"

Francis, the head jailer, a fat Dravidian in a white drill suit and gold spectacles, waved his black hand. "Yes sir, yes sir," he bubbled. "All iss satisfactorily prepared. The hangman iss waiting. We shall proceed."

"Well, quick march, then. The prisoners can't get their breakfast till this job's over."

We set out for the gallows. Two warders marched on either side of the prisoner, with their rifles at the slope; two others marched close against him, gripping him by arm and shoulder, as though at once pushing and supporting him. The rest of us, magistrates and the like, followed behind. Suddenly, when we had gone ten yards, the procession stopped short without any order or warning. A dreadful thing had happened—a dog, come goodness knows whence, had appeared in the yard. It came bounding among us with a loud volley of barks, and leapt round us wagging its whole body, wild with glee at finding so many human beings together. It was a large woolly dog, half Airedale, half pariah. For a moment it pranced round us, and then, before anyone could stop it, it had made a dash for the prisoner and, jumping up, tried to lick his face. Everyone stood aghast, too taken aback even to grab at the dog.

"Who let that bloody brute in here?" said the superintendent angrily. "Catch it, someone!"

A warder, detached from the escort, charged clumsily after the dog, but it danced and gambolled just out of his reach, taking everything as part of the game. A young Eurasian jailer picked up a handful of gravel and tried to stone the dog away, but it dodged the stones and came after us again. Its yaps echoed from the jail walls. The prisoner, in the grasp of the two warders, looked on incuriously, as though this was another formality of the hanging. It was several minutes before someone managed to catch the dog. Then we put my handkerchief through its collar and moved off once more, with the dog still straining and whimpering.

It was about forty yards to the gallows. I watched the bare brown back of the prisoner marching in front of me. He walked clumsily with his bound arms, but quite steadily, with that bobbing gait of the Indian who never straightens his knees. At each step his muscles slid neatly into place, the lock of hair on his scalp danced up and down, his feet printed themselves on the wet gravel. And once, in spite of the men who gripped him by each shoulder, he stepped slightly aside to avoid a puddle on the path.

It is curious, but till that moment I had never realized what it means to destroy a healthy, conscious man. When I saw the prisoner step aside to avoid the puddle I saw the mystery, the unspeakable wrongness, of cutting a life short when it is in full tide. This man was not dying, he was alive just as we are alive. All the organs of his body were working—bowels digesting food, skin renewing itself, nails growing, tissues forming—all toiling away in solemn foolery. His nails would still be growing when he stood on the drop, when he was falling through the air with a tenth-of-a-second to live. His eyes saw the yellow gravel and the grey walls, and his brain still remembered, foresaw, reasoned—reasoned even about puddles. He and we were a party of men walking together, seeing, hearing, feeling, understanding the same world; and in two minutes, with a sudden snap, one of us would be gone—one mind less, one world less.

The gallows stood in a small yard, separate from the main grounds of the prison, and overgrown with tall prickly weeds. It was a brick erection like three sides of a shed, with planking on top, and above that two beams and a crossbar with the rope dangling. The hangman, a grey-haired convict in the white uniform of the prison, was waiting beside his machine. He greeted us with a servile crouch as we entered. At a word from Francis the two warders, gripping the prisoner more closely than ever, half led half pushed him to the gallows and helped him clumsily up the ladder. Then the hangman climbed up and fixed the rope round the prisoner's neck.

We stood waiting, five yards away. The warders had formed in a rough circle round the gallows. And then, when the noose was fixed, the prisoner began crying out to his god. It was a high, reiterated cry of "Ram! Ram! Ram! Ram!" not urgent and fearful like a prayer or cry for help, but steady, rhythmical, almost like the tolling of a bell. The dog answered the sound with a whine. The hangman, still standing on the gallows, produced a small cotton bag like a flour bag and drew it down over the prisoner's face. But the sound, muffled by the cloth, still persisted, over and over again: "Ram! Ram! Ram! Ram! Ram!"

The hangman climbed down and stood ready, holding the lever.

Minutes seemed to pass. The steady, muffled crying from the prisoner went on and on, "Ram! Ram! Ram!" never faltering for an instant. The superintendent, his head on his chest, was slowly poking the ground with his stick; perhaps he was counting the cries, allowing the prisoner a fixed number—fifty, perhaps, or a hundred. Everyone had changed color. The Indians had gone grey like bad coffee, and one or two of the bayonets were wavering. We looked at the lashed, hooded man on the drop, and listened to his cries—each cry another second of life; the same thought was in all our minds: oh, kill him quickly, get it over, stop that abominable noise!

Suddenly the superintendent made up his mind. Throwing up his head he made a swift motion with his stick. "Chalo!" he shouted almost fiercely.

There was a clanking noise, and then dead silence. The prisoner had vanished, and the rope was twisting on itself. I let go of the dog, and it galloped immediately to the back of the gallows; but when it got there it stopped short, barked, and then retreated into a corner of the yard, where it stood among the weeds, looking timorously out at us. We went round the gallows to inspect the prisoner's body. He was dangling with his toes pointed straight downwards, very slowly revolving, as dead as a stone.

The superintendent reached out with his stick and poked the bare brown body; it oscillated slightly. "*He's* all right," said the superintendent. He backed out from under the gallows, and blew out a deep breath. The moody look had gone out of his face quite suddenly. He glanced at his wrist-watch. "Eight minutes past eight. Well, that's all for this morning, thank God."

The warders unfixed bayonets and marched away. The dog, sobered and conscious of having misbehaved itself, slipped after them. We walked out of the gallows yard, past the condemned cells with their waiting prisoners, into the big central yard of the prison. The convicts, under the command of warders armed with lathis, were already receiving their breakfast. They squatted in long rows, each man holding a tin panikin, while two warders with buckets marched round ladling out rice; it seemed quite a homely, jolly scene, after the hanging. An enormous relief had come upon us now that the job was done. One felt an impulse to sing, to break into a run, to snigger. All at once everyone began chattering gaily.

The Eurasian boy walking beside me nodded towards the way we had come, with a knowing smile: "Do you know, sir, our friend [he meant the dead man] when he heard his appeal had been dismissed, he pissed on the floor of his cell. From fright. Kindly take one of my cigarettes, sir. Do you not admire my new silver case, sir? From the boxwalah, two rupees eight annas. Classy European style."

Several people laughed—at what, nobody seemed certain.

Francis was walking by the superintendent, talking garrulously: "Well, sir, all hass passed off with the utmost satisfactoriness. It was all finished—flick! like that. It iss not always so—oah, no! I have known cases where the doctor wass obliged to go beneath the gallows and pull the prissoner's legs to ensure decease. Most disagreeable!"

"Wriggling about, eh? That's bad," said the superintendent.

"Ach, sir, it iss worse when they become refractory! One man, I recall, clung to the bars of hiss cage when we went to take him out. You will scarcely credit, sir, that it took six warders to dislodge him, three pulling at each leg. We reasoned with him. 'My dear fellow,' we said, 'think of all the pain and trouble you are causing to us!' But no, he would not listen! Ach, he wass very troublesome!"

I found that I was laughing quite loudly. Everyone was laughing. Even the superintendent grinned in a tolerant way. "You'd better all come out and have a drink," he said quite genially. "I've got a bottle of whisky in the car. We could do with it."

We went through the big double gates of the prison into the road. "Pulling at his legs!" exclaimed a Burmese magistrate suddenly, and burst into a loud chuckling. We all began laughing again. At that moment Francis' anecdote seemed extraordinarily funny. We all had a drink together, native and European alike, quite amicably. The dead man was a hundred yards away.

ALBERT CAMUS

Albert Camus, regarded by many as the conscience of his age, was killed in an automobile accident in France at the age of 46. Born in Algeria in 1913, he spent his childhood in extreme poverty. L'envers et l'endroit (not yet translated into English) is a moving record of those years. While he was working his way through the University of Algeria, he became interested in the theater, and for a few years managed and acted with a theatrical company. In 1938 he traveled to Europe for the first time. He returned to Algeria, worked as a journalist for Alger Républicain and later for Paris-Soir but left in 1942 to join the French Resistance movement; he edited and wrote many articles—then unsigned—for the underground newspaper

Combat. *After the liberation he continued as editor of* Combat *but resigned in 1945 to devote full time to his writing.*

Camus's reputation blossomed almost overnight. Germaine Brée, a notable student of his work, writes: "Camus's rapid rise to celebrity between 1942 and 1945 is unparalleled in the history of French literature: The Stranger, The Myth of Sisyphus, *the two plays* Caligula *and* The Misunderstanding, *together with Camus's role in the Resistance and the widespread interest in his* Combat *editorials, started his career in meteoric fashion." His fame became international. In 1951 he published* The Rebel, *perhaps the most difficult of his works. In* The Plague *(1947),* The Fall *(1956), and* The Exile and the Kingdom *(1957), a book of short stories, he continued to express his philosophical ideas in fictional terms. In 1957 Camus was awarded the Nobel Prize for literature. The Committee cited his "clearsighted earnestness" which "illuminates the problem of the human conscience of our time."*

Although capital punishment in its broadest sense—the taking away of life—is a recurrent theme in almost all of his work, "Reflections on the Guillotine" (1957) is his one explicit argument on the subject. This long essay was first published in a periodical, and then in Réflexions sur la peine de mort, *a symposium by Arthur Koestler and Camus. Presented here with omissions, it may be read in full in* Resistance, Rebellion, and Death, *ed. and trans. Justin O'Brien (1960).*

FROM REFLECTIONS ON THE GUILLOTINE

Shortly before the war of 1914, an assassin whose crime was particularly repulsive (he had slaughtered a family of farmers, including the children) was condemned to death in Algiers. He was a farm worker who had killed in a sort of bloodthirsty frenzy but had aggravated his case by robbing his victims. The affair created a great stir. It was generally thought that decapitation was too mild a punishment for such a monster. This was the opinion, I have been told, of my father, who was especially aroused by the murder of the children. One of the few things I know about him, in any case, is that he wanted to witness the execution, for the first time in his life. He got up in the dark to go to the place of execution at the other end of town amid a great crowd of people. What he saw that morning he never told anyone. My mother relates merely that he came rushing home, his face distorted, refused to talk, lay down for a moment on the bed, and suddenly began to vomit. He had just discovered the reality hidden under the noble phrases with which it was masked. Instead of thinking of the slaughtered children, he could think of nothing but that quivering body that had just been dropped onto a board to have its head cut off.

Presumably that ritual act is horrible indeed if it manages to overcome the indignation of a simple, straightforward man and if a punishment he considered richly deserved had no other effect in the end than to nauseate him. When the extreme penalty simply causes vomiting on the part of the respectable citizen it is supposed to protect, how can anyone maintain that it is likely, as it ought to be, to bring more peace and order into the community? Rather, it is obviously no less repulsive than the crime, and this new murder, far from making amends for the harm done to the social body, adds a new blot to the first one. Indeed, no one dares speak directly of the ceremony. Officials and journalists who have to talk about it, as if they were aware of both its provocative and its shameful aspects, have made up a sort of ritual language, reduced to stereotyped phrases. Hence we read at breakfast time in a corner of the newspaper that the condemned "has paid his debt to society" or that he has "atoned" or that "at five a.m. justice was done." The officials call the condemned man "the interested party" or "the patient" or refer to him by a number. People write of capital punishment as if they were whispering. In our well-policed society we recognize that an illness is serious from the fact that we don't dare speak of it directly. For a long time, in middle-class families people said no more than that the elder daughter had a "suspicious cough" or that the father had a "growth" because tuberculosis and cancer were looked upon as somewhat shameful maladies. This is probably even truer of capital punishment since everyone strives to refer to it only through euphemisms. It is to the body politic what cancer is to the individual body, with this difference: no one has ever spoken of the necessity of cancer. There is no hesitation, on the other hand, about presenting capital punishment as a regrettable necessity, a necessity that justifies killing because it is necessary, and let's not talk about it because it is regrettable.

But it is my intention to talk about it crudely. Not because I like scandal, nor, I believe, because of an unhealthy streak in my nature. As a writer, I have always loathed avoiding the issue; as a man, I believe that the repulsive aspects of our condition, if they are inevitable, must merely be faced in silence. But when silence or tricks of language contribute to maintaining an abuse that must be reformed or a suffering that can be relieved, then there is no other solution but to speak out and show the obscenity hidden under the verbal cloak. France shares with England and Spain the honor of being one of the last countries this side of the iron curtain to keep capital punishment in its arsenal of repression. The survival of such a primitive rite has been made possible among us only by the thoughtlessness or ignorance of the public, which reacts only with the ceremonial phrases that have been drilled into it. When the imagination sleeps, words are emptied of their meaning: a deaf population absent-mindedly registers the condemnation of a man. But if people are shown the machine, made to touch the wood and steel and to hear the sound of a head falling, then public imagination, suddenly awakened, will repudiate both the vocabulary and the penalty.

When the Nazis in Poland indulged in public executions of hostages, to keep those hostages from shouting words of revolt and liberty they muzzled them with a plaster-coated gag. It would be shocking to compare the fate of those innocent victims with that of condemned criminals. But, aside from the fact that criminals are not the only ones to be guillotined in our country, the method is the same. We smother under padded words a penalty whose legitimacy we could assert only after we had examined the penalty in reality. Instead of saying that the death penalty is first of all necessary and then adding that it is better not to talk about it, it is essential to say what it really is and then say whether, being what it is, it is to be considered as necessary.

So far as I am concerned, I consider it not only useless but definitely harmful, and I must record my opinion here before getting to the subject itself. It would not be fair to imply that I reached this conclusion as a result of the weeks of investigation and research I have just devoted to this question. But it would be just as unfair to attribute my conviction to mere mawkishness. I am far from indulging in the flabby pity characteristic of humanitarians, in which values and responsibilities fuse, crimes are balanced against one another, and innocence finally loses its rights. Unlike many of my well-known contemporaries, I do not think that man is by nature a social animal. To tell the truth, I think just the reverse. But I believe, and this is quite different, that he cannot live henceforth outside of society, whose laws are necessary to his physical survival. Hence the responsibilities must be established by society itself according to a reasonable and workable scale. But the law's final justification is in the good it does or fails to do to the society of a given place and time. For years I have been unable to see anything in capital punishment but a penalty the imagination could not endure and a lazy disorder that my reason condemned. Yet I was ready to think that my imagination was influencing my judgment. But, to tell the truth, I found during my recent research nothing that did not strengthen my conviction, nothing that modified my arguments. On the contrary, to the arguments I already had others were added. Today I share absolutely Koestler's conviction: the death penalty besmirches our society, and its upholders cannot reasonably defend it. Without repeating his decisive defense, without piling up facts and figures that would only duplicate others (and Jean Bloch-Michel's make them useless), I shall merely state reasons to be added to Koestler's; like his, they argue for an immediate abolition of the death penalty.

. . .

A punishment that penalizes without forestalling is indeed called revenge. It is a quasi-arithmetical reply made by society to whoever breaks its primordial law. That reply is as old as man; it is called the law of retaliation. Whoever has done me harm must suffer harm; whoever has put out my eye must lose an eye; and whoever has killed must die. This is an emotion, and a particularly violent one, not a principle. Retaliation is related to nature and instinct, not to law. Law, by definition, cannot obey the same rules as nature. If murder is in the nature of man, the law is not intended to imitate or reproduce that nature. It is intended to correct it. Now, retaliation does no more than ratify and confer the status of a law on a pure impulse of nature. We have all known that impulse, often to our shame, and we know its power, for it comes down to us from the primitive forests. In this regard, we French, who are properly indignant upon seeing the oil king in Saudi Arabia preach international democracy and call in a butcher to cut off a thief's hand with a cleaver, live also in a sort of Middle Ages without even the consolations of faith. We still define justice according to the rules of a crude arithmetic.[1] Can it be said at least that that arithmetic is exact and that justice, even when elementary, even when limited to legal revenge, is safeguarded by the death penalty? The answer must be no.

Let us leave aside the fact that the law of retaliation is inapplicable and that it would seem just as excessive to punish the incendiary by setting fire to his house as it would be insufficient to punish the thief by deducting from his bank account a sum equal to his theft. Let us admit that it is just and necessary to compensate for the murder of the victim by the death of the murderer. But beheading is not simply death. It is just as different, in essence, from the privation of life as a concentration camp is from prison. It is a murder, to be sure, and one that arithmetically pays for the murder committed. But it adds to death a rule, a public premeditation known to the future victim, an organization, in short, which is in itself a source of moral sufferings more terrible than death. Hence there is no equivalence. Many laws consider a premeditated crime more serious than a crime of pure violence. But what then is capital punishment but the most premeditated of murders, to which no criminal's deed, however calculated it may be, can be compared? For there to be equivalence, the death penalty would have to punish a criminal who had warned his victim of the date at which he would inflict a horrible death

---

[1] A few years ago I asked for the reprieve of six Tunisians who had been condemned to death for the murder, in a riot, of three French policemen. The circumstances in which the murder had taken place made difficult any division of responsibilities. A note from the executive office of the President of the Republic informed me that my appeal was being considered by the appropriate organization. Unfortunately, when that note was addressed to me I had already read two weeks earlier that the sentence had been carried out. Three of the condemned men had been put to death and the three others reprieved. The reasons for reprieving some rather than the others were not convincing. But probably it was essential to carry out three executions where there had been three victims.

on him and who, from that moment onward, had confined him at his mercy for months. Such a monster is not encountered in private life.

There, too, when our official jurists talk of putting to death without causing suffering, they don't know what they are talking about and, above all, they lack imagination. The devastating, degrading fear that is imposed on the condemned for months or years[2] is a punishment more terrible than death, and one that was not imposed on the victim. Even in the fright caused by the mortal violence being done to him, most of the time the victim is hastened to his death without knowing what is happening to him. The period of horror is counted out with his life, and hope of escaping the madness that has swept down upon that life probably never leaves him. On the other hand, the horror is parceled out to the man who is condemned to death. Torture through hope alternates with the pangs of animal despair. The lawyer and chaplain, out of mere humanity, and the jailers, so that the condemned man will keep quiet, are unanimous in assuring him that he will be reprieved. He believes this with all his being and then he ceases to believe it. He hopes by day and despairs of it by night.[3] As the weeks pass, hope and despair increase and become equally unbearable. According to all accounts, the color of the skin changes, fear acting like an acid. "Knowing that you are going to die is nothing," said a condemned man in Fresnes. "But not knowing whether or not you are going to live, that's terror and anguish." Cartouche said of the supreme punishment: "Why, it's just a few minutes that have to be lived through." But it is a matter of months, not of minutes. Long in advance the condemned man knows that he is going to be killed and that the only thing that can save him is a reprieve, rather similar, for him, to the decrees of heaven. In any case, he cannot intervene, make a plea himself, or convince. Everything goes on outside of him. He is no longer a man but a thing waiting to be handled by the executioners. He is kept as if he were inert matter, but he still has a consciousness which is his chief enemy.

When the officials whose job it is to kill that man call him a parcel, they know what they are saying. To be unable to do anything against the hand that moves you from one place to another, holds you or rejects you, is this not indeed being a parcel, or a thing, or, better, a hobbled animal? Even then an animal can refuse to eat. The condemned man cannot. He is given the benefit of a special diet (at Fresnes, Diet No. 4 with extra

---

[2] Roemen, condemned to death at the Liberation of France, remained seven hundred days in chains before being executed, and this is scandalous. Those condemned under common law, as a general rule, wait from three to six months for the morning of their death. And it is difficult, if one wants to maintain their chances of survival, to shorten that period. I can bear witness, moreover, to the fact that the examination of appeals for mercy is conducted in France with a seriousness that does not exclude the visible inclination to pardon, insofar as the law and customs permit.

[3] Sunday not being a day of execution, Saturday night is always better in the cell blocks reserved for those condemned to death.

milk, wine, sugar, jam, butter); they see to it that he nourishes himself. If need be, he is forced to do so. The animal that is going to be killed must be in the best condition. The thing or the animal has a right only to those debased freedoms that are called whims. "They are very touchy," a top-sergeant at Fresnes says without the least irony of those condemned to death. Of course, but how else can they have contact with freedom and the dignity of the will that man cannot do without? Touchy or not, the moment the sentence has been pronounced the condemned man enters an imperturbable machine. For a certain number of weeks he travels along in the intricate machinery that determines his every gesture and eventually hands him over to those who will lay him down on the killing machine. The parcel is no longer subject to the laws of chance that hang over the living creature but to mechanical laws that allow him to foresee accurately the day of his beheading.

That day his being an object comes to an end. During the three quarters of an hour separating him from the end, the certainty of a powerless death stifles everything else; the animal, tied down and amenable, knows a hell that makes the hell he is threatened with seem ridiculous. The Greeks, after all, were more humane with their hemlock. They left their condemned a relative freedom, the possibility of putting off or hastening the hour of his death. They gave him a choice between suicide and execution. On the other hand, in order to be doubly sure, we deal with the culprit ourselves. But there could not really be any justice unless the condemned, after making known his decision months in advance, had approached his victim, bound him firmly, informed him that he would be put to death in an hour, and had finally used that hour to set up the apparatus of death. What criminal ever reduced his victim to such a desperate and powerless condition?

This doubtless explains the odd submissiveness that is customary in the condemned at the moment of their execution. These men who have nothing more to lose could play their last card, choose to die of a chance bullet or be guillotined in the kind of frantic struggle that dulls all the faculties. In a way, this would amount to dying freely. And yet, with but few exceptions, the rule is for the condemned to walk toward death passively in a sort of dreary despondency. That is probably what our journalists mean when they say that the condemned died courageously. We must read between the lines that the condemned made no noise, accepted his status as a parcel, and that everyone is grateful to him for this. In such a degrading business, the interested party shows a praise-worthy sense of propriety by keeping the degradation from lasting too long. But the compliments and the certificates of courage belong to the general mystification surrounding the death penalty. For the condemned will often be seemly in proportion to the fear he feels. He will deserve the praise of the press only if his fear or his feeling of isolation is great enough to sterilize him completely. Let there be no misunderstanding.

Some among the condemned, whether political or not, die heroically, and they must be granted the proper admiration and respect. But the majority of them know only the silence of fear, only the impassivity of fright, and it seems to me that such terrified silence deserves even greater respect. When the priest Bela Just offers to write to the family of a young condemned man a few moments before he is hanged and hears the reply: "I have no courage, even for that," how can a priest, hearing that confession of weakness, fail to honor the most wretched and most sacred thing in man? Those who say nothing but leave a little pool on the spot from which they are taken—who would dare say they died as cowards? And how can we describe the men who reduced them to such cowardice? After all, every murderer when he kills runs the risk of the most dreadful of deaths, whereas those who kill him risk nothing except advancement.

No, what man experiences at such times is beyond all morality. Not virtue, nor courage, nor intelligence, nor even innocence has anything to do with it. Society is suddenly reduced to a state of primitive terrors where nothing can be judged. All equity and all dignity have disappeared. "The conviction of innocence does not immunize against brutal treatment. . . . I have seen authentic bandits die courageously whereas innocent men went to their deaths trembling in every muscle."[4] When the same man adds that, according to his experience, intellectuals show more weakness, he is not implying that such men have less courage than others but merely that they have more imagination. Having to face an inevitable death, any man, whatever his convictions, is torn asunder from head to toe.[5] The feeling of powerlessness and solitude of the condemned man, bound and up against the public coalition that demands his death, is in itself an unimaginable punishment. From this point of view, too, it would be better for the execution to be public. The actor in every man could then come to the aid of the terrified animal and help him cut a figure, even in his own eyes. But darkness and secrecy offer no recourse. In such a disaster, courage, strength of soul, even faith may be disadvantages. As a general rule, a man is undone by waiting for capital punishment well before he dies. Two deaths are inflicted on him, the first being worse than the second, whereas he killed but once. Compared to such torture, the penalty of retaliation seems like a civilized law. It never claimed that the man who gouged out one of his brother's eyes should be totally blinded.

. . .

There are, however, major criminals whom all juries would condemn at any time and in any place whatever. Their crimes are not open to doubt, and the evidence brought by the accusation is confirmed by the

---

[4] Bela Just, *La Potence et la Croix* (Fasquelle).

[5] A great surgeon, a Catholic himself, told me that as a result of his experience he did not even inform believers when they had an incurable cancer. According to him, the shock might destroy even their faith.

confessions of the defense. Most likely, everything that is abnormal and monstrous in them is enough to classify them as pathological. But the psychiatric experts, in the majority of cases, affirm their responsibility. Recently in Paris a young man, somewhat weak in character but kind and affectionate, devoted to his family, was, according to his own admission, annoyed by a remark his father made about his coming home late. The father was sitting reading at the dining-room table. The young man seized an ax and dealt his father several blows from behind. Then in the same way he struck down his mother, who was in the kitchen. He undressed, hid his bloodstained trousers in the closet, went to make a call on the family of his fiancée, without showing any signs, then returned home and notified the police that he had just found his parents murdered. The police immediately discovered the bloodstained trousers and, without difficulty, got a calm confession from the parricide. The psychiatrists decided that this man who murdered through annoyance was responsible. His odd indifference, of which he was to give other indications in prison (showing pleasure because his parents' funeral had attracted so many people—"They were much loved," he told his lawyer), cannot, however, be considered as normal. But his reasoning power was apparently untouched.

Many "monsters" offer equally impenetrable exteriors. They are eliminated on the mere consideration of the facts. Apparently the nature or the magnitude of their crimes allows no room for imagining that they can ever repent or reform. They must merely be kept from doing it again, and there is no other solution but to eliminate them. On this frontier, and on it alone, discussion about the death penalty is legitimate. In all other cases the arguments for capital punishment do not stand up to the criticisms of the abolitionists. But in extreme cases, and in our state of ignorance, we make a wager. No fact, no reasoning can bring together those who think that a chance must always be left to the vilest of men and those who consider that chance illusory. But it is perhaps possible, on that final frontier, to go beyond the long opposition between partisans and adversaries of the death penalty by weighing the advisability of that penalty today, and in Europe. With much less competence, I shall try to reply to the wish expressed by a Swiss jurist, Professor Jean Graven, who wrote in 1952 in his remarkable study on the problem of the death penalty: "Faced with the problem that is once more confronting our conscience and our reason, we think that a solution must be sought, not through the conceptions, problems, and arguments of the past, nor through the hopes and theoretical promises of the future, but through the ideas, recognized facts, and necessities of the present."⁶ It is possible, indeed, to debate endlessly as to the benefits or harm attributable to the death penalty through the ages or in an intellectual

---

⁶ *Revue de Criminologie et de Police Technique* (Geneva), special issue, 1952.

vacuum. But it plays a role here and now, and we must take our stand here and now in relation to the modern executioner. What does the death penalty mean to the men of the mid-century?

To simplify matters, let us say that our civilization has lost the only values that, in a certain way, can justify that penalty and, on the other hand, suffers from evils that necessitate its suppression. In other words, the abolition of the death penalty ought to be asked for by all thinking members of our society, for reasons both of logic and of realism.

Of logic, to begin with. Deciding that a man must have the definitive punishment imposed on him is tantamount to deciding that that man has no chance of making amends. This is the point, to repeat ourselves, where the arguments clash blindly and crystallize in a sterile opposition. But it so happens that none among us can settle the question, for we are all both judges and interested parties. Whence our uncertainty as to our right to kill and our inability to convince each other. Without absolute innocence, there is no supreme judge. Now, we have all done wrong in our lives even if that wrong, without falling within the jurisdiction of the laws, went as far as the unknown crime. There are no just people— merely hearts more or less lacking in justice. Living at least allows us to discover this and to add to the sum of our actions a little of the good that will make up in part for the evil we have added to the world. Such a right to live, which allows a chance to make amends, is the natural right of every man, even the worst man. The lowest of criminals and the most upright of judges meet side by side, equally wretched in their solidarity. Without that right, moral life is utterly impossible. None among us is authorized to despair of a single man, except after his death, which transforms his life into destiny and then permits a definitive judgment. But pronouncing the definitive judgment before his death, decreeing the closing of accounts when the creditor is still alive, is no man's right. On this limit, at least, whoever judges absolutely condemns himself absolutely.

Bernard Fallot of the Masuy gang, working for the Gestapo, was condemned to death after admitting the many terrible crimes of which he was guilty, and declared himself that he could not be pardoned. "My hands are too red with blood," he told a prison mate.[7] Public opinion and the opinion of his judges certainly classed him among the irremediable, and I should have been tempted to agree if I had not read a surprising testimony. This is what Fallot said to the same companion after declaring that he wanted to die courageously: "Shall I tell you my greatest regret? Well, it is not having known the Bible I now have here. I assure you that I wouldn't be where I now am." There is no question of giving in to some conventional set of sentimental pictures and calling to mind

---

[7] Jean Bocognano: *Quartier des fauves, prison de Fresnes* (Editions du Fuseau).

Victor Hugo's good convicts. The age of enlightenment, as people say, wanted to suppress the death penalty on the pretext that man was naturally good. Of course he is not (he is worse or better). After twenty years of our magnificent history we are well aware of this. But precisely because he is not absolutely good, no one among us can pose as an absolute judge and pronounce the definitive elimination of the worst among the guilty, because no one of us can lay claim to absolute innocence. Capital judgment upsets the only indisputable human solidarity—our solidarity against death—and it can be legitimized only by a truth or a principle that is superior to man.

In fact, the supreme punishment has always been, throughout the ages, a religious penalty. Inflicted in the name of the king, God's representative on earth, or by priests or in the name of society considered as a sacred body, it denies, not human solidarity, but the guilty man's membership in the divine community, the only thing that can give him life. Life on earth is taken from him, to be sure, but his chance of making amends is left him. The real judgment is not pronounced; it will be in the other world. Only religious values, and especially belief in eternal life, can therefore serve as a basis for the supreme punishment because, according to their own logic, they keep it from being definitive and irreparable. Consequently, it is justified only insofar as it is not supreme.

The Catholic Church, for example, has always accepted the necessity of the death penalty. It inflicted that penalty itself, and without stint, in other periods. Even today it justifies it and grants the State the right to apply it. The Church's position, however subtle, contains a very deep feeling that was expressed directly in 1937 by a Swiss National Councillor from Fribourg during a discussion in the National Council. According to M. Grand, the lowest of criminals when faced with execution withdraws into himself. "He repents and his preparation for death is thereby facilitated. The Church has saved one of its members and fulfilled its divine mission. This is why it has always accepted the death penalty, not only as a means of self-defense, but *as a powerful means of salvation.*[8] . . . Without trying to make of it a thing of the Church, the death penalty can point proudly to its almost divine efficacy, like war."

By virtue of the same reasoning, probably, there could be read on the sword of the Fribourg executioner the words: "Lord Jesus, thou art the judge." Hence the executioner is invested with a sacred function. He is the man who destroys the body in order to deliver the soul to the divine sentence, which no one can judge beforehand. Some may think that such words imply rather scandalous confusions. And, to be sure, whoever clings to the teaching of Jesus will look upon that handsome sword as one more outrage to the person of Christ. In the light of this, it is possible to understand the dreadful remark of the Russian condemned man about to be

---

[8] My italics.

hanged by the Tsar's executioners in 1905 who said firmly to the priest who had come to console him with the image of Christ: "Go away and commit no sacrilege." The unbeliever cannot keep from thinking that men who have set at the center of their faith the staggering victim of a judicial error ought at least to hesitate before committing legal murder. Believers might also be reminded that Emperor Julian, before his conversion, did not want to give official offices to Christians because they systematically refused to pronounce death sentences or to have anything to do with them. For five centuries Christians therefore believed that the strict moral teaching of their master forbade killing. But Catholic faith is not nourished solely by the personal teaching of Christ. It also feeds on the Old Testament, on St. Paul, and on the Church Fathers. In particular, the immortality of the soul and the universal resurrection of bodies are articles of dogma. As a result, capital punishment is for the believer a temporary penalty that leaves the final sentence in suspense, an arrangement necessary only for terrestrial order, an administrative measure which, far from signifying the end for the guilty man, may instead favor his redemption. I am not saying that all believers agree with this, and I can readily imagine that some Catholics may stand closer to Christ than to Moses or St. Paul. I am simply saying that faith in the immortality of the soul allowed Catholicism to see the problem of capital punishment in very different terms and to justify it.

But what is the value of such a justification in the society we live in, which in its institutions and its customs has lost all contact with the sacred? When an atheistic or skeptical or agnostic judge inflicts the death penalty on an unbelieving criminal, he is pronouncing a definitive punishment that cannot be reconsidered. He takes his place on the throne of God,[9] without having the same powers and even without believing in God. He kills, in short, because his ancestors believed in eternal life. But the society that he claims to represent is in reality pronouncing a simple measure of elimination, doing violence to the human community united against death, and taking a stand as an absolute value because society is laying claim to absolute power. To be sure, it delegates a priest to the condemned man, through tradition. The priest may legitimately hope that fear of punishment will help the guilty man's conversion. Who can accept, however, that such a calculation should justify a penalty most often inflicted and received in a quite different spirit? It is one thing to believe before being afraid and another to find faith after fear. Conversion through fire or the guillotine will always be suspect, and it may seem surprising that the Church has not given up conquering infidels through terror. In any case, society that has lost all contact with the sacred can find no advantage in a conversion in which it professes to have no interest. Society decrees a sacred punishment and at the same

---

[9] As everyone knows, the jury's decision is preceded by the words: "Before God and my conscience. . . ."

time divests it both of excuse and of usefulness. Society proceeds sovereignly to eliminate the evil ones from her midst as if she were virtue itself. Like an honorable man killing his wayward son and remarking: "Really, I didn't know what to do with him." She assumes the right to select as if she were nature herself and to add great sufferings to the elimination as if she were a redeeming god.

To assert, in any case, that a man must be absolutely cut off from society because he is absolutely evil amounts to saying that society is absolutely good, and no one in his right mind will believe this today. Instead of believing this, people will more readily think the reverse. Our society has become so bad and so criminal only because she has respected nothing but her own preservation or a good reputation in history. Society has indeed lost all contact with the sacred. But society began in the nineteenth century to find a substitute for religion by proposing herself as an object of adoration. The doctrines of evolution and the notions of selection that accompany them have made of the future of society a final end. The political utopias that were grafted onto those doctrines placed at the end of time a golden age that justified in advance any enterprises whatever. Society became accustomed to legitimizing what might serve her future and, consequently, to making use of the supreme punishment in an absolute way. From then on, society considered as a crime and a sacrilege anything that stood in the way of her plan and her temporal dogmas. In other words, after being a priest, the executioner became a government official. The result is here all around us. The situation is such that this mid-century society which has lost the right, in all logics, to decree capital punishment ought now to suppress it for reasons of realism.

. . .

From the humanitarian idylls of the eighteenth century to the blood-stained gallows the way leads directly, and the executioners of today, as everyone knows, are humanists. Hence we cannot be too wary of the humanitarian ideology in dealing with a problem such as the death penalty. On the point of concluding, I should like therefore to repeat that neither an illusion as to the natural goodness of the human being nor faith in a golden age to come motivates my opposition to the death penalty. On the contrary, its abolition seems to me necessary because of reasoned pessimism, of logic, and of realism. Not that the heart has no share in what I have said. Anyone who has spent weeks with texts, recollections, and men having any contact, whether close or not, with the gallows could not possibly remain untouched by that experience. But, let me repeat, I do not believe, nonetheless, that there is no responsibility in this world and that we must give way to that modern tendency to absolve everything, victim and murderer, in the same confusion. Such purely sentimental confusion is made up of cowardice rather than of generosity and eventually justifies whatever is worst in this world. If you keep on excusing, you eventually give your blessing to the slave camp, to cowardly force, to organized executioners, to the cynicism of great political monsters; you finally hand over your brothers. This can be seen around us. But it so happens, in the present state of the world, that the man of today wants laws and institutions suitable to a convalescent, which will curb him without breaking him and lead him without crushing him. Hurled into the unchecked dynamic movement of history, he needs a natural philosophy and a few laws of equilibrium. He needs, in short, a society based on reason and not the anarchy into which he has been plunged by his own pride and the excessive powers of the State.

I am convinced that abolition of the death penalty would help us progress toward that society. After taking such an initiative, France could offer to extend it to the non-abolitionist countries on both sides of the iron curtain. But, in any case, she should set the example. Capital punishment would then be replaced by hard labor—for life in the case of criminals considered irremediable and for a fixed period in the case of the others. To any who feel that such a penalty is harsher than capital punishment we can only express our amazement that they did not suggest, in this case, reserving it for such as Landru and applying capital punishment to minor criminals. We might remind them, too, that hard labor leaves the condemned man the possibility of choosing death, whereas the guillotine offers no alternative. To any who feel, on the other hand, that hard labor is too mild a penalty, we can answer first that they lack imagination and secondly that privation of freedom seems to them a slight punishment only insofar as contemporary society has taught us to despise freedom.[10]

The fact that Cain is not killed but bears a mark of reprobation in the eyes of men is the lesson we must draw from the Old Testament, to say nothing of the Gospels, instead of looking back to the cruel examples of the Mosaic law. In any case, nothing keeps us from trying out an experiment, limited in duration (ten years, for instance), if our Parliament is still incapable of making up for its votes in favor of alcohol by such a great civilizing step as complete abolition of the penalty. And if, really, public opinion and its representatives cannot give up the law of laziness which simply eliminates what it cannot reform, let us at least —while hoping for a new day of truth—not make of it the "solemn slaughterhouse"[11] that befouls our society. The death penalty as it is now applied, and however rarely it may be, is a revolting butchery, an outrage

---

[10] See the report on the death penalty by Representative Dupont in the National Assembly on 31 May 1791: "A sharp and burning mood consumes the assassin; the thing he fears most is inactivity; it leaves him to himself, and to get away from it he continually braves death and tries to cause death in others; solitude and his own conscience are his real torture. Does this not suggest to you what kind of punishment should be inflicted on him, what is the kind of which he will be most sensitive? *Is it not in the nature of the malady that the remedy is to be found?*" I have italicized the last sentence, for it makes of that little-known Representative a true precursor of our modern psychology.

[11] Tarde.

inflicted on the person and body of man. That truncation, that living
and yet uprooted head, those spurts of blood date from a barbarous
period that aimed to impress the masses with degrading sights. Today
when such vile death is administered on the sly, what is the meaning of
this torture? The truth is that in the nuclear age we kill as we did in
the age of the spring balance. And there is not a man of normal sensitivity who, at the mere thought of such crude surgery, does not feel
nauseated. If the French State is incapable of overcoming habit and giving
Europe one of the remedies it needs, let France begin by reforming the
manner of administering capital punishment. The science that serves to
kill so many could at least serve to kill decently. An anesthetic that would
allow the condemned man to slip from sleep to death (which would be
left within his reach for at least a day so that he could use it freely and
would be administered to him in another form if he were unwilling or
weak of will) would assure his elimination, if you insist, but would put
a little decency into what is at present but a sordid and obscene exhibition.

I suggest such compromises only insofar as one must occasionally despair
of seeing wisdom and true civilization influence those reponsible for our
future. For certain men, more numerous than we think, it is physically
unbearable to know what the death penalty really is and not to be able
to prevent its application. In their way, they suffer that penalty themselves, and without any justice. If only the weight of filthy images weighing upon them were reduced, society would lose nothing. But even
that, in the long run, will be inadequate. There will be no lasting peace
either in the heart of individuals or in social customs until death is outlawed.

Civil Disobedience

When the conscience of the individual is in conflict with the law, which should yield? The issue was expressed fatefully for the United States by Thomas Jefferson in the Declaration of Independence. Today again specific laws and mores are being challenged by men who do not challenge the general principle of law and order. Once again the issue has become a focal point of national debate.

Many people say that civil disobedience within a civilized state is by definition immoral. This argument is felt to be especially cogent in a democracy, where law is man-made and adjustable. We voluntarily relinquish some of our freedom and accept the necessity and authority of the law in order to protect the community and guard it against anarchy. Defiance, then, strikes not only at specific laws but also at the concept of law and order and thus at the system itself. This is the position which Plato presents so forcefully in *The Crito,* part of which is printed below. The counter-argument is presented by Thoreau, one of the most dedicated individualists in our history, who argues for the supreme sovereignty of the individual conscience. Bertrand Russell and Martin Luther King, using both rational argument and passionate appeal, present the case for non-violent civil disobedience today. In weighing their arguments, the reader may also wish to consider two related ideas. One is that such acts as the illegal sit-in may be likened to the strike and picketing of a few generations ago; they are forms of social protest which are attempting to qualify for public acceptance and legality. The other, a paradox pointed out by George Orwell in his essay on Gandhi, is that modern civil disobedience can only be effective in a democratic community. "It is difficult to see," says Orwell, "how Gandhi's methods [passive resistance] could be applied in a country where opponents of the regime disappear in the middle of the night and are never heard of again. Without a free press and the right of assembly, it is impossible not merely to appeal to outside opinion, but to bring a mass movement into being, or even to make your intentions known to your adversary."

PLATO

Plato, one of the greatest philosophers of the western world, was born in Athens. Originally named Aristocles, he was surnamed Plato because of his broad shoulders or—as some would have it—his broad forehead. Early in his life he became a student of Socrates, and his subsequent writings are evidence of the profound influence his teacher had on him. After Socrates' trial, conviction, and death in 399 B.C., Plato spent thirteen years away from Athens, in Italy, Egypt, and parts of Greece. He returned in 386 B.C. and founded the Academy in which he taught until his death in 347 B.C. Aristotle was his student. Plato's extant works are in the form of conversations, or dialogues, in which the leading speaker is usually Socrates. Perhaps the best known of the dialogues is The Republic, *in which Socrates explores the nature of the ideal state. Plato records the last days of Socrates in three early dialogues,* The Apology, The Crito, *and* The Phaedo. *The* Apology *presents Socrates' speech at his trial on charges of corrupting youth and believing in Gods other than the State's divinities. The* Phaedo *records Socrates' last conversation before death. In* The Crito, *Crito visits Socrates in prison and tries to persuade him to escape. We print below, from the Jowett translation, third edition, Socrates' argument for submitting to the death penalty that the law had imposed on him.*

FROM THE CRITO

Socrates . . . Ought a man to do what he admits to be right, or ought he to betray the right?

Crito. He ought to do what he thinks right.

Soc. But if this is true, what is the application? In leaving the prison against the will of the Athenians, do I wrong any? or rather do I not wrong those whom I ought least to wrong? Do I not desert the principles which were acknowledged by us to be just—what do you say?

Cr. I cannot tell, Socrates; for I do not know.

Soc. Then consider the matter in this way:—Imagine that I am about to play truant (you may call the proceeding by any name which you like), and the laws and the government come and interrogate me: 'Tell us, Socrates,' they say; 'what are you about? are you not going by an act of yours to overturn us—the laws, and the whole state, as far as in you lies? Do you imagine that a state can subsist and not be overthrown, in which the decisions of law have no power, but are set aside and trampled upon by individuals?' What will be our answer, Crito, to these and the like words? Any one, and especially a rhetorician, will have a good deal to say on behalf of the law which requires a sentence to be carried out. He will argue that this law should not be set aside; and shall we reply, 'Yes; but the state has injured us and given an unjust sentence.' Suppose I say that?

Cr. Very good, Socrates.

Soc. 'And was that our agreement with you?' the law would answer; 'or were you to abide by the sentence of the state?' And if I were to express my astonishment at their words, the law would probably add: 'Answer, Socrates, instead of opening your eyes—you are in the habit of asking and answering questions. Tell us,—What complaint have you to make against us which justifies you in attempting to destroy us and the state? In the first place did we not bring you into existence? Your father married your mother by our aid and begat you. Say whether you have any objection to urge against those of us who regulate marriage?' None, I should reply. 'Or against those of us who after birth regulate the nurture and education of children, in which you also were trained? Were not the laws, which have the charge of education, right in commanding your father to train you in music and gymnastic?' Right, I should reply. 'Well then, since you were brought into the world and nurtured and educated by us, can you deny in the first place that you are our child and slave, as your fathers were before you? And if this is true you are not on equal terms with us; nor can you think that you have a right to do to us what we are doing to you. Would you have any right to strike or revile or do any other evil to your father or your master, if you had one, because you have been struck or reviled by him, or received some other evil at his hands?—you would not say this? And because we think right to destroy you, do you think that you have any right to destroy us in return, and your country as far as in you lies? Will you, O professor of true virtue, pretend that you are justified in this? Has a philosopher like you failed to discover that our country is more to be valued and higher and holier far than mother or father or any ancestor, and more to be regarded in the eyes of the gods and of men of understanding? also to be soothed, and gently and reverently entreated when angry, even more than a father, and either to be persuaded, or if not persuaded, to be obeyed? And when we are punished by her, whether with imprisonment or stripes, the punishment is to be endured in silence; and if she leads us to wounds or death in battle, thither we follow as is right; neither may any one yield or retreat or leave his rank, but whether in battle or in a court of law, or in any other place, he must do what his city and his country order him; or he must change their view of what is just: and if he may do no violence to his father or mother, much less may he do violence to his country.' What answer shall we make to this, Crito? Do the laws speak truly, or do they not?

Cr. I think that they do.

Soc. Then the laws will say, 'Consider, Socrates, if we are speaking truly that in your present attempt you are going to do us an injury. For, having brought you into the world, and nurtured and educated you, and given you and every other citizen a share in every good which we had to give, we further proclaim to any Athenian by the liberty which we allow him, that if he does not like us when he has become of age and has seen the ways of the city, and made our acquaintance, he may go where he pleases and take his goods with him. None of us laws will forbid him or interfere with him. Any one who does not like us and the city, and who wants to emigrate to a colony or to any other city, may go where he likes, retaining his property. But he who has experience of the manner in which we order justice and administer the state, and still remains, has entered into an implied contract that he will do as we command him. And he who disobeys us is, as we maintain, thrice wrong; first, because in disobeying us he is disobeying his parents; secondly, because we are the authors of his education; thirdly, because he has made an agreement with us that he will duly obey our commands; and he neither obeys them nor convinces us that our commands are unjust; and we do not rudely impose them, but give him the alternative of obeying or convincing us;—that is what we offer, and he does neither.

'These are the sort of accusations to which, as we were saying, you, Socrates, will be exposed if you accomplish your intentions; you, above all other Athenians.' Suppose now I ask, why I rather than anybody else? they will justly retort upon me that I above all other men have acknowledged the agreement. 'There is clear proof,' they will say, 'Socrates, that we and the city were not displeasing to you. Of all Athenians you have been the most constant resident in the city, which, as you never leave, you may be supposed to love. For you never went out of the city either to see the games, except once when you went to the Isthmus, or to any other place unless when you were on military service; nor did you travel as other men do. Nor had you any curiosity to know

other states or their laws: your affections did not go beyond us and
our state; we were your special favourites, and you acquiesced in our
government of you; and here in this city you begat your children, which
is a proof of your satisfaction. Moreover, you might in the course of
the trial, if you had liked, have fixed the penalty at banishment; the
state which refuses to let you go now would have let you go then. But
you pretended that you preferred death to exile, and that you were
not unwilling to die. And now you have forgotten these fine sentiments,
and pay no respect to us the laws, of whom you are the destroyer; and
are doing what only a miserable slave would do, running away and turning your back upon the compacts and agreements which you made as
a citizen. And first of all answer this very question: Are we right in
saying that you agreed to be governed according to us in deed, and
not in word only? Is that true or not?' How shall we answer, Crito?
Must we not assent?

Cr. We cannot help it, Socrates.

Soc. Then will they not say: 'You, Socrates, are breaking the covenants and agreements which you made with us at your leisure, not in
any haste or under any compulsion or deception, but after you have
had seventy years to think of them, during which time you were at
liberty to leave the city, if we were not to your mind, or if our covenants
appeared to you to be unfair. You had your choice, and might have gone
either to Lacedaemon or Crete, both which states are often praised by
you for their good government, or to some other Hellenic or foreign
state. Whereas you, above all other Athenians, seemed to be so fond of
the state, or, in other words, of us her laws (and who would care about
a state which has no laws?), that you never stirred out of her; the halt,
the blind, the maimed were not more stationary in her than you were.
And now you run away and forsake your agreements. Not so, Socrates,
if you will take our advice; do not make yourself ridiculous by escaping
out of the city.

'For just consider, if you transgress and err in this sort of way, what
good will you do either to yourself or to your friends? That your
friends will be driven into exile and deprived of citizenship, or will lose
their property, is tolerably certain; and you yourself, if you fly to one
of the neighbouring cities, as, for example, Thebes or Megara, both of
which are well governed, will come to them as an enemy, Socrates, and
their government will be against you, and all patriotic citizens will cast
an evil eye upon you as a subverter of the laws, and you will confirm
in the minds of the judges the justice of their own condemnation of
you. For he who is a corrupter of the laws is more than likely to be a
corrupter of the young and foolish portion of mankind. Will you then
flee from well-ordered cities and virtuous men? and is existence worth
having on these terms? Or will you go to them without shame, and

talk to them, Socrates? And what will you say to them? What you say here about virtue and justice and institutions and laws being the best things among men? Would that be decent of you? Surely not. But if you go away from well-governed states to Crito's friends in Thessaly, where there is great disorder and licence, they will be charmed to hear the tale of your escape from prison, set off with ludicrous particulars of the manner in which you were wrapped in a goatskin or some other disguise, and metamorphosed as the manner is of runaways; but will there be no one to remind you that in your old age you were not ashamed to violate the most sacred laws from a miserable desire of a little more life? Perhaps not, if you keep them in a good temper; but if they are out of temper you will hear many degrading things; you will live, but how?—as the flatterer of all men, and the servant of all men; and doing what?—eating and drinking in Thessaly, having gone abroad in order that you may get a dinner. And where will be your fine sentiments about justice and virtue? Say that you wish to live for the sake of your children—you want to bring them up and educate them—will you take them into Thessaly and deprive them of Athenian citizenship? Is this the benefit which you will confer upon them? Or are you under the impression that they will be better cared for and educated here if you are still alive, although absent from them; for your friends will take care of them? Do you fancy that if you are an inhabitant of Thessaly they will take care of them, and if you are an inhabitant of the other world that they will not take care of them? Nay; but if they who call themselves friends are good for anything, they will—to be sure they will.

'Listen, then, Socrates, to us who have brought you up. Think not of life and children first, and of justice afterwards, but of justice first, that you may be justified before the princes of the world below. For neither will you nor any that belong to you be happier or holier or juster in this life, or happier in another, if you do as Crito bids. Now you depart in innocence, a sufferer and not a doer of evil; a victim, not of the laws but of men. But if you go forth, returning evil for evil, and injury for injury, breaking the covenants and agreements which you have made with us, and wronging those whom you ought least of all to wrong, that is to say, yourself, your friends, your country, and us, we shall be angry with you while you live, and our brethren, the laws in the world below, will receive you as an enemy; for they will know that you have done your best to destroy us. Listen, then, to us and not to Crito.'

This, dear Crito, is the voice which I seem to hear murmuring in my ears, like the sound of the flute in the ears of the mystic; that voice, I say, is humming in my ears, and prevents me from hearing any other. And I know that anything more which you may say will be vain. Yet speak, if you have anything to say.

Cr. I have nothing to say, Socrates.

Soc. Leave me then, Crito, to fulfil the will of God, and to follow whither he leads.

THOMAS JEFFERSON

On June 11, 1776, the Continental Congress appointed a committee of five—Thomas Jefferson, Benjamin Franklin, John Adams, Robert Livingston, and Roger Sherman—to prepare a declaration of independence. It was decided that Jefferson should first write a draft. He did so, drawing heavily on the natural rights political philosophy of the time, but, as he says, he turned to "neither book nor pamphlet" in its preparation. A few changes were made by Adams and Franklin, and it was then presented to Congress on June 28. On July 2 and 3 Congress debated the form and content of the Declaration, made a few further changes, and on July 4 approved it without dissent. We here credit Jefferson with authorship, although we print the amended and official version taken from the United States Senate Manual.

DECLARATION OF INDEPENDENCE

(In Congress July 4, 1776)

The Unanimous Declaration of the Thirteen United States of America

When in the Course of human events, it becomes necessary for one people to dissolve the political bands which have connected them with another, and to assume among the powers of the earth, the separate and equal station to which the Laws of Nature and of Nature's God entitle them, a decent respect to the opinions of mankind requires that they should declare the causes which impel them to the separation.

We hold these truths to be self-evident, that all men are created equal, that they are endowed by their Creator with certain unalienable Rights, that among these are Life, Liberty and the pursuit of Happiness. That to secure these rights, Governments are instituted among Men, deriving their just powers from the consent of the governed, That whenever any Form of Government becomes destructive of these ends, it is the Right of the People to alter or to abolish it, and to institute new Government, laying its foundation on such principles and organizing its powers in such form, as to them shall seem most likely to effect their Safety and Happiness. Prudence, indeed, will dictate that Governments long established should not be changed for light and transient causes; and accordingly all experience hath shewn that mankind are more disposed to suffer, while evils are sufferable, than to right themselves by abolishing the forms to which they are accustomed. But when a long train of abuses and usurpations, pursuing invariably the same Object evinces a design to reduce them under absolute Despotism, it is their right, it is their duty, to throw off such Government, and to provide new Guards for their future security. Such has been the patient sufferance of these Colonies; and such is now the necessity which constrains them to alter their former Systems of Government. The history of the present King of Great Britain is a history of repeated injuries and usurpations, all having in direct object the establishment of an absolute Tyranny over these States. To prove this, let Facts be submitted to a candid world.

He has refused his Assent to Laws, the most wholesome and necessary for the public good.

He has forbidden his Governors to pass Laws of immediate and pressing importance, unless suspended in their operation till his Assent should be obtained; and when so suspended, he has utterly neglected to attend to them.

He has refused to pass other Laws for the accommodation of large districts of people, unless those people would relinquish the right of Representation in the Legislature, a right inestimable to them and formidable to tyrants only.

He has called together legislative bodies at places unusual, uncomfortable, and distant from the depository of their public Records, for the sole purpose of fatiguing them into compliance with his measures.

He has dissolved Representative Houses repeatedly, for opposing with manly firmness his invasions on the rights of the people.

He has refused for a long time, after such dissolutions, to cause others to be elected; whereby the Legislative powers, incapable of Annihilation, have returned to the People at large for their exercise; the State remaining in the mean time exposed to all the dangers of invasion from without, and convulsions within.

He has endeavoured to prevent the population of these States; for that purpose obstructing the Laws for Naturalization of Foreigners; refusing to pass others to encourage their migrations hither, and raising the conditions of new Appropriations of Lands.

He has obstructed the Administration of Justice, by refusing his Assent to Laws for establishing Judiciary powers.

He has made Judges dependent on his Will alone, for the tenure of their offices, and the amount and payment of their salaries.

He has erected a multitude of New Offices, and sent hither swarms of Officers to harass our people, and eat out their substance.

He has kept among us, in times of peace, Standing Armies without the Consent of our legislatures.

He has affected to render the Military independent of and superior to the Civil power.

He has combined with others to subject us to a jurisdiction foreign to our constitution, and unacknowledged by our laws; giving his Assent to their Acts of pretended Legislation:

For quartering large bodies of armed troops among us:

For protecting them, by a mock Trial, from punishment for any Murders which they should commit on the Inhabitants of these States:

For cutting off our Trade with all parts of the world:

For imposing Taxes on us without our Consent:

For depriving us in many cases, of the benefits of Trial by Jury:

For transporting us beyond Seas to be tried for pretended offences:

For abolishing the free System of English Laws in a neighbouring Province, establishing therein an Arbitrary government, and enlarging its Boundaries so as to render it at once an example and fit instrument for introducing the same absolute rule into these Colonies:

For taking away our Charters, abolishing our most valuable Laws, and altering fundamentally the Forms of our Governments:

For suspending our own Legislatures, and declaring themselves invested with power to legislate for us in all cases whatsoever.

He has abdicated Government here, by declaring us out of his Protection and waging War against us.

He has plundered our seas, ravaged our Coasts, burnt our towns, and destroyed the lives of our people.

He is at this time transporting large Armies of foreign Mercenaries to compleat the works of death, desolation and tyranny, already begun with circumstances of Cruelty & perfidy scarcely paralleled in the most barbarous ages, and totally unworthy the Head of a civilized nation.

He has constrained our fellow Citizens taken Captive on the high Seas to bear Arms against their Country, to become the executioners of their friends and Brethren, or to fall themselves by their Hands.

He has excited domestic insurrections amongst us, and has endeavoured to bring on the inhabitants of our frontiers, the merciless Indian Savages, whose known rule of warfare is an undistinguished destruction of all ages, sexes and conditions.

In every stage of these Oppressions We have Petitioned for Redress in the most humble terms: Our repeated Petitions have been answered only by repeated injury. A Prince, whose character is thus marked by every act which may define a Tyrant, is unfit to be the ruler of a free people.

Nor have We been wanting in attentions to our British brethren. We have warned them from time to time of attempts by their legislature to extend an unwarrantable jurisdiction over us. We have reminded them of the circumstances of our emigration and settlement here. We have appealed to their native justice and magnanimity, and we have conjured them by the ties of our common kindred to disavow these usurpations, which would inevitably interrupt our connections and correspondence. They too have been deaf to the voice of justice and of consanguinity. We must, therefore, acquiesce in the necessity, which denounces our Separation, and hold them, as we hold the rest of mankind. Enemies in War, in Peace Friends.

WE, THEREFORE, the REPRESENTATIVES OF THE UNITED STATES OF AMERICA, IN GENERAL CONGRESS, Assembled, appealing to the Supreme Judge of the world for the rectitude of our intentions, do, in the Name, and by authority of the good People of these Colonies, solemnly PUBLISH and DECLARE, That these United Colonies are, and of Right ought to be FREE AND INDEPENDENT STATES; that they are Absolved from all Allegiance to the British Crown, and that all political connection between them and the State of Great Britain, is and ought to be totally dissolved; and that as FREE AND INDEPENDENT STATES, they have full Power to levy War, conclude Peace, contract Alliances, establish Commerce, and to do all other Acts and Things which INDEPENDENT STATES may of right do. And for the support of this Declaration, with a firm reliance on the protection of divine Providence, we mutually pledge to each other our Lives, our Fortunes and our sacred Honor.

HENRY DAVID THOREAU

A social rebel with high principles, a man who loved nature and solitude, Thoreau is considered by some a memorable individualist, by others a perennial adolescent, and by still others as both. E. B. White has called him a "regular hairshirt of a man." Born in Concord, Mass., in 1817, he was educated at Harvard and after graduation returned to Concord where he first taught school and on later occasions supported himself by making pencils. He became a friend of Emerson, who was at the time leader of Concord's intellectual and spiritual life; he joined the Transcendental Club and contributed frequently to its journal, The Dial. Some have said that Thoreau was the answer to Emerson's plea for an American Scholar (see page 31). From July 4, 1845, to September 6, 1847, Thoreau lived in a hut at nearby Walden Pond, an experience which he recorded in his most famous work, Walden. His stay there was interrupted for one day in the summer of 1846 when he was arrested for not paying the Massachusetts poll tax. He explained his refusal as an act of protest against a government which sanctioned the Mexican War, a war he considered in the interests of Southern slave holders; he later wrote an eloquent defense of civil disobedience which was first published in 1849. This essay, which has become an American classic, is reprinted in full below; the text is that of the Riverside edition of Thoreau's works.

CIVIL DISOBEDIENCE

I heartily accept the motto,—"That government is best which governs least;" and I should like to see it acted up to more rapidly and systematically. Carried out, it finally amounts to this, which also I believe,—"That government is best which governs not at all;" and when men are prepared for it, that will be the kind of government which they will have. Government is at best but an expedient; but most governments are usually, and all governments are sometimes, inexpedient. The objections which have been brought against a standing army, and they are many and weighty, and deserve to prevail, may also at last be brought against a standing government. The standing army is only an arm of the standing government. The government itself, which is only the mode which the people have chosen to execute their will, is equally liable to be abused and perverted before the people can act through it. Witness the present Mexican war, the work of comparatively a few individuals using the standing government as their tool; for, in the outset, the people would not have consented to this measure.

This American government,—what is it but a tradition, though a recent one, endeavoring to transmit itself unimpaired to posterity, but each instant losing some of its integrity? It has not the vitality and force of a single living man; for a single man can bend it to his will. It is a sort of wooden gun to the people themselves. But it is not the less necessary for this; for the people must have some complicated machinery or other, and hear its din, to satisfy that idea of government which they have. Governments show thus how successfully men can be imposed on, even impose on themselves, for their own advantage. It is excellent, we must all allow. Yet this government never of itself furthered any enterprise, but by the alacrity with which it got out of its way. *It* does not keep the country free. *It* does not settle the West. *It* does not educate. The character inherent in the American people has done all that has been accomplished; and it would have done somewhat more, if the government had not sometimes got in its way. For government is an expedient by which men would fain succeed in letting one another alone; and, as has been said, when it is most expedient, the governed are most let alone by it. Trade and commerce, if they were not made of India-rubber, would never manage to bounce over the obstacles which legislators are continually putting in their way; and, if one were to judge these men wholly by the effects of their actions and not partly by their intentions, they would deserve to be classed and punished with those mischievous persons who put obstructions on the railroads.

But, to speak practically and as a citizen, unlike those who call themselves no-government men, I ask for, not at once no government, but *at once* a better government. Let every man make known what kind of government would command his respect, and that will be one step toward obtaining it.

After all, the practical reason why, when the power is once in the hands of the people, a majority are permitted, and for a long period continue, to rule is not because they are most likely to be in the right, nor because this seems fairest to the minority, but because they are physically the strongest. But a government in which the majority rule in all cases cannot be based on justice, even as far as men understand it. Can there not be a government in which majorities do not virtually decide right and wrong, but conscience?—in which majorities decide only those questions to which the rule of expediency is applicable? Must the citizen ever for a moment, or in the least degree, resign his conscience to the legislator? Why has every man a conscience, then? I think that we should be men first, and subjects afterward. It is not desirable to cultivate a respect for the law, so much as for the right. The only obligation which I have a right to assume is to do at any time what I think right. It is truly enough said, that a corporation has no conscience; but a corporation of conscientious men is a corporation *with* a conscience. Law never made men a whit more just; and, by means of their respect for it, even the well-disposed are daily made the agents of injustice. A common and natural result of an undue respect for law is, that you may see a file of soldiers, colonel, captain, corporal, privates, powder-monkeys, and all, marching in admirable order over hill and dale to the wars, against their wills, ay, against their common sense and consciences, which makes it very steep marching indeed, and produces a palpitation of the heart. They have no doubt that it is a damnable business in which they are concerned; they are all peaceably inclined. Now, what are they? Men at all? or small movable forts and magazines, at the service of some unscrupulous man in power? Visit the Navy-Yard, and behold a marine, such a man as an American government can make, or such as it can make a man with its black arts,—a mere shadow and reminiscence of humanity, a man laid out alive and standing, and already, as one may say, buried under arms with funeral accompaniments, though it may be,—

> "Not a drum was heard, not a funeral note,
>   As his corse to the rampart we hurried;
> Not a soldier discharged his farewell shot
>   O'er the grave where our hero we buried."

The mass of men serve the state thus, not as men mainly, but as machines, with their bodies. They are the standing army, and the militia, jailers, constables, posse comitatus, etc. In most cases there is no free exercise whatever of the judgment or of the moral sense; but they put themselves on a level with wood and earth and stones; and wooden men can perhaps be manufactured that will serve the purpose as well. Such command no more respect than men of straw or a lump of dirt. They have the same sort of worth only as horses and dogs. Yet such as these even are commonly esteemed good citizens. Others—as most legislators, politicians, lawyers, ministers, and office-holders—serve the state chiefly with their heads; and, as they rarely make any moral distinctions, they are as likely to serve the Devil, without *intending* it, as God. A very few, as heroes, patriots, martyrs, reformers in the great sense, and *men*, serve the state with their consciences also, and so necessarily resist it for the most part; and they are commonly treated as enemies by it. A wise man will only be useful as a man, and will not submit to be "clay," and "stop a hole to keep the wind away," but leave that office to his dust at least:—

> "I am too high-born to be propertied,
>   To be a secondary at control,
>   Or useful serving-man and instrument
>   To any sovereign state throughout the world."

He who gives himself entirely to his fellow-men appears to them useless and selfish; but he who gives himself partially to them is pronounced a benefactor and philanthropist.

How does it become a man to behave toward this American government to-day? I answer, that he cannot without disgrace be associated with it. I cannot for an instant recognize that political organization as *my* government which is the *slave's* government also.

All men recognize the right of revolution; that is, the right to refuse allegiance to, and to resist, the government, when its tyranny or its inefficiency are great and unendurable. But almost all say that such is not the case now. But such was the case, they think, in the Revolution of '75. If one were to tell me that this was a bad government because it taxed certain foreign commodities brought to its ports, it is most probable that I should not make an ado about it, for I can do without them. All machines have their friction; and possibly this does enough good to counterbalance the evil. At any rate, it is a great evil to make a stir about it. But when the friction comes to have its machine, and oppression and robbery are organized, I say, let us not have such a machine any longer. In other words, when a sixth of the population of a nation which has undertaken to be the refuge of liberty are slaves, and a whole country is unjustly overrun and conquered by a foreign army, and subjected to military law, I think that it is not too soon for honest men to rebel and revolutionize. What makes this duty the more urgent is the fact that the country so overrun is not our own, but ours is the invading army.

Paley, a common authority with many on moral questions, in his chapter on the "Duty of Submission to Civil Government," resolves all civil obligation into expediency; and he proceeds to say, "that so long as the interest of the whole society requires it, that is, so long as the established government cannot be resisted or changed without public inconveniency, it is the will of God that the established government be obeyed, and no longer. . . . This principle being admitted, the justice of every particular case of resistance is reduced to a computation of the quantity of the danger and grievance on the one side, and of the probability and expense of redressing it on the other." Of this, he says, every man shall judge for himself. But Paley appears never to have contemplated those cases to which the rule of expediency does not apply, in which a people, as well as an individual, must do justice, cost what it may. If I have unjustly wrested a plank from a drowning man, I must restore it to him though I drown myself. This, according to Paley, would be inconvenient. But he that would save his life, in such a case, shall lose it. This people must cease to hold slaves, and to make war on Mexico, though it cost them their existence as a people.

In their practice, nations agree with Paley; but does any one think that Massachusetts does exactly what is right at the present crisis?

> "A drab of state, a cloth-o'-silver slut,
> To have her train borne up, and her soul trail in the dirt."

Practically speaking, the opponents to a reform in Massachusetts are not a hundred thousand politicians at the South, but a hundred thousand merchants and farmers here, who are more interested in commerce and agriculture than they are in humanity, and are not prepared to do justice to the slave and to Mexico, *cost what it may*. I quarrel not with far-off foes, but with those who, near at home, coöperate with, and do the bidding of, those far away, and without whom the latter would be harmless. We are accustomed to say, that the mass of men are unprepared; but improvement is slow, because the few are not materially wiser or better than the many. It is not so important that many should be as good as you, as that there be some absolute goodness somewhere; for that will leaven the whole lump. There are thousands who are *in opinion* opposed to slavery and to the war, who yet in effect do nothing to put an end to them; who, esteeming themselves children of Washington and Franklin, sit down with their hands in their pockets, and say that they know not what to do, and do nothing; who even postpone the question of freedom to the question of free-trade, and quietly read the prices-current along with the latest advices from Mexico, after dinner, and, it may be, fall asleep over them both. What is the price-current of an honest man and patriot to-day? They hesitate, and they regret, and sometimes they petition; but they do nothing in earnest and with effect. They will wait, well disposed, for others to remedy the evil, that they may no longer have it to regret. At most, they give only a cheap vote, and a feeble countenance and Godspeed, to the right, as it goes by them. There are nine hundred and ninety-nine patrons of virtue to one virtuous man. But it is easier to deal with the real possessor of a thing than with the temporary guardian of it.

All voting is a sort of gaming, like checkers or backgammon, with a slight moral tinge to it, a playing with right and wrong, with moral questions; and betting naturally accompanies it. The character of the voters is not staked. I cast my vote, perchance, as I think right; but I am not vitally concerned that that right should prevail. I am willing to leave it to the majority. Its obligation, therefore, never exceeds that of expediency. Even voting *for the right* is *doing* nothing for it. It is only expressing to men feebly your desire that it should prevail. A wise man will not leave the right to the mercy of chance, nor wish it to prevail through the power of the majority. There is but little virtue in the action of masses of men. When the majority shall at length vote for the abolition of slavery, it will be because they are indifferent to slavery, or because there is but little slavery left to be abolished by their vote. *They* will then be the only slaves. Only *his* vote can hasten the abolition of slavery who asserts his own freedom by his vote.

I hear of a convention to be held at Baltimore, or elsewhere, for the selection of a candidate for the Presidency, made up chiefly of editors, and men who are politicians by profession; but I think, what is it to any independent, intelligent, and respectable man what decision they may come to? Shall we not have the advantage of his wisdom and honesty, nevertheless? Can we not count upon some independent votes? Are there not many individuals in the country who do not attend conventions? But no: I find that the respectable man, so called, has immediately drifted from his position, and despairs of his country, when his country has more reason to despair of him. He forthwith adopts one of the candidates thus selected as the only *available* one, thus proving that he is himself *available* for any purposes of the demagogue. His vote is of no more worth than that of any unprincipled foreigner or hireling native, who may have been bought. O for a man who is a *man*, and, as my neighbor says, has a bone in his back which you cannot pass your hand through! Our statistics are at fault: the population has been returned too large. How many *men* are there to a square thousand miles in this country? Hardly one. Does not America offer any inducement for men to settle here? The American has dwindled into an Odd Fellow,—one who may be known by the development of his organ of gregariousness, and a manifest lack of intellect and cheerful self-reliance; whose first and chief concern, on coming into the world, is to see that the Almshouses are in good repair; and, before yet he has lawfully donned the virile garb, to collect a fund for the support of the widows and orphans that may be; who, in short, ventures to live only by the aid of the Mutual Insurance company, which has promised to bury him decently.

It is not a man's duty, as a matter of course, to devote himself to the eradication of any, even the most enormous wrong; he may still properly have other concerns to engage him; but it his duty, at least, to wash his hands of it, and, if he gives it no thought longer, not to give it practically his support. If I devote myself to other pursuits and contemplations, I must first see, at least, that I do not pursue them sitting upon another man's shoulders. I must get off him first, that he may pursue his contemplations too. See what gross inconsistency is tolerated. I have heard some of my townsmen say, "I should like to have them order me out to help put down an insurrection of the slaves, or to march to Mexico;— see if I would go;" and yet these very men have each, directly by their allegiance, and so indirectly, at least, by their money, furnished a substitute. The soldier is applauded who refuses to serve in an unjust war by those who do not refuse to sustain the unjust government which makes the war; is applauded by those whose own act and authority he disregards and sets at naught; as if the state were penitent to that degree that it hired one to scourge it while it sinned, but not to that degree that it left off sinning for a moment. Thus, under the name of Order and Civil Government, we are all made at last to pay homage to and support our own meanness. After the first blush of sin comes its indifference; and from immoral it becomes, as it were, *un*moral, and not quite unnecessary to that life which we have made.

The broadest and most prevalent error requires the most disinterested virtue to sustain it. The slight reproach to which the virtue of patriotism is commonly liable, the noble are most likely to incur. Those who, while they disapprove of the character and measures of a government, yield to it their allegiance and support are undoubtedly its most conscientious supporters, and so frequently the most serious obstacles to reform. Some are petitioning the state to dissolve the Union, to disregard the requisitions of the President. Why do they not dissolve it themselves,—the union between themselves and the state,—and refuse to pay their quota into its treasury? Do not they stand in the same relation to the state that the state does to the Union? And have not the same reasons prevented the state from resisting the Union which have prevented them from resisting the state?

How can a man be satisfied to entertain an opinion merely, and enjoy *it?* Is there any enjoyment in it, if his opinion is that he is aggrieved? If you are cheated out of a single dollar by your neighbor, you do not rest satisfied with knowing that you are cheated, or with saying that you are cheated, or even with petitioning him to pay you your due; but you take effectual steps at once to obtain the full amount, and see that you are never cheated again. Action from principle, the perception and the performance of right, changes things and relations; it is essentially revolutionary, and does not consist wholly with anything which was. It not only divides states and churches, it divides families; ay, it divides the *individual*, separating the diabolical in him from the divine.

Unjust laws exist: shall we be content to obey them, or shall we endeavor to amend them, and obey them until we have succeeded, or shall we transgress them at once? Men generally, under such a government as this, think that they ought to wait until they have persuaded the majority to alter them. They think that, if they should resist, the remedy would be worse than the evil. But it is the fault of the government itself that the remedy *is* worse than the evil. *It* makes it worse. Why is it not more apt to anticipate and provide for reform? Why does it not cherish its wise minority? Why does it cry and resist before it is hurt? Why does it not encourage its citizens to be on the alert to point out its faults, and *do* better than it would have them? Why does it always crucify Christ, and excommunicate Copernicus and Luther, and pronounce Washington and Franklin rebels?

One would think, that a deliberate and practical denial of its authority was the only offense never contemplated by government; else, why has it not assigned its definite, its suitable and proportionate penalty? If a man who has no property refuses but once to earn nine shillings for the state, he is put in prison for a period unlimited by any law that I know, and determined only by the discretion of those who placed him there; but if he should steal ninety times nine shillings from the state, he is soon permitted to go at large again.

If the injustice is part of the necessary friction of the machine of government, let it go, let it go: perchance it will wear smooth,—certainly the machine will wear out. If the injustice has a spring, or a pulley, or a rope, or a crank, exclusively for itself, then perhaps you may consider whether the remedy will not be worse than the evil; but if it is of such a nature that it requires you to be the agent of injustice to another, then, I say, break the law. Let your life be a counter friction to stop the machine. What I have to do is to see, at any rate, that I do not lend myself to the wrong which I condemn.

As for adopting the ways which the state has provided for remedying the evil, I know not of such ways. They take too much time, and a man's life will be gone. I have other affairs to attend to. I came into this world, not chiefly to make this a good place to live in, but to live in it, be it good or bad. A man has not everything to do, but something; and because he cannot do *everything*, it is not necessary that he should do *something* wrong. It is not my business to be petitioning the Governor or the Legislature any more than it is theirs to petition me; and if they should not hear my petition, what should I do then? But in this case the state has provided no way: its very Constitution is the evil. This may seem to be harsh and stubborn and unconciliatory; but it is to treat with the utmost kindness and consideration the only spirit that can appreciate or deserves it. So is all change for the better, like birth and death, which convulse the body.

I do not hesitate to say, that those who call themselves Abolitionists should at once effectually withdraw their support, both in person and property, from the government of Massachusetts, and not wait till they constitute a majority of one, before they suffer the right to prevail through them. I think that it is enough if they have God on their side, without waiting for that other one. Moreover, any man more right than his neighbors constitutes a majority of one already.

I meet this American government, or its representative, the state government, directly, and face to face, once a year—no more—in the person of its tax-gatherer; this is the only mode in which a man situated as I am necessarily meets it; and it then says distinctly, Recognize me; and the simplest, the most effectual, and, in the present posture of affairs, the indispensablest mode of treating with it on this head, of expressing your little satisfaction with and love for it, is to deny it then. My civil neighbor, the tax-gatherer, is the very man I have to deal with,—for it is, after all, with men and not with parchment that I quarrel,—and he has voluntarily chosen to be an agent of the government. How shall he ever know well what he is and does as an officer of the government, or as a man, until he is obliged to consider whether he shall treat me, his neighbor, for whom he has respect, as a neighbor and well-disposed man, or as a maniac and disturber of the peace, and see if he can get over this obstruction to his neighborliness without a ruder and more impetuous thought or speech corresponding with his action. I know this well, that if one thousand, if one hundred, if ten men whom I could name,—if ten *honest* men only,—ay, if *one* HONEST man, in this State of Massachusetts, *ceasing to hold slaves*, were actually to withdraw from this copartnership, and be locked up in the county jail therefor, it would be the abolition of slavery in America. For it matters not how small the beginning may seem to be: what is once well done is done forever. But we love better to talk about it: that we say is our mission. Reform keeps many scores of newspapers in its service, but not one man. If my esteemed neighbor, the State's ambassador, who will devote his days to the settlement of the question of human rights in the Council Chamber, instead of being threatened with the prisons of Carolina, were to sit down the prisoner of Massachusetts, that State which is so anxious to foist the sin of slavery upon her sister,—though at present she can discover only an act of inhospitality to be the ground of a quarrel with her,—the Legislature would not wholly waive the subject the following winter.

Under a government which imprisons any unjustly, the true place for a just man is also a prison. The proper place to-day, the only place which Massachusetts has provided for her freer and less desponding spirits, is in her prisons, to be put out and locked out of the State by her own act, as they have already put themselves out by their principles. It is there that the fugitive slave, and the Mexican prisoner on parole, and the Indian come to plead the wrongs of his race should find them; on that separate, but more free and honorable ground, where the State places those who are not *with* her, but *against* her,—the only house in a slave State in which a free man can abide with honor. If any think that their influence would be lost there, and their voices no longer afflict the ear of the State, that they would not be as an enemy within its walls, they do not know by how much truth is stronger than error, nor how much more eloquently and effectively he can combat injustice who has experienced a little in his own person. Cast your whole vote, not a strip of paper merely, but your whole influence. A minority is powerless while it conforms to the majority; it is not even a minority then; but it is irresistible when it clogs by its whole weight. If the alternative is to keep all just men in prison, or give up war and slavery, the State will not hesitate which to choose. If a thousand men were not to pay their tax-bills this year, that would not be a violent and bloody measure, as it would be to pay them, and enable the State to commit violence and shed innocent blood. This is, in fact, the definition of a peaceable revolution, if any such is possible. If the tax-gatherer, or any other public officer, asks me, as one has done, "But what shall I do?" my answer is, "If you really wish to do anything, resign your office." When the subject has refused allegiance, and the officer has resigned his office, then the revolution is accomplished. But even suppose blood should flow. Is there not a sort of blood shed when the conscience is wounded? Through this wound a man's real manhood and immortality flow out, and he bleeds to an everlasting death. I see this blood flowing now.

I have contemplated the imprisonment of the offender, rather than the seizure of his goods,—though both will serve the same purpose,— because they who assert the purest right, and consequently are most dangerous to a corrupt State, commonly have not spent much time in accumulating property. To such the State renders comparatively small service, and a slight tax is wont to appear exorbitant, particularly if they are obliged to earn it by special labor with their hands. If there were one who lived wholly without the use of money, the State itself would hesitate to demand it of him. But the rich man—not to make any invidious comparison—is always sold to the institution which makes him rich. Absolutely speaking, the more money, the less virtue; for money comes between a man and his objects, and obtains them for him; and it was certainly no great virtue to obtain it. It puts to rest many questions which he would otherwise be taxed to answer; while the only new question which it puts is the hard but superfluous one, how to spend it. Thus his moral ground is taken from under his feet. The opportunities of living are diminished in proportion as what are called the "means" are increased. The best thing a man can do for his culture when he is rich is to endeavor to carry out those schemes which he entertained when he was poor. Christ answered the Herodians accord- ing to their condition. "Show me the tribute-money," said he;—and one took a penny out of his pocket;—if you use money which has the image of Cæsar on it, and which he has made current and valuable, that is, *if you are men of the State*, and gladly enjoy the advantages of Cæsar's government, then pay him back some of his own when he demands it. "Render therefore to Cæsar that which is Cæsar's, and to God those things which are God's,"—leaving them no wiser than before as to which was which; for they did not wish to know.

When I converse with the freest of my neighbors, I perceive that, what- ever they may say about the magnitude and seriousness of the question, and their regard for the public tranquillity, the long and the short of the matter is, that they cannot spare the protection of the existing government, and they dread the consequences to their property and families of disobedience to it. For my own part, I should not like to think that I ever rely on the protection of the State. But, if I deny the authority of the State when it presents its tax-bill, it will soon take and waste all my property, and so harass me and my children without end. This is hard. This makes it impossible for a man to live honestly, and at the same time comfortably, in outward respects. It will not be worth the while to accumulate property; that would be sure to go again. You must hire or squat somewhere, and raise but a small crop, and eat that soon. You must live within yourself, and depend upon yourself always tucked up and ready for a start, and not have many affairs. A man may grow rich in Turkey even, if he will be in all respects a good subject of the Turkish government. Confucius said: "If a state is governed by the principles of reason, poverty and misery are subjects of shame; if a state is not governed by the principles of reason, riches and honors are the subjects of shame." No: until I want the protection of Massachusetts to be extended to me in some distant Southern port, where my liberty is endangered, or until I am bent solely on building up an estate at home by peaceful enterprise, I can afford to refuse allegiance to Massachusetts, and her right to my property and life. It costs me less in every sense to incur the penalty of disobedience to the State than it would to obey. I should feel as if I were worth less in that case.

Some years ago, the State met me in behalf of the Church, and commanded me to pay a certain sum toward the support of a clergyman whose preaching my father attended, but never I myself. "Pay," it said, "or be locked up in the jail." I declined to pay. But, unfortunately, another man saw fit to pay it. I did not see why the schoolmaster should be taxed to support the priest, and not the priest the schoolmaster; for I was not the State's schoolmaster, but I supported myself by voluntary subscription. I did not see why the lyceum should not present its tax-bill, and have the State to back its demand, as well as the Church. However, at the request of the selectmen, I condescended to make some such statement as this in writing:—"Know all men by these presents, that I, Henry Thoreau, do not wish to be regarded as a member of any incorporated society which I have not joined." This I gave to the town clerk; and he has it. The State, having thus learned that I did not wish to be regarded as a member of that church, has never made a like demand on me since; though it said that it must adhere to its original presumption that time. If I had known how to name them, I should then have signed off in detail from all the societies which I never signed on to; but I did not know where to find a complete list.

I have paid no poll-tax for six years. I was put into a jail once on this account, for one night; and, as I stood considering the walls of solid stone, two or three feet thick, the door of wood and iron, a foot thick, and the iron grating which strained the light, I could not help being struck with the foolishness of that institution which treated me as if I were mere flesh and blood and bones, to be locked up. I wondered that it should have concluded at length that this was the best use it could put me to, and had never thought to avail itself of my services in some way. I saw that, if there was a wall of stone between me and my townsmen, there was a still more difficult one to climb or break through before they could get to be as free as I was. I did not for a moment feel confined, and the walls seemed a great waste of stone and mortar. I felt as if I alone of all my townsmen had paid my tax. They plainly did not know how to treat me, but behaved like persons who are underbred. In every threat and in every compliment there was a blunder; for they thought that my chief desire was to stand the other side of that stone wall. I could not but smile to see how industriously they locked the door on my meditations, which followed them out again without let or hindrance, and *they* were really all that was dangerous. As they could not reach me, they had resolved to punish my body; just as boys, if they cannot come at some person against whom they have a spite, will abuse his dog. I saw that the State was half-witted, that it was timid as a lone woman with her silver spoons, and that it did not know its friends from its foes, and I lost all my remaining respect for it, and pitied it.

Thus the State never intentionally confronts a man's sense, intellectual or moral, but only his body, his senses. It is not armed with superior wit or honesty, but with superior physical strength. I was not born to be forced. I will breathe after my own fashion. Let us see who is the strongest. What force has a multitude? They only can force me who obey a higher law than I. They force me to become like themselves. I do not hear of *men* being *forced* to live this way or that by masses of men. What sort of life were that to live? When I meet a government which says to me, "Your money or your life," why should I be in haste to give it my money? It may be in a great strait, and not know what to do: I cannot help that. It must help itself; do as I do. It is not worth the while to snivel about it. I am not responsible for the successful working of the machinery of society. I am not the son of the engineer. I perceive that, when an acorn and a chestnut fall side by side, the one does not remain inert to make way for the other, but both obey their own laws, and spring and grow and flourish as best they can, till one, perchance, over-shadows and destroys the other. If a plant cannot live according to its nature, it dies; and so a man.

The night in prison was novel and interesting enough. The prisoners in their shirt-sleeves were enjoying a chat and the evening air in the doorway, when I entered. But the jailer said, "Come, boys, it is time to lock up;" and so they dispersed, and I heard the sound of their steps returning into the hollow apartments. My room-mate was introduced to me by the jailer as "a first-rate fellow and a clever man." When the door was locked, he showed me where to hang my hat, and how he managed matters there. The rooms were whitewashed once a month; and this one, at least, was the whitest, most simply furnished, and probably the neatest apartment in the town. He naturally wanted to know where I came from, and what brought me there; and, when I had told him, I asked him in my turn how he came there, presuming him to be an honest man, of course; and, as the world goes, I believe he was. "Why," said he, "they accuse me of burning a barn; but I never did it." As near as I could discover, he had probably gone to bed in a barn when drunk, and smoked his pipe there; and so a barn was burnt. He had the reputation of being a clever man, had been there some three months waiting for his trial to come on, and would have to wait as much longer; but he was quite domesticated and contented, since he got his board for nothing, and thought that he was well treated.

He occupied one window, and I the other; and I saw that if one stayed there long, his principal business would be to look out the window. I had soon read all the tracts that were left there, and examined where former prisoners had broken out, and where a grate had been sawed off, and heard the history of the various occupants of that room; for I found that even here there was a history and a gossip which never circulated beyond the walls of the jail. Probably this is the only house in the town where verses are composed, which are afterward printed in a circular form, but not published. I was shown quite a long list of verses which were composed by some young men who had been detected in an attempt to escape, who avenged themselves by singing them.

I pumped my fellow-prisoner as dry as I could, for fear I should never see him again; but at length he showed me which was my bed, and left me to blow out the lamp.

It was like traveling into a far country, such as I had never expected to behold, to lie there for one night. It seemed to me that I never had heard the town-clock strike before, nor the evening sounds of the village; for we slept with the windows open, which were inside the grating. It was to see my native village in the light of the Middle Ages, and our Concord was turned into a Rhine stream, and visions of knights and castles passed before me. They were the voices of old burghers that I heard in the streets. I was an involuntary spectator and auditor of whatever was done and said in the kitchen of the adjacent village-inn,—a wholly new and rare experience to me. It was a closer view of my native town. I was fairly inside of it. I never had seen its institutions before. This is one of its peculiar institutions; for it is a shire town. I began to comprehend what its inhabitants were about.

In the morning, our breakfasts were put through the hole in the door, in small oblong-square tin pans, made to fit, and holding a pint of chocolate, with brown bread, and an iron spoon. When they called for the vessels again, I was green enough to return what bread I had left; but my comrade seized it, and said that I should lay that up for lunch or dinner.

Soon after he was let out to work at haying in a neighboring field, whither he went every day, and would not be back till noon; so he bade me good-day, saying that he doubted if he should see me again.

When I came out of prison,—for some one interfered, and paid that tax,—I did not perceive that great changes had taken place on the common, such as he observed who went in a youth and emerged a tottering and gray-headed man; and yet a change had to my eyes come over the scene,—the town, and State, and country,—greater than any that mere time could effect. I saw yet more distinctly the State in which I lived. I saw to what extent the people among whom I lived could be trusted as good neighbors and friends; that their friendship was for summer weather only; that they did not greatly propose to do right; that they were a distinct race from me by their prejudices and superstitions, as the Chinamen and Malays are; that in their sacrifices to humanity they ran no risks, not even to their property; that after all they were not so noble but they treated the thief as he had treated them, and hoped, by a certain outward observance and a few prayers, and by walking in a particular straight though useless path from time to time, to save their souls. This may be to judge my neighbors harshly; for I believe that many of them are not aware that they have such an institution as the jail in their village.

It was formerly the custom in our village, when a poor debtor came out of jail, for his acquaintances to salute him, looking through their fingers, which were crossed to represent the grating of a jail window, "How do ye do?" My neighbors did not thus salute me, but first looked at me, and then at one another, as if I had returned from a long journey. I was put into jail as I was going to the shoemaker's to get a shoe which was mended. When I was let out the next morning, I proceeded to finish my errand, and, having put on my mended shoe, joined a huckleberry party, who were impatient to put themselves under my conduct; and in half an hour,—for the horse was soon tackled,—was in the midst of a huckleberry field, on one of our highest hills, two miles off, and then the State was nowhere to be seen.

This is the whole history of "My Prisons."

I have never declined paying the highway tax, because I am as desirous of being a good neighbor as I am of being a bad subject; and as for supporting schools, I am doing my part to educate my fellow-countrymen now. It is for no particular item in the tax-bill that I refuse to pay it. I simply wish to refuse allegiance to the State, to withdraw and stand aloof from it effectually. I do not care to trace the course of my dollar, if I could, till it buys a man or a musket to shoot one with,—the dollar is innocent,—but I am concerned to trace the effects of my allegiance. In fact, I quietly declare war with the State, after my fashion, though I will still make what use and get what advantage of her I can, as is usual in such cases.

If others pay the tax which is demanded of me, from a sympathy with the State, they do but what they have already done in their own case, or rather they abet injustice to a greater extent than the State requires. If they pay the tax from a mistaken interest in the individual taxed, to save his property, or prevent his going to jail, it is because they have not considered wisely how far they let their private feelings interfere with the public good.

This, then, is my position at present. But one cannot be too much on his guard in such a case, lest his action be biased by obstinacy or an undue regard for the opinions of men. Let him see that he does only what belongs to himself and to the hour.

I think sometimes, Why, this people mean well, they are only ignorant; they would do better if they knew how: why give your neighbors this pain to treat you as they are not inclined to? But I think again, This is no reason why I should do as they do, or permit others to suffer much greater pain of a different kind. Again, I sometimes say to myself, When many millions of men, without heat, without ill will, without personal feeling of any kind, demand of you a few shillings only, without the possibility, such is their constitution, of retracting or altering their present demand, and without the possibility, on your side, of appeal to any other millions, why expose yourself to this overwhelming brute force? You do not resist cold and hunger, the winds and the waves, thus obstinately; you quietly submit to a thousand similar necessities. You do not put your head into the fire. But just in proportion as I regard this as not wholly a brute force, but partly a human force, and consider that I have relations to those millions as to so many millions of men, and not of mere brute or inanimate things, I see that appeal is possible, first and instantaneously, from them to the Maker of them, and, secondly, from them to themselves. But if I put my head deliberately into the fire, there is no appeal to fire or to the Maker of fire, and I have only myself to blame. If I could convince myself that I have any right to be satisfied with men as they are, and to treat them accordingly, and not according, in some respects, to my requisitions and expectations of what they and I ought to be, then, like a good Mussulman and fatalist, I should endeavor to be satisfied with things as they are, and say it is the will of God. And, above all, there is this difference between resisting this and a purely brute or natural force, that I can resist this with some effect; but I cannot expect, like Orpheus, to change the nature of the rocks and trees and beasts.

I do not wish to quarrel with any man or nation. I do not wish to split hairs, to make fine distinctions, or set myself up as better than my neighbors. I seek rather, I may say, even an excuse for conforming to the laws of the land. I am but too ready to conform to them. Indeed, I have reason to suspect myself on this head; and each year, as the tax-gatherer comes round, I find myself disposed to review the acts and position of the general and State governments, and the spirit of the people, to discover a pretext for conformity.

> "We must affect our country as our parents,
> And if at any time we alienate
> Our love or industry from doing it honor,
> We must respect effects and teach the soul
> Matter of conscience and religion,
> And not desire of rule or benefit."

I believe that the State will soon be able to take all my work of this sort out of my hands, and then I shall be no better a patriot than my fellow-countrymen. Seen from a lower point of view, the Constitution, with all its faults, is very good; the law and the courts are very respectable; even this State and this American government are, in many respects, very admirable, and rare things, to be thankful for, such as a great many have described them; but seen from a point of view a little higher, they are what I have described them; seen from a higher still, and the highest, who shall say what they are, or that they are worth looking at or thinking of at all?

However, the government does not concern me much, and I shall bestow the fewest possible thoughts on it. It is not many moments that I live under a government, even in this world. If a man is thought-free, fancy-free, imagination-free, that which *is not* never for a long time appearing *to be* to him, unwise rulers or reformers cannot fatally interrupt him.

I know that most men think differently from myself; but those whose lives are by profession devoted to the study of these or kindred subjects content me as little as any. Statesmen and legislators, standing so completely within the institution, never distinctly and nakedly behold it. They speak of moving society, but have no resting-place without it. They may be men of a certain experience and discrimination, and have no doubt invented ingenious and even useful systems, for which we sincerely thank them; but all their wit and usefulness lie within certain not very wide limits. They are wont to forget that the world is not governed by policy and expediency. Webster never goes behind government, and so cannot speak with authority about it. His words are wisdom to those legislators who contemplate no essential reform in the existing government; but for thinkers, and those who legislate for all time, he never once glances at the subject. I know of those whose serene and wise speculations on this theme would soon reveal the limits of his mind's range and hospitality. Yet, compared with the cheap professions of most reformers, and the still cheaper wisdom and eloquence of politicians in general, his are almost the only sensible and valuable words, and we thank Heaven for him. Comparatively, he is always strong, original, and, above all, practical. Still, his quality

is not wisdom, but prudence. The lawyer's truth is not Truth, but consistency or a consistent expediency. Truth is always in harmony with
herself, and is not concerned chiefly to reveal the justice that may consist
with wrong-doing. He well deserves to be called, as he has been called,
the Defender of the Constitution. There are really no blows to be given
by him but defensive ones. He is not a leader, but a follower. His leaders
are the men of '87. "I have never made an effort," he says, "and never
propose to make an effort; I have never countenanced an effort, and never
mean to countenance an effort, to disturb the arrangement as originally
made, by which the various States came into the Union." Still thinking of
the sanction which the Constitution gives to slavery, he says, "Because
it was a part of the original compact,—let it stand." Notwithstanding his
special acuteness and ability, he is unable to take a fact out of its merely
political relations, and behold it as it lies absolutely to be disposed of by the
intellect,—what, for instance, it behooves a man to do here in America
to-day with regard to slavery,—but ventures, or is driven, to make some
such desperate answer as the following, while professing to speak absolutely, and as a private man,—from which what new and singular code
of social duties might be inferred? "The manner," says he, "in which
the governments of those States where slavery exists are to regulate it is
for their own consideration, under their responsibility to their constituents,
to the general laws of propriety, humanity, and justice, and to God.
Associations formed elsewhere, springing from a feeling of humanity, or
any other cause, have nothing whatever to do with it. They have never
received any encouragement from me, and they never will."

They who know of no purer sources of truth, who have traced up its
stream no higher, stand, and wisely stand, by the Bible and the Constitution, and drink at it there with reverence and humility; but they who
behold where it comes trickling into this lake or that pool, gird up their
loins once more, and continue their pilgrimage toward its fountain-head.

No man with a genius for legislation has appeared in America. They
are rare in the history of the world. There are orators, politicians, and
eloquent men, by the thousand; but the speaker has not yet opened his
mouth to speak who is capable of settling the much-vexed questions of
the day. We love eloquence for its own sake, and not for any truth which
it may utter, or any heroism it may inspire. Our legislators have not yet
learned the comparative value of free-trade and of freedom, of union,
and of rectitude, to a nation. They have no genius or talent for comparatively humble questions of taxation and finance, commerce and manufactures and agriculture. If we were left solely to the wordy wit of
legislators in Congress for our guidance, uncorrected by the seasonable
experience and the effectual complaints of the people, America would not
long retain her rank among the nations. For eighteen hundred years,
though perchance I have no right to say it, the New Testament has been
written; yet where is the legislator who has wisdom and practical talent

enough to avail himself of the light which it sheds on the science of legislation?

The authority of government, even such as I am willing to submit to,—for I will cheerfully obey those who know and can do better than I, and in many things even those who neither know nor can do so well,—is still an impure one: to be strictly just, it must have the sanction and consent of the governed. It can have no pure right over my person and property but what I concede to it. The progress from an absolute to a limited monarchy, from a limited monarchy to a democracy, is a progress toward a true respect for the individual. Even the Chinese philosopher was wise enough to regard the individual as the basis of the empire. Is a democracy, such as we know it, the last improvement possible in government? Is it not possible to take a step further towards recognizing and organizing the rights of man? There will never be a really free and enlightened State until the State comes to recognize the individual as a higher and independent power, from which all its own power and authority are derived, and treats him accordingly. I please myself with imagining a State at last which can afford to be just to all men, and to treat the individual with respect as a neighbor; which even would not think it inconsistent with its own repose if a few were to live aloof from it, not meddling with it, nor embraced by it, who fulfilled all the duties of neighbors and fellow-men. A State which bore this kind of fruit, and suffered it to drop off as fast as it ripened, would prepare the way for a still more perfect and glorious State, which also I have imagined, but not yet anywhere seen.

BERTRAND RUSSELL

Bertrand Russell, philosopher, mathematician, educator, prolific essayist, controversial social critic, and pacifist leader, was born in England in 1872, the son of a family prominent in English history since the early sixteenth century. Educated (and since 1944 a Fellow) at Trinity College, Cambridge, he has also taught or lectured at Harvard, Chicago, UCLA, and many other schools in this country. His career has been both dis-

tinguished and lively and has often brought him into the center of public attention. He won early renown for his Principia Mathematica (1910–1913), written with Alfred North Whitehead, and early notoriety when he served a jail sentence as a conscientious objector in World War I. His academic visit to America in 1940 caused a furor when a New York State Supreme Court order forbade his appointment as Professor of Philosophy at CCNY, presumably because of his controversial views on sex and marriage, and when unsuccessful attempts were made to oust him from a lectureship at Harvard that same year. In 1950 he won the Nobel Prize for literature "in recognition of his manysided and significant authorship in which he has constantly figured as a defender of humanity and freedom of thought." In the last decade, Russell has devoted a large part of his efforts to pacifist activities. In 1961 he was once again jailed, this time for inciting pacifist demonstrators to a "breach of peace." More recently he has founded the Bertrand Russell Peace Foundation and the Atlantic Peace Foundation. This essay below, which we have entitled "The Committee of 100," is taken from A Matter of Life (1963), a collection of essays (edited by Clara Urquhart) concerned with "the moral sickness of which nuclear danger is but the most frightening symptom."

Russell's bibliography is so extensive that we can do no more than suggest a few of his best known volumes. These include Introduction to Mathematical Philosophy *(1919),* Sceptical Essays *(1928),* Marriage and Morals *(1929),* Education and the Social Order *(1932),* In Praise of Idleness *(1935),* A History of Western Philosophy *(1945),* Authority and the Individual *(1949),* Why I Am Not a Christian *(1957), and* Has Man a Future? *(1963).*

THE COMMITTEE OF 100

The Committee of 100, as your readers are aware, calls for non-violent civil disobedience on a large scale as a means of inducing the British Government (and others, we hope, in due course) to abandon nuclear weapons and the protection that they are supposed to afford. Many critics have objected that civil disobedience is immoral, at any rate where the government is democratic. It is my purpose to combat this view, not in general, but in the case of non-violent civil disobedience on behalf of certain aims advocated by the Committee of 100.

It is necessary to begin with some abstract principles of ethics. There are, broadly speaking, two types of ethical theory. One of these, which is exemplified in the Decalogue, lays down rules of conduct which are supposed to hold in all cases, regardless of the effects of obeying them. The other theory, while admitting that some rules of conduct are valid in a very great majority of cases, is prepared to consider the consequences of actions and to permit breaches of the rules where the consequences of obeying the rules are obviously undesirable. In practice, most people adopt the second point of view, and only appeal to the first in controversies with opponents.

Let us take a few examples. Suppose a physically powerful man, suffering from hydrophobia, was about to bite your children, and the only way of preventing him was to kill him. I think very few people would think you unjustified in adopting this method of saving your children's lives. Those who thought you justified would not deny that the prohibition of murder is *almost* always right. Probably they would go on to say that this particular sort of killing should not be called 'murder'. They would define 'murder' as 'unjustifiable homicide'. In that case, the precept that murder is wrong becomes a tautology, but the ethical question remains: 'What sort of killing is to be labelled as murder?' Or take, again, the commandment not to steal. Almost everybody would agree that in an immense majority of cases it is right to obey this commandment. But suppose you were a refugee, fleeing with your family from persecution, and you could not obtain food except by stealing. Most people would agree that you would be justified in stealing. The only exceptions would be those who approved of the tyranny from which you were trying to escape.

There have been many cases in history where the issue was not so clear. In the time of Pope Gregory VI, simony was rife in the Church. Pope Gregory VI, by means of simony, became Pope and did so in order to abolish simony. In this he was largely successful, and final success was achieved by his disciple and admirer, Pope Gregory VII, who was one of the most illustrious of Popes. I will not express an opinion on the conduct of Gregory VI, which has remained a controversial issue down to the present day.

The only rule, in all such doubtful cases, is to consider the consequences of the action in question. We must include among these consequences the bad effect of weakening respect for a rule which is usually right. But, even when this is taken into account, there will be cases where even the most generally acceptable rule of conduct should be broken.

So much for general theory. I will come now one step nearer to the moral problem with which we are concerned.

What is to be said about a rule enjoining respect for law? Let us first consider the arguments in favour of such a rule. Without law, a civilized community is impossible. Where there is general disrespect for the law, all kinds of evil consequences are sure to follow. A notable example was the failure of prohibition in America. In this case it became obvious that the only cure was a change in the law, since it was impossible to obtain general respect for the law as it stood. This view prevailed, in spite of the fact that those who broke the law were not actuated by what are called conscientious motives. This case made it obvious that respect for the law has two sides. If there is to be respect for the law, the law must be generally considered to be worthy of respect.

The main argument in favour of respect for law is that, in disputes between two parties, it substitutes a neutral authority for private bias which would be likely in the absence of law. The force which the law can exert is, in most such cases, irresistible, and therefore only has to be invoked in the case of a minority of reckless criminals. The net result is a community in which most people are peaceful. These reasons for the reign of law are admitted in the great majority of cases, except by anarchists. I have no wish to dispute their validity save in exceptional circumstances.

There is one very large class of cases in which the law does not have the merit of being impartial as between the disputants. This is when one of the disputants is the state. The state makes the laws and, unless there is a very vigilant public opinion in defence of justifiable liberties, the state will make the law such as suits its own convenience, which may not be what is for the public good. In the Nuremberg trials war criminals were condemned for obeying the orders of the state, though their condemnation was only possible after the state in question had suffered military defeat. But it is noteworthy that the powers which defeated Germany all agreed that failure to practise civil disobedience may deserve punishment.

Those who find fault with the particular form of civil disobedience which I am concerned to justify maintain that breaches of the law, though they may be justified under a despotic régime, can never be justified in a democracy. I cannot see any validity whatever in this contention. There are many ways in which nominally democratic governments can fail to carry out principles which friends of democracy should respect. Take, for example, the case of Ireland before it achieved independence. Formally, the Irish had the same democratic rights as the British. They could send representatives to Westminster and plead their case by all the received democratic processes. But, in spite of this, they were in a minority which, if they had confined themselves to legal methods, would have been permanent. They won their independence by breaking the law. If they had not broken it, they could not have won.

There are many other ways in which governments, which are nominally democratic, fail to be so. A great many questions are so complex that only a few experts can understand them. When the bank rate is raised or lowered, what proportion of the electorate can judge whether it was right to do so? And, if anyone who has no official position criticizes the action of the Bank of England, the only witnesses who can give authoritative evidence will be men responsible for what has been done, or closely connected with those who are responsible. Not only in questions of finance, but still more in military and diplomatic questions, there is in every civilized state a well-developed technique of concealment. If the government wishes some fact to remain unknown, almost all major organs of publicity will assist in concealment. In such cases it often happens that the truth can only be made known, if at all, by persistent and self-sacrificing efforts involving obloquy and perhaps disgrace. Sometimes, if the matter rouses sufficient passion, the truth comes to be known in the end. This happened, for example, in the Dreyfus Case. But where the matter is less sensational the ordinary voter is likely to be left permanently in ignorance.

For such reasons democracy, though much less liable to abuses than dictatorship, is by no means immune to abuses of power by those in authority or by corrupt interests. If valuable liberties are to be preserved there have to be people willing to criticize authority and even, on occasion, to disobey it.

Those who most loudly proclaim their respect for law are in many cases quite unwilling that the domain of law should extend to international relations. In relations between states the only law is still the law of the jungle. What decides a dispute is the question of which side can cause the greatest number of deaths to the other side. Those who do not accept this criterion are apt to be accused of lack of patriotism. This makes it impossible not to suspect that law is only valued where it already exists, and not as an alternative to war.

This brings me at last to the particular form of non-violent civil disobedience which is advocated and practised by the Committee of 100. Those who study nuclear weapons and the probable course of nuclear war are divided into two classes. There are, on the one hand, people employed by governments, and, on the other hand, unofficial people who are actuated by a realization of the dangers and catastrophes which are probable if governmental policies remain unchanged. There are a number of questions in dispute. I will mention a few of them. What is the likelihood of a nuclear war by accident? What is to be feared from fallout? What proportion of the population is likely to survive an all-out nuclear war? On every one of these questions independent students find that official apologists and policy-makers give answers which, to an unbiased inquirer, appear grossly and murderously misleading. To make known to the general population what independent inquirers believe to be the true answers to these questions is a very difficult matter. Where the truth is difficult to ascertain there is a natural inclination to believe what official authorities assert. This is especially the case when what they assert enables people to dismiss uneasiness as needlessly alarmist. The major organs of publicity feel themselves part of the Establishment and are very reluctant to take a course which the Establishment will frown on. Long and frustrating experience has proved, to those among us who have endeavoured to make unpleasant facts known, that orthodox methods, alone, are insufficient. By means of civil disobedience a certain kind of publicity becomes possible. What we do is reported, though as far as possible our reasons for what we do are not mentioned. The policy of suppressing our reasons, however, has only very partial success. Many people are roused to inquire into questions which they had been willing to ignore. Many people, especially among the young, come to share the opinion that governments, by means of lies and evasions, are luring whole populations to destruction. It seems not unlikely that, in the end, an irresistible popular movement of protest will compel governments to allow their subjects to continue to exist. On the basis of long experience, we are convinced that this object cannot be achieved by law-abiding methods alone. Speaking for myself, I regard this as the most important reason for adopting civil disobedience.

Another reason for endeavouring to spread knowledge about nuclear warfare is the extreme imminence of the peril. Legally legitimate methods of spreading this knowledge have been proved to be very slow, and we believe, on the basis of experience, that only such methods as we have adopted can spread the necessary knowledge before it is too late. As things stand, a nuclear war, probably by accident, may occur at any moment. Each day that passes without such a war is a matter of luck, and it cannot be expected that luck will hold indefinitely. Any day, at any hour, the whole population of Britain may perish. Strategists and negotiators play a leisurely game in which procrastination is one of the received methods. It is urgent that the populations of East and West compel both sides to realize that the time at their disposal is limited and that, while present methods continue, disaster is possible at any moment, and almost certain sooner or later.

There is, however, still another reason for employing non-violent civil disobedience which is very powerful and deserves respect. The programmes of mass extermination, upon which vast sums of public money are being spent, must fill every humane person with feelings of utter horror. The West is told that communism is wicked; the East is told that capitalism is wicked. Both sides deduce that the nations which favour either are to be 'obliterated', to use Khrushchev's word. I do not doubt that each side is right in thinking that a nuclear war would destroy the other side's 'ism', but each side is hopelessly mistaken if it thinks that a nuclear war could establish its own 'ism'. Nothing that either East or West desires can result from a nuclear war. If both sides could be made to understand this, it would become possible for both sides to realize that there can be no victory for either, but only total defeat for both. If this entirely obvious fact were publicly admitted in a joint statement by Khrushchev and Kennedy, a compromise method of coexistence could be negotiated giving each side quite obviously a thousand times more of what it wants than could be achieved by war. The utter uselessness of war, in the present age, is completely obvious except to those who have been so schooled in past traditions that they are incapable of thinking in terms of the world that we now have to live in. Those of us who protest against nuclear weapons and nuclear war cannot acquiesce in a world in which each man owes such freedom as remains to him to the capacity of his government to cause many hundreds of millions of deaths by pressing a button. This is to us an abomination, and rather than seem to acquiesce in it we are willing, if necessary, to become outcasts and to suffer whatever obloquy and whatever hardship may be involved in standing aloof from the governmental framework. This thing is a horror. It is something in the shadow of which nothing good can flourish. I am convinced that, on purely political grounds, our reasoned case is unanswerable. But, beyond all political considerations, there is the determination not to be an accomplice in the worst crime that human beings have ever contemplated. We are shocked, and rightly shocked, by Hitler's extermination of six million Jews, but the governments of East and West calmly contemplate the possibility of a massacre at least a hundred times greater than that perpetrated by Hitler. Those who realize the magnitude of this horror cannot even *seem* to acquiesce in the policies from which it springs. It is this feeling, much more than any political calculation, that gives fervour and strength to our movement, a kind of fervour and a kind of strength which, if a nuclear war does not soon end us all, will make our movement grow until it reaches the point where governments can no longer refuse to let mankind survive.

MARTIN LUTHER KING, Jr.

Martin Luther King was born in Georgia in 1929 and educated at Morehouse College, Crozer Theological Seminary, and Boston University. He became a Baptist minister in Montgomery, Alabama, in 1954. The next year he launched the now famous Montgomery bus boycott. Since then Dr. King has become a forceful advocate of non-violent disobedience in the civil rights struggle. Founder and President of the Southern Christian Leadership Conference, he was a leader of the 1963 "March on Washington" and a participant in many of the demonstrations against segregation which followed in its wake. In 1964 he received the Nobel Peace Prize.

A leading spokesman for civil rights, his writings include Stride

Toward Freedom *(1958)*, Strength to Love *(1963)*, *and* Why We Can't Wait *(1964)*, *which includes a revised version of the letter printed below, and an author's note in which he says that "This response to a published statement by eight fellow clergymen from Alabama . . . was composed under somewhat constricting circumstances. Begun on the margins of the newspaper in which the statement appeared while I was in jail, the letter was continued on scraps of writing paper supplied by a friendly Negro trusty, and concluded on a pad my attorneys were eventually permitted to leave me. Although the text remains in substance unaltered, I have indulged in the author's prerogative of polishing it for publication." For its greater immediacy, we present here the unrevised version of the letter, together with the public statement which occasioned it.*

PUBLIC STATEMENT BY EIGHT
ALABAMA CLERGYMEN

April 12, 1963

We the undersigned clergymen are among those who, in January, issued "An Appeal for Law and Order and Common Sense," in dealing with racial problems in Alabama. We expressed understanding that honest convictions in racial matters could properly be pursued in the courts, but urged that decisions of those courts should in the meantime be peacefully obeyed.

Since that time there had been some evidence of increased forbearance and a willingness to face facts. Responsible citizens have undertaken to work on various problems which cause racial friction and unrest. In Birmingham, recent public events have given indication that we all have opportunity for a new constructive and realistic approach to racial problems.

However, we are now confronted by a series of demonstrations by some of our Negro citizens, directed and led in part by outsiders. We recognize the natural impatience of people who feel that their hopes are slow in being realized. But we are convinced that these demonstrations are unwise and untimely.

We agree rather with certain local Negro leadership which has called for honest and open negotiation of racial issues in our area. And we believe this kind of facing of issues can best be accomplished by citizens of our own metropolitan area, white and Negro, meeting with their knowledge and experience of the local situation. All of us need to face that responsibility and find proper channels for its accomplishment.

Just as we formerly pointed out that "hatred and violence have no sanction in our religious and political traditions," we also point out that such actions as incite to hatred and violence, however technically peaceful those actions may be, have not contributed to the resolution of our local problems. We do not believe that these days of new hope are days when extreme measures are justified in Birmingham.

We commend the community as a whole, and the local news media and law enforcement officials in particular, on the calm manner in which these demonstrations have been handled. We urge the public to continue to show restraint should the demonstrations continue, and the law enforcement officials to remain calm and continue to protect our city from violence.

We further strongly urge our own Negro community to withdraw support from these demonstrations, and to unite locally in working peacefully for a better Birmingham. When rights are consistently denied, a cause should be pressed in the courts and in negotiations among local leaders, and not in the streets. We appeal to both our white and Negro citizenry to observe the principles of law and order and common sense.

Signed by:
   C. C. J. CARPENTER, DD., LL.D., Bishop of Alabama
   JOSEPH A. DURICK, D.D., Auxiliary Bishop, Diocese of Mobile-Birmingham
   Rabbi MILTON L. GRAFMAN, Temple Emanu-El, Birmingham, Alabama
   Bishop PAUL HARDIN, Bishop of the Alabama-West Florida Conference of the Methodist Church
   Bishop NOLAN B. HARMON, Bishop of the North Alabama Conference of the Methodist Church
   GEORGE M. MURRAY, D.D., LL.D., Bishop Coadjutor, Episcopal Diocese of Alabama
   EDWARD V. RAMAGE, Moderator, Synod of the Alabama Presbyterian Church in the United States
   EARL STALLINGS, Pastor, First Baptist Church, Birmingham, Alabama

LETTER FROM BIRMINGHAM JAIL

MARTIN LUTHER KING, JR.
Birmingham City Jail
April 16, 1963

Bishop C. C. J. CARPENTER
Bishop JOSEPH A. DURICK
Rabbi MILTON L. GRAFMAN
Bishop PAUL HARDIN
Bishop NOLAN B. HARMON
The Rev. GEORGE M. MURRAY
The Rev. EDWARD V. RAMAGE
The Rev. EARL STALLINGS

My dear Fellow Clergymen,

While confined here in the Birmingham City Jail, I came across your recent statement calling our present activities "unwise and untimely." Seldom, if ever, do I pause to answer criticism of my work and ideas. If I sought to answer all of the criticisms that cross my desk, my secretaries would be engaged in little else in the course of the day and I would have no time for constructive work. But since I feel that you are men of genuine good will and your criticisms are sincerely set forth, I would like to answer your statement in what I hope will be patient and reasonable terms.

I think I should give the reason for my being in Birmingham, since you have been influenced by the argument of "outsiders coming in." I have the honor of serving as president of the Southern Christian Leadership Conference, an organization operating in every Southern state with headquarters in Atlanta, Georgia. We have some eighty-five affiliate organizations all across the South—one being the Alabama Christian Movement for Human Rights. Whenever necessary and possible we share staff, educational, and financial resources with our affiliates. Several months ago our local affiliate here in Birmingham invited us to be on call to engage in a nonviolent direct action program if such were deemed necessary. We readily consented and when the hour came we lived up to our promises. So I am here, along with several members of my staff, because we were invited here. I am here because I have basic organizational ties here. Beyond this, I am in Birmingham because injustice is here. Just as the eighth century prophets left their little villages and carried their "thus saith the Lord" far beyond the boundaries of their home town, and just as the Apostle Paul left his little village of Tarsus and carried the gospel of

Jesus Christ to practically every hamlet and city of the Graeco-Roman world, I too am compelled to carry the gospel of freedom beyond my particular home town. Like Paul, I must constantly respond to the Macedonian call for aid.

Moreover, I am cognizant of the interrelatedness of all communities and states. I cannot sit idly by in Atlanta and not be concerned about what happens in Birmingham. Injustice anywhere is a threat to justice everywhere. We are caught in an inescapable network of mutuality tied in a single garment of destiny. Whatever affects one directly affects all indirectly. Never again can we afford to live with the narrow, provincial "outside agitator" idea. Anyone who lives inside the United States can never be considered an outsider anywhere in this country.

You deplore the demonstrations that are presently taking place in Birmingham. But I am sorry that your statement did not express a similar concern for the conditions that brought the demonstrations into being. I am sure that each of you would want to go beyond the superficial social analyst who looks merely at effects, and does not grapple with underlying causes. I would not hesitate to say that it is unfortunate that so-called demonstrations are taking place in Birmingham at this time, but I would say in more emphatic terms that it is even more unfortunate that the white power structure of this city left the Negro community with no other alternative.

In any nonviolent campaign there are four basic steps: (1) collection of the facts to determine whether injustices are alive; (2) negotiation; (3) self-purification; and (4) direct action. We have gone through all of these steps in Birmingham. There can be no gainsaying of the fact that racial injustice engulfs this community. Birmingham is probably the most thoroughly segregated city in the United States. Its ugly record of police brutality is known in every section of this country. Its unjust treatment of Negroes in the courts is a notorious reality. There have been more unsolved bombings of Negro homes and churches in Birmingham than any city in this nation. These are the hard, brutal, and unbelievable facts. On the basis of these conditions Negro leaders sought to negotiate with the city fathers. But the political leaders consistently refused to engage in good faith negotiation.

Then came the opportunity last September to talk with some of the leaders of the economic community. In these negotiating sessions certain promises were made by the merchants—such as the promise to remove the humiliating racial signs from the stores. On the basis of these promises Rev. Shuttlesworth and the leaders of the Alabama Christian Movement for Human Rights agreed to call a moratorium on any type of demonstrations. As the weeks and months unfolded we realized that we were the victims of a broken promise. The signs remained. As in so many experiences of the past we were confronted with blasted hopes, and the dark shadow of a deep disappointment settled upon us. So we had no alternative except that of preparing for direct action, whereby we would present our very bodies as a means of laying our case before the conscience of the local and national community. We were not unmindful of the difficulties involved. So we decided to go through a process of self-purification. We started having workshops on nonviolence and repeatedly asked ourselves the questions, "Are you able to accept blows without retaliating?" "Are you able to endure the ordeals of jail?"

We decided to set our direct action program around the Easter season, realizing that with the exception of Christmas, this was the largest shopping period of the year. Knowing that a strong economic withdrawal program would be the by-product of direct action, we felt that this was the best time to bring pressure on the merchants for the needed changes. Then it occurred to us that the March election was ahead, and so we speedily decided to postpone action until after election day. When we discovered that Mr. Connor was in the run-off, we decided again to postpone action so that the demonstrations could not be used to cloud the issues. At this time we agreed to begin our nonviolent witness the day after the run-off.

This reveals that we did not move irresponsibly into direct action. We too wanted to see Mr. Connor defeated; so we went through postponement after postponement to aid in this community need. After this we felt that direct action could be delayed no longer.

You may well ask, "Why direct action? Why sit-ins, marches, etc.? Isn't negotiation a better path?" You are exactly right in your call for negotiation. Indeed, this is the purpose of direct action. Nonviolent direct action seeks to create such a crisis and establish such creative tension that a community that has constantly refused to negotiate is forced to confront the issue. It seeks so to dramatize the issue that it can no longer be ignored. I just referred to the creation of tension as a part of the work of the nonviolent resister. This may sound rather shocking. But I must confess that I am not afraid of the word tension. I have earnestly worked and preached against violent tension, but there is a type of constructive nonviolent tension that is necessary for growth. Just as Socrates felt that it was necessary to create a tension in the mind so that individuals could rise from the bondage of myths and half-truths to the unfettered realm of creative analysis and objective appraisal, we must see the need of having nonviolent gadflies to create the kind of tension in society that will help men rise from the dark depths of prejudice and racism to the majestic heights of understanding and brotherhood. So the purpose of the direct action is to create a situation so crisis-packed that it will inevitably open the door to negotiation. We, therefore, concur with you in your call for negotiation. Too long has our beloved Southland been bogged down in the tragic attempt to live in monologue rather than dialogue.

One of the basic points in your statement is that our acts are untimely. Some have asked, "Why didn't you give the new administration time to act?" The only answer that I can give to this inquiry is that the new administration must be prodded about as much as the outgoing one before it acts. We will be sadly mistaken if we feel that the election of Mr. Boutwell will bring the millennium to Birmingham. While Mr. Boutwell is much more articulate and gentle than Mr. Connor, they are both segregationists dedicated to the task of maintaining the status quo. The hope I see in Mr. Boutwell is that he will be reasonable enough to see the futility of massive resistance to desegregation. But he will not see this without pressure from the devotees of civil rights. My friends, I must say to you that we have not made a single gain in civil rights without determined legal and non-violent pressure. History is the long and tragic story of the fact that privileged groups seldom give up their privileges voluntarily. Individuals may see the moral light and voluntarily give up their unjust posture; but as Reinhold Niebuhr has reminded us, groups are more immoral than individuals.

We know through painful experience that freedom is never voluntarily given by the oppressor; it must be demanded by the oppressed. Frankly I have never yet engaged in a direct action movement that was "well timed," according to the timetable of those who have not suffered unduly from the disease of segregation. For years now I have heard the word "Wait!" It rings in the ear of every Negro with a piercing familiarity. This "wait" has almost always meant "never." It has been a tranquilizing thalidomide, relieving the emotional stress for a moment, only to give birth to an ill-formed infant of frustration. We must come to see with the distinguished jurist of yesterday that "justice too long delayed is justice denied." We have waited for more than three hundred and forty years for our constitutional and God-given rights. The nations of Asia and Africa are moving with jet-like speed toward the goal of political independence, and we still creep at horse and buggy pace toward the gaining of a cup of coffee at a lunch counter.

I guess it is easy for those who have never felt the stinging darts of segregation to say wait. But when you have seen vicious mobs lynch your mothers and fathers at will and drown your sisters and brothers at whim; when you have seen hate filled policemen curse, kick, brutalize, and even kill your black brothers and sisters with impunity; when you see the vast majority of your twenty million Negro brothers smothering in an airtight cage of poverty in the midst of an affluent society; when you suddenly find your tongue twisted and your speech stammering as you seek to explain to your six-year-old daughter why she can't go to the public amusement park that has just been advertised on television, and see tears welling up in her little eyes when she is told that Funtown is closed to colored children, and see the depressing clouds of inferiority begin to form in her little mental sky, and see her begin to distort her little personality by unconsciously developing a bitterness toward white people; when you have to concoct an answer for a five-year-old son asking in agonizing pathos: "Daddy, why do white people treat colored people so mean?"; when you take a cross country drive and find it necessary to sleep night after night in the uncomfortable corners of your automobile because no motel will accept you; when you are humiliated day in and day out by nagging signs reading "white" men and "colored"; when your first name becomes "nigger" and your middle name becomes "boy" (however old you are) and your last name becomes "John," and when your wife and mother are never given the respected title "Mrs."; when you are harried by day and haunted by night by the fact that you are a Negro, living constantly at tip-toe stance never quite knowing what to expect next, and plagued with inner fears and outer resentments; when you are forever fighting a degenerating sense of "nobodiness";—then you will understand why we find it difficult to wait. There comes a time when the cup of endurance runs over, and men are no longer willing to be plunged into an abyss of injustice where they experience the bleakness of corroding despair. I hope, sirs, you can understand our legitimate and unavoidable impatience.

You express a great deal of anxiety over our willingness to break laws. This is certainly a legitimate concern. Since we so diligently urge people to obey the Supreme Court's decision of 1954 outlawing segregation in the public schools, it is rather strange and paradoxical to find us consciously breaking laws. One may well ask, "How can you advocate breaking some laws and obeying others?" The answer is found in the fact that there are two types of laws. There are *just* laws and there are *unjust* laws. I would be the first to advocate obeying just laws. One has not only a legal but moral responsibility to obey just laws. Conversely, one has a moral responsibility to disobey unjust laws. I would agree with Saint Augustine that "An unjust law is no law at all."

Now what is the difference between the two? How does one determine when a law is just or unjust? A just law is a man-made code that squares with the moral law or the law of God. An unjust law is a code that is out of harmony with the moral law. To put it in the terms of Saint Thomas Aquinas, an unjust law is a human law that is not rooted in eternal and natural law. Any law that uplifts human personality is just. Any law that degrades human personality is unjust. All segregation statutes are unjust because segregation distorts the soul and damages the personality. It gives the segregator a false sense of superiority and the segregated a false sense of inferiority. To use the words of Martin Buber, the great Jewish philosopher, segregation substitutes an "I-it" relationship for the "I-thou" relationship, and ends up relegating persons to the status of things. So segregation is not only politically, economically, and sociologically unsound, but it is morally wrong and sinful. Paul Tillich has said that sin is separation. Isn't segregation an existential expression of man's tragic separation, an expression of his awful estrangement, his terrible sinfulness? So I can urge men to obey the 1954 decision of the Supreme Court because it is morally right, and I can urge them to disobey segregation ordinances because they are morally wrong.

Let us turn to a more concrete example of just and unjust laws. An unjust law is a code that a majority inflicts on a minority that is not binding on itself. This is *difference* made legal. On the other hand a just law is a code that a majority compels a minority to follow that it is willing to follow itself. This is *sameness* made legal.

Let me give another explanation. An unjust law is a code inflicted upon a minority which that minority had no part in enacting or creating because they did not have the unhampered right to vote. Who can say the legislature of Alabama which set up the segregation laws was democratically elected? Throughout the state of Alabama all types of conniving methods are used to prevent Negroes from becoming registered voters and there are some counties without a single Negro registered to vote despite the fact that the Negro constitutes a majority of the population. Can any law set up in such a state be considered democratically structured?

These are just a few examples of unjust and just laws. There are some instances when a law is just on its face but unjust in its application. For instance, I was arrested Friday on a charge of parading without a permit. Now there is nothing wrong with an ordinance which requires a permit for a parade, but when the ordinance is used to preserve segregation and to deny citizens the First Amendment privilege of peaceful assembly and peaceful protest, then it becomes unjust.

I hope you can see the distinction I am trying to point out. In no sense do I advocate evading or defying the law as the rabid segregationist would do. This would lead to anarchy. One who breaks an unjust law must do it *openly, lovingly* (not hatefully as the white mothers did in New Orleans when they were seen on television screaming "nigger, nigger, nigger") and with a willingness to accept the penalty. I submit that an individual who breaks a law that conscience tells him is unjust, and willingly accepts the penalty by staying in jail to arouse the conscience of the community over its injustice, is in reality expressing the very highest respect for law.

Of course there is nothing new about this kind of civil disobedience. It was seen sublimely in the refusal of Shadrach, Meshach, and Abednego to obey the laws of Nebuchadnezzar because a higher moral law was involved. It was practiced superbly by the early Christians who were willing to face hungry lions and the excruciating pain of chopping blocks, before submitting to certain unjust laws of the Roman Empire. To a degree academic freedom is a reality today because Socrates practiced civil disobedience.

We can never forget that everything Hitler did in Germany was "legal" and everything the Hungarian freedom fighters did in Hungary was "illegal." It was "illegal" to aid and comfort a Jew in Hitler's Germany.

But I am sure that, if I had lived in Germany during that time, I would have aided and comforted my Jewish brothers even though it was illegal. If I lived in a communist country today where certain principles dear to the Christian faith are suppressed, I believe I would openly advocate disobeying these antireligious laws.

I must make two honest confessions to you, my Christian and Jewish brothers. First I must confess that over the last few years I have been gravely disappointed with the white moderate. I have almost reached the regrettable conclusion that the Negroes' great stumbling block in the stride toward freedom is not the White Citizens' "Counciler" or the Ku Klux Klanner, but the white moderate who is more devoted to "order" than to justice; who prefers a negative peace which is the absence of tension to a positive peace which is the presence of justice; who constantly says "I agree with you in the goal you seek, but I can't agree with your methods of direct action"; who paternalistically feels that he can set the time-table for another man's freedom; who lives by the myth of time and who constantly advises the Negro to wait until a "more convenient season." Shallow understanding from people of good will is more frustrating than absolute misunderstanding from people of ill will. Lukewarm acceptance is much more bewildering than outright rejection.

I had hoped that the white moderate would understand that law and order exist for the purpose of establishing justice, and that when they fail to do this they become the dangerously structured dams that block the flow of social progress. I had hoped that the white moderate would understand that the present tension in the South is merely a necessary phase of the transition from an obnoxious negative peace, where the Negro passively accepted his unjust plight, to a substance-filled positive peace, where all men will respect the dignity and worth of human personality. Actually, we who engage in nonviolent direct action are not the creators of tension. We merely bring to the surface the hidden tension that is already alive. We bring it out in the open where it can be seen and dealt with. Like a boil that can never be cured as long as it is covered up but must be opened with all its pus-flowing ugliness to the natural medicines of air and light, injustice must likewise be exposed, with all of the tension its exposing creates, to the light of human conscience and the air of national opinion before it can be cured.

In your statement you asserted that our actions, even though peaceful, must be condemned because they precipitate violence. But can this assertion be logically made? Isn't this like condemning the robbed man because his possession of money precipitated the evil act of robbery? Isn't this like condemning Socrates because his unswerving commitment to truth and his philosophical delvings precipitated the misguided popular mind to make him drink the hemlock? Isn't this like condemning Jesus because His unique God consciousness and never-ceasing devotion to His will precipitated the evil act of crucifixion? We must come to see, as federal courts have consistently affirmed, that it is immoral to urge an individual to withdraw his efforts to gain his basic constitutional rights because the quest precipitates violence. Society must protect the robbed and punish the robber.

I had also hoped that the white moderate would reject the myth of time. I received a letter this morning from a white brother in Texas which said: "All Christians know that the colored people will receive equal rights eventually, but is it possible that you are in too great of a religious hurry? It has taken Christianity almost 2000 years to accomplish what it has. The teachings of Christ take time to come to earth." All that is said here grows out of a tragic misconception of time. It is the strangely irrational notion that there is something in the very flow of time that will inevitably cure all ills. Actually time is neutral. It can be used either destructively or constructively. I am coming to feel that the people of ill will have used time much more effectively than the people of good will. We will have to repent in this generation not merely for the vitriolic words and actions of the bad people, but for the appalling silence of the good people. We must come to see that human progress never rolls in on wheels of inevitability. It comes through the tireless efforts and persistent work of men willing to be co-workers with God, and without this hard work time itself becomes an ally of the forces of social stagnation.

We must use time creatively, and forever realize that the time is always ripe to do right. Now is the time to make real the promise of democracy, and transform our pending national elegy into a creative psalm of brotherhood. Now is the time to lift our national policy from the quicksand of racial injustice to the solid rock of human dignity.

You spoke of our activity in Birmingham as extreme. At first I was rather disappointed that fellow clergymen would see my nonviolent efforts as those of the extremist. I started thinking about the fact that I stand in the middle of two opposing forces in the Negro community. One is a force of complacency made up of Negroes who, as a result of long years of oppression, have been so completely drained of self-respect and a sense of "somebodiness" that they have adjusted to segregation, and of a few Negroes in the middle class who, because of a degree of academic and economic security, and because at points they profit by segregation, have unconsciously become insensitive to the problems of the masses. The other force is one of bitterness and hatred and comes perilously close to advocating violence. It is expressed in the various black nationalist groups that are springing up over the nation, the largest and best known being Elijah Muhammad's Muslim movement. This movement is nourished by the contemporary frustration over the continued existence of racial discrimination. It is made up of people who have lost faith in America, who have absolutely repudiated Christianity, and who have concluded that the white man is an incurable "devil." I have tried to stand between these two forces saying that we need not follow the "do-nothingism" of the complacent or the hatred and despair of the black nationalist. There is the more excellent way of love and nonviolent protest. I'm grateful to God that, through the Negro church, the dimension of nonviolence entered our struggle. If this philosophy had not emerged I am convinced that by now many streets of the South would be flowing with floods of blood. And I am further convinced that if our white brothers dismiss us as "rabble rousers" and "outside agitators"—those of us who are working through the channels of nonviolent direct action—and refuse to support our nonviolent efforts, millions of Negroes, out of frustration and despair, will seek solace and security in black nationalist ideologies, a development that will lead inevitably to a frightening racial nightmare.

Oppressed people cannot remain oppressed forever. The urge for freedom will eventually come. This is what has happened to the American Negro. Something within has reminded him of his birthright of freedom; something without has reminded him that he can gain it. Consciously and unconsciously, he has been swept in by what the Germans call the *Zeitgeist*, and with his black brothers of Africa, and his brown and yellow brothers of Asia, South America, and the Caribbean, he is moving with a sense of cosmic urgency toward the promised land of racial justice. Recognizing this vital urge that has engulfed the Negro community, one should readily understand public demonstrations. The Negro has many pent-up resentments and latent frustrations. He has to get them out. So let him march sometime; let him have his prayer pilgrimages to the city hall; understand why he must have sit-ins and freedom rides. If his repressed emotions do not come out in these nonviolent ways, they will come out in ominous expressions of violence. This is not a threat; it is a fact of history. So I have not said to my people, "Get rid of your discontent." But I have tried to say that this normal and healthy discontent can be channeled through the creative outlet of nonviolent direct action. Now this approach is being dismissed as extremist. I must admit that I was initially disappointed in being so categorized.

But as I continued to think about the matter I gradually gained a bit of satisfaction from being considered an extremist. Was not Jesus an extremist in love? "Love your enemies, bless them that curse you, pray for them that despitefully use you." Was not Amos an extremist for justice— "Let justice roll down like waters and righteousness like a mighty stream." Was not Paul an extremist for the gospel of Jesus Christ—"I bear in my body the marks of the Lord Jesus." Was not Martin Luther an extremist— "Here I stand; I can do none other so help me God." Was not John Bunyan an extremist—"I will stay in jail to the end of my days before I make a butchery of my conscience." Was not Abraham Lincoln an extremist—"This nation cannot survive half slave and half free." Was not Thomas Jefferson an extremist—"We hold these truths to be self evident that all men are created equal." So the question is not whether we will be extremist but what kind of extremist will we be. Will we be extremists for hate or will we be extremists for love? Will we be extremists for the preservation of injustice—or will we be extremists for the cause of justice? In that dramatic scene on Calvary's hill three men were crucified. We must never forget that all three were crucified for the same crime—the crime of extremism. Two were extremists for immorality, and thus fell below their environment. The other, Jesus Christ, was an extremist for love, truth, and goodness, and thereby rose above His environment. So, after all, maybe the South, the nation, and the world are in dire need of creative extremists.

I had hoped that the white moderate would see this. Maybe I was too optimistic. Maybe I expected too much. I guess I should have realized that few members of a race that has oppressed another race can understand or appreciate the deep groans and passionate yearnings of those that have been oppressed, and still fewer have the vision to see that injustice must be rooted out by strong, persistent, and determined action. I am thankful, however, that some of our white brothers have grasped the meaning of this social revolution and committed themselves to it. They are still all too small in quantity, but they are big in quality. Some like Ralph McGill, Lillian Smith, Harry Golden, and James Dabbs have written about our struggle in eloquent, prophetic, and understanding terms. Others have marched with us down nameless streets of the South. They have languished in filthy, roach-infested jails, suffering the abuse and brutality of angry policemen who see them as "dirty nigger lovers." They, unlike so many of their moderate brothers and sisters, have recognized the urgency of the moment and sensed the need for powerful "action" antidotes to combat the disease of segregation.

Let me rush on to mention my other disappointment. I have been so greatly disappointed with the white Church and its leadership. Of course there are some notable exceptions. I am not unmindful of the fact that each of you has taken some significant stands on this issue. I commend you, Rev. Stallings, for your Christian stand on this past Sunday, in welcoming Negroes to your worship service on a non-segregated basis. I commend the Catholic leaders of this state for integrating Springhill College several years ago.

But despite these notable exceptions I must honestly reiterate that I have been disappointed with the Church. I do not say that as one of those negative critics who can always find something wrong with the Church. I say it as a minister of the gospel, who loves the Church; who was nurtured in its bosom; who has been sustained by its spiritual blessings and who will remain true to it as long as the cord of life shall lengthen.

I had the strange feeling when I was suddenly catapulted into the leadership of the bus protest in Montgomery several years ago that we would have the support of the white Church. I felt that the white ministers, priests, and rabbis of the South would be some of our strongest allies. Instead, some have been outright opponents, refusing to understand the freedom movement and misrepresenting its leaders; all too many others have been more cautious than courageous and have remained silent behind the anesthetizing security of stained glass windows.

In spite of my shattered dreams of the past, I came to Birmingham with the hope that the white religious leadership of this community would see the justice of our cause and, with deep moral concern, serve as the channel through which our just grievances could get to the power structure. I had hoped that each of you would understand. But again I have been disappointed.

I have heard numerous religious leaders of the South call upon their worshippers to comply with a desegregation decision because it is the law, but I have longed to hear white ministers say follow this decree because integration is morally right and the Negro is your brother. In the midst of blatant injustices inflicted upon the Negro, I have watched white churches stand on the sideline and merely mouth pious irrelevancies and sanctimonious trivialities. In the midst of a mighty struggle to rid our nation of racial and economic injustice, I have heard so many ministers say, "Those are social issues with which the Gospel has no real concern," and I have watched so many churches commit themselves to a completely other-worldly religion which made a strange distinction between body and soul, the sacred and the secular.

So here we are moving toward the exit of the twentieth century with a religious community largely adjusted to the status quo, standing as a tail light behind other community agencies rather than a headlight leading men to higher levels of justice.

I have travelled the length and breadth of Alabama, Mississippi, and all the other Southern states. On sweltering summer days and crisp autumn mornings I have looked at her beautiful churches with their spires pointing heavenward. I have beheld the impressive outlay of her massive religious education buildings. Over and over again I have found myself asking: "Who worships here? Who is their God? Where were their voices when the lips of Governor Barnett dripped with words of interposition and nullification? Where were they when Governor Wallace gave the clarion call for defiance and hatred? Where were their voices of support when tired, bruised, and weary Negro men and women decided to rise from the dark dungeons of complacency to the bright hills of creative protest?"

Yes, these questions are still in my mind. In deep disappointment, I have wept over the laxity of the Church. But be assured that my tears have been tears of love. There can be no deep disappointment where there is not deep love. Yes, I love the Church; I love her sacred walls. How could I do otherwise? I am in the rather unique position of being the son, the grandson, and the great grandson of preachers. Yes, I see the Church as the body of Christ. But, oh! How we have blemished and scarred that body through social neglect and fear of being nonconformist.

There was a time when the Church was very powerful. It was during that period when the early Christians rejoiced when they were deemed worthy to suffer for what they believed. In those days the Church was not merely a thermometer that recorded the ideas and principles of popular opinion; it was a thermostat that transformed the mores of society. Wherever the early Christians entered a town the power structure got disturbed and immediately sought to convict them for being "disturbers of the peace" and "outside agitators." But they went on with the conviction that they were a "colony of heaven" and had to obey God rather than man. They were small in number but big in commitment. They were too God-intoxicated to be "astronomically intimidated." They brought an end to such ancient evils as infanticide and gladiatorial contest.

Things are different now. The contemporary Church is so often a weak, ineffectual voice with an uncertain sound. It is so often the arch-supporter of the status quo. Far from being disturbed by the presence of the Church, the power structure of the average community is consoled by the Church's silent and often vocal sanction of things as they are.

But the judgment of God is upon the Church as never before. If the Church of today does not recapture the sacrificial spirit of the early Church, it will lose its authentic ring, forfeit the loyalty of millions, and be dismissed as an irrelevant social club with no meaning for the twentieth century. I am meeting young people every day whose disappointment with the Church has risen to outright disgust.

Maybe again I have been too optimistic. Is organized religion too inextricably bound to the status quo to save our nation and the world? Maybe I must turn my faith to the inner spiritual Church, the church within the Church, as the true *ecclesia* and the hope of the world. But again I am thankful to God that some noble souls from the ranks of organized religion have broken loose from the paralyzing chains of conformity and joined us as active partners in the struggle for freedom. They have left their secure congregations and walked the streets of Albany, Georgia, with us. They have gone through the highways of the South on torturous rides for freedom. Yes, they have gone to jail with us. Some have been kicked out of their churches and lost the support of their bishops and fellow ministers. But they have gone with the faith that right defeated is stronger than evil triumphant. These men have been the leaven in the lump of the race. Their witness has been the spiritual salt that has preserved the true meaning of the Gospel in these troubled times. They have carved a tunnel of hope through the dark mountain of disappointment.

I hope the Church as a whole will meet the challenge of this decisive hour. But even if the Church does not come to the aid of justice, I have no despair about the future. I have no fear about the outcome of our struggle in Birmingham, even if our motives are presently misunderstood. We will reach the goal of freedom in Birmingham and all over the nation, because the goal of America is freedom. Abused and scorned though we may be, our destiny is tied up with the destiny of America. Before the pilgrims landed at Plymouth, we were here. Before the pen of Jefferson etched across the pages of history the majestic words of the Declaration of Independence, we were here. For more than two centuries our fore-parents labored in this country without wages; they made cotton "king"; and they built the homes of their masters in the midst of brutal injustice and shameful humiliation—and yet out of a bottomless vitality they continued to thrive and develop. If the inexpressible cruelties of slavery could not stop us, the opposition we now face will surely fail. We will win our freedom because the sacred heritage of our nation and the eternal will of God are embodied in our echoing demands.

I must close now. But before closing I am impelled to mention one other point in your statement that troubled me profoundly. You warmly commended the Birmingham police force for keeping "order" and "preventing violence." I don't believe you would have so warmly commended the police force if you had seen its angry violent dogs literally biting six unarmed, nonviolent Negroes. I don't believe you would so quickly commend the policemen if you would observe their ugly and inhuman treatment of Negroes here in the city jail; if you would watch them push and curse old Negro women and young Negro girls; if you would see them slap and kick old Negro men and young Negro boys; if you will observe them, as they did on two occasions, refuse to give us food because we wanted to sing our grace together. I'm sorry that I can't join you in your praise for the police department.

It is true that they have been rather disciplined in their public handling of the demonstrators. In this sense they have been rather publicly "nonviolent." But for what purpose? To preserve the evil system of segregation. Over the last few years I have consistently preached that nonviolence demands that the means we use must be as pure as the ends we seek. So I have tried to make it clear that it is wrong to use immoral means to attain moral ends. But now I must affirm that it is just as wrong, or even more so, to use moral means to preserve immoral ends. Maybe Mr. Connor and his policemen have been rather publicly nonviolent, as Chief Prichett was in Albany, Georgia, but they have used the moral means of nonviolence to maintain the immoral end of flagrant racial injustice. T. S. Eliot has said that there is no greater treason than to do the right deed for the wrong reason.

I wish you had commended the Negro sit-inners and demonstrators of Birmingham for their sublime courage, their willingness to suffer, and their amazing discipline in the midst of the most inhuman provocation. One day the South will recognize its real heroes. They will be the James Merediths, courageously and with a majestic sense of purpose, facing jeering and hostile mobs and the agonizing loneliness that characterizes the life of the pioneer. They will be old, oppressed, battered Negro women, symbolized in a seventy-two year old woman of Montgomery, Alabama, who rose up with a sense of dignity and with her people decided not to ride the segregated buses, and responded to one who inquired about her tiredness with ungrammatical profundity: "My feets is tired, but my soul is rested." They will be young high school and college students, young ministers of the gospel and a host of the elders, courageously and nonviolently sitting in at lunch counters and willingly going to jail for conscience sake. One day the South will know that when these disinherited children of God sat down at lunch counters they were in reality standing up for the best in the American dream and the most sacred values in our Judeo-Christian heritage, and thus carrying our whole nation back to great wells of democracy which were dug deep by the founding fathers in the formulation of the Constitution and the Declaration of Independence.

Never before have I written a letter this long (or should I say a book?). I'm afraid that it is much too long to take your precious time. I can assure you that it would have been much shorter if I had been writing from a comfortable desk, but what else is there to do when you are alone for days in the dull monotony of a narrow jail cell other than write long letters, think strange thoughts, and pray long prayers?

If I have said anything in this letter that is an overstatement of the truth and is indicative of an unreasonable impatience, I beg you to forgive me. If I have said anything in this letter that is an understatement of the truth and is indicative of my having a patience that makes me patient with anything less than brotherhood, I beg God to forgive me.

I hope this letter finds you strong in the faith. I also hope that circumstances will soon make it possible for me to meet each of you, not as an integrationist or a civil rights leader, but as a fellow clergyman and a Christian brother. Let us all hope that the dark clouds of racial prejudice will soon pass away and the deep fog of misunderstanding will be lifted from our fear-drenched communities and in some not too distant tomorrow the radiant stars of love and brotherhood will shine over our great nation with all of their scintillating beauty.

Yours for the cause of
Peace and Brotherhood

MARTIN LUTHER KING, JR.

Censorship

Censorship is at least as old as the ancient world. Protagoras' treatise, *Concerning Gods,* was burned in fifth-century B.C. Athens; the attacks on Cleon in Aristophanes' *The Acharnians* led to an Athenian "censorship" law; and the Romans had, of course, their Censors. But it was the invention of printing which brought forth the more systematic censorship of the modern world.

Until the nineteenth century, political and religious censorship caused the greatest debate. Milton's classic *Areopagitica*—not reprinted here because of its great length—attacked the licensing act of 1643 "in order to deliver the press from the restraints with which it was encumbered." "God," writes Milton, "trusts [man] with the gift of reason to be his own chooser"; he thus presents an argument against censorship of any kind.

Political censorship is still an issue today; to see this we do not need to turn to the obvious example of totalitarian governments. Although we in America tend to take "freedom of the press" for granted, we accept direct censorship for "security" reasons, and our press can be subjected to powerful indirect censorship, both from the government and from itself. The essays below, however, focus on the ancient concern with moral censorship—often debated today in terms of pornography and obscenity. Plato and Father Gardiner speak for the necessity of censorship in moral education. Walter Lippmann explains censorship as basically a conservative implement, used to defend the existing order against rebel attack. Henry Miller and Judge Woolsey present different arguments—much more different in tone than in attitude—against literary censorship.

PLATO

FROM THE REPUBLIC

We present below two excerpts from The Republic—*one from Book II and one from Book X—the Jowett translation, third edition. For information on Plato and his works, see page 153.*

•

[*Socrates is speaking to Adeimantus*]

. . .

You know also that the beginning is the most important part of any work, especially in the case of a young and tender thing; for that is the time at which the character is being formed and the desired impression is more readily taken.

Quite true.

And shall we just carelessly allow children to hear any casual tales which may be devised by casual persons, and to receive into their minds ideas for the most part the very opposite of those which we should wish them to have when they are grown up?

We cannot.

Then the first thing will be to establish a censorship of the writers of fiction, and let the censors receive any tale of fiction which is good, and reject the bad; and we will desire mothers and nurses to tell their children the authorised ones only. Let them fashion the mind with such tales, even more fondly than they mould the body with their hands; but most of those which are now in use must be discarded.

Of what tales are you speaking? he said.

You may find a model of the lesser in the greater, I said; for they are necessarily of the same type, and there is the same spirit in both of them.

Very likely, he replied; but I do not as yet know what you would term the greater.

Those, I said, which are narrated by Homer and Hesiod, and the rest of the poets, who have ever been the great story-tellers of mankind.

But which stories do you mean, he said; and what fault do you find with them?

A fault which is most serious, I said; the fault of telling a lie, and, what is more, a bad lie.

But when is this fault committed?

Whenever an erroneous representation is made of the nature of gods and heroes,—as when a painter paints a portrait not having the shadow of a likeness to the original.

Yes, he said, that sort of thing is certainly very blameable; but what are the stories which you mean?

First of all, I said, there was that greatest of all lies, in high places, which the poet told about Uranus, and which was a bad lie too,—I mean what Hesiod says that Uranus did, and how Cronus retaliated on him. The doings of Cronus, and the sufferings which in turn his son inflicted upon him, even if they were true, ought certainly not to be lightly told to young and thoughtless persons; if possible, they had better be buried in silence. But if there is an absolute necessity for their mention, a chosen few might hear them in a mystery, and they should sacrifice not a common [Eleusinian] pig, but some huge and unprocurable victim; and then the number of the hearers will be very few indeed.

Why, yes, said he, those stories are extremely objectionable.

Yes, Adeimantus, they are stories not to be repeated in our State; the young man should not be told that in committing the worst of crimes he is far from doing anything outrageous; and that even if he chastises his father when he does wrong, in whatever manner, he will only be following the example of the first and greatest among the gods.

I entirely agree with you, he said; in my opinion those stories are quite unfit to be repeated.

Neither, if we mean our future guardians to regard the habit of quarrelling among themselves as of all things the basest, should any word be said to them of the wars in heaven, and of the plots and fightings of the gods against one another, for they are not true. No, we shall never mention the battles of the giants, or let them be embroidered on garments; and we shall be silent about the innumerable other quarrels of gods and heroes with their friends and relatives. If they would only believe us we would tell them that quarrelling is unholy, and that never up to this time has there been any quarrel between citizens; this is what old men and old women should begin by telling children; and when they grow up, the poets also should be told to compose for them in a similar spirit. But the narrative of Hephaestus binding Here his mother, or how on another occasion Zeus sent him flying for taking her part when she was being beaten, and all the battles of the gods in Homer—these tales must not be admitted into our State, whether they are supposed to have an allegorical meaning or not. For a young person cannot judge what is allegorical and what is literal; anything that he receives into his mind at that age is likely to become indelible and unalterable; and therefore it is most important that the tales which the young first hear should be models of virtuous thoughts.

There you are right, he replied; but if any one asks where are such models to be found and of what tales are you speaking—how shall we answer him?

I said to him, You and I, Adeimantus, at this moment are not poets, but founders of a State: now the founders of a State ought to know the general forms in which poets should cast their tales, and the limits which must be observed by them, but to make the tales is not their business.

Very true, he said; but what are these forms of theology which you mean?

Something of this kind, I replied:—God is always to be represented as he truly is, whatever be the sort of poetry, epic, lyric or tragic, in which the representation is given.

Right.

And is he not truly good? and must he not be represented as such?

Certainly.

And no good thing is hurtful?

No, indeed.

And that which is not hurtful hurts not?

Certainly not.

And that which hurts not does no evil?

No.

And can that which does no evil be a cause of evil?

Impossible.

And the good is advantageous?

Yes.

And therefore the cause of well-being?

Yes.

It follows therefore that the good is not the cause of all things, but of the good only?

Assuredly.

Then God, if he be good, is not the author of all things, as the many assert, but he is the cause of a few things only, and not of most things that occur to men. For few are the goods of human life, and many are the evils, and the good is to be attributed to God alone; of the evils the causes are to be sought elsewhere, and not in him.

That appears to me to be most true, he said.

Then we must not listen to Homer or to any other poet who is guilty of the folly of saying that two casks

'Lie at the threshold of Zeus, full of lots, one of good, the other of evil lots,'

and that he to whom Zeus gives a mixture of the two

   'Sometimes meets with evil fortune, at other times with good;'

but that he to whom is given the cup of unmingled ill,

      'Him wild hunger drives o'er the beauteous earth.'

And again—

      'Zeus, who is the dispenser of good and evil to us.'

And if any one asserts that the violation of oaths and treaties, which was really the work of Pandarus, was brought about by Athene and Zeus, or that the strife and contention of the gods was instigated by Themis and Zeus, he shall not have our approval; neither will we allow our young men to hear the words of Aeschylus, that

'God plants guilt among men when he desires utterly to destroy a house.'

And if a poet writes of the sufferings of Niobe—the subject of the tragedy in which these iambic verses occur—or of the house of Pelops, or of the Trojan war or on any similar theme, either we must not permit him to say that these are the works of God, or if they are of God, he must devise some explanation of them such as we are seeking; he must say that God did what was just and right, and they were the better for being punished; but that those who are punished are miserable, and that God is the author of their misery—the poet is not to be permitted to say; though he may say that the wicked are miserable because they require to be punished, and are benefited by receiving punishment from God; but that God being good is the author of evil to any one is to be strenuously denied, and not to be said or sung or heard in verse or prose by any one whether old or young in any well-ordered commonwealth. Such a fiction is suicidal, ruinous, impious.

   I agree with you, he replied, and am ready to give my assent to the law.

   Let this then be one of our rules and principles concerning the gods, to which our poets and reciters will be expected to conform—that God is not the author of all things, but of good only. . . .

            [Socrates is speaking to Glaucon]
                     • • •

   Hear and judge: The best of us, as I conceive, when we listen to a passage of Homer, or one of the tragedians, in which he represents some pitiful hero who is drawling out his sorrows in a long oration, or weeping, and smiting his breast—the best of us, you know, delight in giving way to sympathy, and are in raptures at the excellence of the poet who stirs our feelings most.

Yes, of course I know.

But when any sorrow of our own happens to us, then you may observe that we pride ourselves on the opposite quality—we would fain be quiet and patient; this is the manly part, and the other which delighted us in the recitation is now deemed to be the part of a woman.

Very true, he said.

Now can we be right in praising and admiring another who is doing that which any one of us would abominate and be ashamed of in his own person?

No, he said, that is certainly not reasonable.

Nay, I said, quite reasonable from one point of view.

What point of view?

If you consider, I said, that when in misfortune we feel a natural hunger and desire to relieve our sorrow by weeping and lamentation, and that this feeling which is kept under control in our own calamities is satisfied and delighted by the poets;—the better nature in each of us, not having been sufficiently trained by reason or habit, allows the sympathetic element to break loose because the sorrow is another's; and the spectator fancies that there can be no disgrace to himself in praising and pitying any one who comes telling him what a good man he is, and making a fuss about his troubles; he thinks that the pleasure is a gain, and why should he be supercilious and lose this and the poem too? Few persons ever reflect, as I should imagine, that from the evil of other men something of evil is communicated to themselves. And so the feeling of sorrow which has gathered strength at the sight of the misfortunes of others is with difficulty repressed in our own.

How very true!

And does not the same hold also of the ridiculous? There are jests which you would be ashamed to make yourself, and yet on the comic stage, or indeed in private, when you hear them, you are greatly amused by them, and are not at all disgusted at their unseemliness;—the case of pity is repeated;—there is a principle in human nature which is disposed to raise a laugh, and this which you once restrained by reason, because you were afraid of being thought a buffoon, is now let out again; and having stimulated the risible faculty at the theatre, you are betrayed unconsciously to yourself into playing the comic poet at home.

Quite true, he said.

And the same may be said of lust and anger and all the other affections, of desire and pain and pleasure, which are held to be inseparable from every action—in all of them poetry feeds and waters the passions instead of drying them up; she lets them rule, although they ought to be con‹ trolled, if mankind are ever to increase in happiness and virtue.

I cannot deny it.

Therefore, Glaucon, I said, whenever you meet with any of the eulo-gists of Homer declaring that he has been the educator of Hellas, and that he is profitable for education and for the ordering of human things, and that you should take him up again and again and get to know him and regulate your whole life according to him, we may love and honour those who say these things—they are excellent people, as far as their lights extend; and we are ready to acknowledge that Homer is the greatest of poets and first of tragedy writers; but we must remain firm in our conviction that hymns to the gods and praises of famous men are the only poetry which ought to be admitted into our State. For if you go beyond this and allow the honeyed muse to enter, either in epic or lyric verse, not law and the reason of mankind, which by common consent have ever been deemed best, but pleasure and pain will be the rulers in our State. . . .

HAROLD C. GARDINER

Harold C. Gardiner was born in Washington, D.C., in 1904 and educated at St. Andrew on Hudson, Woodstock College, and Cambridge University, where he received the Ph.D. In 1935 he was ordained as a priest in the Catholic Church. He has been Board Chairman of the Catholic Book of the Month Club, a member of the Catholic Press Association, and since 1940, literary editor of America, *a national Catholic weekly. His many books include* The Great Books: A Christian Appraisal, *4 vols. (1949–1952);* Fifty Years of the American Novel *(1951);* Catholic Viewpoint on Censorship *(1957), from which we reprint Chapter 1 below;* In All Conscience, *with F. Getlein (1960); and* Movies, Words and Art *(1961).*

AUTHORITY AND THE ROLE OF COERCION

It may seem like taking a very long running start indeed in order to essay a modest broad jump, but any discussion of the problems of modern, and especially American, censorship cannot be sensibly undertaken without laying first a basis for argumentation by sketching the Catholic philosophy on the state and on human freedom. It is to be hoped that the term "Catholic philosophy" will not annoy those not of the Catholic faith who may chance to read these words. The phrase is not used in the sense of describing a "sectarian" system of thought. The philosophy referred to is indeed more aptly termed the *philosophia perennis,* for its roots lie far back in the Judaic and Greco-Roman world, were developed by the medieval Christian philosophers, and have borne fruit in the thinking of the framers of our Declaration of Independence. Many philosophers, political scientists, thinkers on the problems of government and the relations of Church and state hold, at least in general outline, the philosophy of the state and of human freedom that will be sketched in this and the following chapter.

To begin at the beginning, this philosophy holds that the state is a "natural" institution. This means that man, by his very nature, spontaneously but inevitably forms a community with his fellow men; that man is, of his very nature, a "social" being. Since man's nature comes from God, and since man's impulses toward communal living are a natural consequence of his being man, this gravitation is also God-given. This is seen most obviously in the institution of marriage. The first society to which man is naturally drawn, both by the exigencies of his nature and by his historical development, is the familial society. This seminal society, however, proves itself to be inadequate for the fulfillment of man's deepest desires and needs, and so man is induced again by the very bent of his nature to associate with other families—for mutual sociability, protection, comfort, development, and so on.

But, together with his impulses toward societal living, man, even in society, still possesses his individual will, his particular desires and ambitions. Given this fact, itself another God-given attribute, society is faced immediately with the problem of a number of individuals and families trying to get along together for some common purpose, toward some mutually agreed goal—protection against outside inimical forces, let us say, or the development of agricultural ways and means. Obviously there arises the necessity of some compromise; individual differences must be resolved; somebody, or some group selected to deliberate and speak for the whole community, has to make the decisions. And so arises, just as naturally and just as clearly God-given in origin as man's societal nature itself, the institution of authority.

It is not to be thought that authority in a community takes its origin from deficiency. The necessity of authority does not spring from sin—as though only in a group of fallible and fumbling human beings is authority a necessity. Far from being a necessary evil, authority results from the very perfection of the human beings it is destined to weld into community life. Authority arises from the fact of each individual's free will:

it is because each one has free will that individuality must be harnessed, so to speak, if the individuals are to pull as a team for the cohesion and advancement of the community.

Authority in a community, then, has more than what is called a "substitutional" function—that is, a function that makes up for some inherent deficiency in the body to be governed. To be sure, some of the obvious instances of authority that spring to mind show us authority being exercised because there is some sort of "deficiency" in those governed. So parents, for example, exercise their authority over minor children because the children cannot yet know what is best for them. But even if children became overnight as wise and kind and prudent as their parents, parental authority would still exist (though its open exercise might be minimized) because of the very fact that common action in the family demands a source from which decisions must come.

Now the reason for this rather long disquisition on a fundamental concept, which most men of good will find no difficulty in accepting, is that a consequence that is largely overlooked may be brought to light. The consequence is simply and perhaps, to some, startlingly this: authority is not only to be respected but *loved*. If the common purpose of a family—mutual love, peace, prosperity, and so on—is a purpose worthy of love, then the authority that directs the family to that purpose is worthy of love, and not only because authority is the human instrument through which the common purpose may be achieved, but because, just as the family and its essential purposes are natural (i.e., God-instituted), so the authority is natural (i.e., God-instituted).

This is true not merely from a consideration of the origin of society and of the authority which is necessary for the very existence of society, but from a consideration of the purpose or end for which society exists. That end or purpose, in general, is the common good, the good of society as a whole as distinguished from the good of the individuals who make up the whole. Individuals dwell in familial society in such fashion that desires, ambitions, modes of action that might be most delectable for the individual are forgone, sacrificed (or sublimated, as the current phrase goes) for the sake of the good of the whole family. Mother's craving for the mink coat or father's passion for golf yields—or should—to the needs of the family for decent prosperity. Individuals and families dwelling in civil society also conspire, or should conspire, to a common end, which we call the common good and which can be summed up in the phrase "peace and prosperity." An individual or a family yields to some extent its dominion over its wealth and property through the machinery of taxes, for example, not because they like to, but because it is for the common good.

Authority, therefore, is to be respected and loved, not only because it comes, reductively, as the philosophers would say, from God, but because, in its legitimate exercise, it also leads (reductively) to God, because such exercise of authority leads to the common good which is also willed by God.

This philosophy of authority is not only down-to-earth, it reaches to heaven in its sublimity. It may sound like the veriest idealism, but it is not for that reason utopian. Common sense alone will tell us that, if authority is not loved, the vagaries to which any exercise of human authority is subject will sooner or later bring that authority to be feared or hated. It is perhaps almost inevitable, because of the earthiness of our human emotions, that a neutral and sort of bloodless respect for authority cannot long hold the field. This is especially true since authority is not infrequently vested in a person or a party one feels he cannot validly respect. In such a case, if the *principle* of authority is not loved, its imposition by one who is not respected comes easily to bring law and order under fear, suspicion, and hatred. Then one will obey because he must, not because he loves the common good which is, of itself, as the goal of societal action, lovable.

As has been hinted above, it does not follow from this line of thought that any and every *enactment* of authority must be loved. Some enactments may be onerous (such as the paying of taxes) but just; in this case the enactment must be respected, not only in thought, but in actual fulfillment. Other enactments may be ill-considered (such as our late Prohibition law) or unjust; in this case there is recourse, in a properly constituted state, to redress. So we have the system of constitutional checks and balances by which the enactments of the legislative arm are subject to review by the judiciary; thus the goal of the common good, though lost sight of for a time, may be restored as the only proper purpose of the state.

But the principle remains unshaken. Authority, as the necessary instrument by which the parts of the societal whole may conspire to a common end, is an object of love.

The particular relevance of this principle to the problem of censorship will become clear, it is to be hoped, throughout the whole course of this book. Its particular relevance here depends on another aspect of law and authority which must now fit into this preliminary chapter.

One of the essential postulates of law is authority's coercive power. If a society is to strive with any hope of success toward a common goal —peace and prosperity in a commonwealth—the authority governing that society must not only be able to pass laws and to reassess those laws constantly as circumstances change (the role of the interpretations of our Supreme Court); it must also be enabled to enforce those laws and to exact penalties for their violation. This is obviously the point at which respect for authority, let alone love for it, as we have been considering above, comes in for its severest test. It is one thing to be all in favor of sane traffic laws and even to love them in a theoretical sort of way while you are snug in your armchair or gleefully watching some road hog getting his comeuppance at the hands of a traffic cop. It is quite another thing to love the authority that slaps a ticket on you because you temporarily forgot your respect for (and love of) the law. Coercion is never pleasant for those being coerced and, quite obviously, coercion can overstep proper bounds and turn into injustice and tyranny. But coercion that is exercised as a means to prevent the frustration of the common good is as worthy of respect and love as is the authority it is designed to uphold.

One consideration that may serve to put the coercive aspect of law and authority into proper perspective is a consideration of the educative or pedagogical quality of coercion. Restrictions merely for the sake of restriction are never proper or valid, either morally or politically. Such restrictions would be purely the result of the whim of the authority— or, worse, of malice. Restrictions are valid only if they are for the sake of a greater good, a greater liberty. To be restrained to drive your car at not more than fifty miles an hour is an improper infringement of your liberty, *unless* that very restriction allows drivers in general (and pedestrians) a reasonably assured freedom from danger to life and limb.

This principle is so valid that not even the restrictions which God's law puts on our human actions are good *merely* because they are restrictions. The negative precepts of the Ten Commandments look always to a positive freedom. "Thou shalt not commit adultery" means that if you avoid this threat to the stability, happiness, and holiness of married union you will be freed from a burden so that you may go on from there to the fullness of married life as God intends it. The negative precepts, accordingly, may be looked upon as simply clearing away the roadblocks thrown up by our pride and sensuality so that the greater freedom may operate, and that freedom is positive and glorious: "You shall *love* God with your whole heart and with your whole soul and with all your mind, and your neighbor as yourself," or, more gloriously still, "as Christ has loved you."

If the coercive aspect of law and authority is looked on in this way, as a means toward a greater freedom, the pedagogical aspect of coercion becomes clear. Coercion by way of consequence instructs the members of a society (family or state), although the instruction may be painful, that there *is* a common good which the offending member may have been habitually ignoring or temporarily forgetting. St. Thomas Aquinas has much to say on this matter of the pedagogical value of coercion, especially in his *Summa Theologica* (1a–2ae, 95, 1). Here, for instance, is one commentary on the teaching of the Saint:

"Every man needs education and virtuous training. Paternal training, whose proper instrument is persuasion, provides sufficiently for the training of youths who are prone to virtue; on the contrary, those who are prone to vice must be prevented by coercion from doing wrong. . . . By compelling bad boys from doing wrong, a twofold result is secured: first, the tranquillity of honest people is assured; secondly, the bad boys themselves get used to acting honestly, so that they may finally become virtuous, having become able to do voluntarily what they previously did by fear of punishment.

"This elevated conception of the pedagogical function of coercion rests upon the psychological fact that a good habit generated by fear, although non-virtuous in its origin, makes virtue easier, the substitution of good will for fear taking place easily when the exterior acts of virtue have become habitual. Coercion, in the long run, paves the way for persuasion, because habitual automatism turns to voluntariness."[1]

The skeptic or the cynic will probably retort that this concept of the pedagogical value of coercion is a pipe dream and that it is extremely doubtful that the wrongdoer is ever so persuaded by force and restraint that he comes to will and love the good. This happy result is certainly to be discerned frequently enough in the sanctuary of conscience: the sinner, restrained by the fear of hell, for instance, can and does come to love the good. But the point of this discussion is quite other. It may be that in the sphere of external activity—in civic, social, and political life—the mere fact of restraint or coercion rarely convinces the wrongdoer of the good to be desired. It may be that the extortionist or the blackmailer or the arsonist, clapped into jail to restrain his felonous acts, is simply biding his time and meditating ways and means to resume his ill-advised manner of life.

But those who are not so coerced, those who are concerned with the problems of respect for law and authority—they are the ones who ought to be able to consider with dispassion this whole matter of the coercive aspect of authority. The sorry fact of the matter is, however, that all too frequently the very ones who ought to be concerned with the very highest and most exalted concepts of the law are often the ones who, perhaps all unwittingly, are whittling away at one of the very foundations of respect for law—the foundation of its coercive power. So, in this matter of censorship, protests by such organizations as the American Civil Liberties Union against any and all exercises of "censorship" all too often sound as though they are based on the assumption that all coercion exercised by authority is a bad and evil thing, both in itself and in its consequences. Thus, for instance, the following statement issued by the Authors League of America (as reported in the New York *Times* for May 9, 1957):

"[The League has noted] with increasing concern, in the decade since the Second World War, a drift in our national life toward censorship. . . . The impetus in this authoritarian drift is coming mainly from groups who above all should hold totalitarianism in abhorrence: a few religious organizations and a few patriotic organizations, where zeal has overcome wisdom . . .

---

[1] Yves Simon, *Nature and Functions of Authority* (Milwaukee: Marquette University Press, 1940), p. 54.

"The Authors League denies the right of any individual or group in the United States to set limits on the freedom to write, which includes the freedom of publication, distribution and performance of writings."

The obvious drift of this statement, of course, is directed toward groups which endeavor to "censor" outside the operation of the law; but two overtones, it is to be suspected, are also evident. The first is that "censorship" is *ipso facto* "totalitarian." This is a point to be proved, not merely asserted. Beyond that seems to lie the confusion against which this whole chapter is directed: namely, that all coercion or restraint imposed by society on the individual is wrong.

This consideration, however, needs further development in the following chapter, in which we shall discuss more fully the problem of human freedom in the face of legitimate authority. Underlying the false estimate of coercion as being merely a negating and restrictive aspect of authority is the equally false assumption that whatever, especially in a democracy, curtails freedom (but what *type* of freedom is rarely defined, though here lies the specific problem) impedes "progress." The Catholic concept, on the other hand, holds that the very idea of human progress implies necessarily the correlative idea of measure and restraint, internally in a man's own conscience and motives, and externally through the operation of law and of social forces which are not formally legal.

The suspicion that the coercive aspects of authority and law are not to be tolerated by free men is a holdover from the philosophic liberalism of the nineteenth century. The most familiar expression of this bent of mind is found in the cant expression that "ideas have to make their way in the market place." Perhaps the most cogent phrasing of this philosophy is found in the following passage:

"If we refrain from coercing a man for his own good, it is not because his good is indifferent to us, but because it cannot be furthered by coercion. The difficulty is founded on the nature of the good, itself, which on its personal side depends on the spontaneous flow of feeling checked and guided not by external restraint, but by rational self-control. To try to form character by coercion is to destroy it in the making. Personality is not built up from without but grows from within, and the function of the outer order is not to create it, but to provide for it the most suitable conditions for growth. Thus, to the common question whether it is possible to make men good by Act of Parliament, the reply is that it is not possible to compel morality because morality is the act or character of a free agent, but that it is possible to create the conditions under which morality can develop, and among these not the least important is freedom from compulsion by others."[2]

Commenting on this statement, Yves Simon pithily remarks: "The point

---

[2] L. T. Hobhouse, *Liberalism* (New York: Holt, 1911), p. 143.

is, precisely, that good habits possibly determined by coercion are to be numbered among these 'conditions under which morality can develop.' "[3]

Again, these liberals and their modern progeny claim that "an absolute freedom of thought and expression [is] justified, their idea being that in any circumstances whatever, truth can but profit by unrestricted freedom."[4] Let truth go out and jostle with error in the market place, they proclaim, do not restrain or limit error and the expression of it, and the truth will always win out. Now, certainly the Catholic position entertains the utmost respect for the power of truth (*magna est veritas et praevalebit*) and for its ultimate triumph, but that respect is not so naïve as to believe that here and now, in these circumstances, when the truth should already have won and its delayed victory imperils the common good, error must be left uncontrolled. Professor Simon puts his finger on this liberal philosophical error when he says:

"The contribution of error to the development of truth is but a happy occurrence, whose regularity is not guaranteed by any steady principle. Liberals ascribe to accidental occurrences a regularity that accident does not admit of. At the *heart of Liberalism* lies an almost religious belief in a kind of Demiurge immanent in the stream of contingent events, or better, identical with the very stream of contingencies. . . . Owing to this benevolent Spirit of Nature, contingency and chance are supposed to result indefectibly in happy achievements. Wrong use of the human freedom, in the long run at least, does not matter. Regarding both truth-values and economic values, the Liberal confidently relies upon the *laissez faire laissez passer* system. Liberalism is an *optimistic naturalism*."[5]

Another aspect of the "optimistic naturalism" of philosophic liberalism is the rather naïve idolatry of the power of mere education, and by that is meant any educative process that insists exclusively on the freedom to examine and learn. With reference to the problem of censorship, the argument would run that if only "good" books, movies, and what not were made increasingly widespread for the consuming public they would inevitably drive out the "bad." This stand is based, as will be evident, on the prior assumption that the truth will always vanquish error if allowed to compete on an equal footing. But any "equal footing" rests on the further assumption that all men are equal in taste, inclination to virtue, powers of self-control, and a host of other qualities. Surely it is a fact of experience, which even the foes of all and every censorship are themselves constrained to admit, that some people who have indeed been exposed to "good" literature throughout many years of education still seem to prefer the "art" and "girlie" magazines to the reasonably priced classics that can be found on the very same newsstands.

This is not to underestimate the power of education but simply to restate that the educative process, no less than the process of law, neces-

---

[3] *Op. cit.*, p. 56.   [4] *Ibid.*, p. 59.   [5] *Ibid.*, pp. 61–62.

sarily entails a restrictive or coercive element. If the goal of education is a glorious and positive "do"—*do* grow into the full stature of integral manhood—it can be reached only by some inculcation of many a "don't"—*don't* dissipate your energies, debauch your potentialities by running after goals that are unworthy of a man. C. S. Lewis, in his thoughtful and challenging little book, *The Abolition of Man*, has much to say on this entire subject. Here is a small passage which underlines the thought that education alone is not enough to make a man virtuous:

"It still remains true that no justification of virtue will enable a man to be virtuous. Without the aid of *trained* [emphasis supplied] emotions, the intellect is powerless against the animal organism. I had sooner play cards with a man who was quite sceptical about ethics, but bred to believe that 'a gentleman does not cheat,' than against an irreproachable moral philosopher who had been brought up among sharpers. In battle it is not syllogisms that will keep the reluctant nerves and muscles to their post in the third hour of the bombardment."[6]

But the training of the emotions, of the will, of just and noble sentiments, what Plato calls the "spirited element," is something that implicates all sorts of restraining elements in education. The young trainee cannot be thrown out, naked and unarmed, into the market place of clashing ideas and expected to see at once—or perhaps ever—the beauty and force of the truth. Mere exposure to "facts" will never add up to human education. As Mr. Lewis remarks of one he calls the "Innovator" (he is the holder of the thesis that man will always obey the truth if exposed to it): "[He] is trying to get a conclusion in the imperative mood out of premises in the indicative mood; and though he continues trying to all eternity he cannot succeed, for the thing is impossible."[7] To put the potential reader, for instance, in the presence of "good" and "bad" literature, before an openly pornographic book and a wholesome one, and say, "See, the one is good and the other bad," will never, of itself, induce in the reader the conclusion, "I ought to read the one and avoid the other." The premises for that conclusion have to come from a deeper source than the mere struggle between truth and error in the market place. Part of the source is the restrictive or coercive aspect of both law and education.

This stage of our discussion leads immediately into the thorny problem of the proper balance between law (and education) and human freedom. Before we go on to that, however, let us try to gather together some conclusions.

The Catholic viewpoint is that law is to be loved because it is rational and because of its origin and purpose. Its origin is from God; its ultimate purpose is rationally to assure greater freedom.

---

[6] C. S. Lewis, *The Abolition of Man* (New York: Macmillan, 1947), p. 15.
[7] *Ibid.*, p. 20.

One of the necessary postulates of law (or of the exercise of law through authority) is the community's coercive power, the restriction and punishment of evil-doing, of infringements of the law. This onerous element is not less to be loved than the expansive aspects, for it is destined for the same purpose, to facilitate the exercise of freedom.

It follows, therefore, that society, which has the right and duty to establish laws for the common good, has, by the same title, the right *and the duty* to exercise coercion. It would seem superfluous to emphasize this truth were it not for the fact that most of the controversy about censorship seems to rest fundamentally at exactly this crux. A great number of those who oppose censorship in any shape or form deny implicitly (though they may never advert to the fact) that society has the *right* to censor—especially the state in a pluralistic society like the one in which we live. We aver in these pages that the state not only has the *right* but is solemnly bound by the *duty* to censor, under certain circumstances.

It seems odd that this can apparently be the stand of opponents of censorship, since they are quite ready to admit other coercive powers of the state. No one of them would question the right of the state to arrest traffic-law violators, for instance, or to throw dope peddlers into jail, but when it comes to any restrictions or controls in the matter of freedom of expression, they will not only deny the state's duty to protect the common good, but will even call into question its right.

It is hard, no doubt, to reconcile the divergent statements of such organizations as the American Civil Liberties Union. In the "Statement on Censorship Activity by Private Organizations and the National Office of Decent Literature," issued to the press in May 1957, for instance, we read, on the one hand: "Since *any kind* [emphasis supplied] of censorship infringes that constitutionally guaranteed freedom of the press which protects the free exchange of ideas in our country, it is imperative that the American people be warned of the danger in which their freedom stands." Again: "The First and Fourteenth Amendments to the United States Constitution, and the constitutions of the several States, prohibit governmental abridgment of freedom of the press. If one may read, one must be able to buy; if one may buy, others must be able to print and sell." But on the other hand, the American Civil Liberties Union is constrained to recognize that the phrase, "any kind of censorship," is far too wide, for it goes on to state: "If curbs are to be placed on freedom of the press, and these curbs must be based on a clear and present danger of a substantive harm from the publication, they can be imposed only by our courts, through full legal process."

If the Constitution prohibits governmental abridgment of freedom of the press, how can the courts be exercising "full legal process" when they impose curbs, even under "clear and present danger"?

I do not see how the Union can have it both ways, and I believe their fundamental drive is to abolish all kinds of control on all possible kinds of expression and that their stand is that the "full legal process" under which the courts now act is itself unconstitutional. And this, if I am not reading too sinister a purpose into the convictions of men of good will, springs, it seems incontrovertible to me, from a false concept of the nature of coercion in the authority of government.

A further example. In *The Freedom to Read,* published for the National Book Committee, the authors state: "We have argued on philosophic grounds [we shall advert to these arguments in our next chapter] that censorship is unsound, impractical and undesirable." Yet in the very next sentence they go on to say: "On political grounds, recognizing that censorship in the broad sense has been and is being practiced, we shall consider how its operation can be kept strictly in conformity with law and the preservation of rights, in order that it shall not impede directly or indirectly the freedom of expression by which, among other consequences, the dangers of censorship may become more generally recognized."[8] But, again, here is an inconsistency. If censorship is indeed "unsound, impractical and undesirable," then any "law" dealing with it ought to be concerned wholly and solely with eliminating it, lock, stock, and barrel.

The thought will not die that we are back at a basic misapprehension —that any restriction of "freedom" is a block to "progress," and hence that any coercive aspects of the law are always, by their nature, bad aspects and should therefore not only be held to a minimum, which all admit, but eliminated altogether.

Inevitably we come at this point to a consideration of "freedom." Is it an absolute? What is it? Is it the only and essentially indispensable atmosphere under which "progress" can flourish? Before we essay some thoughts on this and, obviously, on its connection with the problems of censorship, let us close this chapter with a pertinent thought from St. Thomas:

"Laws are passed to ensure the smooth running of the commonwealth. Unrestricted rights are not allowed in any civil constitution. Even in a democratic state, where the whole people exercise power, rights are not absolute but relative, though from the equal liberty of all subjects under the law the state may be described as predominantly equalitarian. The statutes passed by a democracy may be just, not because they reach pure and perfect justice, but because they fit the purpose of the regime."[9]

Perhaps, after all is said and done, the opponents of all and any censorship, who are, it would seem, the proponents of freedom as an absolute,

---

[8] By Richard McKeon, Robert K. Merton, and Walter Gellhorn (New York: R. R. Bowker Co., 1957), p. 11.

[9] Commentary in *V Ethics,* lect. 2. This quotation from St. Thomas is taken from the rich store to be found in *St. Thomas Aquinas: Philosophical Texts,* by Thomas Gilby (New York: Oxford Press, 1951), especially from the sections on "Law" and "Community and Society," pp. 352–93.

are devoted to a false ideal of law which does not take sufficiently into account the fact that law, as we know it, is for poor, fallible, striving human beings who *need* the pedagogy of coercion and restraint no less than the expansive skies of liberty and freedom.

WALTER LIPPMANN

Walter Lippmann has been called the Dean of American newspapermen. Born in 1889, he was educated at Harvard and then taught philosophy there as an assistant to George Santayana. He joined the staff of The New Republic *at its founding in 1914, interrupted his journalistic career to serve as assistant to the Secretary of War—doing special work on peace negotiating—and then moved to an editorial position on the* New York World. *In 1931 he joined the staff of the* New York Herald Tribune. *His writings have been syndicated in newspapers throughout the country, and his column "Today and Tomorrow" won him Pulitzer Prizes in 1958 and 1962. The 1958 award cited the "wisdom, perception, and high sense of responsibility with which he has commented for many years on national and international affairs." He has also received numerous honorary degrees and such foreign decorations as the Legion of Honor from France and the Order of Leopold from Norway. His many books include* Liberty and the News *(1920),* Public Opinion *(1922),* The Good Society *(1937),* The Public Philosophy *(1955),* The Coming Tests with Russia *(1961), and* Western Unity and the Common Market *(1962). The essay we present below is Chapter 8 of* Men of Destiny, *first published in 1928.*

THE NATURE OF THE BATTLE
OVER CENSORSHIP

Not long ago I was at work in my study writing, when, as was her custom, the lady across the way burst into song. There was something about that lady's voice which prevented the use of a human intelligence, and I called upon the janitor to give her my compliments and then silence her. She replied with a good deal of conviction that this was a free country and she would sing when the spirit moved her; if I did not like it, I could retire to the great open spaces.

The lady and I both love liberty, I think. But she loves her liberty whereas I love mine. There does not seem to be a theory of liberty which can be used to decide between us. Lord Acton, for example, was a great historian of the problem of liberty, but as between the lady and myself, I see no help from him when he says that "by liberty I mean the assurance that every man shall be protected in doing what he believes his duty against the influence of authority and majorities, custom and opinion." It was the lady's custom to feel it her duty to practice her singing at the precise moment when I felt it my duty to write an article. The janitor never seemed so completely convinced as I was that mine was much the higher form of duty until he had had a chance on the day after Christmas to compare the lady's gift with mine. Then apparently he read John Stuart Mill, learned that "the sole end for which mankind are warranted, individuals or collectively, in interfering with the liberty of action of any of their number, is self-protection." I got protection and it cost me a box of Corona Coronas, twenty-five dollars, and an old overcoat.

I am somewhat persuaded that no one has ever succeeded in defining the area of liberty more precisely than I did in this case. The classic attempts by Milton and Mill end, if you examine them, in vagueness and compromise. Milton, for example, would have granted freedom of opinion to every one but the Papists and the Atheists; Mill was prepared to suppress any one who did "evil" to "others," leaving it to the others, it would seem, to decide what was evil. Had Milton been asked why Papists and Atheists should be denied the freedom he asked for Dissenters, he would probably have said that they would abuse their freedom. Mill argued that if you gave too much liberty to some men there would be none left for other men. He may have been right, but when you admit this to be true you have disposed of the claim that there is a clear and universal doctrine of liberty.

A theory of liberty is usually stated in general terms, but in fact its real meaning in concrete cases is derived from the nature of these cases themselves. Milton worked out his doctrine of liberty as a weapon which the Puritans could use against the Stuarts; Mill wrote for Victorian England during the ascendancy of the middle class, in that short interval between the downfall of the squirearchy and before the rise of the great corporations. He addressed himself to a section of the English people which did not then contemplate the possibility of really serious divisions of opinion.

The history of Luther's ideas shows how closely related is a theory of liberty to the specific needs of the man who preaches it. When Luther first came into conflict with the Holy See he stood very much alone. There was at that time no Protestant Church, the German princes had not taken him up, he had not worked out a Protestant theology. At this juncture he made his famous utterance on behalf of liberty, saying that "Princes are not to be obeyed when they command submission to superstitious errors, but their aid is not to be invoked in support of the word of God." Facing a bull of excommunication, living in fear of assassination, he preached that heretics must be converted by Scripture and not by fire, otherwise the hangman would be the greatest doctor. But later when the religious revolution had won in Germany, it developed, like all revolutions, beyond anything that Luther had desired. In the name of that right of private judgment and dissent which he had proclaimed against Leo X, there arose heresies within the heresy, the sects of Zwingli and the Anabaptists, and the red jacobinism of the Peasants' War. Luther was horrified at these threats against the security of the Church he had founded. "Out of the gospel and divine truth come devilish lies," he cried, "from the blood in our body comes corruption." The devil, he said, having failed to put him down by the help of the Pope, was seeking his destruction through the preachers of treason and blood. He exhorted the nobles to crush the rebels without mercy. "If there are innocent persons among them, God will surely save and preserve them as He did with Lot and Jeremiah."

Lord Acton, from whom I have taken this account, says that in appealing to the sword Luther had in reality reverted to his original teaching, and that the notion of liberty, whether civil or religious, was hateful to his despotic nature and contrary to his interpretation of Scripture. It remains a fact that Luther had at one time preached the revolutionary doctrine of the right of private judgment, and that this doctrine was worked out to justify his own rebellion against Rome.

II

Heywood Broun and Margaret Leech say in their book on Anthony Comstock that "anything remotely bearing upon sex was to his mind obscene." This helps to explain Comstock, but it is quite misleading if it is meant as an account of Comstockery. This crusading is not a one-man affair, and the psychopathology of the vice crusader does not, I think, give a convincing explanation of his success in enlisting the support of the community. Obviously American society from the Civil War to the World War was not composed entirely or even largely of Anthony Comstocks. Yet for forty years the vice crusade was carried on with the consent of the community punctuated only here and there by the jeers of a minority. Comstock got his support not because of what he believed about the uncleanness of sex but because of what he did toward suppressing those particular manifestations of sex which respectable people wished to have suppressed.

The patrons of his society, the public officials, the clergy, and the fathers and mothers who backed him were not much interested in, and many were no doubt embarrassed by, his idiotic assaults on September Morn and the nude classics. They were thinking of the tons of plainly indecent books and pictures he destroyed rather than the occasional masterpiece which he insulted.

A realistic study of censorship will show, I believe, that it is almost wholly directed against the unadjusted outsiders. It is not the idea as such which the censor attacks, whether it be heresy or radicalism or obscenity. He attacks the circulation of the idea among the classes which in his judgment are not to be trusted with the idea.

The censor himself may be cited as proof of this assertion that the danger is believed to be not in the idea itself but in the peculiar corruptibility of a certain part of the community. The censor exposes himself daily to every corrupting influence. I do not know, of course, what goes on in the dreams of those who compile the Index Expurgatorius, spend their days reading bolshevik pamphlets in the Department of Justice, see all the prohibited films and read all the dirty books. They may in their unconscious minds come to doubt God, insult the flag, and despise chastity. But whatever the private consequences may be, outwardly the censors remain doubly convinced of the sanctity of the institution they are protecting. No one has ever been known to decline to serve on a committee to investigate radicals on the ground that so much exposure to their doctrines would weaken his patriotism, nor on a vice commission on the ground that it would impair his morals. Anything may happen inside the censor, but what counts is that in his outward appearances after his ordeal by temptation he is more than ever a paragon of the conforming virtues. Perhaps his appetites are satisfied by an inverted indulgence, but to a clear-sighted conservative that does not really matter. The conservative is not interested in innocent thoughts. He is interested in loyal behavior.

Apart from certain residual tabus which have the power to cause irrational fear, the essence of censorship has always been, not to suppress subversive ideas as such, but to withhold them from those who are young or unprivileged or otherwise undependable. The purpose of censorship is to prevent overt rebellion against the state, the church, the family, and the economic system. Where there is no danger of overt action there is rarely any interference with freedom.

That is why there has so often been amazing freedom of opinion within an aristocratic class which at the same time sanctioned the ruthless suppression of heterodox opinion among the common people. When the Inquisition was operating most effectively against the bourgeois who had lapsed into heresy, the princes of the Church and the nobles enjoyed the freedom of the Renaissance. There are indeed historians who point out that the Inquisition was not concerned with Jews, Mohammedans and infidels but almost entirely with Christians who had lapsed. For the evil which the Inquisition attacked was not disbelief as such but disloyalty to the Church.

An old Roman maxim said: *de internis non iudicat praetor*, the judge is not concerned with subjective things. Neither is the censor. He does not bother about the internal freedom of an aristocracy, the free speculation which has long been practiced within the Jesuit order, the private candor of politicians and journalists, the unimpressed realism of bankers about business men. Opinions in such a medium are free because they are safe. There is no organic disposition to run wild because the mind is free.

For purposes of argument the advocates of censorship will often pretend that they are worried about the intrinsic viciousness of an idea. Advocates of censorship are often muddle-headed and therefore not clear as to why they are doing what they are doing. But actions speak louder than words, and when you look at censorship as a whole it is plain that it is actually applied in proportion to the vividness, the directness, and the intelligibility of the medium which circulates the subversive idea. The moving picture is perhaps the most popular medium of expression there is; it speaks clearly to the lowest and the most immature intelligence. It is therefore forbidden to present many scenes which the theater is free to present. There are less theaters and the seats cost more. In America, at least, the theater is now largely confined to the metropolitan centers, and it is patronized by a well-to-do, comparatively mature, and sophisticated audience. It is only when a play goes into a long run and begins to be seen by the very general public, as was "The Captive," for example, that the authorities are compelled to pay much attention to protests from the guardians of morality. The scandal about "The Captive" was at bottom its success. Had it been played for a limited run in a theater attended by the sophisticated, it would not have been clubbed to death. But when "The Captive" had run four months on Broadway it had exhausted its mature audience; it was then being patronized by much simpler people, and it was from them and from those who heard from them that the demand for suppression arose and gradually became irresistible.

The newspapers and magazines of general circulation are much freer than the stage. They discuss regularly matters which if presented on the stage would bring out the police reserves. Men are much less moved by what they read than by what they see, and literacy is a recent and uncertain accomplishment of the human race. The proprietors of the tabloids found this out a few years ago and it has been a very profitable discovery. They have produced a new type of paper which is consciously adapted to a low and hurried intelligence. But the essence of tabloid journalism is that it caters with extreme skill to the unadjusted and unprivileged part of the community. It offers them not rebellion but vicarious satisfaction, and therefore it is a kind of narcotic bolshevism as distinguished from the stimulant bolshevism that Lenin preached. There is some protest against the tabloids, but it is not as yet very severe, because the tabloids are in effect a substitute for rebellion rather than a cause of it. Nevertheless they are suspect because, like the moving picture, they reach the suspect classes, and one may confidently predict that if censorship is ever applied to American newspapers it will be due to some breach of the peace which is ascribed to the tabloids. Unless they turn respectable, as some of them show signs of doing, the logic of their formula will compel them to explore newer and newer excitements. They will experiment until at last they bring down upon themselves the wrath of the established community.

The novel is even freer than the press to-day because it is an even denser medium of expression. And in the jargon of a learned treatise a man may if he likes discuss with equanimity the advantages and disadvantages of incest among the Egyptian Pharaohs, or assassination as a method of social reform. For the practical limitations on the freedom of thought and speech are fixed by the estimate of those who have the power to suppress as to how effectively a dangerous idea is being presented to those who might be disposed to rebel.

III

Any one who with a moderately objective mind examines our own great controversies about freedom and suppression cannot fail, I think, to realize how little their avowed theory has to do with the attitude men take. The arguments which men used to justify the nullification of the Fifteenth Amendment in Georgia are now heard in Massachusetts to justify the nullification of the Eighteenth Amendment. The same corporate interests which object to regulation at home as an intolerable form of paternalism insist when they go abroad that the government shall protect them as if they were helpless children. The word "liberty" as used to-day may mean the open shop if an employer is speaking, a closed shop if a labor leader is speaking. There is no commonly accepted definition of liberty. The government of human affairs consists in finding a compromise among conflicting interests: liberty is the watchword used by an interest to justify it in doing what it would like to do, and authority is the watchword of an interest that does not wish to be interfered with by some other interest while it is doing what it wishes to do.

In concrete questions the verbal encounter throws little light on the issue. Suppression through some form of censorship is a means of defense, and, speaking broadly, suppression is practiced by the guardians of the state, the church, the family, and property. The support of censorship is to be found among those who feel themselves to be in harmony with the purposes of the institution that is attacked—that is to say, among officials and party workers and the classes who depend most upon the protection of the state, among churchmen and the devout, among parents, teachers, the guardians of the young, among the elderly and the sexually settled, and also among the impotent and inhibited—all those in short whose manner of life would become confused if the particular institution were radically altered. They are the reserves of conservatism from which are mobilized the legions of defense against the irregular forces of the outsiders—the immature, the unprivileged, the unsettled, and the unadjusted, by whom rebellions are made.

The defenders of authority assume that a considerable part of the people, including all children, are not attached by fixed and reliable habits to the existing order. Being unattached they are impressionable, and might therefore be seduced by agitators. They do not have within themselves, inherent in their characters, that interested loyalty to things as they are which makes men immune to subversive influences. In matters of this sort we must remember that the words "right" and "wrong" mean simply friendly or hostile to the purposes of the institution in question; that is why it is said that the outsiders do not have the interest of the institution sufficiently at heart to feel instinctively the difference between right and wrong. They cannot be allowed to judge for themselves because they are without the premises of sound judgment. They are not unconsciously loyal, and their impressions have to be controlled by the insiders who are intuitively right-minded.

The rationalist argument for liberty, as stated for example by Mill, does not meet this powerful dogma squarely. That, it seems to me, is why the stock theories of liberty are persuasive only to the party which is in rebellion and to a few neutrals who are not vitally concerned with the quarrel. The doctrinaires of liberty base their theory on the assumption that almost all men have the ability to weigh evidence and choose reasonably. Whether almost all men have the ability or not, they certainly do not use it. They are governed by their interests as they conceive them by consulting their feelings about them. The men who ever reach a conclusion which is contrary to their bias and their convenience are too few to make any important difference in the course of events. I have taken into account the fact that some men will sacrifice their lives, their fortunes, and their reputations in the pursuit of an ideal or under the compulsion of some deep necessity of which they may not be wholly aware. The hero and the saint would not be so distinguished if their conduct were normal. For the run of men and women, who make up human society, the thing which decides their attitude in a concrete and critical issue is not evidence, argument and repartee, but whether they are attached to or repelled by the institution which is under fire

The neutrally-minded person with a somewhat liberal disposition often misunderstands this conflict because it does not really touch him. He merely apprehends it as he apprehends the news that forty miners have been trapped in a mine. But your rebel knows his side of the conflict as the doomed miners know their anguish, in a way that a disinterested mind can never know it. The rebel feels his rebellion not as a plea for this or that reform but as an unbearable tension in his viscera. He must break down the cause of his frustration or jump out of his own skin. The true conservative has the same sort of organic need: his institution is to him a mainstay of his being; it exists not as an idea but in the very structure of his character, and the threat to destroy it fills him with anxiety and with fury.

The battles of liberty are organic conflicts between the adjusted and the unadjusted.

March, 1927.

HENRY MILLER

Henry Miller is an American novelist who was born in New York City in 1891. At 18 he spent two months at City College, then traveled in the Southwest and Alaska with the money his father had given him to go to Cornell University. When he returned home the next year he went to work in his father's tailor shop; later he became an employment manager for Western Union Telegraph Company; and still later he operated a Greenwich Village speakeasy. In 1930 he took up residence in France for nine years. He returned to New York in 1940, traveled widely, wrote voluminously, and for a long time settled in Big Sur, California.

Because of its history in United States courts, the best known of Mr. Miller's many novels is probably Tropic of Cancer *(1934). Among his other books are* Tropic of Capricorn *(1938),* Sexus *(1949),* Plexus *(1953),* The Colossus of Maroussi *(1941), and more recently* Nexus *(1960),* To Paint Is to Love Again *(1960), and* Stand Still Like the Hummingbird *(1962). He has also written several pieces on literary censorship, among them the letter we print below, addressed to a Norwegian lawyer.*

DEFENSE OF THE FREEDOM
TO READ

Big Sur, California
February 27, 1959

Mr. Trygve Hirsch
Oslo, Norway

Dear Mr. Hirsch:

To answer your letter of January 19th requesting a statement of me which might be used in the Supreme Court trial to be conducted in March or April of this year. . . . It is difficult to be more explicit than I was in my letter of September 19th, 1957, when the case against my book *Sexus* was being tried in the lower courts of Oslo. However, here are some further reflections which I trust will be found *à propos*.

When I read the decision of the Oslo Town Court, which you sent me some months ago, I did so with mingled feelings. If occasionally I was obliged to roll with laughter—partly because of the inept translation, partly because of the nature and the number of infractions listed—I trust no one will take offense. Taking the world for what it is, and the men who make and execute the laws for what they are, I thought the decision as fair and honest as any theorem of Euclid's. Nor was I unaware of, or indifferent to, the efforts made by the Court to render an interpretation beyond the strict letter of the law. (An impossible task, I would say, for if laws are made for men and not men for laws, it is also true that certain individuals are made for the law and can only see things through the eyes of the law.)

I failed to be impressed, I must confess, by the weighty, often pompous or hypocritical, opinions adduced by scholars, literary pundits, psychologists, medicos and such like. How could I be when it is precisely such single-minded individuals, so often wholly devoid of humor, at whom I so frequently aim my shafts?

Rereading this lengthy document today, I am more than ever aware of the absurdity of the whole procedure. (How lucky I am not to be indicted as a "pervert" or "degenerate," but simply as one who makes sex pleasurable and innocent!) Why, it is often asked, when he has so much else to give, did he have to introduce these disturbing, controversial scenes dealing with sex? To answer that properly, one would have to go back to the womb—with or without the analyst's guiding hand. Each one—priest, analyst, barrister, judge—has his own answer, usually a ready-made one. But none go far enough, none are deep enough, inclusive enough. The divine answer, of course, is—first remove the mote from your own eye!

If I were there, in the dock, my answer would probably be—"Guilty! Guilty on all ninety-seven counts! To the gallows!" For when I take the short, myopic view, I realize that I was guilty even before I wrote the book. Guilty, in other words, because I am the way I am. The marvel is that I am walking about as a free man. I should have been condemned the moment I stepped out of my mother's womb.

In that heart-rending account of my return to the bosom of the family which is given in *Reunion in Brooklyn*, I concluded with these words, and I meant them, each and every one of them: "I regard the entire world as my home. I inhabit the earth, not a particular portion of it labeled America, France, Germany, Russia. . . . I owe allegiance to mankind, not to a particular country, race or people. I answer to God, not to the Chief Executive, whoever he may happen to be. I am here on earth to work out my own private destiny. My destiny is linked with that of every other living creature inhabiting this planet—perhaps with those on other planets too, who knows? I refuse to jeopardize my destiny by regarding life within the narrow rules which are laid down to circumscribe it. I dissent from the current view of things, as regards murder, as regards religion, as regards society, as regards our well-being. I will try to live my life in accordance with the vision I have of things eternal. I say 'Peace to you all!' and if you don't find it, it's because you haven't looked for it."

It is curious, and not irrelevant, I hope, to mention at this point the reaction I had upon reading Homer recently. At the request of the publisher, Gallimard, who is bringing out a new edition of *The Odyssey*, I wrote a short Introduction to this work. I had never read *The Odyssey* before, only *The Iliad*, and that but a few months ago. What I wish to say is that, after waiting sixty-seven years to read these universally esteemed classics, I found much to disparage in them. In *The Iliad*, or "the butcher's manual," as I call it, more than in *The Odyssey*. But it would never occur to me to request that they be banned or burned. Nor did I fear, on finishing them, that I would leap outdoors, axe in hand, and run amok. My boy, who was only nine when he read *The Iliad* (in a child's version), my boy who confesses to "liking murder once in a while," told me he was fed up with Homer, with all the killing and all the nonsense about the gods. But I have never feared that this son of mine, now going on eleven, still an avid reader of our detestable "Comics," a devotee of Walt Disney (who is not to my taste at all), an ardent movie fan, particularly of the "Westerns," I have never feared, I say, that he will grow up to be a killer. (Not even if the Army claims him!) I would rather see his mind absorbed by other interests, and I do my best to provide them, but, like all of us, he is a product of the age. No need, I trust, for me to elaborate on the dangers which confront us all, youth especially, in *this* age. The point is that with each age the menace varies. Whether it be witchcraft, idolatry, leprosy, cancer, schizophrenia, communism, fascism, or what, we have ever to do battle. Seldom do we really vanquish the enemy, in whatever guise he presents himself. At best we become immunized. But we never know, nor are we able to prevent in advance, the dangers which lurk around the corner. No matter how knowledgeable, no matter how wise, no matter how prudent and cautious, we all have an Achilles' heel. Security is not the lot of man. Readiness, alertness, responsiveness—these are the sole defenses against the blows of fate.

I smile to myself in putting the following to the honorable members of the Court, prompted as I am to take the bull by the horns. Would it please the Court to know that by common opinion I pass for a sane, healthy, normal individual? That I am not regarded as a "sex addict," a pervert, or even a neurotic? Nor as a writer who is ready to sell his soul for money? That, as a husband, a father, a neighbor, I am looked upon as "an asset" to the community? Sounds a trifle ludicrous, does it not? Is this the same *enfant terrible,* it might be asked, who wrote the unmentionable *Tropics, The Rosy Crucifixion, The World of Sex, Quiet Days in Clichy?* Has he reformed? Or is he simply in his dotage now?

To be precise, the question is—are the author of these questionable works and the man who goes by the name of Henry Miller one and the same person? My answer is yes. And I am also one with the protagonist of these "autobiographical romances." That is perhaps harder to swallow. But why? Because I have been "utterly shameless" in revealing every aspect of my life? I am not the first author to have adopted the confessional approach, to have revealed life nakedly, or to have used language supposedly unfit for the ears of school girls. Were I a saint recounting his life of sin, perhaps these bald statements relating to my sex habits would be found enlightening, particularly by priests and medicos. They might even be found instructive.

But I am not a saint, and probably never will be one. Though it occurs to me, as I make this assertion, that I have been called that more than once, and by individuals whom the Court would never suspect capable of holding such an opinion. No, I am not a saint, thank heavens! nor even a propagandist of a new order. I am simply a man, a man born to write, who has taken as his theme the story of his life. A man who has made it clear, in the telling, that it was a good life, a rich life, a merry life, despite the ups and downs, despite the barriers and obstacles (many of his own making), despite the handicaps imposed by stupid codes and conventions. Indeed, I hope that I have made more than that clear, because whatever I may say about my own life which is only *a* life, is merely a means of talking about life itself, and what I have tried, desperately sometimes, to make clear is this, that I look upon life itself as good, good no matter on what terms, that I believe it is *we* who make it unlivable, *we*, not the gods, not fate, not circumstance.

Speaking thus, I am reminded of certain passages in the Court's decision which reflect on my sincerity as well as on my ability to think straight. These passages contain the implication that I am often deliberately obscure as well as pretentious in my "metaphysical and surrealistic" flights. I am only too well aware of the diversity of opinion which these "excursi" elicit in the minds of my readers. But how am I to answer such accusations, touching as they do the very marrow of my literary being? Am I to say, "You don't know what you are talking about"? Ought I to muster impressive names—"authorities"—to counterbalance these judgments? Or would it not be simpler to say, as I have before—"Guilty! Guilty on all counts, your Honor!"

Believe me, it is not impish, roguish perversity which leads me to pronounce, even quasi-humorously, this word "guilty." As one who thoroughly and sincerely believes in what he says and does, even when wrong, is it not more becoming on my part to admit "guilt" than attempt to defend myself against those who use this word so glibly? Let us be honest. Do those who judge and condemn me—not in Oslo necessarily, but the world over—do these individuals truly believe me to be a culprit, to be "the enemy of society," as they often blandly assert? What is it that disturbs them so? Is it the existence, the prevalence, of immoral, amoral, or unsocial behavior, such as is described in my works, or is it the exposure of such behavior in print? Do people of our day and age really behave in this "vile" manner or are these actions merely the product of a "diseased" mind? (Does one refer to such authors as Petronius, Rabelais, Rousseau, Sade, to mention but a few, as "diseased minds"?) Surely some of you must have friends or neighbors, in good standing too, who have indulged in this questionable behavior, or worse. As a man of the world, I know only too well that the appanage of a priest's frock, a judicial robe, a teacher's uniform provides no guarantee of immunity to the temptations of the flesh. We are all in the same pot, we are all guilty, or innocent, depending on whether we take the frog's view or the Olympian view. For the once I shall refrain from pretending to measure or apportion guilt, to say, for example, that a criminal is more guilty, or less, than a hypocrite. We do not have crime, we do not have war, revolution, crusades, inquisitions, persecution and intolerance because some among us are wicked, mean-spirited, or murderers at heart; we have this malignant condition of human affairs because all of us, the righteous as well as the ignorant and the malicious, lack true forbearance, true compassion, true knowledge and understanding of human nature.

To put it as succinctly and simply as possible, here is my basic attitude

toward life, my prayer, in other words: "Let us stop thwarting one another, stop judging and condemning, stop slaughtering one another."
I do not implore you to suspend or withhold judgment of me or my
work. Neither I nor my work is that important. (One cometh, another
goeth.) What concerns me is the harm you are doing to yourselves. I
mean by perpetuating this talk of guilt and punishment, of banning and
proscribing, of whitewashing and blackballing, of closing your eyes
when convenient, of making scapegoats when there is no other way out.
I ask you pointblank—does the pursuance of your limited role enable
you to get the most out of life? When you write me off the books, so
to speak, will you find your food and wine more palatable, will you
sleep better, will you be a better man, a better husband, a better father
than before? These are the things that matter—what happens to *you*,
not what you do to *me*.

I know that the man in the dock is not supposed to ask questions, he
is there to answer. But I am unable to regard myself as a culprit. I am
simply "out of line." Yet I am in the tradition, so to say. A list of my
precursors would make an impressive roster. This trial has been going
on since the days of Prometheus. Since before that. Since the days of
the Archangel Michael. In the not too distant past there was one who was
given the cup of hemlock for being "the corrupter of youth." Today
he is regarded as one of the sanest, most lucid minds that ever was. We
who are always being arraigned before the bar can do no better than
to resort to the celebrated Socratic method. Our only answer is to return
the question.

There are so many questions one could put to the Court, to any
Court. But would one get a response? Can the Court of the Land ever
be put in question? I am afraid not. The judicial body is a sacrosanct
body. This is unfortunate, as I see it, for when issues of grave import
arise the last court of reference, in my opinion, should be the public.
When justice is at stake responsibility cannot be shifted to an elect few
without injustice resulting. No Court could function if it did not follow
the steel rails of precedent, taboo and prejudice.

I come back to the lengthy document representing the decision of the
Oslo Town Court, to the tabulation of all the infractions of the moral
code therein listed. There is something frightening as well as dishearten-
ing about such an indictment. It has a medieval aspect. And it has nothing to do with justice. Law itself is made to look ridiculous. Once again
let me say that it is not the courts of Oslo or the laws and codes of Norway which I inveigh against; everywhere in the civilized world there
is this mummery and flummery manifesting as the Voice of Inertia. The
offender who stands before the Court is not being tried by his peers but
by his dead ancestors. The moral codes, operative only if they are in
conformance with natural or divine laws, are not safeguarded by these

flimsy dikes; on the contrary, they are exposed as weak and ineffectual barriers.

Finally, here is the crux of the matter. Will an adverse decision by this court or any other court effectively hinder the further circulation of this book? The history of similar cases does not substantiate such an eventuality. If anything, an unfavorable verdict will only add more fuel to the flames. Proscription only leads to resistance; the fight goes on underground, becomes more insidious therefore, more difficult to cope with. If only one man in Norway reads the book and believes with the author that one has the right to express himself freely, the battle is won. You cannot eliminate an idea by suppressing it, and the idea which is linked with this issue is one of freedom to read what one chooses. Freedom, in other words, to read what is bad for one as well as what is good for one —or, what is simply innocuous. How can one guard against evil, in short, if one does not know what evil is?

But it is not something evil, not something poisonous, which this book *Sexus* offers the Norwegian reader. It is a dose of life which I administered to myself first, and which I not only survived but thrived on. Certainly I would not recommend it to infants, but then neither would I offer a child a bottle of *aqua vite*. I can say one thing for it unblushingly —compared to the atom bomb, it is full of life-giving qualities.

Henry Miller.

JOHN M. WOOLSEY

John Munro Woolsey (1877–1945) was educated at Yale University and the Columbia Law School, where he founded the Columbia Law Review. *He was admitted to the New York Bar in 1901 and worked in private law offices—specializing in admiralty law—until he was appointed U. S. District Judge by President Hoover in 1929. It was in this capacity that he handed down the celebrated decision on James Joyce's novel* Ulysses. *The decision was upheld by the Federal Circuit Court of Appeals, and the* Random House 1934 edition of Ulysses *thus became the first legally*

printed edition of the book in any English-speaking country. The decision is here reprinted from the Modern Library edition of Ulysses.

U. S. A. v. ONE. BOOK *ULYSSES*

UNITED STATES DISTRICT COURT

SOUTHERN DISTRICT OF NEW YORK

United States of America, *Libelant* v. One Book called "Ulysses" Random House, Inc., *Claimant*	OPINION A. 110-59

On cross motions for a decree in a libel of confiscation, supplemented by a stipulation—hereinafter described—brought by the United States against the book "Ulysses" by James Joyce, under Section 305 of the Tariff Act of 1930, Title 19 United States Code, Section 1305, on the ground that the book is obscene within the meaning of that Section, and, hence, is not importable into the United States, but is subject to seizure, forfeiture and confiscation and destruction.

United States Attorney—by Samuel C. Coleman, Esq., and Nicholas Atlas, Esq., of counsel—for the United States, in support of motion for a decree of forfeiture, and in opposition to motion for a decree dismissing the libel.

Messrs. Greenbaum, Wolff & Ernst,—by Morris L. Ernst, Esq., and Alexander Lindey, Esq., of counsel—attorneys for claimant Random House, Inc., in support of motion for a decree dismissing the libel, and in opposition to motion for a decree of forfeiture.

WOOLSEY, J:

The motion for a decree dismissing the libel herein is granted, and, consequently, of course, the Government's motion for a decree of forfeiture and destruction is denied.

Accordingly a decree dismissing the libel without costs may be entered herein.

I. The practice followed in this case is in accordance with the suggestion made by me in the case of *United States v. One Book Entitled "Contraception"*, 51 F. (2d) 525, and is as follows:

After issue was joined by the filing of the claimant's answer to the libel for forfeiture against "Ulysses", a stipulation was made between the United States Attorney's office and the attorneys for the claimant providing:

1. That the book "Ulysses" should be deemed to have been annexed to and to have become part of the libel just as if it had been incorporated in its entirety therein.

2. That the parties waived their right to a trial by jury.

3. That each party agreed to move for decree in its favor.

4. That on such cross motions the Court might decide all the questions of law and fact involved and render a general finding thereon.

5. That on the decision of such motions the decree of the Court might be entered as if it were a decree after trial.

It seems to me that a procedure of this kind is highly appropriate in libels for the confiscation of books such as this. It is an especially advantageous procedure in the instant case because on account of the length of "Ulysses" and the difficulty of reading it, a jury trial would have been an extremely unsatisfactory, if not an almost impossible, method of dealing with it.

II. I have read "Ulysses" once in its entirety and I have read those passages of which the Government particularly complains several times. In fact, for many weeks, my spare time has been devoted to the consideration of the decision which my duty would require me to make in this matter.

"Ulysses" is not an easy book to read or to understand. But there has been much written about it, and in order properly to approach the consideration of it it is advisable to read a number of other books which have now become its satellites. The study of "Ulysses" is, therefore, a heavy task.

III. The reputation of "Ulysses" in the literary world, however, warranted my taking such time as was necessary to enable me to satisfy myself as to the intent with which the book was written, for, of course, in any case where a book is claimed to be obscene it must first be determined, whether the intent with which it was written was what is called, according to the usual phrase, pornographic,—that is, written for the purpose of exploiting obscenity.

If the conclusion is that the book is pornographic that is the end of the inquiry and forfeiture must follow.

But in "Ulysses", in spite of its unusual frankness, I do not detect anywhere the leer of the sensualist. I hold, therefore, that it is not pornographic.

IV. In writing "Ulysses", Joyce sought to make a serious experiment in a new, if not wholly novel, literary genre. He takes persons of the lower middle class living in Dublin in 1904 and seeks not only to describe what they did on a certain day early in June of that year as they went about the City bent on their usual occupations, but also to tell what many of them thought about the while.

Joyce has attempted—it seems to me, with astonishing success—to show how the screen of consciousness with its ever-shifting kaleidoscopic impressions carries, as it were on a plastic palimpsest, not only what is in the focus of each man's observation of the actual things about him, but also in a penumbral zone residua of past impressions, some recent and some drawn up by association from the domain of the subconscious. He shows how each of these impressions affects the life and behavior of the character which he is describing.

What he seeks to get is not unlike the result of a double or, if that is possible, a multiple exposure on a cinema film which would give a clear foreground with a background visible but somewhat blurred and out of focus in varying degrees.

To convey by words an effect which obviously lends itself more appropriately to a graphic technique, accounts, it seems to me, for much of the obscurity which meets a reader of "Ulysses". And it also explains another aspect of the book, which I have further to consider, namely, Joyce's sincerity and his honest effort to show exactly how the minds of his characters operate.

If Joyce did not attempt to be honest in developing the technique which he has adopted in "Ulysses" the result would be psychologically misleading and thus unfaithful to his chosen technique. Such an attitude would be artistically inexcusable.

It is because Joyce has been loyal to his technique and has not funked its necessary implications, but has honestly attempted to tell fully what his characters think about, that he has been the subject of so many attacks and that his purpose has been so often misunderstood and misrepresented. For his attempt sincerely and honestly to realize his objective has required him incidentally to use certain words which are generally considered dirty words and has led at times to what many think is a too poignant preoccupation with sex in the thoughts of his characters.

The words which are criticized as dirty are old Saxon words known to almost all men and, I venture, to many women, and are such words as would be naturally and habitually used, I believe, by the types of folk whose life, physical and mental, Joyce is seeking to describe. In respect of the recurrent emergence of the theme of sex in the minds of his characters, it must always be remembered that his locale was Celtic and his season Spring.

Whether or not one enjoys such a technique as Joyce uses is a matter of taste on which disagreement or argument is futile, but to subject that technique to the standards of some other technique seems to me to be little short of absurd.

Accordingly, I hold that "Ulysses" is a sincere and honest book and I think that the criticisms of it are entirely disposed of by its rationale.

V. Furthermore, "Ulysses" is an amazing *tour de force* when one considers the success which has been in the main achieved with such a difficult objective as Joyce set for himself. As I have stated, "Ulysses" is not an easy book to read. It is brilliant and dull, intelligible and obscure by turns. In many places it seems to me to be disgusting, but although it contains, as I have mentioned above, many words usually considered dirty, I have not found anything that I consider to be dirt for dirt's sake. Each word of the book contributes like a bit of mosaic to the detail of the picture which Joyce is seeking to construct for his readers.

If one does not wish to associate with such folk as Joyce describes, that is one's own choice. In order to avoid indirect contact with them one may not wish to read "Ulysses"; that is quite understandable. But when such a real artist in words, as Joyce undoubtedly is, seeks to draw a true picture of the lower middle class in a European city, ought it to be impossible for the American public legally to see that picture?

To answer this question it is not sufficient merely to find, as I have found above, that Joyce did not write "Ulysses" with what is commonly called pornographic intent, I must endeavor to apply a more objective standard to his book in order to determine its effect in the result, irrespective of the intent with which it was written.

VI. The statute under which the libel is filed only denounces, in so far as we are here concerned, the importation into the United States from any foreign country of "any obscene book". Section 305 of the Tariff Act of 1930, Title 19 United States Code, Section 1305. It does not marshal against books the spectrum of condemnatory adjectives found, commonly, in laws dealing with matters of this kind. I am, therefore, only required to determine whether "Ulysses" is obscene within the legal definition of that word.

The meaning of the word "obscene" as legally defined by the Courts is: tending to stir the sex impulses or to lead to sexually impure and lustful thoughts. *Dunlop* v. *United States*, 165 U. S. 486, 501; *United States* v. *One Book Entitled "Married Love"*, 48 F. (2d) 821, 824; *United States* v. *One Book Entitled "Contraception"*, 51 F. (2d) 525, 528; and compare *Dysart* v. *United States*, 272 U. S. 655, 657; *Swearingen* v. *United States*, 161 U. S. 446, 450; *United States* v. *Dennett*, 39 F. (2d) 564, 568 (C. C. A. 2); *People* v. *Wendling*, 258 N. Y. 451, 453.

Whether a particular book would tend to excite such impulses and thoughts must be tested by the Court's opinion as to its effect on a person with average sex instincts—what the French would call *l'homme moyen sensuel*—who plays, in this branch of legal inquiry, the same role of hypothetical reagent as does the "reasonable man" in the law of torts and "the man learned in the art" on questions of invention in patent law.

The risk involved in the use of such a reagent arises from the inherent tendency of the trier of facts, however fair he may intend to be, to make his reagent too much subservient to his own idiosyncrasies. Here, I have attempted to avoid this, if possible, and to make my reagent herein more objective than he might otherwise be, by adopting the following course:

After I had made my decision in regard to the aspect of "Ulysses", now under consideration, I checked my impressions with two friends of mine who in my opinion answered to the above stated requirement for my reagent.

These literary assessors—as I might properly describe them—were called on separately, and neither knew that I was consulting the other. They are men whose opinion on literature and on life I value most highly. They had both read "Ulysses", and, of course, were wholly unconnected with this cause.

Without letting either of my assessors know what my decision was, I gave to each of them the legal definition of obscene and asked each whether in his opinion "Ulysses" was obscene within that definition.

I was interested to find that they both agreed with my opinion: that reading "Ulysses" in its entirety, as a book must be read on such a test as this, did not tend to excite sexual impulses or lustful thoughts but that its net effect on them was only that of a somewhat tragic and very powerful commentary on the inner lives of men and women.

It is only with the normal person that the law is concerned. Such a test as I have described, therefore, is the only proper test of obscenity in the case of a book like "Ulysses" which is a sincere and serious attempt to devise a new literary method for the observation and description of mankind.

I am quite aware that owing to some of its scenes "Ulysses" is a rather strong draught to ask some sensitive, though normal, persons to take. But my considered opinion, after long reflection, is that whilst in many places the effect of "Ulysses" on the reader undoubtedly is somewhat emetic, nowhere does it tend to be an aphrodisiac.

"Ulysses" may, therefore, be admitted into the United States.

JOHN M. WOOLSEY
UNITED STATES DISTRICT JUDGE

December 6, 1933

Social Implications of Race

The opening pages of Ruth Benedict's book *Race: Science and Politics* (1940) serve as a better introduction to this section than any we could devise. Arthur de Gobineau's chapter demonstrates a theoretical position of the nineteenth century, one which Hitler later used to sanction his devastating policy and which thus illustrates crudely how "social science" can be used to further political ends. Professor Dobzhansky, writing in 1963, brings a modern scientific mind to bear on the concepts of "race" and "equality." Orwell's description of a North African city as seen through the eyes of a white European sounds a note of warning, and serves to introduce the last four selections. They present, from varying points of view and in varying styles and tone, the American dilemma of Negro and White.

RUTH BENEDICT

FROM RACISM—THE *ISM* OF THE MODERN WORLD

As an introduction to this section, we reprint here the opening pages of the first chapter of Ruth Benedict's Race: Science and Politics *(1940). Information on the author and her writing follows index.*

•

As early as the late 1880's a French pro-Aryan, Vacher de Lapouge, wrote: "I am convinced that in the next century millions will cut each other's throats because of 1 or 2 degrees more or less of cephalic index." On the surface it appears a fantastic reason for world wars, and it was certainly a reason new under the sun. Was he right? What could it mean? The cephalic index is the quotient of the greatest breadth of the head divided by its length, and some tribes and peoples over the world run to high indices and some to low. Narrow heads are found among uncivilized primitives and among powerful and cultivated Western Europeans; broad heads are too. Neither the narrow heads of the whole world nor the broad heads stack up to show any obvious monopoly of glorious destiny or any corner on ability or virtue. Even in any one European nation or in America men of achievement have been some of them narrow-headed and some broad-headed. What could it mean that "millions will cut each other's throats" because of the shape of the top of their skulls?

In the long history of the world men have given many reasons for killing each other in war: envy of another people's good bottom land or of their herds, ambition of chiefs and kings, different religious beliefs, high spirits, revenge. But in all these wars the skulls of the victims on both sides were generally too similar to be distinguished. Nor had the war leaders incited their followers against their enemies by referring to the shapes of their heads. They might call them the heathen, the barbarians, the heretics, the slayers of women and children, but never our enemy Cephalic Index 82.

It was left for high European civilization to advance such a reason for war and persecution and to invoke it in practice. In other words, racism is a creation of our own time. It is a new way of separating the sheep from the goats. The old parable in the New Testament separated mankind as individuals: on the one hand those who had done good, and on the other those who had done evil. The new way divides them by hereditary bodily characteristics—shape of the head, skin colour, nose form, hair texture, colour of the eyes—and those who have certain hallmarks are known by these signs to be weaklings and incapable of civilization, and those with the opposite are the hope of the world. Racism is the new Calvinism which asserts that one group has the stigmata of superiority and the other has those of inferiority. According to racism we know our enemies, not by their aggressions against us, not by their creed or language, not even by their possessing wealth we want to take, but by noting their hereditary anatomy. For the leopard cannot change his spots and by these you know he is a leopard.

For the individual, therefore, racism means that damnation or salvation in this world is determined at conception; an individual's good life cannot tip the balance in his favour and he cannot live a bad life if his physical type is the right sort. By virtue of birth alone each member of the "race" is high caste and rightly claims his place in the sun at the expense of men of other "races." He need not base his pride upon personal achievement nor upon virtue; he was born high caste.

From this postulate racism makes also an assertion about race: that the "good" anatomical hallmarks are the monopoly of a pure race which has always throughout history manifested its glorious destiny. The racialists have rewritten history to provide the scion of such a race with a long and glamorous group ancestry as gratifying as an individual coat of arms, and they assure him that the strength and vigour of his race are immutable and guaranteed by the laws of Nature. He must, however, guard this pure blood from contamination by that of lesser breeds, lest degeneration follow and his race lose its supremacy. All over the world for the last generation this doctrine has been invoked in every possible kind of conflict: sometimes national, between peoples as racially similar as the French and Germans; sometimes across the colour line, as in Western fears of the Yellow Peril; sometimes in class conflicts, as in France; sometimes in conflicts between immigrants who arrived a little earlier and those who came a little later, as in America. It has become a bedlam.

Where all people claim to be tallest, not all can be right. In this matter of races, can the sciences to which they all appeal judge among the babel of contradictory claims and award the decision? Or is it a matter of false premises and bastard science? It is essential, if we are to live in this modern world, that we should understand Racism and be able to judge its arguments. We must know the facts first of Race, and then of this doctrine that has made use of them. For Racism is an *ism* to which everyone in the world today is exposed; for or against, we must take sides. And the history of the future will differ according to the decision which we make.

JOSEPH ARTHUR, COMTE DE GOBINEAU

Joseph Arthur de Gobineau (1816–1882), French diplomat, Orientalist, and man of letters, was educated first by private tutors and later at a college in Switzerland. In 1849 he was appointed "chef de cabinet" by Alexis de Tocqueville, then Foreign Minister, and subsequently served in many other diplomatic posts. His writings include books on Asiatic religion and philosophy and on the Renaissance, but of most interest to us here is his four-volume Essai sur l'inégalité des races humaines *(1853–1855), translated in 1915 by Adrian Collins as* The Inequality of Human Races. *In these volumes M. Gobineau proposes that Aryan racial purity can be maintained only by preserving and strengthening the Nordic strains, a theory which later became fashionable in German intellectual circles and must have influenced Nazi ideology. We present below the concluding chapter of this work, originally entitled "Recapitulation: The Respective Characteristics of the Three Great Races; the Superiority of the White Type, and, Within this Type, of the Aryan Family."*

THE RESPECTIVE CHARACTERISTICS
OF THE THREE GREAT RACES

I have shown the unique place in the organic world occupied by the human species, the profound physical, as well as moral, differences separating it from all other kinds of living creatures. Considering it by itself, I have been able to distinguish, on physiological grounds alone, three great and clearly marked types, the black, the yellow, and the white. However uncertain the aims of physiology may be, however meagre its resources, however defective its methods, it can proceed thus far with absolute certainty.

The negroid variety is the lowest, and stands at the foot of the ladder. The animal character, that appears in the shape of the pelvis, is stamped on the negro from birth, and foreshadows his destiny. His intellect will always move within a very narrow circle. He is not however a mere brute, for behind his low receding brow, in the middle of his skull, we can see signs of a powerful energy, however crude its objects. If his mental faculties are dull or even non-existent, he often has an intensity of desire, and so of will, which may be called terrible. Many of his senses, especially taste and smell, are developed to an extent unknown to the other two races.[1]

The very strength of his sensations is the most striking proof of his inferiority. All food is good in his eyes, nothing disgusts or repels him. What he desires is to eat, to eat furiously, and to excess; no carrion is too revolting to be swallowed by him. It is the same with odours; his inordinate desires are satisfied with all, however coarse or even horrible. To these qualities may be added an instability and capriciousness of feeling, that cannot be tied down to any single object, and which, so far as he is concerned, do away with all distinctions of good and evil. We might even say that the violence with which he pursues the object that has aroused his senses and inflamed his desires is a guarantee of the desires being soon satisfied and the object forgotten. Finally, he is equally careless of his own life and that of others: he kills willingly, for the sake of killing; and this human machine, in whom it is so easy to arouse emotion, shows, in face of suffering, either a monstrous indifference or a cowardice that seeks a voluntary refuge in death.

The yellow race is the exact opposite of this type. The skull points forward, not backward. The forehead is wide and bony, often high and projecting. The shape of the face is triangular, the nose and chin showing none of the coarse protuberances that mark the negro. There is further a general proneness to obesity, which, though not confined to the yellow type, is found there more frequently than in the others. The yellow man has little physical energy, and is inclined to apathy; he commits none of the strange excesses so common among negroes. His desires are feeble, his will-power rather obstinate than violent; his longing for material pleasures, though constant, is kept within bounds. A rare glutton by nature, he shows far more discrimination in his choice of food. He tends to mediocrity in everything; he understands easily enough anything not too deep or sublime. He has a love of utility and a respect

---

[1] "Taste and smell in the negro are as powerful as they are undiscriminating. He eats everything, and odours which are revolting to us are pleasant to him" (Pruner).

for order, and knows the value of a certain amount of freedom. He is practical, in the narrowest sense of the word. He does not dream or theorize; he invents little, but can appreciate and take over what is useful to him. His whole desire is to live in the easiest and most comfortable way possible. The yellow races are thus clearly superior to the black. Every founder of a civilization would wish the backbone of his society, his middle class, to consist of such men. But no civilized society could be created by them; they could not supply its nerve-force, or set in motion the springs of beauty and action.

We come now to the white peoples. These are gifted with reflective energy, or rather with an energetic intelligence. They have a feeling for utility, but in a sense far wider and higher, more courageous and ideal, than the yellow races; a perseverance that takes account of obstacles and ultimately finds a means of overcoming them; a greater physical power, an extraordinary instinct for order, not merely as a guarantee of peace and tranquillity, but as an indispensable means of self-preservation. At the same time, they have a remarkable, and even extreme, love of liberty, and are openly hostile to the formalism under which the Chinese are glad to vegetate, as well as to the strict despotism which is the only way of governing the negro.

The white races are, further, distinguished by an extraordinary attachment to life. They know better how to use it, and so, as it would seem, set a greater price on it; both in their own persons and those of others, they are more sparing of life. When they are cruel, they are conscious of their cruelty; it is very doubtful whether such a consciousness exists in the negro. At the same time, they have discovered reasons why they should surrender this busy life of theirs, that is so precious to them. The principal motive is honour, which under various names has played an enormous part in the ideas of the race from the beginning. I need hardly add that the word honour, together with all the civilizing influences connoted by it, is unknown to both the yellow and the black man.

On the other hand, the immense superiority of the white peoples in the whole field of the intellect is balanced by an inferiority in the intensity of their sensations. In the world of the senses, the white man is far less gifted than the others, and so is less tempted and less absorbed by considerations of the body, although in physical structure he is far the most vigorous.[2]

Such are the three constituent elements of the human race. I call them secondary types, as I think myself obliged to omit all discussion of the Adamite man. From the combination, by intermarriage, of the varieties of these types come the tertiary groups. The quaternary formations are produced by the union of one of these tertiary types, or of a pure-blooded

---

[2] Martius observes that the European is superior to the coloured man in the pressure of the nervous fluid (*Reise in Brasilien*, vol. i, p. 259).

tribe, with another group taken from one of the two foreign species.

Below these categories others have appeared—and still appear. Some of these are very strongly characterized, and form new and distinct points of departure, coming as they do from races that have been completely fused. Others are incomplete, and ill-ordered, and, one might even say, anti-social, since their elements, being too numerous, too disparate, or too barbarous, have had neither the time nor the opportunity for combining to any fruitful purpose. No limits, except the horror excited by the possibility of infinite intermixture, can be assigned to the number of these hybrid and chequered races that make up the whole of mankind.

It would be unjust to assert that every mixture is bad and harmful. If the three great types had remained strictly separate, the supremacy would no doubt have always been in the hands of the finest of the white races, and the yellow and black varieties would have crawled for ever at the feet of the lowest of the whites. Such a state is so far ideal, since it has never been beheld in history; and we can imagine it only by recognizing the undisputed superiority of those groups of the white races which have remained the purest.

It would not have been all gain. The superiority of the white race would have been clearly shown, but it would have been bought at the price of certain advantages which have followed the mixture of blood. Although these are far from counterbalancing the defects they have brought in their train, yet they are sometimes to be commended. Artistic genius, which is equally foreign to each of the three great types, arose only after the intermarriage of white and black. Again, in the Malayan variety, a human family was produced from the yellow and black races that had more intelligence than either of its ancestors. Finally, from the union of white and yellow, certain intermediary peoples have sprung, who are superior to the purely Finnish tribes as well as to the negroes.

I do not deny that these are good results. The world of art and great literature that comes from the mixture of blood, the improvement and ennoblement of inferior races—all these are wonders for which we must needs be thankful. The small have been raised. Unfortunately, the great have been lowered by the same process; and this is an evil that nothing can balance or repair. Since I am putting together the advantages of racial mixtures, I will also add that to them is due the refinement of manners and beliefs, and especially the tempering of passion and desire. But these are merely transitory benefits, and if I recognize that the mulatto, who may become a lawyer, a doctor, or a business man, is worth more than his negro grandfather, who was absolutely savage, and fit for nothing, I must also confess that the Brahmans of primitive India, the heroes of the Iliad and the Shahnameh, the warriors of Scandinavia—the glorious shades of noble races that have disappeared—give us a higher and more brilliant idea of humanity, and were more active, intelligent, and trusty instruments of civilization and grandeur than the peoples, hybrid a hundred times over, of the present day. And the blood even of these was no longer pure.

However it has come about, the human races, as we find them in history, are complex; and one of the chief consequences has been to throw into disorder most of the primitive characteristics of each type. The good as well as the bad qualities are seen to diminish in intensity with repeated intermixture of blood; but they also scatter and separate off from each other, and are often mutually opposed. The white race originally possessed the monopoly of beauty, intelligence, and strength. By its union with other varieties, hybrids were created, which were beautiful without strength, strong without intelligence, or, if intelligent, both weak and ugly. Further, when the quantity of white blood was increased to an indefinite amount by successive infusions, and not by a single admixture, it no longer carried with it its natural advantages, and often merely increased the confusion already existing in the racial elements. Its strength, in fact, seemed to be its only remaining quality, and even its strength served only to promote disorder. The apparent anomaly is easily explained. Each stage of a perfect mixture produces a new type from diverse elements, and develops special faculties. As soon as further elements are added, the vast difficulty of harmonizing the whole creates a state of anarchy. The more this increases, the more do even the best and richest of the new contributions diminish in value, and by their mere presence add fuel to an evil which they cannot abate. If mixtures of blood are, to a certain extent, beneficial to the mass of mankind, if they raise and ennoble it, this is merely at the expense of mankind itself, which is stunted, abased, enervated, and humiliated in the persons of its noblest sons. Even if we admit that it is better to turn a myriad of degraded beings into mediocre men than to preserve the race of princes whose blood is adulterated and impoverished by being made to suffer this dishonourable change, yet there is still the unfortunate fact that the change does not stop here; for when the mediocre men are once created at the expense of the greater, they combine with other mediocrities, and from such unions, which grow ever more and more degraded, is born a confusion which, like that of Babel, ends in utter impotence, and leads societies down to the abyss of nothingness whence no power on earth can rescue them.

Such is the lesson of history. It shows us that all civilizations derive from the white race, that none can exist without its help, and that a society is great and brilliant only so far as it preserves the blood of the noble group that created it, provided that this group itself belongs to the most illustrious branch of our species.

Of the multitude of peoples which live or have lived on the earth,

ten alone have risen to the position of complete societies. The remainder
have gravitated round these more or less independently, like planets
round their suns. If there is any element of life in these ten civilizations
that is not due to the impulse of the white races, any seed of death that
does not come from the inferior stocks that mingled with them, then
the whole theory on which this book rests is false. On the other hand,
if the facts are as I say, then we have an irrefragable proof of the nobility
of our own species. Only the actual details can set the final seal of truth
on my system, and they alone can show with sufficient exactness the
full implications of my main thesis, that peoples degenerate only in consequence of the various admixtures of blood which they undergo; that
their degeneration corresponds exactly to the quantity and quality of
the new blood, and that the rudest possible shock to the vitality of a
civilization is given when the ruling elements in a society and those developed by racial change have become so numerous that they are clearly
moving away from the homogeneity necessary to their life, and it therefore becomes impossible for them to be brought into harmony and so
acquire the common instincts and interests, the common logic of existence,
which is the sole justification for any social bond whatever. There is
no greater curse than such disorder, for however bad it may have made
the present state of things, it promises still worse for the future.

NOTE.—The "ten civilizations" mentioned in the last paragraph are as
follows. They are fully discussed in the subsequent books of the "Inequality of Races," of which the present volume forms the first.

I. The Indian civilization, which reached its highest point round the
Indian Ocean, and in the north and east of the Indian Continent, south-
east of the Brahmaputra. It arose from a branch of a white people, the
Aryans.

II. The Egyptians, round whom collected the Ethiopians, the Nubians,
and a few smaller peoples to the west of the oasis of Ammon. This society was created by an Aryan colony from India, that settled in the
upper valley of the Nile.

III. The Assyrians, with whom may be classed the Jews, the Phœni-
cians, the Lydians, the Carthaginians, and the Hymiarites. They owed their
civilizing qualities to the great white invasions which may be grouped
under the name of the descendants of Shem and Ham. The Zoroastrian
Iranians who ruled part of Central Asia under the names of Medes,
Persians, and Bactrians, were a branch of the Aryan family.

IV. The Greeks, who came from the same Aryan stock, as modified
by Semitic elements.

V. The Chinese civilization, arising from a cause similar to that operating in Egypt. An Aryan colony from India brought the light of civilization to China also. Instead however of becoming mixed with black

peoples, as on the Nile, the colony became absorbed in Malay and yellow races, and was reinforced, from the north-west, by a fair number of white elements, equally Aryan but no longer Hindu.

VI. The ancient civilization of the Italian peninsula, the cradle of Roman culture. This was produced by a mixture of Celts, Iberians, Aryans, and Semites.

VII. The Germanic races, which in the fifth century transformed the Western mind. These were Aryans.

VIII.–X. The three civilizations of America, the Alleghanian, the Mexican, and the Peruvian.

Of the first seven civilizations, which are those of the Old World, six belong, at least in part, to the Aryan race, and the seventh, that of Assyria, owes to this race the Iranian Renaissance, which is, historically, its best title to fame. Almost the whole of the Continent of Europe is inhabited at the present time by groups of which the basis is white, but in which the non-Aryan elements are the most numerous. There is no true civilization, among the European peoples, where the Aryan branch is not predominant.

In the above list no negro race is seen as the initiator of a civilization. Only when it is mixed with some other can it even be initiated into one.

Similarly, no spontaneous civilization is to be found among the yellow races; and when the Aryan blood is exhausted stagnation supervenes.

ADOLF HITLER

❦

Adolf Hitler (1889–1945), Austrian born, became the Nazi Dictator of Germany. After a brief and unsuccessful venture in art (he was refused admission to the Viennese Academy) and after a number of years of odd jobs and poverty, he left Vienna in 1913 and settled in Munich. During World War I he volunteered in the Bavarian army and rose to the rank of Corporal. He returned to Munich in 1918 and began dabbling in politics. In 1920, with a handful of followers, he founded his own party which grew into the National Socialist German Workers' (Nazi) party. The Munich

Putsch of 1923, an abortive attempt to overthrow the state government of Bavaria, gained him national attention and a thirteen-month jail sentence. It was during these months in jail that Hitler wrote the first volume of Mein Kampf (My Struggle), *published in 1925, which he intended to call "A Four and One-Half Year Struggle against Lies, Stupidity, and Cowardice: Settling Accounts with the Destroyers of the Nationalist Socialist Movement." The second volume was published in the following year, 1926. The book enjoyed only a small circulation at first, but a few years before Hitler came to power sales began to rise and soon* Mein Kampf *was a best seller second only to the Bible. Hitler was made chancellor in 1933 and after Hindenburg's death in 1934 was elected Führer for life. He is thought to have committed suicide in Berlin, on April 29, 1945.*

Today Hitler's name has become a byword for psychotic inhumanity; Mein Kampf *has been called a satanic Bible. Partly autobiographical, it not only outlines his program for world conquest but also broadcasts his hatred of Jews and his aim to restore to the Aryan "race" its sense of superiority. The selection we reprint below is the beginning of the eleventh chapter of Volume 1 of* Mein Kampf, *translated by Ralph Manheim.*

NATION AND RACE

There are some truths which are so obvious that for this very reason they are not seen or at least not recognized by ordinary people. They sometimes pass by such truisms as though blind and are most astonished when someone suddenly discovers what everyone really ought to know. Columbus's eggs lie around by the hundreds of thousands, but Columbuses are met with less frequently.

Thus men without exception wander about in the garden of Nature; they imagine that they know practically everything and yet with few exceptions pass blindly by one of the most patent principles of Nature's rule: the inner segregation of the species of all living beings on this earth.

Even the most superficial observation shows that Nature's restricted form of propagation and increase is an almost rigid basic law of all the innumerable forms of expression of her vital urge. Every animal mates only with a member of the same species. The titmouse seeks the titmouse, the finch the finch, the stork the stork, the field mouse the field mouse, the dormouse the dormouse, the wolf the she-wolf, etc.

Only unusual circumstances can change this, primarily the compulsion of captivity or any other cause that makes it impossible to mate within the same species. But then Nature begins to resist this with all possible means, and her most visible protest consists either in refusing further capacity for propagation to bastards or in limiting the fertility of later offspring; in most cases, however, she takes away the power of resistance to disease or hostile attacks.

This is only too natural.

Any crossing of two beings not at exactly the same level produces a medium between the level of the two parents. This means: the offspring will probably stand higher than the racially lower parent, but not as high as the higher one. Consequently, it will later succumb in the struggle against the higher level. Such mating is contrary to the will of Nature for a higher breeding of all life. The precondition for this does not lie in associating superior and inferior, but in the total victory of the former. The stronger must dominate and not blend with the weaker, thus sacrificing his own greatness. Only the born weakling can view this as cruel, but he after all is only a weak and limited man; for if this law did not prevail, any conceivable higher development of organic living beings would be unthinkable.

The consequence of this racial purity, universally valid in Nature, is not only the sharp outward delimitation of the various races, but their uniform character in themselves. The fox is always a fox, the goose a goose, the tiger a tiger, etc., and the difference can lie at most in the varying measure of force, strength, intelligence, dexterity, endurance, etc., of the individual specimens. But you will never find a fox who in his inner attitude might, for example, show humanitarian tendencies toward geese, as similarly there is no cat with a friendly inclination toward mice.

Therefore, here, too, the struggle among themselves arises less from inner aversion than from hunger and love. In both cases, Nature looks on calmly, with satisfaction, in fact. In the struggle for daily bread all those who are weak and sickly or less determined succumb, while the struggle of the males for the female grants the right or opportunity to propagate only to the healthiest. And struggle is always a means for improving a species' health and power of resistance and, therefore, a cause of its higher development.

If the process were different, all further and higher development would cease and the opposite would occur. For, since the inferior always predominates numerically over the best, if both had the same possibility of preserving life and propagating, the inferior would multiply so much more rapidly that in the end the best would inevitably be driven into the background, unless a correction of this state of affairs were undertaken. Nature does just this by subjecting the weaker part to such severe living conditions that by them alone the number is limited, and by not permitting the remainder to increase promiscuously, but making a new and ruthless choice according to strength and health.

No more than Nature desires the mating of weaker with stronger individuals, even less does she desire the blending of a higher with a lower race, since, if she did, her whole work of higher breeding, over perhaps hundreds of thousands of years, might be ruined with one blow.

Historical experience offers countless proofs of this. It shows with terrifying clarity that in every mingling of Aryan blood with that of lower peoples the result was the end of the cultured people. North America, whose population consists in by far the largest part of Germanic elements who mixed but little with the lower colored peoples, shows a different humanity and culture from Central and South America, where the predominantly Latin immigrants often mixed with the aborigines on a large scale. By this one example, we can clearly and distinctly recognize the effect of racial mixture. The Germanic inhabitant of the American continent, who has remained racially pure and unmixed, rose to be master of the continent; he will remain the master as long as he does not fall a victim to defilement of the blood.

The result of all racial crossing is therefore in brief always the following:

(a) Lowering of the level of the higher race;

(b) Physical and intellectual regression and hence the beginning of a slowly but surely progressing sickness.

To bring about such a development is, then, nothing else but to sin against the will of the eternal creator.

And as a sin this act is rewarded.

When man attempts to rebel against the iron logic of Nature, he comes into struggle with the principles to which he himself owes his existence as a man. And this attack must lead to his own doom.

Here, of course, we encounter the objection of the modern pacifist, as truly Jewish in its effrontery as it is stupid! 'Man's rôle is to overcome Nature!'

Millions thoughtlessly parrot this Jewish nonsense and end up by really imagining that they themselves represent a kind of conqueror of Nature; though in this they dispose of no other weapon than an idea, and at that such a miserable one, that if it were true no world at all would be conceivable.

But quite aside from the fact that man has never yet conquered Nature in anything, but at most has caught hold of and tried to lift one or another corner of her immense gigantic veil of eternal riddles and secrets, that in reality he invents nothing but only discovers everything, that he does not dominate Nature, but has only risen on the basis of his knowledge of various laws and secrets of Nature to be lord over those other living creatures who lack this knowledge—quite aside from all this, an idea cannot overcome the preconditions for the development and being of humanity, since the idea itself depends only on man. Without human beings there is no human idea in this world, therefore, the idea as such is always conditioned by the presence of human beings and hence of all the laws which created the precondition for their existence.

And not only that! Certain ideas are even tied up with certain men. This applies most of all to those ideas whose content originates, not in an exact scientific truth, but in the world of emotion, or, as it is so beautifully and clearly expressed today, reflects an 'inner experience.' All these ideas, which have nothing to do with cold logic as such, but represent only pure expressions of feeling, ethical conceptions, etc., are chained to the existence of men, to whose intellectual imagination and creative power they owe their existence. Precisely in this case the preservation of these definite races and men is the precondition for the existence of these ideas. Anyone, for example, who really desired the victory of the pacifistic idea in this world with all his heart would have to fight with all the means at his disposal for the conquest of the world by the Germans; for, if the opposite should occur, the last pacifist would die out with the last German, since the rest of the world has never fallen so deeply as our own people, unfortunately, has for this nonsense so contrary to Nature and reason. Then, if we were serious, whether we liked it or not, we would have to wage wars in order to arrive at pacifism. This and nothing else was what Wilson, the American world savior, intended, or so at least our German visionaries believed—and thereby his purpose was fulfilled.

In actual fact the pacifistic-humane idea is perfectly all right perhaps when the highest type of man has previously conquered and subjected the world to an extent that makes him the sole ruler of this earth. Then this idea lacks the power of producing evil effects in exact proportion as its practical application becomes rare and finally impossible. Therefore, first struggle and then we shall see what can be done. Otherwise mankind has passed the high point of its development and the end is not the domination of any ethical idea but barbarism and consequently chaos. At this point someone or other may laugh, but this planet once moved through the ether for millions of years without human beings and it can do so again some day if men forget that they owe their higher existence, not to the ideas of a few crazy ideologists, but to the knowledge and ruthless application of Nature's stern and rigid laws.

Everything we admire on this earth today—science and art, technology and inventions—is only the creative product of a few peoples and originally perhaps of *one* race. On them depends the existence of this whole culture. If they perish, the beauty of this earth will sink into the grave with them.

However much the soil, for example, can influence men, the result of the influence will always be different depending on the races in question. The low fertility of a living space may spur the one race to the highest achievements; in others it will only be the cause of bitterest poverty and final undernourishment with all its consequences. The inner nature of peoples is always determining for the manner in which outward influences will be effective. What leads the one to starvation trains the other to hard work.

All great cultures of the past perished only because the originally creative race died out from blood poisoning.

The ultimate cause of such a decline was their forgetting that all culture depends on men and not conversely; hence that to preserve a certain culture the man who creates it must be preserved. This preservation is bound up with the rigid law of necessity and the right to victory of the best and stronger in this world.

Those who want to live, let them fight, and those who do not want to fight in this world of eternal struggle do not deserve to live.

Even if this were hard—that is how it is! Assuredly, however, by far the harder fate is that which strikes the man who thinks he can overcome Nature, but in the last analysis only mocks her. Distress, misfortune, and diseases are her answer.

The man who misjudges and disregards the racial laws actually forfeits the happiness that seems destined to be his. He thwarts the triumphal march of the best race and hence also the precondition for all human progress, and remains, in consequence, burdened with all the sensibility of man, in the animal realm of helpless misery.

* * *

It is idle to argue which race or races were the original representative of human culture and hence the real founders of all that we sum up under the word 'humanity.' It is simpler to raise this question with regard to the present, and here an easy, clear answer results. All the human culture, all the results of art, science, and technology that we see before us today, are almost exclusively the creative product of the Aryan. This very fact admits of the not unfounded inference that he alone was the founder of all higher humanity, therefore representing the prototype of all that we understand by the word 'man.' He is the Prometheus of mankind from whose bright forehead the divine spark of genius has sprung at all times, forever kindling anew that fire of knowledge which illumined the night of silent mysteries and thus caused man to climb the path to mastery over the other beings of this earth. Exclude him—and perhaps after a few thousand years darkness will again descend on the earth, human culture will pass, and the world turn to a desert.

. . .

THEODOSIUS DOBZHANSKY

*Professor Dobzhansky, born in Russia in 1900, is an internationally known
authority on genetics and evolution. As a Fellow of the International
Education Board of the Rockefeller Foundation, he worked at Columbia
University and at the California Institute of Technology from 1927 to
1929. He was invited to stay on at the California Institute of Technology,
joined its faculty, and by 1936 was named full professor. In 1940 he returned to Columbia as Professor of Zoology. As specialist, Professor
Dobzhansky has devoted over thirty years of study to the mechanics of
heredity in the fruit fly; as humanist, he has been concerned with the
philosophical and social implications of modern biology. His writings
include* Genetics and the Origin of Species *(1937), which earned him the
Daniel Giraud Elliot medal and prize from the National Academy of
Sciences in 1941;* Heredity, Race and Society, *in collaboration with
L. C. Dunn (1946);* Evolution, Genetics, and Man *(1955);* The Biological
Basis of Human Freedom *(1956); and* Mankind Evolving: The Evolution
of the Human Species *(1962). The article we present below first appeared
in* Eugenics Quarterly, *December, 1963.*

GENETICS OF RACE EQUALITY

The crucial fact of our age is that people almost everywhere now take
the idea of human equality quite seriously. It is no longer accepted as
nature's law that people with darker skins are destined to be servants
and those with lighter ones, masters. Children of those at the bottom of
the social ladder no longer acquiesce in being placed automatically in a
similar position. Everybody is entitled to equality. But what is equality?
On the authority of the Declaration of Independence, it is a self-evident
truth "that all men were created equal." Yet we hear that biology and
genetics have demonstrated conclusively that men are unequal. Do bi-

ology and genetics really contradict what the Declaration of Independence holds to be self-evident? Or are the words "equal" and "unequal" being used in different senses? Just what have biology and genetics discovered that is relevant to the probem of equality or inequality?

Two geometric figures are said to be equal if they are identical in size and shape and coincide when superimposed on each other. Human equality, whether of persons or of groups, obviously means nothing of this sort. We generally have no difficulty distinguishing between persons whom we meet; the similarity of so-called identical twins strikes us as something unusual and remarkable. In fact, no two persons, not even identical twins, are ever truly identical. Every human being is in some respects unlike any other. This is not something that modern biology has recently found, but a matter of simple observation, so amply documented by the experience of everyone that its validity can hardly be questioned. Every person is, indeed, an individual, unique and unrepeatable. However, diversity and unlikeness, whether of individuals or of groups such as races, should not be confused with inequality. Nor should the affirmation of equality be taken to imply identity or uniformity.

Biology and genetics have some relevance to the problem of human equality. They have ushered in a new understanding of the nature and causes of human diversity. This nature resides in the remarkable chemical substances, the deoxyribonucleic acids, which are the principal constituents of the genes carried in the chromosomes of cell nuclei. Human genes are products of the evolutionary history of the human species, or the changes which were taking place in response to the environments in which our ancestors were living.

At this point one is tempted to discuss technicalities, which, although interesting and even fascinating in their own right, are not absolutely indispensable to our main theme. I shall resist the temptation. The essentials, developed from the seminal discoveries made by Gregor Mendel almost a century ago, can be stated quite simply. How many kinds of genes we inherit from our ancestors is not known with precision; there are at least thousands, and there may be tens of thousands, of genes carried in each human sex cell. An individual carries, then, thousands or tens of thousands of *pairs* of genes—one member of each pair being of maternal and the other of paternal origin.

What happens when the individual comes, in its turn, to form sex cells—egg cells or spermatozoa? It follows from Mendel's findings that each sex cell receives one or the other, the maternal or the paternal, member of every gene pair, but not a mixture of the two. A sex cell which receives a maternal copy of a gene A may, however, receive either the maternal or the paternal copy of the gene B, of the gene C, etc. Taking 1000 as a minimum estimate of the number of genes, it turns out that an individual is potentially capable of forming 2^{1000} kinds of sex cells containing different assortments of the maternal and paternal (or grand-maternal and grandpaternal) genes. I say *potentially*, because 2^{1000} is a number far greater than that of the atoms in the universe. Even if only one tenth—i.e. 100—of the maternal and paternal genes are different, the potentially possible number of kinds of sex cells is 2^{100}, which is a 31-place figure, vastly greater than the number of the sex cells produced.

All this adds up to something pretty simple after all: not even brothers and sisters, children of the same parents, are at all likely to have the same genes. No matter how many people may be born, despite any possible "population explosion," a tremendous majority of the potentially possible human nature will never be realized. A carping critic may remark that we hardly needed to learn genetics to discover what we know from everyday observation, that no two persons are ever alike. Genetics does, however, demonstrate something less commonplace when applied to analysis of the racial diversity among men.

Since our neighbors and even our closest relatives are all distinguishably different persons, it is not in the least surprising that people living in remote lands, or people whose ancestors came from such lands, are more noticeably different. We are inclined, however, to treat the diversity of groups in a manner rather different from diversity of individuals. If asked to describe your brother, or a cousin, or a fellow next door, you will probably say that he is somewhat taller (or shorter), darker (or lighter), heavier (or slimmer) than you, and you may add that he is inclined to be kind or easily angered, lazy or impatient, etc. A person whose ancestors lived in America before Columbus is, however, likely to be referred to as an Indian, and one whose ancestors came from trop-ical Africa, as a Negro.

Up to a point, this is, of course, legitimate. People of African ancestry usually have such conspicuous traits as a dark skin, kinky hair, broad nose, full lips, etc. One should not, however, forget that individual Indians, or Negroes, differ among themselves as much as do persons of the white race or any other race or group. When a group of people is given a name, a stereotype is likely to be invented; and oddly enough, the fewer persons of a given group one knows, the more rigid are the stereotypes of what all Indians, or Negroes, or Irishmen, or Jews are supposed to be. Most unreasonable of all, persons are then likely to be treated not according to what they are as individuals but according to the stereotype of the group to which they belong. This is as unwar-rantable biologically as it is ethically iniquitous.

Biologists have found between a million and two million species of animals and plants. An individual animal belongs to a certain species. It is, for example, either a horse *(Equus caballus)*, or an ass *(Equus asinus)*, or a sterile species hybrid (mule); but it cannot belong to two species at the same time. When anthropologists and biologists started to describe and classify races of men and animals, they treated races the same way as they treated species. Each was catalogued and given a name. But then difficulties arose. Biologists are sometimes in doubt as to whether certain forms should be regarded as belonging to the same or to two different species; however, with enough material, and given careful study, the doubts can usually be resolved. There is, however, no agreement among anthropologists concerning how many races there are in the human species. Opinions vary from three to more than two hundred. This is not a matter of insufficient data; the more studies are made on human populations, the less clear-cut the races become.

The difficulty is fundamental. Biological species are genetically closed systems; races are genetically open ones. Species do not interbreed and do not exchange genes, or do so rarely; they are reproductively isolated. The gene pools of the species man, chimpanzee, gorilla, and orang are quite separate; gene interchanges do not occur between these species. The biological meaning of this separation is evolutionary independence. Two species may have arisen from a common ancestor who lived long ago, but they embarked on separate evolutionary courses when they became species. No matter how favorable a new gene arising by mutation in the human species may be, it will not benefit the species chimpanzee nor vice versa.

Not so with races. Mankind, the human species, was a single evolutionary unit, at least, since mid-Pleistocene (the Ice Age). It continues to be a single unit, all segregations and apartheids notwithstanding. Wherever different human populations are sympatric—i.e. geographically intermingled in a common territory as castes or as religions or linguistic groups—some miscegenation and gene exchange crops up. More important still is the interbreeding and gene flow among populations of neighboring territories. It is a relative innovation in mankind that some racially distinct populations live sympatrically, like Negroes and Whites over a considerable part of the United States. Before, say, 2000 B.C., the human races, like races of most animal species, were largely allopatric, living in different territories. However, the peripheral gene flow, the gene exchange between allopatric but neighboring populations, whether human or animal, is and always was a regular occurrence.

This continuous, sometimes slow, but unfailing gene flow between neighboring clans, tribes, nations, and races upholds the biological and evolutionary unity of mankind. There may be no recorded case of a marriage of an Eskimo with, say, a Melanesian or a Bushman, but there are genetic links between all these populations via the geographically intervening groups. In contrast with distinct species, a beneficial change arising in any population anywhere in the world may become a part of the common biological endowment of all races of mankind. This genetic oneness of mankind has been growing steadily since the development of material cultures has made travel and communication between the inhabitants of different countries progressively more and more rapid and easy. What should be stressed however, is that mankind has not become a meaningful biological entity just recently, since men began to travel often and far. The human species was such an entity even before it became recognizably human.

Races, on the contrary, are not, and never were, groups clearly defined biologically. The gene flow between human populations makes race boundaries always more or less blurred. Consider three groups of people, for example: Scandinavians, Japanese, and Congolese. Every individual will probably be easily placeable in one of the three races—White, Mongoloid, and Negroid. It will however, be far from easy to delimit these races if one observes also the inhabitants of the countries geographically intermediate between Scandinavia, Japan, and Congo, respectively. Intermediate countries have intermediate populations, or populations which differ in some characteristics from all previously outlined races. One may try to get out of the difficulty by recognizing several intermediate races; or else, one may speculate that the races were nicely distinct at some time in the past, and got mixed up lately owing to miscegenation. This helps not at all. The more races one sets up, the fuzzier their boundaries become. And the difficulty is by no means confined to man; it occurs as well in many biological species where it cannot be blamed on recent miscegenation.

Populations which inhabit different countries differ more often in relative frequencies of genetically simple traits than in any single trait being present in all individuals of one population and always absent in another population. Not only are the differences thus relative rather than absolute; but, to make things more complex still, the variations of different characters are often independent or at least not strongly correlated. Some populations may be clearly different in a gene A but rather similar in a gene B, while other populations may be different in B but less so in A. This makes the drawing of any lines separating different races a rather arbitrary procedure, and results in the notorious inability of anthropologists to agree on any race classification yet proposed. Race classifiers might have indeed preferred to find simple and tidy races, in which every person would show just the characteristics that his race is supposed to possess. Nature has not been obliging enough to make the races conform to this prescription. Exactly the same difficulties which a student of races encounters in the human species are met with also by zoologists who are working with species of nonhuman animals, and arguments have actually been put forward that animals have no races, or at least that the races should not be described and named. Where, then, are races found? If they are nowhere to be found, then what are these visibly different populations of the human species which are usually referred to as races?

Much needed light on the nature of population or race difference came from studies on the genetics of chemical constituents of the human blood.

As far back as 1900, Landsteiner discovered four blood types, or blood groups, distinguishable by simple laboratory tests. These blood groups—called O, A, B, and AB—are inherited very simply, according to Mendel's laws. Brothers and sisters and parents and children may, and quite often do, differ in blood types. An enormous number of investigations have been made, especially in recent years, on the distribution of the blood types among peoples in various parts of the world. Any race or population can be described in terms of the percentages of the four blood types. Almost everywhere persons of all four types are found, but in different proportions. Thus B and AB bloods are commonest among peoples of central Asia and India, A bloods in western Europe and in some American Indians, while many American Indian tribes belong predominantly or even exclusively to the group O.

Several other blood group systems have been discovered, including the Rhesus system, usually referred to as the Rh factor. The genes for these blood groups behave in general like those for the "classical" O-A-B-AB blood types. For example, one of the variants (alleles) of the Rhesus gene occurs much more often in the populations of Africa than elsewhere. But mark this well—this gene does occur, albeit infrequently, in human populations almost everywhere in the world, and it is quite certain that it has not spread so widely owing to a Negro admixture in recent centuries.

These facts are profoundly significant. Consider the following situation, which is by no means unusual. A person of European origin, say an Englishman or a Frenchman, has O-type blood, while his brother has B blood. In this particular respect, these brothers differ from each other, while one of them resembles many American Indians with O bloods, and the other matches numerous persons in Asia and elsewhere who have B bloods. Or else, one of the brothers may have the kind of Rhesus blood type most characteristic of the Africans, and the other brother may have blood more like a majority of his European neighbors. Such characteristics, of which the persons concerned are usually quite unaware, may become vitally important in some circumstances. If an individual with O-type blood needs a blood transfusion, then O-type blood from a donor of no matter what race will be safe, while the blood of the recipient's brother may be dangerous if that brother has A, B, or AB blood.

Though not different in principle from the blood types, the genetics of skin color and similar traits is considerably more complex. The color difference between Negro and White skin is due to joint action of several genes, each of which by itself makes the skin only a little darker or lighter. Geneticists have studied the inheritance of skin pigmentation for half a century, yet exactly how many genes are involved is still unknown. The skin color is obviously variable among the so-called "white" as well as among the "black" peoples, some individuals being darker and others, lighter. If we were able to map the geographic distribution of each separate skin color gene as thoroughly as it has been done for some blood group genes, the race differences would probably be resolved into gene frequency differences. It is fair to say that the studies on blood types and similar traits have, so far at least, helped more to understand races than to classify them.

Thus every race includes persons with diverse genetic endowments. Genetic studies show that race differences are compounded of the same kinds of genetic elements in which individuals within a race also differ. An individual must always be judged according to what he is, not according to the place of origin of his ancestors. Races may be defined as populations which differ in frequencies, or in prevalence, of some genes. Race differences are relative, not absolute.

This modern race concept, based on findings of genetics, appears to differ from the traditional view so much that it has provoked some misunderstanding and opposition. The use of traits like the blood groups to elucidate the nature of the races of which mankind is composed may seem a questionable procedure. To distinguish races, should one use, rather, traits like the skin pigmentation in place of the blood types? Some blood types can be found almost anywhere in the world; on the other hand, pale skins (other than albino) do not occur among the natives of equatorial Africa or of New Guinea, and black skins are not found among the natives of Europe. This objection is beside the point. The blood types are useful because their genetic nature is relatively simple and well understood. The classification of the human races need not be based on any one trait; the behavior of the blood types helps, however, to understand the behavior of other traits, including the skin color.

To sum up, the races of man are not integrated biological entities of the sort biological species are. Race boundaries are blurred by the more or less slow but long-sustained gene exchange. The number of races that should be recognized is arbitrary in the sense that it is a matter of convention and convenience whether one should give names to only a few "major" or also to a larger number of "minor" races. An anthropologist who maintains that there are exactly five or any other fixed number of races, or who resolves to cut the Gordian Knot—mankind has no races— is nurturing illusions. On the other hand, there need be nothing arbitrary about race differences; human populations are racially distinct if they differ in the frequencies of some genes, and not distinct if they do not so differ. The presence of race differences can be ascertained, and if they are present, their magnitude can be measured.

The problem that inevitably arises in any discussion of individual and race equality is how consequential the differences among humans really are. Man's bodily structures do not differentiate him very strikingly from other living creatures; it is the psychic, intellectual, or spiritual side of human nature that is truly distinctive of Man. Physical race differences supply only the externally visible marks by which the geographic origin of people, or rather of their ancestors, can be identified. The blood types, nose shapes, and skin colors of people whom we meet are so much less important to us than their dispositions, intelligence, and rectitude. It is a person's personality that matters.

The diversity of personalities would seem to be as great, and surely more telling, than the diversity of skin colors or other physical traits. And, though the biological basis of both kinds of diversity is the same in principle, it is different enough in its outward manifestations that the difference constitutes a genuine problem. This is the perennial nature-nurture problem. The confusion and polemics with which it was beset for a long time were due in part to the problem having been wrongly stated—which human traits are due to heredity and which to environment. No trait can arise unless the heredity of the organism makes it possible, and no heredity operates outside of environments. A meaningful way is to ask what part of the diversity observed in a given population is conditioned by the genetic differences between persons composing this population, and what part is due to the upbringing, education, and other environmental variables. Furthermore, the issue must be investigated and solved separately for each function, trait or characteristic that comes under consideration. Suppose one collects good data on the genetic and environmental components of the observed diversity in the intelligence quotients, or on the resistance to tuberculosis. This would not tell us anything about the diversity of temperaments or about resistance to cancer.

Even correctly stated, the nature-nurture problem remains a formidable one. Dogmatic statements abound on both the hereditarian and the environmentalist side of the controversy, and they usually say much about their authors but not much about the subject at issue. The plain truth is that it is not known just how influential are the genetic variables in psychic or personality traits or how plastic these traits might be in different environments that can be contrived by modern technology, medicine, and educational methods. There is no way in practice to arrange for a large group of people to be brought up under controlled and uniform conditions in order to see how similar or different they would develop. The converse experiment—observing identical twins, individuals with similar heredities brought up in different environments—is possible, but opportunities for such observations are scarcer than one would wish they were.

Some partisans of human equality got themselves in the untenable position of arguing that mankind is genetically uniform with respect to intelligence, ability, and other psychic traits. Actually it is, I think, fair to say that whenever any variable trait in man was at all adequately studied genetically, evidence was found of at least some, though perhaps slight, contribution of genetic differences. Being equal has to be compatible with being different, and different in characters that are relevant to the specifically human estate, not alone in "skin-deep" traits like skin color.

The current civil rights movement in the United States has elicited a rash of racist pamphlets which pretend to prove, very "scientifically" of course, that races cannot be equal because they differ in the average brain size, the average I.Q., etc. Now, there is no reason to believe that small differences in the brain volumes are any indication of different mental capacities; the I.Q. tests are not reliable when administered to people of different sociocultural backgrounds, and in any case they cannot be taken as anything approaching a measurement of human worth. Be all that as it may, the striking fact—which not even the racists can conceal—is that the race differences in the averages are much smaller than the variations within any race. In other words, large brains and high I.Q.'s of persons of every race are much larger and higher than the averages for their own or any other race. And conversely, the low variants in every race are much below the average for any race. This is a situation quite analogous to what is known about race differences in such traits as blood groups and is in perfect accord with theoretical expectations in populations which exchange genes.

It is impossible in an article such as the present one to summarize and to evaluate critically the abundant but often unreliable and contradictory data on the nature-nurture situation in man. It is more useful to consider here some fundamentals that must be kept in mind in dealing with such data. An all too often forgotten and yet most basic fact is that the genes determine, not traits or characters, but the ways in which the organism responds to the environments. One inherits, not the skin color and intelligence, but only genes which make the development of certain colors and intelligence possible. To state the same thing with a slightly different emphasis, the gene complement determines the path which the development of a person will take, given the sequence of the environments which this person encounters in the process of living. Any developmental process, whether physiological or psychological, can be influenced or modified by genetic as well as by environmental variables. The realization of heredity is manageable, within limits, by physiological and social engineering. What the limits are depends upon our understanding of the developmental processes involved. Modern medicine is able to control the manifestations of some hereditary diseases which not so long ago were incurable. This does not make hereditary defects and diseases harmless or unimportant; even if they can be cured, it is better for the individual and for his society to have no necessity of being cured. This does give substance to the hope that hereditary need be, not destiny, but conditioning.

Although the mode of inheritance of physical and psychic traits in man is fundamentally the same, their developmental plasticity—the ability to respond to modifying influences of the environment—is different. There is no known way to alter the blood group with which a person is born; it is possible to modify one's skin color, making it somewhat darker or lighter by sun tanning or by lack of sun exposure; the development of personality traits is very much dependent on the family and social environments in which an individual is brought up and lives. The great lability of psychic traits is at least one of the reasons why it is so hard, not only to measure precisely the role played by heredity in their variations, but even to prove unambiguously that some of these traits are influenced by heredity at all. The more environmentally labile is a trait, the more critical it is for its investigation to have the environment under control; this is difficult or impossible to achieve with man.

The great environmental plasticity of psychic traits in man is no biological accident. It is an important, even crucial, evolutionary adaptation which distinguishes man from other creatures, including those nearest to him in the zoological system. It is by brain, not by brawn, that man controls his environment. Mankind's singular and singularly powerful adaptive instrument is culture. Culture is not inherited through genes, it is acquired by learning from other human beings. The ability to learn, and thus to acquire a culture and to become a member of a society is, however, given by the genetic endowment that is mankind's distinctive biological attribute. In a sense, human genes have surrendered their primacy in human evolution to an entirely new, nonbiological or superorganic agent, culture. However, it should not be forgotten that this agent is entirely dependent on the human genotype.

A pseudobiological fallacy—dangerous because it is superficially so plausible—alleges that the differences in psychic traits among human individuals and races are genetically fixed to about the same extent as they are among races or breeds of domestic animals. This overlooks the fact that the behavior of a breed of horses or of dogs is always a part of a complex of characters that are deliberately selected by the breeders to fit the animals for its intended use. A hunting dog with a temperament of a Pekingese, a great Dane behaving like a fox terrier, a draft horse as highstrung as a race horse or vice versa—all these monstrosities would be worthless or even dangerous to their human masters. Man has seen to it that the genes that stabilize the desirable behavior traits in his domestic animals be fixed and the genes that predispose for variable or undesirable behavior be eliminated.

What is biologically as well as sociologically requisite in man is the exact opposite—not to fix rigidly his qualities, but to be able to learn whatever mode of behavior fits a job to be done, the mores of the group of which one happens to be a member, a conduct befitting the circumstances and opportunities. Man's paramount adaptive trait is his educability. The biological evolution of mankind has accordingly so shaped the human genotype that an educability is a universal property of all nonpathological individuals. It is a diagnostic character of mankind as a species, not of only some of its races. This universality is no accident either. In all cultures, primitive or advanced, the vital ability is to be able to learn whatever is necessary to become a competent member of some group or society. In advanced civilizations the variety of function has grown so enormously that learning has come to occupy a considerable fraction of the life span. Even where, as in India, the society was splintered for centuries into castes specialized for different occupations, the ability to learn new professions or trades has been preserved.

Champions of human equality have traditionally been environmentalists, conspicuously distrustful of genetic determinisms. Historically their attitude has been useful in counterbalancing the influence of those racist hereditarians who tried to justify the denial of equality of opportunity to most people on the pretext that the latter are genetically inferior. The environmentalists, however, went too far in their protest. They simply failed to understand that to be equal is not the same thing as to be alike. Equality is a sociological, not a biological, ideal. A society may grant equality to its citizens, but it cannot make them alike. What is more, in a society composed of genetically identical individuals, equality would be meaningless; individuals would have to be assigned for different occupations by drawing lots or in some other arbitrary manner. The ideal of equality of opportunity is precious, because it holds out a hope that persons and groups diverse in their endowments may enjoy a feeling of belonging and of partnership and may work for the common good in whatever capacity without loss of their human dignity. Men must be dealt with primarily on the basis of their humanity and also on the basis of their potentialities and accomplishments as individuals; the practice of treating them according to their race or color is a nefarious one.

Genetic diversity is a blessing, not a curse. Any society—particularly any civilized society—has a multitude of diverse vocations and callings to be filled, and new ones are constantly emerging. The human genetically secured educability enables most individuals of all races to be trained for most occupations. This is certainly the basic and fundamental adaptive quality of all mankind; yet this is in no way incompatible with a genetically conditioned diversity of preferences and special abilities. Music is an obnoxious noise to some, ecstatic pleasure to others. Some have a bodily frame that can be trained for championship in wrestling, or running, or sprinting, or weight lifting. Some can develop phenomenal abilities for chess playing, or painting, or composing poetry. Can anybody develop a skill in any of these occupations if he makes sufficient effort? Possibly many people could, to some extent. The point is, however, that what comes easily to some requires great exertion from others, and even then the accomplishment is mediocre at best. The willingness to strive derives, however, at least in part, from a feeling that the labor is rewarded by the thrill of accomplishment or in some other way. There is little stimulus to exert oneself if the results of the exertions are likely to be pitifully small. And it is also possible that there is such a thing as predisposition to striving and effort.

It is a perversion of the ethic of equality to endeavor to reduce everybody to a uniform level of achievement. "From each according to his ability" is the famous motto of Marxian socialism, and it behooves democracy to grant no less recognition to the diversity of human individualities. This is not an apology for "rugged individualism"; the "ruggedness" amounts often to indifference or even contempt for individualities of others. Equality is, however, not an end in itself, but a means to an end, which can only be the self-actualization of human individuals and the fullest possible realization of their socially valuable capacities and potentialities. Individuals and groups will arrange their lives differently, in accordance with their diverse notions of what form of happiness they wish to pursue. Their contributions to mankind's store of achievements will be different in kind and in magnitude. The point is, however, that everybody should be able to contribute to the limit of his ability. To deny the equality of opportunity to persons or groups is evil, because it results in wastage of talent, ability, and aptitude, besides being contrary to the basic ethic of humanity.

GEORGE ORWELL

MARRAKECH

This essay, written in 1939, is included in George Orwell's collection entitled Such, Such Were the Joys *(1953). For information on the author and his writings, see page 74.*

•

As the corpse went past the flies left the restaurant table in a cloud and rushed after it, but they came back a few minutes later.

The little crowd of mourners—all men and boys, no women—threaded their way across the market-place between the piles of pomegranates and the taxis and the camels, wailing a short chant over and over again. What really appeals to the flies is that the corpses here are never put into coffins, they are merely wrapped in a piece of rag and carried on a rough wooden bier on the shoulders of four friends. When the friends get to the burying-ground they hack an oblong hole a foot or two deep, dump the body in it and fling over it a little of the dried-up, lumpy earth, which is like broken brick. No gravestone, no name, no identifying mark of any kind. The burying-ground is merely a huge waste of hummocky earth, like a derelict building-lot. After a month or two no one can even be certain where his own relatives are buried.

When you walk through a town like this—two hundred thousand inhabitants, of whom at least twenty thousand own literally nothing except the rags they stand up in—when you see how the people live, and still more how easily they die, it is always difficult to believe that you are walking among human beings. All colonial empires are in reality founded upon that fact. The people have brown faces—besides, there are so many of them! Are they really the same flesh as yourself? Do they even have names? Or are they merely a kind of undifferentiated brown stuff, about as individual as bees or coral insects? They rise out of the earth, they sweat and starve for a few years, and then they sink back into the nameless mounds of the graveyard and nobody notices that they are gone. And even the graves themselves soon fade back into the soil. Sometimes, out for a walk, as you break your way through the prickly pear, you notice that it is rather bumpy underfoot, and only a certain regularity in the bumps tells you that you are walking over skeletons.

I was feeding one of the gazelles in the public gardens.

Gazelles are almost the only animals that look good to eat when they are still alive, in fact, one can hardly look at their hindquarters without thinking of mint sauce. The gazelle I was feeding seemed to know that this thought was in my mind, for though it took the piece of bread I was holding out it obviously did not like me. It nibbled rapidly at the bread, then lowered its head and tried to butt me, then took another nibble and then butted again. Probably its idea was that if it could drive me away the bread would somehow remain hanging in mid-air.

An Arab navvy working on the path nearby lowered his heavy hoe and sidled slowly towards us. He looked from the gazelle to the bread and from the bread to the gazelle, with a sort of quiet amazement, as though he had never seen anything quite like this before. Finally he said shyly in French:

"*I* could eat some of that bread."

I tore off a piece and he stowed it gratefully in some secret place under his rags. This man is an employee of the Municipality.

When you go through the Jewish quarters you gather some idea of what the medieval ghettoes were probably like. Under their Moorish rulers the Jews were only allowed to own land in certain restricted areas, and after centuries of this kind of treatment they have ceased to bother about overcrowding. Many of the streets are a good deal less than six feet wide, the houses are completely windowless, and sore-eyed children cluster everywhere in unbelievable numbers, like clouds of flies. Down the centre of the street there is generally running a little river of urine.

In the bazaar huge families of Jews, all dressed in the long black robe and little black skull-cap, are working in dark fly-infested booths that look like caves. A carpenter sits cross-legged at a prehistoric lathe, turning chair-legs at lightning speed. He works the lathe with a bow in his right hand and guides the chisel with his left foot, and thanks to a lifetime of sitting in this position his left leg is warped out of shape. At his side his grandson, aged six, is already starting on the simpler parts of the job.

I was just passing the coppersmiths' booths when somebody noticed that I was lighting a cigarette. Instantly, from the dark holes all round, there was a frenzied rush of Jews, many of them old grandfathers with flowing grey beards, all clamouring for a cigarette. Even a blind man somewhere at the back of one of the booths heard a rumour of cigarettes and came crawling out, groping in the air with his hand. In about a minute I had used up the whole packet. None of these people, I suppose, works less than twelve hours a day, and every one of them looks on a cigarette as a more or less impossible luxury.

As the Jews live in self-contained communities they follow the same trades as the Arabs, except for agriculture. Fruit-sellers, potters, silver-smiths, blacksmiths, butchers, leatherworkers, tailors, water-carriers, beg-gars, porters—whichever way you look you see nothing but Jews. As a matter of fact there are thirteen thousand of them, all living in the space of a few acres. A good job Hitler wasn't here. Perhaps he was on his way, however. You hear the usual dark rumours about the Jews, not only from the Arabs but from the poorer Europeans.

"Yes, mon vieux, they took my job away from me and gave it to a Jew. The Jews! They're the real rulers of this country, you know. They've got all the money. They control the banks, finance—everything."

"But," I said, "isn't it a fact that the average Jew is a labourer working for about a penny an hour?"

"Ah, that's only for show! They're all moneylenders really. They're cunning, the Jews."

In just the same way, a couple of hundred years ago, poor old women used to be burned for witchcraft when they could not even work enough magic to get themselves a square meal.

theme

All people who work with their hands are partly invisible, and the more important the work they do, the less visible they are. Still, a white skin is always fairly conspicuous. In northern Europe, when you see a labourer ploughing a field, you probably give him a second glance. In a hot country, anywhere south of Gibraltar or east of Suez, the chances are that you don't even see him. I have noticed this again and again. In a tropical landscape one's eye takes in everything except the human beings. It takes in the dried-up soil, the prickly pear, the palm tree and the distant mountain, but it always misses the peasant hoeing at his patch. He is the same colour as the earth, and a great deal less interesting to look at.

It is only because of this that the starved countries of Asia and Africa are accepted as tourist resorts. No one would think of running cheap trips to the Distressed Areas. But where the human beings have brown skins their poverty is simply not noticed. What does Morocco mean to a Frenchman? An orange-grove or a job in Government service. Or to an Englishman? Camels, castles, palm trees, Foreign Legionnaires, brass trays, and bandits. One could probably live there for years without noticing that for nine-tenths of the people the reality of life is an endless, back-breaking struggle to wring a little food out of an eroded soil.

Most of Morocco is so desolate that no wild animal bigger than a hare can live on it. Huge areas which were once covered with forest have turned into a treeless waste where the soil is exactly like broken-up brick. Nevertheless a good deal of it is cultivated, with frightful labour. Everything is done by hand. Long lines of women, bent double like inverted capital L's, work their way slowly across the fields, tearing up the prickly weeds with their hands, and the peasant gathering lucerne for fodder pulls it up stalk by stalk instead of reaping it, thus saving an inch or two on each stalk. The plough is a wretched wooden thing, so frail that one can easily carry it on one's shoulder, and fitted underneath with a rough iron spike which stirs the soil to a depth of about four inches. This is as much as the strength of the animals is equal to. It is usual to plough with a cow and a donkey yoked together. Two donkeys would not be quite strong enough, but on the other hand two cows would cost a little more to feed. The peasants possess no harrows, they merely plough the soil several times over in different directions, finally leaving it in rough furrows, after which the whole field has to be shaped with hoes into small oblong patches to conserve water. Except for a day or two after the rare rainstorms there is never enough water. Along the edges of the fields channels are hacked out to a depth of thirty or forty feet to get at the tiny trickles which run through the subsoil.

Every afternoon a file of very old women passes down the road outside my house, each carrying a load of firewood. All of them are mummified with age and the sun, and all of them are tiny. It seems to be generally the case in primitive communities that the women, when they get beyond a certain age, shrink to the size of children. One day a poor old creature who could not have been more than four feet tall crept past me under a vast load of wood. I stopped her and put a five-sou piece (a little more than a farthing) into her hand. She answered with a shrill wail, almost a scream, which was partly gratitude but mainly surprise. I suppose that from her point of view, by taking any notice of her, I seemed almost to be violating a law of nature. She accepted her status as an old woman, that is to say as a beast of burden. When a family is travelling it is quite usual to see a father and a grown-up son riding ahead on donkeys, and an old woman following on foot, carrying the baggage.

But what is strange about these people is their invisibility. For several weeks, always at about the same time of day, the file of old women had hobbled past the house with their firewood, and though they had registered themselves on my eyeballs I cannot truly say that I had seen them. Firewood was passing—that was how I saw it. It was only that one day I happened to be walking behind them, and the curious up-and-down motion of a load of wood drew my attention to the human being beneath it. Then for the first time I noticed the poor old earth-coloured bodies, bodies reduced to bones and leathery skin, bent double under the crushing weight. Yet I suppose I had not been five minutes on Moroccan soil before I noticed the overloading of the donkeys and was infuriated by it. There is no question that the donkeys are damnably treated. The Moroccan donkey is hardly bigger than a St. Bernard dog, it carries a load which in the British Army would be considered too much for a fifteen-hands mule, and very often its pack-saddle is not taken off its back for weeks together. But what is peculiarly pitiful is that it is the most willing creature on earth, it follows its master like a dog and does not need either bridle or halter. After a dozen years of devoted work it suddenly drops dead, whereupon its master tips it into the ditch and the village dogs have torn its guts out before it is cold.

This kind of thing makes one's blood boil, whereas—on the whole—the plight of the human beings does not. I am not commenting, merely pointing to a fact. People with brown skins are next door to invisible. Anyone can be sorry for the donkey with its galled back, but it is generally owing to some kind of accident if one even notices the old woman under her load of sticks.

As the storks flew northward the Negroes were marching southward—a long, dusty column, infantry, screw-gun batteries, and then more infantry, four or five thousand men in all, winding up the road with a clumping of boots and a clatter of iron wheels.

They were Senegalese, the blackest Negroes in Africa, so black that sometimes it is difficult to see whereabouts on their necks the hair begins. Their splendid bodies were hidden in reach-me-down khaki uniforms, their feet squashed into boots that looked like blocks of wood, and every tin hat seemed to be a couple of sizes too small. It was very hot and the men had marched a long way. They slumped under the weight of their packs and the curiously sensitive black faces were glistening with sweat.

As they went past a tall, very young Negro turned and caught my eye. But the look he gave me was not in the least the kind of look you might expect. Not hostile, not contemptuous, not sullen, not even inquisitive. It was the shy, wide-eyed Negro look, which actually is a look of profound respect. I saw how it was. This wretched boy, who is a French citizen and has therefore been dragged from the forest to scrub floors and catch syphilis in garrison towns, actually has feelings of reverence before a white skin. He has been taught that the white race are his masters, and he still believes it.

But there is one thought which every white man (and in this connection it doesn't matter twopence if he calls himself a socialist) thinks when he sees a black army matching past. "How much longer can we go on kidding these people? How long before they turn their guns in the other direction?"

It was curious, really. Every white man there had this thought stowed somewhere or other in his mind. I had it, so had the other onlookers, so had the officers on their sweating chargers and the white N.C.O.'s marching in the ranks. It was a kind of secret which we all knew and were too clever to tell; only the Negroes didn't know it. And really it was like watching a flock of cattle to see the long column, a mile or two miles of armed men, flowing peacefully up the road, while the great white birds drifted over them in the opposite direction, glittering like scraps of paper.

[1939]

PERRY MORGAN

Perry Morgan is Managing Editor of the Charlotte (N.C.) News. *Educated at the University of Georgia, he has also studied as a Nieman Fellow at Harvard. He has worked on newspapers in Georgia, Michigan, Virginia, and North Carolina and has won several prizes for editorial and news writing. The article we reprint below first appeared in the January, 1962, issue of* Esquire.

THE CASE FOR THE
WHITE SOUTHERNER

When the good citizens of New Rochelle, New York, were accused last year of admitting Jim Crow to their schools, they denied it. When they were taken to court, they resisted. When the judge looked and saw old Jim sitting there plain as day and ordered his removal, a solid citizen of New Rochelle cried: "Nobody understands our situation."

New Rochelle is located in the Piety Belt that denounces racial discrimination and has it, too. The law is against it, but the majority of people are for it. Beginning in 1930, Judge Irving R. Kaufman found, the New Rochelle school board had confined Negro pupils exclusively to one school. This was the Lincoln School (presumably after Abraham Lincoln who signed the Emancipation Proclamation) from which transfers were denied even though all-white schools had twice as many vacant seats as children registered at Lincoln. Even after Judge Kaufman ordered Jim Crow expelled, a school board majority concocted a desegregation plan designed to sneak old Jim back into school by the side door. The judge, however, was adamant.

The Piety Belt is a varied land populated by people of good conscience. Their forefathers, according to much-loved myth, fought a war to free the slaves. And for the century since, by preachment and earnest exhortation, they have urged the white Southerner to conquer the evil in his heart and treat the Negro as a free and equal American. They have looked away to Dixie Land with fury and scorn and earnestly have hoped the down-trodden Negro would never doubt the constancy of their faith.

Abundance of precept, however, has been accompanied by a stringent shortage of example in the Piety Belt. Negroes migrating into the North early noted that, although the law was on their side, the people lacked some of the warmth and fellowship to which they were accustomed. "Up North," the saying sprang up, "they don't care how high you get just so you don't get too close; down South, they don't care how close you get, just so you don't get too high." The point has not lost its sharpness.

The South has been given far too much credit for ingenuity in shaping the law to its own purposes. The Southern lawyer seeking to circumvent the Supreme Court decision really had to look no farther than Phila-delphia to find the model for what in the South the Northern press sniffily defines as "token integration." According to a Public Affairs Committee study by Will Maslow and Richard Cohen, "more Negro children attend what are in fact segregated schools in the major cities of the North than attend officially segregated schools in urban areas of the South." Note the authors: "When Lieutenant Nellie Forbush, the Navy nurse in *South Pacific*, tells the world she hails from Little Rock, she is greeted from Maine to Madagascar with hoots, catcalls and other indigenous expressions of disapproval . . . yet Little Rock . . . has fewer Negroes than the South Side of Chicago. More significant, school segregation is as prevalent in that corner of Chicago as it is in the Arkansas capital." So much for the soul of John Brown—in bivouac.

The non-Southerner naturally has ready excuses for this paradox. It is difficult to admit guilt. Having hidden his complicity in the crime of slavery for a century he cannot bring himself to face the fact now that the victim has caught up with him. His schools stagger from crisis to crisis under the weight of a vast influx of Negro children who lack the capacity to keep up with their white classmates. Achievement levels are dropping. The more affluent whites are fleeing. One school superintendent told *Look* Magazine's George B. Leonard, Jr. that a third of the children in his elementary schools may end up not only unemployed, but unemployable. But, as Leonard wrote, this is a shrouded crisis. Though Dr. James B. Conant has deplored the lack of statistics, school officials cannot publicly face the "delicate and complex matter of racial prejudice." Instead, "they cling to the vain old hope that racial prejudice will disappear if you pretend race does not exist."

So earnest is the innocent resident of the Piety Belt in his explanations that he forgets the white Southerner has heard them all before. In fact, he holds the patents on them. The Negro came to *him* on Yankee slave ships from the jungle. Yet in trying to shake the Northerner from his silly pretensions, *Look* indulged its own in a headline saying "*America's large cities are paying the grim price of a century of rural and Southern educational neglect.*"

Southern neglect? God in heaven! By his standards of the time the Northerner perhaps had excuse for visiting unmerciful vengeance upon the whites of the defeated Confederacy. But what of the freed man in whose name, and out of strategic necessity, the Civil War was given a sacred cause through Lincoln's Emancipation Proclamation? Leaving the freed man and the white man together in a pit of poverty, pain and ignorance, the victorious Northerner turned to a feast of prosperity whose cynicism sickened and dismayed Henry Adams and other sensitive souls.

On reflection, though, it is not quite accurate to say the North merely wrought ruin and departed. More precisely, with a host of exploiting devices, it leeched out of a destroyed region many of the pitiful resources left for its meager sustenance. Long before Franklin D. Roosevelt rediscovered America's own viciously exploited colony to the South, the Piety Belt was grieving for the downtrodden in faraway corners of the world.

The white Southerner and the Negro climbed out of the pit together, and unassisted. It was a long, grim and demeaning journey, and if it scarred the Negro it also scarred the white. For its part in the crime of slavery, as Gerald Johnson has written, the South has paid and paid and paid. It owes neither the North nor the world apologies for its stewardship of the human dilemma deposited on American shores three centuries ago. What qualifications the Negro now brings in support of his demand for full participation in the world's most difficult citizenship, he has from the white Southerner. If he goes North with an inferior education, he was given that by a white man who has never been able to afford adequate schools for his own children.

The Southerner has believed a lot of comforting bushwa about his own region—moonlight, magnolias and all the rest. But having some little experience with the Negro problem, he is altogether disinclined to believe the North's nonsense too. He has observed that wherever the two races exist together in significant numbers—in London, Capetown or New Rochelle—walls are thrown up, and that when laws oppose, the walls somehow curve around the laws.

The case for the white Southerner is that he is a human being with a normal complement of virtues and vices. If he himself has been too much concerned with defending and vaunting his virtues, the North has been overly fascinated with condemning his vices. A Union officer made that point a century ago, as W. D. Workman has recalled, and so did Harriet Beecher Stowe when she got around to looking for herself.

Let the misunderstood citizen of affluent New Rochelle mark well this unique fact: twice in a hundred years the South has been forced to recast the laws, the mood and the mind of its people. In both cases, though it had no model for judgment, the nation decided to substitute revolutionary for evolutionary processes. The latter, to be sure, were still working injustices when the Supreme Court interrupted in 1954, but they had wrought profound changes too. The South at that point had begun rapidly to repair the spiritual and material ravages of a grim host of decades of poverty, ignorance, pain, disease and economic exploitation. A growing middle class was bringing a new stability to political processes flawed and half-paralyzed by the racial factor. The region had begun to surmount the bleak, crippling pessimism that was the natural inheritance of the past and to take new and promising initiatives even in the field of race relations. Great strides had been taken in education, medicine and agriculture. The fabled Southern female was slaving in field and factory, and sometimes both, to send sons and daughters to college and break once and for all the harsh grip of hoe and row. The winds of hope and progress, in sum, were quickening.

Then came May 17, 1954, and an historic decision concerned as much with conjectural foreign-policy needs for a purer national image as with the needs of the American Negro. Never before, not even in the Dred Scott case which wrecked the court's power and prestige on the reefs of Northern outrage, had there issued a writ touching so profoundly and personally the lives of so many millions of individuals. Yet out of his profound innocence, the Northerner fully expected the South—by taking thought—to swiftly swallow its sociological medicine, cleanse the national conscience and miraculously reorder its ancient social rhythms.

Be it noted that the court itself had no such expectations. Far less momentous writs of the court had failed before to run beyond the narrow bounds of the District of Columbia. Less than two decades had passed since the court had prevented its dismemberment by reversing —lock, stock, and barrel—its whole philosophy toward the New Deal.

The court, nonetheless, had set out to make a social laboratory out of a vast region whose history had led, in Robert Penn Warren's phrase, to a massive "fear of abstraction—the instinctive fear that the massiveness of experience, the concreteness of life, will be violated." Now, suddenly, so far as the rank-and-file Southerner knew, the most fearful of all abstractions had been struck into the law of the land. Once again, the vast engine of the Federal Government that had ground his fathers down was to undertake a transformation of his and his children's lives. Once again, the national press would smoke with moral rebuke and condemnation. Already, the NAACP was promising to wrap up the whole revolution in a year or two and, as at least one NAACP official gave as his personal opinion, intermarriage certainly *was* one goal of the revolution.

If this travail would make the world love America more, the Southerner asked himself, what would it do to his children? The very essence of the Supreme Court decision was admission that in the mass the Negro was culturally inferior. And the white schools themselves, despite tax support proportionally greater than the national average, sorely needed strengthening. Thus it was that the most liberal Southerner—and the South has a strain of liberalism unsurpassed for courage and toughness —was forced to ponder earnestly when the learned and gentle William Polk asked: "If the Negro is entitled to lift himself by enforced association with the white man, why should not the white man be entitled to prevent himself from being pulled down by enforced association with the Negro?"

And there were other questions for the heart: What would happen to the virtues of that paternalism which had bound black and white together in a relationship that, however unprogressive, was often warmly human in its sharing? If the Southerner *knew* he did not understand the lesser figure in this bond, was it not frightening to be forced to comprehend that this friendly, agreeable and sympathetic soul that jollied him and nursed his children was in reality a total stranger who changed vocabularies at quitting time?

Walter Lippmann once remarked that "all deliberate speed" in, say, Alabama might mean admission of Negro students to graduate schools of white universities by the tenth anniversary of the court's ruling. Lippmann offered a piercing insight into the fantastic complexity of rejiggering human attitudes plus calm acceptance that wherever such engineering is attempted social turbulence, fear and instability clog and distort the normal channels of social and political leadership. This, really, was not so strange a point—having been written down indelibly in blood and anguish throughout human history. But unhappily, American understanding that is capable of leaping an ocean often sinks midstream in the Potomac River.

As applied to Algeria, for example, the faithful reader of The New York *Times* and auditor of national television understands the difficulty very well. He sees clearly, for it has been movingly and expertly explained, why proud French generals, exquisitely mannered and magnificently educated, yielded to righteousness, insolence and finally to armed rebellion against the great de Gaulle himself at a moment when the very existence of France seemed at stake. Nor can the literate Northerner have failed to understand why in the teeth of the furies and the face of inevitable defeat the French *colon* incessantly riots to retain a way of life that must—and will—go with the wind. The parallels, of course, cannot be drawn too closely, but it says something meaningful about the universal frailties of the human condition.

But, in fairness, the Southerner who would be understood must not overly complain about the myopia of the Northern eye as it skims swiftly over the iron segregation of its Negro ghettos to focus intently upon the South. For if the Supreme Court decisions created opportunities and even felt necessities for false prophecy and senseless doctrine in the South, the market also turned bullish in the North.

Hearken to that admirable and sincerely self-righteous Senator from Illinois, Paul Douglas, regularly informing the South that it simply must throw off the palpable sins of segregation, get right with God and be born again in the image of the Americans for Democratic Action. Yes, verily, and let us not fret so much with the deliberateness of our speed. Keating of New York pats his foot. Ditto Javits and so also Clark of Pennsylvania and other evangelists of instant racial equality.

Let us not impute a lack of charity to these gentlemen. Indeed, they have the faith of their fathers. To befriend a recalcitrant South, they are ready at the drop of a hat to enact a force bill or to employ with Federal monies sociological shepherds to lead the region to redemption. And though all this piety falls sweetly upon the ears of Harlem and South Chicago, with their balances of power and their largely separate and patently unequal schools, it would be idle to charge these gentlemen with insincerity. Moreover, it would be immaterial. The Ku Klux Klan has been full of thugs who wielded the whip with absolute—and terrible— sincerity. John Brown, sainted by the sages of Concord for exploits including the insane murder and mutilation of five non-slaveholders in one night, was the acme of sincerity.

In the light of this heritage, then, which later unconstitutionally forced the fateful Fourteenth Amendment upon the South, does not Paul Douglas' impatience begin to seem entirely reasonable? And, in fact, isn't it understandable if just a bit insane that the last Democratic National Convention would declare an intention to abolish *all* literacy tests for voting in order finally and fully to extend the franchise to the Negro in the South . . . even in those many places where, as stubborn fact has it, he outnumbers the white? The answer is yes, of course, if one is prepared to admit that in the light of the Southerner's entirely different heritage the nation in 1954 would have foreseen that Faubus' rabble would for a time drown out the never-stilled voices of hope, faith and charity in the South. The answer is yes, if one is prepared, as the editors of The New York *Times* are not, to comprehend the resentment of Southerners when with merciless stupidity and frightening innocence "freedom riders" depart the ghettos and, with headlines and television cameras going on before, venture forth to tempt the violent boob from his lair.

Let us not turn so quickly away from this violent man, however. He, too, has a history. Perhaps he is kin to the tenant, Gudger, from whose barren, wasted life James Agee fashioned, in the 1930's, poignant prose for his *Let Us Now Praise Famous Men:*

"Gudger has no home, no land, no mule: none of the more important farming implements. He must get all of these of his landlord (who), for his share of the corn and cotton, also advances him rations money during four months of the year, March through June, and his fertilizer. Gudger pays him back with his labor and with the labor of his family. At the end of the season he pays him back further; with half his corn, with half his cottonseed. Out of his own half of these crops he also pays him back the rations money, plus interest, and his share of the fertilizer, plus interest, and such other debts, plus interest, as he may have incurred. What is left, once doctor bills and other debts have been deducted, is his year's earnings. . . ." Or perhaps this man screaming in the street was related to Ricketts who, with hope of good times, "went $400 into debt on a fine young pair of mules. One of the mules died before it had made its first crop; and the other died the year after; against his fear, amounting to full horror, of sinking to the half-crop level where nothing is owned, Ricketts went into debt for other, inferior mules; his cows went one by one into debts and desperate exchanges and by sickness; he got congestive chills; his wife got pellagra; a number of his children died; he got appendicitis and lay for days on end under the icecap; his wife's pellagra got into her brain; for ten consecutive years now, though they have lived on so little rations money and have turned nearly all their cottonseed money toward their debts, they have not cleared or had any hope of clearing a cent at the end of the year."

In all his variety from a Klansman plotting an atrocity to a school-board member secretly urging Negroes to apply for admission to the upper-class schools to the wan little interracial groups meeting in the church parlor, the white Southerner is a creature of a heritage that he can no more reject than a mother can reject her children. Splotched with evil, to be sure, that heritage also is compounded of triumphs of endurance, of courage, of selflessness that moved a world. Simply because it is gone does not mean it is forgotten or, indeed, could be forgotten. For if the "good Southerner" could break the bonds with the "bad Southerner" to whom he is bound irrevocably by ties, of blood, religion, race, memory, myth and love of land, where would he seek a new code of conduct? Not in the North, surely, for the Southerner knows in his bones what the historians know in fact: that the North has no moral credentials to preach in this matter, that whatever virtues that region may accidentally have earned by "freeing the slaves" was corrupted by a conscienceless "Reconstruction" of a freed man without freedom and a white man without hope or even youth. For the Negro there was no jubilee-jubilo. For neither white nor black was there a Marshall Plan.

The Southerner's senses told him rightly he had no corner on the corrupting of the American dream. He knew that the zeal of the abolitionist was not the reflection of a higher Northern morality—that to the North there was also greed, cynicism and calculation. He knew there was a reason that when the Supreme Court first came to the Fourteenth Amendment that charter of human freedom was converted to one of corporate privilege.

All this is remembered by the defeated as naturally as it is forgotten by the victorious. All this is the stubborn stuff of the barrier reef in the Potomac that keeps the white Northerner and Southerner forever strangers and prolongs the sterile ritual of finger-pointing that has woven both Paul Douglas and Orval Faubus into the sardonic and not-so-secret mirth of Negro intellectuals. Connoisseurs of that humor must await with relish the answer to the riddle: "What's the difference between a group of distressed Negroes being driven into a church by a white mob in Montgomery and another group being driven out of a church by a white mob in Chicago?" Only a dense literalist would torture that riddle with legalisms.

The legalisms remain, of course, and the white Southerner will make his peace with them. And though some of his number take secret pride in having been able with courage and statecraft to hew a path to compliance through a dense thicket of difficulties, he does not forget that the New Order requires most of the "poor white" Southerner who has been given least. He wonders, watching the flight to the suburbs and the proliferation of private pools, clubs and schools, if the grand design of 1954 does not trend North and South toward integration of the impoverished. Knowing something of the Negro's own intense concern for shadings of color that can reject as "too dark" a baby offered for adoption, he ponders earnestly whether the sociologists in their toneless tracts have not assumed too much in their vaunted knowledge of human nature. He understands the Negro professional man's remark to Harry Ashmore that he can always get a contribution for the cause but never an apartment in a New York Jewish neighborhood. He admires the frankness of another successful Negro who, having come up from squalor by dint of great determination, found himself "too busy to practice sociology." He can simultaneously admire the courage of a young Negro sit-in demonstrator, detest the white louts profaning the Confederate flag and wonder all the while whether the sit-ins will sabotage better job opportunities for Negroes. He is bound to wonder, too, if the Negro ever will turn from the faults of the white man's society to grapple with those grievous failings of his own that crowd the dockets of crime, disease and illegitimacy. For as the North ceaselessly has reminded the white Southerner, there is a limit to the number of excuses to be found in deprivation.

Writing that, I see in my mind's eye a white woman with a fifth-grade education, who, driven finally from the tyranny of the field, took a town job that paid $26 a month for sixteen hours a day in labor and transit, and who from this meager sum bought schoolbooks for three children; who, after washing their single sets of clothes at midnight, rose for work at 4 a.m. to leave biscuit dough in the oven and a stern note not to be late for school; who in all her life never bought unless she could pay and carries within her still a fierce independence that denies her pleasure from any gift, but who finds pleasure in giving. She is a Baptist who voted for Kennedy, but, may Myrdal forgive her, she is "prejudiced" against the Negro.

Not for the white Southerner is the sweet and innocent assurance of the slogan. No man better than he knows from mourning a dozen "New Souths" that died a-borning how swiftly the high rhetoric of progress can collapse into a wail and turn him back to the bleak rewards of the beloved and immemorial land.

He moves hesitantly, uncertainly into the New Order. Some of him dares to hope that this time a truly expanding economy will bathe both races in prosperity's magical sprays of tolerance. But he would also hope that some of the virtues of the old might be retained and perhaps even recognized beyond his borders: that in the new patterns the old civility and generosity and, yes, even the romanticism might find a cranny.

For if his fathers' dreams of a noble breed of learned men carried within itself a fatal flaw, was it otherwise so wild a dream? Was it one that a man—glimpsing it, as it were, in a smashed antique mirror—could quite relinquish in an age when men moved as ants beneath the edifice of the Great Machine?

The white Southerner will not fail his nation, nor himself. Out of the aged anguish and conflict of the human heart, the strongest of him will accommodate the pressures of the New Order into something comprehensible to the kin of Gudger and Ricketts and to the Negro who in the company of the white Southerner has at least learned to read the Declaration of Independence.

It may be true that the white Southerner could have done better in the past and that today he could move more swiftly to accommodate the New Order in the tangled skein of the old. Many of his own courageous prophets tell him so, and millions of his number are not averse to taking new paths laid out with care and reason.

It may be, as this loyal son believes, that the grinding mills of the New Order will in time refine the South's great virtues into a new statecraft that will not suffer by comparison with the wisdom and vision of the old.

Certain it is that few beyond are equipped to judge the Southerner's stewardship of the human dilemma the North so long ignored, but soon must face.

The white Southerner fears not history's judgment so much as the misjudgments of the non-Southerner who, armored in innocence and shielded by mass anonymity, sometimes forgets that allegiance to high principle purchases neither wisdom nor political responsibility.

WILLIAM FAULKNER

LETTER TO THE NORTH

Only on very rare occasions did Faulkner feel it necessary to speak out on public problems. He did so in the following article, published in Life, *March 5, 1956. Information on the author and his writings follows index.*

•

My family has lived for generations in one same small section of north Mississippi. My great-grandfather held slaves and went to Virginia in command of a Mississippi infantry regiment in 1861. I state this simply as credentials for the sincerity and factualness of what I will try to say.

From the beginning of this present phase of the race problem in the South, I have been on record as opposing the forces in my native country which would keep the condition out of which this present evil and trouble has grown. Now I must go on record as opposing the forces outside the South which would use legal or police compulsion to eradicate that evil overnight. I was against compulsory segregation. I am just as strongly against compulsory integration. Firstly of course from principle. Secondly because I don't believe compulsion will work.

There are more Southerners than I who believe as I do and have taken the same stand I have taken, at the same price of contumely and insult and threat from other Southerners which we foresaw and were willing to accept because we believed we were helping our native land which we love, to accept a new condition which it must accept whether it wants to or not. That is, by still being Southerners, yet not being a part of the general majority Southern point of view; by being present yet detached, committed and attainted neither by Citizens' Council nor NAACP; by being in the middle, being in a position to say to any incipient irrevocability: "Wait, wait now, stop and consider first."

But where will we go, if that middle becomes untenable? If we have to vacate it in order to keep from being trampled? Apart from the legal aspect, apart even from the simple incontrovertible immorality of discrimination by race, there was another simply human quantity which drew us to the Negro's side: the simple human instinct to champion the underdog.

But if we, the (comparative) handful of Southerners I have tried to postulate, are compelled by the simple threat of being trampled if we don't get out of the way, to vacate that middle where we could have worked to help the Negro improve his condition—compelled to move for the reason that no middle any longer exists—we will have to make a new choice. And this time the underdog will not be the Negro, since he, the Negro, will now be a segment of the topdog, and so the underdog will be that white embattled minority who are our blood and kin. These non-Southern forces will now say, "Go then. We don't want you because we won't need you again." My reply to that is, "Are you sure you won't?"

So I would say to the NAACP and all the organizations who would compel immediate and unconditional integration: "Go slow now. Stop now for a time, a moment. You have the power now; you can afford to withhold for a moment the use of it as a force. You have done a good job, you have jolted your opponent off-balance and he is now vulnerable. But stop there for a moment; don't give him the advantage of a chance to cloud the issue by that purely automatic sentimental appeal to that same universal human instinct for automatic sympathy for the underdog simply because he is under."

And I would say this too. The rest of the United States knows next to nothing about the South. The present idea and picture which they hold of a people decadent and even obsolete through inbreeding and illiteracy— the inbreeding a result of the illiteracy and the isolation—as to be a kind of species of juvenile delinquents with a folklore of blood and violence, yet who, like juvenile delinquents, can be controlled by firmness once they are brought to believe that the police mean business, is as baseless and illusory as that one a generation ago of (oh yes, we subscribed to it too) columned porticoes and magnolias. The rest of the United States assumes that this condition in the South is so simple and so uncomplex that it can be changed tomorrow by the simple will of the national majority backed by legal edict. In fact, the North does not even recognize what it has seen in its own newspapers.

I have at hand an editorial from the New York *Times* of February 10th on the rioting at the University of Alabama because of the admission of Miss Lucy, a Negro. The editorial said: "This is the first time that force and violence have become part of the question." That is not correct. To all Southerners, no matter which side of the question of racial equality they supported, the first implication, and—to the Southerner—even promise, of force and violence was the Supreme Court decision itself. After that, by any standards at all and following as inevitably as night and day, was the case of the three white teen-agers, members of a field trip group from a Mississippi high school (and, as teen-agers do, probably wearing the bright particolored blazers or jackets blazoned across the back with the name of the school) who were stabbed in passing on a Washington street by Negroes they had never seen before and who apparently had never seen them before either; and that of the Till boy and the two Mississippi juries which freed the defendants from both charges; and of the Mississippi garage attendant killed by a white man because, according to the white man, the Negro filled the tank of the white man's car full of gasoline when all the white man wanted was two dollars' worth.

This problem is far beyond a mere legal one. It is even far beyond the moral one it is and still was a hundred years ago in 1860, when many Southerners, including Robert Lee, recognized it as a moral one at the very instant when they in turn elected to champion the underdog because that underdog was blood and kin and home. The Northerner is not even aware yet of what that war really proved. He assumes that it merely proved to the Southerner that he was wrong. It didn't do that because the Southerner already knew he was wrong and accepted that gambit even when he knew it was the fatal one. What that war should have done, but failed to do, was to prove to the North that the South will go to any length, even that fatal and already doomed one, before it will accept alteration of its racial condition by mere force of law or economic threat.

Since I went on record as being opposed to compulsory racial inequality, I have received many letters. A few of them approved. But most of them were in opposition. And a few of these were from Southern Negroes, the only difference being that they were polite and courteous instead of being threats and insults, saying in effect: "Please, Mr. Faulkner, stop talking and be quiet. You are a good man and you think you are helping us. But you are not helping us. You are doing us harm. You are playing into the hands of the NAACP so that they are using you to make trouble for our race that we don't want. Please hush, you look after your white folks' trouble and let us take care of ours." This one in particular was a long one, from a woman who was writing for and in the name of the pastor and the entire congregation of her church. It went on to say that the Till boy got exactly what he asked for, coming down there with his Chicago ideas, and that all his mother wanted was to make money out of the role of her bereavement. Which sounds exactly like the white people in the South who justified and even defended the crime by declining to find that it was one.

We have had many violent inexcusable personal crimes of race against race in the South, but since 1919 the major examples of communal race tension have been more prevalent in the North, like the Negro family who were refused acceptance in the white residential district in Chicago, and the Korean-American who suffered for the same reason in Anaheim,

Calif. Maybe it is because our solidarity is not racial, but instead is the majority white segregationist plus the Negro minority like my correspondent above, who prefer peace to equality. But suppose the line of demarcation should become one of the race; the white minority like myself compelled to join the white segregation majority no matter how much we oppose the principle of inequality; the Negro minority who want peace compelled to join the Negro majority who advocate force, no matter how much that minority wanted only peace?

So the Northerner, the liberal, does not know the South. He can't know it from his distance. He assumes that he is dealing with a simple legal theory and a simple moral idea. He is not. He is dealing with a fact: the fact of an emotional condition of such fierce unanimity as to scorn the fact that it is a minority and which will go to any length and against any odds at this moment to justify and, if necessary, defend that condition and its right to it.

So I would say to all the organizations and groups which would force integration on the South by legal process: "Stop now for a moment. You have shown the Southerner what you can do and what you will do if necessary; give him a space in which to get his breath and assimilate that knowledge; to look about and see that (1) Nobody is going to force integration on him from the outside; (2) That he himself faces an obsolescence in his own land which only he can cure; a moral condition which not only must be cured but a physical condition which has got to be cured if he, the white Southerner, is to have any peace, is not to be faced with another legal process or maneuver every year, year after year, for the rest of his life."

JAMES BALDWIN

James Baldwin was born in Harlem in 1924, the oldest of nine children, and graduated from DeWitt Clinton High School where he was editor of the literary magazine. After the death of his father in 1943 he lived in Greenwich Village, working by day as handyman, office boy, or factory worker and writing at night. A Rosenwald Fellowship received in 1948 enabled him to go to Paris, where he wrote his first two novels, Go Tell It on the Mountain *(1952) and* Giovanni's Room *(1956), and the essays published as* Notes of a Native Son *(1955). In 1957 he returned to America and since then has become one of the most articulate literary spokesmen of the civil rights movement.* The Fire Next Time *(1963), two searing articles, or letters, on the relationship between the American Negro and the American white man, secured his reputation as an essayist. Baldwin's writing has won him many awards, among them a Guggenheim Fellowship (1954), a* Partisan Review *Fellowship (1956), and the National Institute of Arts and Letters Award (1956).* Nobody Knows My Name, *a collection of essays, was selected as one of the outstanding books of 1961 by the Notable Book Council of the American Library Association. The essay we present below is Chapter 7 of this collection.*

FAULKNER AND DESEGREGATION

Any real change implies the breakup of the world as one has always known it, the loss of all that gave one an identity, the end of safety. And at such a moment, unable to see and not daring to imagine what the future will now bring forth, one clings to what one knew, or thought one knew; to what one possessed or dreamed that one possessed. Yet, it is only when a man is able, without bitterness or self-pity, to surrender a dream he has long cherished or a privilege he has long possessed that he is set free— he has set himself free—for higher dreams, for greater privileges. All men have gone through this, go through it, each according to his degree, throughout their lives. It is one of the irreducible facts of life. And remembering this, especially since I am a Negro, affords me almost my only means of understanding what is happening in the minds and hearts of white Southerners today.

For the arguments with which the bulk of relatively articulate white Southerners of good will have met the necessity of desegregation have no value whatever as arguments, being almost entirely and helplessly dishonest, when not, indeed, insane. After more than two hundred years in slavery and ninety years of quasi-freedom, it is hard to think very highly of William Faulkner's advice to "go slow." "They don't mean go slow," Thurgood Marshall is reported to have said, "they mean don't go." Nor is the squire of Oxford very persuasive when he suggests that white Southerners, left to their own devices, will realize that their own social structure looks silly to the rest of the world and correct it of their own accord. It has looked silly, to use Faulkner's rather strange adjective, for a long time; so far from trying to correct it, Southerners, who seem to be characterized by a species of defiance most perverse when it is most despairing, have clung to it, at incalculable cost to themselves, as the only conceivable and as an absolutely sacrosanct way of life. They have never seriously conceded that their social structure was mad. They have insisted, on the contrary, that everyone who criticized it was mad.

Faulkner goes further. He concedes the madness and moral wrongness of the South but at the same time he raises it to the level of a mystique which makes it somehow unjust to discuss Southern society in the same terms in which one would discuss any other society. "Our position is wrong and untenable," says Faulkner, "but it is not wise to keep an emotional people off balance." This, if it means anything, can only mean that this "emotional people" have been swept "off balance" by the pressure of recent events, that is, the Supreme Court decision outlawing segregation. When the pressure is taken off—and not an instant before—this "emotional people" will presumably find themselves once again on balance and will then be able to free themselves of an "obsolescence in [their] own land" in their own way and, of course, in their own time. The question left begging is what, in their history to date, affords any evidence that they have any desire or capacity to do this. And it is, I suppose, impertinent to ask just what Negroes are supposed to do while the South works out what, in Faulkner's rhetoric, becomes something very closely resembling a high and noble tragedy.

The sad truth is that whatever modifications have been effected in the social structure of the South since the Reconstruction, and any alleviations of the Negro's lot within it, are due to great and incessant pressure, very little of it indeed from within the South. That the North has been guilty of Pharisaism in its dealing with the South does not negate the fact that much of this pressure has come from the North. That some—not nearly as many as Faulkner would like to believe—Southern Negroes prefer, or are afraid of changing, the status quo does not negate the fact that it is the Southern Negro himself who, year upon year, and generation upon generation, has kept the Southern waters troubled. As far as the Negro's life in the South is concerned, the NAACP is the only organization which has struggled, with admirable single-mindedness and skill, to raise him to the level of a citizen. For this reason alone, and quite apart from the individual heroism of many of its Southern members, it cannot be equated, as Faulkner equates it, with the pathological Citizen's Council. One organization is working within the law and the other is working against and outside it. Faulkner's threat to leave the "middle of the road" where he has, presumably, all these years, been working for the benefit of Negroes, reduces itself to a more or less up-to-date version of the Southern threat to secede from the Union.

Faulkner—among so many others!—is so plaintive concerning this "middle of the road" from which "extremist" elements of both races are driving him that it does not seem unfair to ask just what he has been doing there until now. Where is the evidence of the struggle he has been carrying on there on behalf of the Negro? Why, if he and his enlightened confreres in the South have been boring from within to destroy segregation, do they react with such panic when the walls show any signs of falling? Why—and how—does one move from the middle of the road where one was aiding Negroes into the streets—to shoot them?

Now it is easy enough to state flatly that Faulkner's middle of the road does not—cannot—exist and that he is guilty of great emotional and intellectual dishonesty in pretending that it does. I think this is why he clings to his fantasy. It is easy enough to accuse him of hypocrisy when he speaks of man being "indestructible because of his simple will to freedom." But he is not being hypocritical; he means it. It is only that Man is one thing—a rather unlucky abstraction in this case—and the Negroes he has always known, so fatally tied up in his mind with his grandfather's slaves, are quite another. He is at his best, and is perfectly sincere, when he declares, in *Harpers*, "To live anywhere in the world today and be against equality because of race or color is like living in Alaska and being against snow. We have already got snow. And as with the Alaskan, merely to live in armistice with it is not enough. Like the Alaskan, we had better use it." And though this seems to be flatly opposed to his statement (in an interview printed in *The Reporter*) that, if it came to a contest between the federal government and Mississippi, he would fight for Mississippi, "even if it meant going out into the streets and shooting Negroes," he means that, too. Faulkner means everything he says, means them all at once, and with very nearly the same intensity. This is why his statements demand our attention. He has perhaps never before more concretely expressed what it means to be a Southerner.

What seems to define the Southerner, in his own mind at any rate, is his relationship to the North, that is to the rest of the Republic, a relationship which can at the very best be described as uneasy. It is apparently very difficult to be at once a Southerner and an American; so difficult that many of the South's most independent minds are forced into the American exile; which is not, of course, without its aggravating, circular effect on the interior and public life of the South. A Bostonian, say, who leaves Boston is not regarded by the citizenry he has abandoned with the same venomous distrust as is the Southerner who leaves the South. The citizenry of Boston do not consider that they have been abandoned, much less betrayed. It is only the American Southerner who seems to be fighting, in his own entrails, a peculiar, ghastly, and perpetual war with all the rest of the country. ("Didn't you say," demanded a Southern woman of Robert Penn Warren, "that you was born down here, used to live right near here?" And when he agreed that this was so: "Yes . . . but you never said where you living now!")

The difficulty, perhaps, is that the Southerner clings to two entirely antithetical doctrines, two legends, two histories. Like all other Americans, he must subscribe, and is to some extent controlled by the beliefs and the principles expressed in the Constitution; at the same time, these beliefs and principles seem determined to destroy the South. He is, on the one hand, the proud citizen of a free society and, on the other, is committed to a society which has not yet dared to free itself of the necessity of naked and brutal oppression. He is part of a country which boasts that it has never lost a war; but he is also the representative of a conquered nation. I have not seen a single statement of Faulkner's concerning desegregation which does not inform us that his family has lived in the same part of Mississippi for generations, that his great-grandfather owned slaves, and that his ancestors fought and died in the Civil War. And so compelling is the image of ruin, gallantry and death thus evoked that it demands a positive effort of the imagination to remember that slaveholding Southerners were not the only people who perished in that war. Negroes and Northerners were also blown to bits. American history, as opposed to Southern history, proves that Southerners were not the only slaveholders, Negroes were not even the only slaves. And the segregation which Faulkner sanctifies by references to Shiloh, Chickamauga, and Gettysburg does not extend back that far, is in fact scarcely as old as the century. The "racial condition" which Faulkner will not have changed by "mere force of law or economic threat" was imposed by precisely these means. The Southern tradition, which is, after all, all that Faulkner is talking about, is not a tradition at all: when Faulkner evokes it, he is simply evoking a legend which contains an accusation. And that accusation, stated far more simply than it should be, is that the North, in winning the war, left the South only one means of asserting its identity and that means was the Negro.

"My people owned slaves," says Faulkner, "and the very obligation we have to take care of these people is morally bad." "This problem is . . . far beyond the moral one it is and still was a hundred years ago, in 1860, when many Southerners, including Robert Lee, recognized it as a moral one at the very instant they in turn elected to champion the underdog because that underdog was blood and kin and home." But the North escaped scot-free. For one thing, in freeing the slave, it established a moral superiority over the South which the South has not learned to live with until today; and this despite—or possibly because of—the fact that this moral superiority was bought, after all, rather cheaply. The North was no better prepared than the South, as it turned out, to make citizens of former slaves, but it was able, as the South was not, to wash its hands of the matter. Men who knew that slavery was wrong were forced, nevertheless, to fight to perpetuate it because they were unable to turn against "blood and kin and home." And when blood and kin and home were defeated, they found themselves, more than ever, committed: committed, in effect, to a way of life which was as unjust and crippling as it was inescapable. In sum, the North, by freeing the slaves of their masters, robbed the masters of any possibility of freeing themselves of the slaves.

When Faulkner speaks, then, of the "middle of the road," he is simply speaking of the hope—which was always unrealistic and is now all but smashed—that the white Southerner, with no coercion from the rest of the nation, will lift himself above his ancient, crippling bitterness and refuse to add to his already intolerable burden of blood-guiltiness. But this hope would seem to be absolutely dependent on a social and psychological stasis which simply does not exist. "Things have been getting better," Faulkner tells us, "for a long time. Only six Negroes were killed by whites in Mississippi last year, according to police figures." Faulkner surely knows how little consolation this offers a Negro and he also knows something about "police figures" in the Deep South. And he knows, too, that murder is not the worst thing that can happen to a man, black or white. But murder may be the worst thing a man can do. Faulkner is not trying to save Negroes, who are, in his view, already saved; who, having refused to be destroyed by terror, are far stronger than the terrified white populace; and who have, moreover, fatally, from his point of view, the weight of the federal government behind them. He is trying to save "whatever good remains in those white people." The time he pleads for is the time in which the Southerner will come to terms with himself, will cease fleeing from his conscience, and achieve, in the words of Robert Penn Warren, "moral identity." And he surely believes, with Warren, that "Then in a country where moral identity is hard to come by, the South, because it has had to deal concretely with a moral problem, may offer some leadership. And we need any we can get. If we are to break out of the national rhythm, the rhythm between complacency and panic."

But the time Faulkner asks for does not exist—and he is not the only Southerner who knows it. There is never time in the future in which we will work out our salvation. The challenge is in the moment, the time is always now.

NORMAN PODHORETZ

Norman Podhoretz was born in New York City and educated at Columbia College and Cambridge University, England, where he was a Fulbright Scholar and a Kellet Fellow. A precociously talented writer and critic, he was appointed editor of Commentary *in 1960, at the age of thirty. He has been a frequent contributor to magazines, and recently published a ten-year collection of his articles, entitled* Doings and Undoings: The Fifties and After in American Writing *(1964). The article we print below first appeared in* Commentary, *February, 1963.*

MY NEGRO PROBLEM—AND OURS

> If we—and . . . I mean the relatively conscious whites and the
> relatively conscious blacks, who must, like lovers, insist on, or
> create, the consciousness of the others—do not falter in our duty
> now, we may be able, handful that we are, to end the racial
> nightmare, and achieve our country, and change the history of
> the world.
>
> —James Baldwin

Two ideas puzzled me deeply as a child growing up in Brooklyn during the 1930's in what today would be called an integrated neighborhood. One of them was that all Jews were rich; the other was that all Negroes were persecuted. These ideas had appeared in print; therefore they must be true. My own experience and the evidence of my senses told me they were not true, but that only confirmed what a day-dreaming boy in the provinces—for the lower-class neighborhoods of New York belong as surely to the provinces as any rural town in North Dakota—discovers very early: *his* experience is unreal and the evidence of his senses is not to be trusted. Yet even a boy with a head full of fantasies incongruously synthesized out of Hollywood movies and English novels cannot altogether deny the reality of his own experience—especially when there is so much deprivation in that experience. Nor can he altogether gainsay the evidence of his own senses—especially such evidence of the senses as comes from being repeatedly beaten up, robbed, and in general hated, terrorized, and humiliated.

And so for a long time I was puzzled to think that Jews were supposed to be rich when the only Jews I knew were poor, and that Negroes were supposed to be persecuted when it was the Negroes who were doing the only persecuting I knew about—and doing it, moreover, to *me*. During the early years of the war, when my older sister joined a left-wing youth organization, I remember my astonishment at hearing her passionately denounce my father for thinking that Jews were worse off than Negroes. To me, at the age of twelve, it seemed very clear that Negroes were better off than Jews—indeed, than *all* whites. A city boy's world is contained within three or four square blocks, and in my world it was the whites, the Italians and Jews, who feared the Negroes, not the other way around. The Negroes were tougher than we were, more ruthless, and on the whole they were better athletes. What could it mean, then, to say that they were badly off and that we were more fortunate? Yet my sister's opinions, like print, were sacred, and when she told me about exploitation and economic forces I believed her. I believed her, but I was still afraid of Negroes. And I still hated them with all my heart.

It had not always been so—that much I can recall from early childhood. When did it start, this fear and this hatred? There was a kindergarten in the local public school, and given the character of the neighborhood, at least half of the children in my class must have been Negroes. Yet I have no memory of being aware of color differences at that age, and I know from observing my own children that they attribute no significance to such differences even when they begin noticing them. I think there was a day—first grade? second grade?—when my best friend Carl hit me on the way home from school and announced that he wouldn't play with me any more because I had killed Jesus. When I ran home to my mother crying for an explanation, she told me not to pay any attention to such foolishness, and then in Yiddish she cursed the *goyim* and the *schwartzes*, the *schwartzes* and the *goyim*. Carl, it turned out, was a *schwartze*, and so was added a third to the categories into which people were mysteriously divided.

Sometimes I wonder whether this is a true memory at all. It is blazingly vivid, but perhaps it never happened: can anyone really remember back to the age of six? There is no uncertainty in my mind, however, about the years that followed. Carl and I hardly ever spoke, though we met in school every day up through the eighth or ninth grade. There would be embarrassed moments of catching his eye or of his catching mine—for whatever it was that had attracted us to one another as very small children remained alive in spite of the fantastic barrier of hostility that had grown up between us, suddenly and out of nowhere. Nevertheless, friendship would have been impossible, and even if it had been possible, it would have been unthinkable. About that, there was nothing anyone could do by the time we were eight years old.

Item: The orphanage across the street is torn down, a city housing project begins to rise in its place, and on the marvelous vacant lot next to the old orphanage they are building a playground. Much excitement and anticipation as Opening Day draws near. Mayor LaGuardia himself comes to dedicate this great gesture of public benevolence. He speaks of neighborliness and borrowing cups of sugar, and of the playground he says that children of all races, colors, and creeds will learn to live together in harmony. A week later, some of us are swatting flies on the playground's inadequate little ball field. A gang of Negro kids, pretty much our own age, enter from the other side and order us out of the park. We refuse, proudly and indignantly, with superb masculine fervor. There is a fight, they win, and we retreat, half whimpering, half with bravado. My first nauseating experience of cowardice. And my first appalled realization that there are people in the world who do not seem to be afraid of anything, who act as though they have nothing to lose. Thereafter the playground becomes a battleground, sometimes quiet, sometimes the scene of athletic competition between Them and Us. But rocks are thrown as often as baseballs. Gradually we abandon the place and use the streets instead. The streets are safer, though we do not admit this to ourselves. We are not, after all, sissies—that most dreaded epithet of an American boyhood.

Item: I am standing alone in front of the building in which I live. It is late afternoon and getting dark. That day in school the teacher had asked a surly Negro boy named Quentin a question he was unable to answer. As usual I had waved my arm eagerly ("Be a good boy, get good marks, be smart, go to college, become a doctor") and, the right answer bursting from my lips, I was held up lovingly by the teacher as an example to the class. I had seen Quentin's face—a very dark, very cruel, very Oriental-looking face—harden, and there had been enough threat in his eyes to make me run all the way home for fear that he might catch me outside.

Now, standing idly in front of my own house, I see him approaching from the project accompanied by his little brother who is carrying a baseball bat and wearing a grin of malicious anticipation. As in a nightmare, I am trapped. The surroundings are secure and familiar, but terror is suddenly present and there is no one around to help. I am locked to the spot. I will not cry out or run away like a sissy, and I stand there, my heart wild, my throat clogged. He walks up, hurls the familiar epithet ("Hey, mo'f——r"), and to my surprise only pushes me. It is a violent push, but not a punch. A push is not as serious as a punch. Maybe I can still back out without entirely losing my dignity. Maybe I can still say, "Hey,

c'mon Quentin, whaddya wanna do *that* for. I dint do nothin' to *you*,"
and walk away, not too rapidly. Instead, before I can stop myself, I push
him back—a token gesture—and I say, "Cut that out, I don't wanna fight,
I ain't got nothin' to fight about." As I turn to walk back into the building,
the corner of my eye catches the motion of the bat his little brother has
handed him. I try to duck, but the bat crashes colored lights into my head.

The next thing I know, my mother and sister are standing over me, both
of them hysterical. My sister—she who was later to join the "progressive"
youth organization—is shouting for the police and screaming imprecations
at those dirty little black bastards. They take me upstairs, the doctor
comes, the police come. I tell them that the boy who did it was a stranger,
that he had been trying to get money from me. They do not believe me,
but I am too scared to give them Quentin's name. When I return to school
a few days later, Quentin avoids my eyes. He knows that I have not
squealed, and he is ashamed. I try to feel proud, but in my heart I know
that it was fear of what his friends might do to me that had kept me silent,
and not the code of the street.

Item: There is an athletic meet in which the whole of our junior high
school is participating. I am in one of the seventh-grade rapid-advance
classes, and "segregation" has now set in with a vengeance. In the last
three or four years of the elementary school from which we have just
graduated, each grade had been divided into three classes, according to
"intelligence." (In the earlier grades the divisions had either been arbitrary
or else unrecognized by us as having anything to do with brains.) These
divisions by IQ, or however it was arranged, had resulted in a preponderance of Jews in the "1" classes and a corresponding preponderance of
Negroes in the "3's," with the Italians split unevenly along the spectrum.
At least a few Negroes had always made the "1's," just as there had always
been a few Jewish kids among the "3's" and more among the "2's" (where
Italians dominated). But the junior high's rapid-advance class of which I
am now a member is overwhelmingly Jewish and entirely white—except
for a shy lonely Negro girl with light skin and reddish hair.

The athletic meet takes place in a city-owned stadium far from the
school. It is an important event to which a whole day is given over. The
winners are to get those precious little medallions stamped with the New
York City emblem that can be screwed into a belt and that prove the
wearer to be a distinguished personage. I am a fast runner, and so I am
assigned the position of anchor man on my class's team in the relay race.
There are three other seventh-grade teams in the race, two of them all
Negro, as ours is all white. One of the all-Negro teams is very tall—their
anchor man waiting silently next to me on the line looks years older than
I am, and I do not recognize him. He is the first to get the baton and
crosses the finishing line in a walk. Our team comes in second, but a few
minutes later we are declared the winners, for it has been discovered that
the anchor man on the first-place team is not a member of the class. We

are awarded the medallions, and the following day our home-room teacher makes a speech about how proud she is of us for being superior athletes as well as superior students. We want to believe that we deserve the praise, but we know that we could not have won even if the other class had not cheated.

That afternoon, walking home, I am waylaid and surrounded by five Negroes, among whom is the anchor man of the disqualified team. "Gimme my medal, mo'f——r," he grunts. I do not have it with me and I tell him so. "Anyway, it ain't yours," I say foolishly. He calls me a liar on both counts and pushes me up against the wall on which we sometimes play handball. "Gimme my mo'f——n' medal," he says again. I repeat that I have left it home. "Le's search the li'l mo'f——r," one of them suggests, "he prolly got it *hid* in his mo'f——n' *pants*." My panic is now unmanageable. (How many times had I been surrounded like this and asked in soft tones, "Len' me a nickle, boy." How many times had I been called a liar for pleading poverty and pushed around, or searched, or beaten up, unless there happened to be someone in the marauding gang like Carl who liked me across that enormous divide of hatred and who would therefore say, "Aaah, c'mon, le's git someone else, *this* boy ain't got no money on 'im.") I scream at them through tears of rage and self-contempt, "Keep your f——n' filthy lousy black hands offa me! I swear I'll get the cops." This is all they need to hear, and the five of them set upon me. They bang me around, mostly in the stomach and on the arms and shoulders, and when several adults loitering near the candy store down the block notice what is going on and begin to shout, they run off and away.

I do not tell my parents about the incident. My team-mates, who have also been waylaid, each by a gang led by his opposite number from the disqualified team, have had their medallions taken from them, and they never squeal either. For days, I walk home in terror, expecting to be caught again, but nothing happens. The medallion is put away into a drawer, never to be worn by anyone.

Obviously experiences like these have always been a common feature of childhood life in working-class and immigrant neighborhoods, and Negroes do not necessarily figure in them. Wherever, and in whatever combination, they have lived together in the cities, kids of different groups have been at war, beating up and being beaten up: micks against kikes against wops against spicks against polacks. And even relatively homogeneous areas have not been spared the warring of the young: one block against another, one gang (called in my day, in a pathetic effort at gentility, an "S.A.C.," or social-athletic club) against another. But the Negro-white conflict had—and no doubt still has—a special intensity and was conducted with a ferocity unmatched by intramural white battling.

In my own neighborhood, a good deal of animosity existed between the Italian kids (most of whose parents were immigrants from Sicily) and the Jewish kids (who came largely from East European immigrant families). Yet everyone had friends, sometimes close friends, in the other "camp," and we often visited one another's strange-smelling houses, if not for meals, then for glasses of milk, and occasionally for some special event like a wedding or a wake. If it happened that we divided into warring factions and did battle, it would invariably be half-hearted and soon patched up. Our parents, to be sure, had nothing to do with one another and were mutually suspicious and hostile. But we, the kids, who all spoke Yiddish or Italian at home, were Americans, or New Yorkers, or Brooklyn boys: we shared a culture, the culture of the street, and at least for a while this culture proved to be more powerful than the opposing cultures of the home.

Why, *why* should it have been so different as between the Negroes and us? How was it borne in upon us so early, white and black alike, that we were enemies beyond any possibility of reconciliation? Why did we hate one another so?

I suppose if I tried, I could answer those questions more or less adequately from the perspective of what I have since learned. I could draw upon James Baldwin—what better witness is there?—to describe the sense of entrapment that poisons the soul of the Negro with hatred for the white man whom he knows to be his jailer. On the other side, if I wanted to understand how the white man comes to hate the Negro, I could call upon the psychologists who have spoken of the guilt that white Americans feel toward Negroes and that turns into hatred for lack of acknowledging itself as guilt. These are plausible answers and certainly there is truth in them. Yet when I think back upon my own experience of the Negro and his of me, I find myself troubled and puzzled, much as I was as a child when I heard that all Jews were rich and all Negroes persecuted. How could the Negroes in my neighborhood have regarded the whites across the street and around the corner as jailers? On the whole, the whites were not so poor as the Negroes, but they were quite poor enough, and the years were years of Depression. As for white hatred of the Negro, how could guilt have had anything to do with it? What share had these Italian and Jewish immigrants in the enslavement of the Negro? What share had they—downtrodden people themselves breaking their own necks to eke out a living—in the exploitation of the Negro?

No, I cannot believe that we hated each other back there in Brooklyn because they thought of us as jailers and we felt guilty toward them. But does it matter, given the fact that we all went through an unrepresentative confrontation? I think it matters profoundly, for if we managed the job of hating each other so well without benefit of the aids to hatred that are supposedly at the root of this madness everywhere else, it must mean that the madness is not yet properly understood. I am far from pretending that I understand it, but I would insist that no view of the problem will begin to approach the truth unless it can account for a case like the one I have been trying to describe. Are the elements of any such view available to us?

At least two, I would say, are. One of them is a point we frequently come upon in the work of James Baldwin, and the other is a related point always stressed by psychologists who have studied the mechanisms of prejudice. Baldwin tells us that one of the reasons Negroes hate the white man is that the white man refuses to *look* at him: the Negro knows that in white eyes all Negroes are alike; they are faceless and therefore not altogether human. The psychologists, in their turn, tell us that the white man hates the Negro because he tends to project those wild impulses that he fears in himself onto an alien group which he then punishes with his contempt. What Baldwin does *not* tell us, however, is that the principle of facelessness is a two-way street and can operate in both directions with no difficulty at all. Thus, in my neighborhood in Brooklyn, *I* was as faceless to the Negroes as they were to me, and if they hated me because I never looked at them, I must also have hated them for never looking at *me*. To the Negroes, my white skin was enough to define me as the enemy, and in a war it is only the uniform that counts and not the person.

So with the mechanism of projection that the psychologists talk about: it too works in both directions at once. There is no question that the psychologists are right about what the Negro represents symbolically to the white man. For me as a child the life lived on the other side of the playground and down the block on Ralph Avenue seemed the very embodiment of the values of the street—free, independent, reckless, brave, masculine, erotic. I put the word "erotic" last, though it is usually stressed above all others, because in fact it came last, in consciousness as in importance. What mainly counted for me about Negro kids of my own age was that they were "bad boys." There were plenty of bad boys among the whites—this was, after all, a neighborhood with a long tradition of crime as a career open to aspiring talents—but the Negroes were *really* bad, bad in a way that beckoned to one, and made one feel inadequate. *We* all went home every day for a lunch of spinach-and-potatoes; *they* roamed around during lunch hour, munching on candy bars. In winter *we* had to wear itchy woolen hats and mittens and cumbersome galoshes; *they* were bare-headed and loose as they pleased. *We* rarely played hookey, or got into serious trouble in school, for all our street-corner bravado; *they* were defiant, forever staying out (to do what delicious things?), forever making disturbances in class and in the halls, forever being sent to the principal and returning uncowed. But most important of all, they were *tough;* beautifully, enviably tough, not giving a damn for anyone or anything. To hell with the teacher, the truant officer, the cop; to hell with the whole of the adult world that held *us* in its grip and that we never had the courage to rebel against except sporadically and in petty ways.

This is what I saw and envied and feared in the Negro: this is what finally made him faceless to me, though some of it, of course, was actually there. (The psychologists also tell us that the alien group which becomes the object of a projection will tend to respond by trying to live up to what is expected of them.) But what, on his side, did the Negro see in me that made me faceless to *him?* Did he envy me my lunches of spinach-and-potatoes and my itchy woolen caps and my prudent behavior in the face of authority, as I envied him his noon-time candy bars and his bare head in winter and his magnificent rebelliousness? Did those lunches and caps spell for him the prospect of power and riches in the future? Did they mean that there were possibilities open to me that were denied to him? Very likely they did. But if so, one also supposes that he feared the impulses within himself toward submission to authority no less powerfully than I feared the impulses in myself toward defiance. If I represented the jailer to him, it was not because I was oppressing him or keeping him down: it was because I symbolized for him the dangerous and probably pointless temptation toward greater repression, just as he symbolized for me the equally perilous tug toward greater freedom. I personally was to be rewarded for this repression with a new and better life in the future, but how many of my friends paid an even higher price and were given only gall in return.

We have it on the authority of James Baldwin that all Negroes hate whites. I am trying to suggest that on their side all whites—all American whites, that is—are sick in their feelings about Negroes. There are Negroes, no doubt, who would say that Baldwin is wrong, but I suspect them of being less honest than he is, just as I suspect whites of self-deception who tell me they have no special feeling toward Negroes. Special feelings about color are a contagion to which white Americans seem susceptible even when there is nothing in their background to account for the susceptibility. Thus everywhere we look today in the North, we find the curious phenomenon of white middle-class liberals with no previous personal experience of Negroes—people to whom Negroes have always been faceless in virtue rather than faceless in vice—discovering that their abstract commitment to the cause of Negro rights will not stand the test of a direct confrontation. We find such people fleeing in droves to the suburbs as the Negro population in the inner city grows; and when they stay in the city we find them sending their children to private school rather than to the "integrated" public school in the neighborhood. We find them resisting the demand that gerrymandered school districts be re-zoned for the purpose of overcoming de facto segregation; we find them judiciously considering whether the Negroes (for their own good, of course) are not perhaps pushing too hard; we find them clucking their tongues over Negro militancy; we find them speculating on the question of whether there may not, after all, be something in the theory that the races are biologically different; we find them saying that it will take a very long time for Negroes to achieve full equality, no matter what anyone does; we find them deploring the rise of black nationalism and expressing the solemn hope that the leaders of the Negro community will discover ways of containing the impatience and incipient violence within the Negro ghettos.[1]

But that is by no means the whole story; there is also the phenomenon of what Kenneth Rexroth once called "crow-jimism." There are the broken-down white boys like Vivaldo Moore in Baldwin's *Another Country* who go to Harlem in search of sex or simply to brush up against something that looks like primitive vitality, and who are so often punished by the Negroes they meet for crimes that they would have been the last ever to commit and of which they themselves have been as sorry victims as any of the Negroes who take it out on them. There are the writers and intellectuals and artists who romanticize Negroes and pander to them, assuming a guilt that is not properly theirs. And there are all the white liberals who permit Negroes to blackmail them into adopting a double standard of moral judgment, and who lend themselves—again assuming the responsibility for crimes they never committed—to cunning and contemptuous exploitation by Negroes they employ or try to befriend.

And what about me? What kind of feelings do I have about Negroes today? What happened to me, from Brooklyn, who grew up fearing and envying and hating Negroes? Now that Brooklyn is behind me, do I fear them and envy them and hate them still? The answer is yes, but not in the same proportions and certainly not in the same way. I now live on the upper west side of Manhattan, where there are many Negroes and many Puerto Ricans, and there are nights when I experience the old apprehensiveness again, and there are streets that I avoid when I am walking in the dark, as there were streets that I avoided when I was a child. I find that I am not afraid of Puerto Ricans, but I cannot restrain my nervousness whenever I pass a group of Negroes standing in front of a bar or sauntering down the street. I know now, as I did not know when I was a child, that power is on my side, that the police are working for me and not for them. And knowing this I feel ashamed and guilty, like the good liberal I have grown up to be. Yet the twinges of fear and the resentment they bring and the self-contempt they arouse are not to be gainsaid.

But envy? Why envy? And hatred? Why hatred? Here again the intensities have lessened and everything has been complicated and qualified by the guilts and the resulting over-compensations that are the heritage of the enlightened middle-class world of which I am now a member. Yet just as in childhood I envied Negroes for what seemed to me their superior masculinity, so I envy them today for what seems to me their

---

[1] For an account of developments like these, see "The White Liberal's Retreat" by Murray Friedman in the January 1963 *Atlantic Monthly*.

superior physical grace and beauty. I have come to value physical grace
very highly, and I am now capable of aching with all my being when I
watch a Negro couple on the dance floor, or a Negro playing baseball
or basketball. They are on the kind of terms with their own bodies that
I should like to be on with mine, and for that precious quality they seem
blessed to me.

The hatred I still feel for Negroes is the hardest of all the old feelings
to face or admit, and it is the most hidden and the most overlarded by
the conscious attitudes into which I have succeeded in willing myself.
It no longer has, as for me it once did, any cause or justification (except,
perhaps, that I am constantly being denied my right to an honest expression of the things I earned the right as a child to feel). How, then,
do I know that this hatred has never entirely disappeared? I know it from
the insane rage that can stir in me at the thought of Negro anti-Semitism;
I know it from the disgusting prurience that can stir in me at the sight
of a mixed couple; and I know it from the violence that can stir in me
whenever I encounter that special brand of paranoid touchiness to which
many Negroes are prone.

This, then, is where I am; it is not exactly where I think all other white
liberals are, but it cannot be so very far away either. And it is because
I am convinced that we white Americans are—for whatever reason, it
no longer matters—so twisted and sick in our feelings about Negroes that
I despair of the present push toward integration. If the pace of progress
were not a factor here, there would perhaps be no cause for despair:
time and the law and even the international political situation are on the
side of the Negroes, and ultimately, therefore, victory—of a sort, anyway
—must come. But from everything we have learned from observers who
ought to know, pace has become as important to the Negroes as substance.
They want equality and they want it *now*, and the white world is yielding to their demand only as much and as fast as it is absolutely being compelled to do. The Negroes know this in the most concrete terms
imaginable, and it is thus becoming increasingly difficult to buy them
off with rhetoric and promises and pious assurances of support. And so
within the Negro community we find more and more people declaring
—as Harold R. Isaacs recently put it in these pages[2]—that they want *out:*
people who say that integration will never come, or that it will take a
hundred or a thousand years to come, or that it will come at too high a
price in suffering and struggle for the pallid and sodden life of the American middle class that at the very best it may bring.

The most numerous, influential, and dangerous movement that has
grown out of Negro despair with the goal of integration is, of course,
the Black Muslims. This movement, whatever else we may say about it,
must be credited with one enduring achievement: it inspired James Bald-

---

[2] "Integration and the Negro Mood," December 1962.

win to write an essay[3] which deserves to be placed among the classics of our language. Everything Baldwin has ever been trying to tell us is distilled here into a statement of overwhelming persuasiveness and prophetic magnificence. Baldwin's message is and always has been simple. It is this: "Color is not a human or personal reality; it is a political reality." And Baldwin's demand is correspondingly simple: color must be forgotten, lest we all be smited with a vengeance "that does not really depend on, and cannot really be executed by, any person or organization, and that cannot be prevented by any police force or army: historical vengeance, a cosmic vengeance based on the law that we recognize when we say, 'Whatever goes up must come down.'" The Black Muslims Baldwin portrays as a sign and a warning to the intransigent white world. They come to proclaim how deep is the Negro's disaffection with the white world and all its works, and Baldwin implies that no American Negro can fail to respond somewhere in his being to their message: that the white man is the devil, that Allah has doomed him to destruction, and that the black man is about to inherit the earth. Baldwin of course knows that this nightmare inversion of the racism from which the black man has suffered can neither win nor even point to the neighborhood in which victory might be located. For in his view the neighborhood of victory lies in exactly the opposite direction: the transcendence of color through love.

Yet the tragic fact is that love is not the answer to hate—not in the world of politics, at any rate. Color is indeed a political rather than a human or a personal reality and if politics (which is to say power) has made it into a human and a personal reality, then only politics (which is to say power) can unmake it once again. But the way of politics is slow and bitter, and as impatience on the one side is matched by a setting of the jaw on the other, we move closer and closer to an explosion and blood may yet run in the streets.

Will this madness in which we are all caught never find a resting-place? Is there never to be an end to it? In thinking about the Jews I have often wondered whether their survival as a distinct group was worth one hair on the head of a single infant. Did the Jews have to survive so that six million innocent people should one day be burned in the ovens of Auschwitz? It is a terrible question and no one, not God himself, could ever answer it to my satisfaction. And when I think about the Negroes in America and about the image of integration as a state in which the Negroes would take their rightful place as another of the protected minorities in a pluralistic society, I wonder whether they really believe in their hearts that such a state can actually be attained, and if so *why* they should wish to survive as a distinct group. I think I know why the Jews

---

[3] Originally published last November in the *New Yorker* under the title "Letter From a Region in My Mind," it has just been reprinted (along with a new introduction) by Dial Press under the title *The Fire Next Time.*

once wished to survive (though I am less certain as to why we still do): they not only believed that God had given them no choice, but they were tied to a memory of past glory and a dream of imminent redemption. What does the American Negro have that might correspond to this? His past is a stigma, his color is a stigma, and his vision of the future is the hope of erasing the stigma by making color irrelevant, by making it disappear as a fact of consciousness.

I share this hope, but I cannot see how it will ever be realized unless color does *in fact* disappear: and that means not integration, it means assimilation, it means—let the brutal word come out—miscegenation. The Black Muslims, like their racist counterparts in the white world, accuse the "so-called Negro leaders" of secretly pursuing miscegenation as a goal. The racists are wrong, but I wish they were right, for I believe that the wholesale merging of the two races is the most desirable alternative for everyone concerned. I am not claiming that this alternative can be pursued programmatically or that it is immediately feasible as a solution; obviously there are even greater barriers to its achievement than to the achievement of integration. What I am saying, however, is that in my opinion the Negro problem can be solved in this country in no other way.

I have told the story of my own twisted feelings about Negroes here, and of how they conflict with the moral convictions I have since developed, in order to assert that such feelings must be acknowledged as honestly as possible so that they can be controlled and ultimately disregarded in favor of the convictions. It is *wrong* for a man to suffer because of the color of his skin. Beside that clichéd proposition of liberal thought, what argument can stand and be respected? If the arguments are the arguments of feeling, they must be made to yield; and one's own soul is not the worst place to begin working a huge social transformation. Not so long ago, it used to be asked of white liberals, "Would you like your sister to marry one?" When I was a boy and my sister was still unmarried, I would certainly have said no to that question. But now I am a man, my sister is already married, and I have daughters. If I were to be asked today whether I would like a daughter of mine "to marry one," I would have to answer: "No, I wouldn't *like* it at all. I would rail and rave and rant and tear my hair. And then I hope I would have the courage to curse myself for raving and ranting, and to give her my blessing. How dare I withhold it at the behest of the child I once was and against the man I now have a duty to be?"

Technology and
Human Values

None of the essays gathered below deals solely or even mainly with the benefits we have derived from technology. In the first place, the matter is too plain, too axiomatic, to require elaborate treatment. The reader does not have to be reminded of the achievements of American industry, of the rise in our standard of living, of the medical alleviation of our pain and the lengthening of our lives. The successful application of science to our practical problems has been truly described as "one of the miracles of mankind." But unless it be in the course of passionate partisan defense of free enterprise or of the democratic way of life, almost no responsible writer today can discuss technological progress without considerable misgivings and without considerable acknowledgment of the losses that seem often to accompany the gains. These misgivings were already felt by Jonathan Swift when applied science was still in its infancy. Lerner and Ellul write with the experience of two hundred years of the industrial age behind them, and Mowrer, focusing on the single problem, population, wryly speculates on our "progress" in the future. The satirical story by E. B. White invites, among other things, some speculation on its relation to Swift's. In one form or another, all of these writers ask the same question: In the pursuit of material progress, in the pride of technical know-how, what human values have we lost?

JONATHAN SWIFT

Swift (1667–1745), born of an English family in Dublin, became an Anglican clergyman during a period of disappointment over his hopes for a political career in England. He nevertheless pursued politics and by 1710 had achieved a powerful position in the Tory party. In 1713 he was rewarded for his service to the Tory government—in the manner of those times—with the Deanship of St. Patrick's, Dublin. However, he spent little time in Ireland until the fall of the Tory party forced his return the following year; for the rest of his life he became a champion of the Irish people against English oppression. Meanwhile, he had become an intimate of the best English writers of his time, a leading political pamphleteer, and had begun the series of writings that make him the greatest of English satirists. Especially notable are A Tale of a Tub *and* The Battle of the Books, *published in 1704,* A Modest Proposal *(1720), and the incomparable* Gulliver's Travels *(1726). It is from the third part of this work, "A Voyage to Laputa, Balnibarbi, Luggnagg, Glubbdubdrib, and Japan," that the present account (Chapter 5) is taken. Some of the specific details in the description would have been recognized by Swift's contemporaries as comic versions of actual experiments reported in the* Transactions of the Royal Society, *the leading scientific group in England. The suggestion for the abolition of words probably refers to Thomas Sprat's ideal of an economical scientific prose that would express "so many 'Things,' almost in an equal number of 'Words.'" Critics have sometimes been inclined to apologize for the attitude towards scientific experiment here expressed by Swift. They point out that no one at the time (Sir Isaac Newton was still alive) could have predicted the enormous achievements of science and technology, and Swift does seem to have attacked "projectors" in part because of the impracticality of their schemes. But*

*in the context of the other readings in this section, the reader may find
that Swift's satire still contains some prophecy in it.*

THE GRAND ACADEMY
OF LAGADO

This Academy is not an entire single Building, but a Continuation of several Houses on both Sides of a Street; which growing waste, was purchased and applyed to that Use.

I was received very kindly by the Warden, and went for many Days to the Academy. Every Room hath in it one or more Projectors; and I believe I could not be in fewer than five Hundred Rooms.

The first Man I saw was of a meagre Aspect, with sooty Hands and Face, his Hair and Beard long, ragged and singed in several Places. His Clothes, Shirt, and Skin were all of the same Colour. He had been Eight Years upon a Project for extracting Sun-Beams out of Cucumbers, which were to be put into Vials hermetically sealed, and let out to warm the Air in raw inclement Summers. He told me, he did not doubt in Eight Years more, that he should be able to supply the Governors Gardens with Sun-shine at a reasonable Rate; but he complained that his Stock was low, and intreated me to give him something as an Encouragement to Ingenuity, especially since this had been a very dear Season for Cucumbers. I made him a small Present, for my Lord had furnished me with Money on purpose, because he knew their Practice of begging from all who go to see them.

I went into another Chamber, but was ready to hasten back, being almost overcome with a horrible Stink. My Conductor pressed me forward, conjuring me in a Whisper to give no Offence, which would be highly resented; and therefore I durst not so much as stop my Nose. The Projector of this Cell was the most ancient Student of the Academy. His Face and Beard were of a pale Yellow; his Hands and Clothes dawbed over with Filth. When I was presented to him, he gave me a very close Embrace, (a Compliment I could well have excused.) His Employment from his first coming into the Academy, was an Operation to reduce human Excrement to its original Food, by separating the several Parts, removing the Tincture which it receives from the Gall, making the Odour exhale, and scumming off the Saliva. He had a weekly Allowance from the Society, of a Vessel filled with human Ordure, about the Bigness of a *Bristol* Barrel.

I saw another at work to calcine Ice into Gunpowder; who likewise shewed me a Treatise he had written concerning the Malleability of Fire, which he intended to publish.

There was a most ingenious Architect who had contrived a new Method for building Houses, by beginning at the Roof, and working downwards to the Foundation; which he justified to me by the like Practice of those two prudent Insects the Bee and the Spider.

There was a Man born blind, who had several Apprentices in his own Condition: Their Employment was to mix Colours for Painters, which their Master taught them to distinguish by feeling and smelling. It was indeed my Misfortune to find them at that Time not very perfect in their Lessons; and the Professor himself happened to be generally mistaken: This Artist is much encouraged and esteemed by the whole Fraternity.

In another Apartment I was highly pleased with a Projector, who had found a Device of plowing the Ground with Hogs, to save the Charges of Plows, Cattle, and Labour. The Method is this: In an Acre of Ground you bury at six Inches Distance, and eight deep, a Quantity of Acorns, Dates, Chesnuts, and other Maste or Vegetables whereof these Animals are fondest; then you drive six Hundred or more of them into the Field, where in a few Days they will root up the whole Ground in search of their Food, and make it fit for sowing, at the same time manuring it with their Dung. It is true, upon Experiment they found the Charge and Trouble very great, and they had little or no Crop. However, it is not doubted that this Invention may be capable of great Improvement.

I went into another Room, where the Walls and Ceiling were all hung round with Cobwebs, except a narrow Passage for the Artist to go in and out. At my Entrance he called aloud to me not to disturb his Webs. He lamented the fatal Mistake the World had been so long in of using Silk-Worms, while we had such plenty of domestick Insects, who infinitely excelled the former, because they understood how to weave as well as spin. And he proposed farther, that by employing Spiders, the Charge of dying Silks would be wholly saved; whereof I was fully convinced when he shewed me a vast Number of Flies most beautifully coloured, wherewith he fed his Spiders; assuring us, that the Webs would take a Tincture from them; and as he had them of all Hues, he hoped to fit every Body's Fancy, as soon as he could find proper Food for the Flies, of certain Gums, Oyls, and other glutinous Matter, to give a Strength and Consistence to the Threads.

There was an Astronomer who had undertaken to place a Sun-Dial upon the great Weather-Cock on the Town-House, by adjusting the annual and diurnal Motions of the Earth and Sun, so as to answer and coincide with all accidental Turnings of the Wind.

I was complaining of a small Fit of the Cholick; upon which my Conductor led me into a Room, where a great Physician resided, who was famous for curing that Disease by contrary Operations from the same Instrument. He had a large Pair of Bellows, with a long slender Muzzle of Ivory. This he conveyed eight Inches up the Anus, and drawing in the Wind, he affirmed he could make the Guts as lank as a dried Bladder. But when the Disease was more stubborn and violent, he let in the Muzzle while the Bellows was full of Wind, which he discharged into the Body of the Patient; then withdrew the Instrument to replenish it, clapping his Thumb strongly against the Orifice of the Fundament; and this being repeated three or four Times, the adventitious Wind would rush out, bringing the noxious along with it (like Water put into a Pump) and the Patient recovers. I saw him try both Experiments upon a Dog, but could not discern any Effect from the former. After the latter, the Animal was ready to burst, and made so violent a Discharge, as was very offensive to me and my Companions. The Dog died on the Spot, and we left the Doctor endeavouring to recover him by the same Operation.

I visited many other Apartments, but shall not trouble my Reader with all the Curiosities I observed, being studious of Brevity.

I had hitherto seen only one Side of the Academy, the other being appropriated to the Advancers of speculative Learning; of whom I shall say something when I have mentioned one illustrious Person more, who is called among them *the universal Artist*. He told us, he had been Thirty Years employing his Thoughts for the Improvement of human Life. He had two large Rooms full of wonderful Curiosities, and Fifty Men at work. Some were condensing Air into a dry tangible Substance, by extracting the Nitre, and letting the aqueous or fluid Particles percolate: Others softening Marble for Pillows and Pin-cushions; others petrifying the Hoofs of a living Horse to preserve them from foundring. The Artist himself was at that Time busy upon two great Designs: The first, to sow Land with Chaff, wherein he affirmed the true seminal Virtue to be contained, as he demonstrated by several Experiments which I was not skilful enough to comprehend. The other was, by a certain Composition of Gums, Minerals, and Vegetables outwardly applied, to prevent the Growth of Wool upon two young Lambs; and he hoped in a reasonable Time to propagate the Breed of naked Sheep all over the Kingdom.

We crossed a Walk to the other Part of the Academy, where, as I have already said, the Projectors in speculative Learning resided.

The first Professor I saw was in a very large Room, with Forty Pupils about him. After Salutation, observing me to look earnestly upon a Frame, which took up the greatest Part of both the Length and Breadth of the Room; he said, perhaps I might wonder to see him employed in a Project for improving speculative Knowledge by practical and mechanical Operations. But the World would soon be sensible of its Usefulness; and he flattered himself, that a more noble exalted Thought never sprang in any other Man's Head. Every one knew how laborious the usual Method is of attaining to Arts and Sciences; whereas by his Contrivance, the most ignorant Person at a reasonable Charge, and with a little bodily Labour, may write Books in Philosophy, Poetry, Politicks, Law, Mathematicks and Theology, without the least Assistance from Genius or Study. He then led me to the Frame, about the Sides whereof all his Pupils stood in Ranks. It was Twenty Foot square, placed in the Middle of the

Room. The Superficies was composed of several Bits of Wood, about the
Bigness of a Dye, but some larger than others. They were all linked
together by slender Wires. These Bits of Wood were covered on every
Square with Paper pasted on them; and on these Papers were written all
the Words of their Language in their several Moods, Tenses, and Declen-
sions, but without any Order. The Professor then desired me to observe,
for he was going to set his Engine at work. The Pupils at his Command
took each of them hold of an Iron Handle, whereof there were Forty
fixed round the Edges of the Frame; and giving them a sudden Turn, the
whole Disposition of the Words was entirely changed. He then commanded Six and Thirty of the Lads to read the several Lines softly as they
appeared upon the Frame; and where they found three or four Words
together that might make Part of a Sentence, they dictated to the four
remaining Boys who were Scribes. This Work was repeated three or four
Times, and at every Turn the Engine was so contrived that the Words
shifted into new Places, as the square Bits of Wood moved upside down.

Six Hours a-Day the young Students were employed in this Labour; and
the Professor shewed me several Volumes in large Folio already collected,
of broken Sentences, which he intended to piece together; and out of
those rich Materials to give the World a compleat Body of all Arts and
Sciences; which however might be still improved, and much expedited, if
the Publick would raise a Fund for making and employing five Hundred
such Frames in *Lagado*, and oblige the Managers to contribute in common
their several Collections.

He assured me, that this Invention had employed all his Thoughts
from his Youth; that he had emptied the whole Vocabulary into his
Frame, and made the strictest Computation of the general Proportion there
is in Books between the Numbers of Particles, Nouns, and Verbs, and
other Parts of Speech.

I made my humblest Acknowledgments to this illustrious Person for
his great Communicativeness; and promised if ever I had the good Fortune
to return to my native Country, that I would do him Justice, as the sole
Inventer of this wonderful Machine; the Form and Contrivance of which
I desired Leave to delineate upon Paper as in the Figure here annexed. I
told him, although it were the Custom of our Learned in *Europe* to steal
Inventions from each other, who had thereby at least this Advantage, that
it became a Controversy which was the right Owner; yet I would take
such Caution, that he should have the Honour entire without a Rival.

We next went to the School of Languages, where three Professors sat
in Consultation upon improving that of their own Country.

The first Project was to shorten Discourse by cutting Polysyllables into
one, and leaving out Verbs and Participles; because in Reality all things
imaginable are but Nouns.

The other, was a Scheme for entirely abolishing all Words whatsoever:
And this was urged as a great Advantage in Point of Health as well as

Brevity. For, it is plain, that every Word we speak is in some Degree a Diminution of our Lungs by Corrosion; and consequently contributes to the shortning of our Lives. An Expedient was therefore offered, that since Words are only Names for *Things*, it would be more convenient for all Men to carry about them, such *Things* as were necessary to express the particular Business they are to discourse on. And this Invention would certainly have taken Place, to the great Ease as well as Health of the Subject, if the Women in Conjunction with the Vulgar and Illiterate had not threatned to raise a Rebellion, unless they might be allowed the Liberty to speak with their Tongues, after the Manner of their Fore-fathers: Such constant irreconcileable Enemies to Science are the common People. However, many of the most Learned and Wise adhere to the new Scheme of expressing themselves by *Things;* which hath only this Incon-venience attending it; that if a Man's Business be very great, and of various Kinds, he must be obliged in Proportion to carry a greater Bundle of *Things* upon his Back, unless he can afford one or two strong Servants to attend him. I have often beheld two of those Sages almost sinking under the Weight of their Packs, like Pedlars among us; who when they met in the Streets would lay down their Loads, open their Sacks, and hold Conversation for an Hour together; then put up their Implements, help each other to resume their Burthens, and take their Leave.

But, for short Conversations a Man may carry Implements in his Pockets and under his Arms, enough to supply him, and in his House he cannot be at a Loss; therefore the Room where Company meet who prac-tice this Art, is full of all *Things* ready at Hand, requisite to furnish Matter for this Kind of artificial Converse.

Another great Advantage proposed by this Invention, was, that it would serve as an universal Language to be understood in all civilized Nations, whose Goods and Utensils are generally of the same Kind, or nearly resembling, so that their Uses might easily be comprehended. And thus, Embassadors would be qualified to treat with foreign Princes or Ministers of State, to whose Tongues they were utter Strangers.

I was at the Mathematical School, where the Master taught his Pupils after a Method scarce imaginable to us in *Europe*. The Proposition and Demonstration were fairly written on a thin Wafer, with Ink composed of a Cephalick Tincture. This the Student was to swallow upon a fasting Stomach, and for three Days following eat nothing but Bread and Water. As the Wafer digested, the Tincture mounted to his Brain, bearing the Proposition along with it. But the Success hath not hitherto been answer-able, partly by some Error in the *Quantum* or Composition, and partly by the Perverseness of Lads; to whom this Bolus is so nauseous, that they generally steal aside, and discharge it upwards before it can operate; neither have they been yet persuaded to use so long an Abstinence as the Prescription requires.

MAX LERNER

THE CULTURE
OF MACHINE LIVING

This is Chapter 6 of the fourth part of America as a Civilization. *Information on the author and his works follows index.*

•

Any principle that comes to dominate a culture can do so only by making itself part of the life processes of the people. This has happened in the case of America, and it is one of the reasons we can speak seriously, and not as a literary flourish, of the culture of machine living. Siegfried Giedion points out that the machine has mechanized such fundamentals as the soil (mechanized agriculture), bread (mechanized milling), death (assembly-line slaughtering pens and the use of by-products by the big meat packers), and the household (the kitchen revolution, the household-appliance revolution, mechanized laundering, and the mechanized bathroom). The analysis can be carried further. Mechanization has extended to transport (boats, trains, autos, busses, trucks, subways, planes), to living outside the home (hotels, motels, sleeping cars, "automats"), and to the basic phases of the communications revolution (newsprint, book publishing, magazines, telephone, telegraph, movies, radio, TV).

Aside from these arterial forms of American living there is also the interminable gadgetry. From the automatic vending machines to the automatic gas stations, from the gadgeted car to the gadgeted bed, America has taken on the aspect of a civilization cluttered with artifacts and filled with the mechanized bric-a-brac of machine living. The Big Technology of the mass-production industries is supplemented by the Little Technology of everyday living.

One could draw a gloomy picture of machine living in America and depict it as the Moloch swallowing the youth and resilience of American manhood. From Butler's *Erewhon* to Capek's *R.U.R.*, European thinkers have seized on the machine as the cancer of modern living. Some have even suggested that there is a daimon in Western man, and especially in the American, that is driving him to the monstrous destruction of his instinctual life and indeed of his whole civilization.

Part of the confusion flows from the failure to distinguish at least three phases of the machine culture. One is what I have just described: *machine living* as such, the use of machinery in work and in leisure and in the constant accompaniments of the day. The second is cultural *standardization*, aside from the machine, but a standardization that flows from machine production. The third is *conformism* in thought, attitude, and action. All three are parts of the empire of the machine but at varying removes and with different degrees of danger for the human spirit.

The danger in machine living itself is chiefly the danger of man's arrogance in exulting over the seemingly easy triumphs over Nature which he calls "progress," so that he cuts himself off increasingly from the organic processes of life itself. Thus with the soil: the erosion of the American earth is not, as some seem to believe, the result of the mechanization of agriculture; a farmer can use science and farm technology to the full, and he need not exhaust or destroy his soil but can replenish it, as has been shown in the TVA, which is itself a triumph of technology. But the machines have been accompanied by a greed for quick results and an irreverence for the soil which are responsible for destroying the balance between man and the environment. What is true of the soil is true of the household: the mechanized household appliances have not destroyed the home or undermined family life; rural electrification has made the farmer's wife less a drudge, and the mass production of suburban houses has given the white-collar family a better chance than it had for sun and living space. What threatens family life is not the "kitchen revolution" or the "housing revolution" but the restless malaise of the spirit, of which the machine is more product than creator.

Even in a society remarkable for its self-criticism the major American writers have not succumbed to the temptation of making the machine into a Devil. Most of the novelists have amply expressed the frustrations of American life, and some (Dreiser, Dos Passos, Farrell and Algren come to mind) have mirrored in their style the pulse beats of an urban mechanized civilization. But except for a few isolated works, like Elmer Rice's *Adding Machine* and Eugene O'Neill's *Dynamo*, the writers have refrained from the pathetic fallacy of ascribing the ills of the spirit to the diabolism of the machine. The greatest American work on technology and its consequences—Lewis Mumford's massive four-volume work starting with *Man and Technics* and ending with *The Conduct of Life* —makes the crucial distinction between what is due to the machine itself and what is due to the human institutions that guide it and determine its uses.

It is here, moving from machine living to cultural standardization, that the picture becomes bleaker. Henry Miller's phrase for its American form is "the air-conditioned nightmare." Someone with a satiric intent could do a withering take-off on the rituals of American standardization.

Most American babies (he might say) are born in standardized hospitals, with a standardized tag put around them to keep them from getting confused with other standardized products of the hospital. Many of them grow up either in uniform rows of tenements or of small-town or suburban houses. They are wheeled about in standard perambulators, shiny or shabby as may be, fed from standardized bottles with standardized nipples according to standardized formulas, and tied up with standardized diapers. In childhood they are fed standardized breakfast foods out of standardized boxes with pictures of standardized heroes on them. They are sent to monotonously similar schoolhouses, where almost uniformly standardized teachers ladle out to them standardized information out of standardized textbooks. They pick up the routine wisdom of the streets in standard slang and learn the routine terms which constrict the range of their language within dishearteningly narrow limits. They wear out standardized shoes playing standardized games, or as passive observers they follow through standardized newspaper accounts or standardized radio and TV programs the highly ritualized antics of grown-up professionals playing the same games. They devour in millions of uniform pulp comic books the prowess of standardized supermen.

As they grow older they dance to canned music from canned juke boxes, millions of them putting standard coins into standard slots to get standardized tunes sung by voices with standardized inflections of emotion. They date with standardized girls in standardized cars. They see automatons thrown on millions of the same movie and TV screens, watching stereotyped love scenes adapted from made-to-order stories in standardized magazines.

They spend the days of their years with monotonous regularity in factory, office, and shop, performing routinized operations at regular intervals. They take time out for standardized "coffee breaks" and later a quick standardized lunch, come home at night to eat processed or canned food, and read syndicated columns and comic strips. Dressed in standardized clothes they attend standardized club meetings, church services, and socials. They have standardized fun at standardized big-city conventions. They are drafted into standardized armies, and if they escape the death of mechanized warfare they die of highly uniform diseases, and to the accompaniment of routine platitudes they are buried in standardized graves and celebrated by standardized obituary notices.

Caricature? Yes, perhaps a crude one, but with a core of frightening validity in it. Every society has its routines and rituals, the primitive groups being sometimes more tyrannously restricted by convention than the industrial societies. The difference is that where the primitive is bound by the rituals of tradition and group life, the American is bound by the rituals of the machine, its products, and their distribution and consumption.

The role of the machine in this standardized living must be made clear. The machine mechanizes life, and since mass production is part of Big Technology, the machine also makes uniformity of life possible. But it does not compel such uniformity. The American who shaves with an electric razor and his wife who buys a standardized "home permanent" for her hair do not thereby have to wear a uniformly vacuous expression through the day. A newspaper that uses the press association wire stories and prints from a highly mechanized set of presses does not thereby have to take the same view of the world that every other paper takes. A novelist who uses a typewriter instead of a quill pen does not have to turn out machine-made historical romances.

The answer is that some do and some don't. What the machine and the mass-produced commodities have done has been to make conformism easier. To buy and use what everyone else does, and live and think as everyone else does, becomes a short cut involving no need for one's own thinking. Those Americans have been captured by conformist living who have been capturable by it.

Cultural stereotypes are an inherent part of all group living, and they become sharper with mass living. There have always been unthinking people leading formless, atomized lives. What has happened in America is that the economics of mass production has put a premium on uniformity, so that America produces more units of more commodities (although sometimes of fewer models) than other cultures. American salesmanship has sought out every potential buyer of a product, so that standardization makes its way by the force of the distributive mechanism into every life. Yet for the person who has a personality pattern and style of his own, standardization need not mean anything more than a set of conveniences which leave a larger margin of leisure and greater scope for creative living. "That we may be enamored by the negation brought by the machine," as Frank Lloyd Wright has put it, "may be inevitable for a time. But I like to imagine this novel negation to be only a platform underfoot to enable a greater splendor of life to be ours than any known to Greek or Roman, Goth or Moor. We should know a life beside which the life they knew would seem not only limited in scale and narrow in range but pale in richness of the color of imagination and integrity of spirit."

Which is to say that technology is the shell of American life, but a shell that need not hamper or stultify the modes of living and thinking. The real dangers of the American mode of life are not in the machine or even in standardization as much as they are in conformism. The dangers do not flow from the contrivances that men have fashioned to lighten their burdens, or from the material abundance which, if anything, should make a richer cultural life possible. They flow rather from the mimesis of the dominant and successful by the weak and mediocre, from the intolerance of diversity, and from the fear of being thought different from one's fellows. This is the essence of conformism.

It would be hard to make the connection between technology and conformism, unless one argues that men fashion their minds in the image of their surroundings, and that in a society of automatism, human beings themselves will become automatons. But this is simply not so. What relation there is between technology and conformism is far more subtle and less mystical. It is a double relation. On the one hand, as Jefferson foresaw, the simpler society of small-scale manufacture did not involve concentration of power in a small group, was not vulnerable to breakdown, and did not need drastic governmental controls; a society of big-scale industry has shown that it does. In that sense the big machines carry with them an imperative toward the directed society, which in turn—whether in war or peace—encourages conformism. On the second score, as De Tocqueville saw, a society in which there is no recognized elite group to serve as the arbiter of morals, thought, and style is bound to be a formless one in which the ordinary person seeks to heal his insecurity by attuning himself to the "tyranny of opinion"—to what others do and say and what they think of him. He is ruled by imitation and prestige rather than a sense of his own worth.

These are dangerous trends, but all of social living is dangerous. The notable fact is that in spite of its machines and standardization America has proved on balance less conformist than some other civilizations where the new technology has played less of a role. One thinks of the totalitarian experience of Italy, of Spain and Portugal, of Germany, of Russia and the East European countries, of Japan, of China. Some, like the Germans, the Japanese, and the Russian and Chinese Communists have been seized with an admiration for the machine; the others have had clerical and feudal traditions, and have lagged in industrial development. The totalitarian spirit can come to reside in a culture no matter what the shell of its technology is. There is no unvarying relation between machines and rigidity of living and thinking.

Americans have, it is true, an idolatry of production and consumption as they have an idolatry of success. But they have not idolized authority or submitted unquestioningly to human or supernatural oracles. They have had their cranks, eccentrics, and anarchists, and they still cling to individualism, even when it is being battered hard. It will take them some time before they can become "man in equipoise," balancing what science and the machine can do as against the demands of the life processes. But where they have failed, the failure has been less that of the machines they have wrought than of the very human fears, greeds, and competitive drives that have accompanied the building of a powerful culture.

It has been suggested that the American, like the Faustian, made a bargain with the Big Technology: a bargain to transform his ways of life and thought in the image of the machine, in return for the range of power and riches the machine would bring within his reach. It is a fine allegory. But truer than the Faustian bargain, with its connotations of the sale of one's soul to the Devil, is the image of Prometheus stealing fire from the gods in order to light a path of progress for men. The path is not yet clear, nor the meaning of progress, nor where it is leading: but the bold intent, the irreverence, and the secular daring have all become part of the American experience.

JACQUES ELLUL

Jacques Ellul, born in Bordeaux in 1912, has studied at the Universities of Bordeaux and Paris. He holds a doctorate in law and is now Professor of Law at Bordeaux. Among his various writings, those on technology have attracted the greatest attention in the United States. His book La Technique *(1954) appeared in English as* The Technological Society *(1964). He is also the author of* Le fondement théologique du droit *(1946), translated in 1960* (The Theological Foundation of Law); Présence au monde moderne *(1948);* Histoire des institutions, *two vols. (1955–56); and* Propagandes *(1962). The present essay, translated by John Wilkinson, appeared in* The Technological Order, *ed. Carl F. Stover (Detroit, 1963). Wilkinson remarks that " 'Technique' as it is used by Ellul is most nearly equivalent to what we commonly think of as 'the technological order' or 'the technological society.' "*

TECHNICAL PROGRESS
IS ALWAYS AMBIGUOUS

It cannot be maintained that technical progress is in itself either good or bad. In the evolution of Technique, contradictory elements are always indissolubly connected. Let us consider these elements under the following four rubrics:

1. All technical progress exacts a price;
2. Technique raises more problems than it solves;
3. Pernicious effects are inseparable from favorable effects; and
4. Every technique implies unforeseeable effects.

1. ALL TECHNICAL PROGRESS EXACTS A PRICE

What is meant here is not that technical progress exacts a price in money or in intellectual effort, but that, when technical progress adds something on the one hand, it inevitably subtracts something on the other. It is always difficult to interpret satisfactorily the bald statement that "technical progress is an established fact," because some people cling to traditional social forms, tending to deny any value at all to such progress, and deeming that nothing can be called progress if it casts doubt on established social values. Other persons, on the contrary, hold that Technique produces extraordinary things of a prodigious novelty, bringing about the consequent disappearance of all sorts of valueless junk.

The fact is that, viewed objectively, technological progress produces values of unimpeachable merit, while simultaneously destroying values no less important. As a consequence, it cannot be maintained that there is absolute progress or absolute regress.

Let me give a few simple examples of this reciprocal action. In the first place, let us consider the fact that modern man, thanks to hygiene in particular and to technical progress in general, enjoys a greater life span than ever before. Life expectancy in France today is approximately 60 years, compared, say, to 35 years in 1890 and 30 years about 1800.[1] But, even with this indubitable extension of the average life span, all physicians are in agreement that, proportionately to this extension, life has become very much more precarious, i.e., our general state of health has become very much more fragile. Human beings of the present have neither the same resistance as their ancestors to disease or to natural conditions, nor the same endurance; they suffer from a certain nervous "fragility" and a loss of general vitality, sensitiveness of their senses, and so on. In the 60 years during which such studies have been carried out, regression in all these respects has been marked. Thus, though we live longer, we live a reduced life with nothing resembling the vital energy of our ancestors. It is clear that diminution on the one hand has been accompanied by augmentation on the other.

In the sphere of labor, the technical progress of the present has effected

---

[1] I must remark that I am very sceptical of the way in which mean life spans are calculated for periods antedating 1800. When the historian says that life expectancy was 20 years in the thirteenth century, his statement can hardly be looked upon as more than a mere joke. There are no means *in principle* of establishing life expectancies for the past.

a considerable economy of muscular effort; but, at the same time this progress has come to demand a greater and greater nervous effort so that tension and wear and tear on our nerves have inversely increased. Here again, a kind of equilibrium has asserted itself between savings and expense.

To take an instance from the sphere of economics, technical progress allows the creation of new industries. But a just view of the matter would compel us to take into consideration the accompanying destruction of resources. To take a French example, the so-called Lacq case is beginning to be well known. An industrial complex for the exploitation of sulphur and natural gas has been established at Lacq, a simple technical fact. But, from the economic point of view, this is far from being the case, since a serious agricultural problem has arisen because of the excessive destruction of farm products in the region. Up to now, the government has not seen fit to take the matter seriously, although it has been officially estimated in reports to the Chamber that, for 1960, agricultural losses have aggregated two billion francs. Now, the vineyards of Jurançon are being attacked by the sulfurous gases and are disappearing, a not inconsiderable economic loss.

To calculate from the economist's point of view the profits of an industry of this kind, it would at the minimum be necessary to deduct the value of what has been destroyed, in this case two billion francs. It would likewise be necessary to deduct the very considerable expenses of all the necessary protective devices, hospitals (which, incidentally, have not yet been constructed), schools,—in short, of the whole urban complex which has not yet been brought into being but which is nevertheless indispensable. We must have knowledge of how to calculate the *whole*. The Lacq enterprise, counting all the expenses of which we have been speaking, must be reckoned a "deficit" enterprise.

Our last example has to do with the problem of the intellectual culture of the masses. True, today's technical means permit a mass culture to exist. Television allows people who never visited a theatre in their lives to see performances of the great classics. *Paris-Match*, through its articles, allows masses of people who would be in total ignorance without such articles to attain to a certain literary (and even to a certain aesthetic) culture. But, on the other side of the ledger, it must be recorded that this same technical progress leads to an ever increasing cultural superficiality. Technical progress absolutely forbids certain indispensable conditions of a genuine culture, viz., reflection and opportunity for assimilation. We are indeed witnessing the creation of knowledge, since we are in possession of the means of knowing what we could never have known before; but it is nevertheless a superficial development because it is one which is purely *quantitative*.

The intellectual no longer has any time to meditate on a book and must choose between two alternatives: *Either* he reads through a whole collection of books rapidly, of which a little later but a few fragments survive—

scattered bits of vague knowledge; *or*, he takes a year to peruse a few books thoroughly. I should like to know who today has the time to take Pascal or Montaigne seriously. To do them justice would require months and months; but today's Technique forbids any such thing. Exactly the same holds for the problem of the "Musée Imaginaire," which Malraux has put so well. We can be in contact with the whole painting and sculpture of humanity; but this availability has no cultural value comparable to that enjoyed by Poussin, who, in his voyage to Rome, passed several years in studying, statue by statue, the ensemble of artistic works at his disposal. He clearly knew nothing of Polynesian or Chinese art, but what he did know had infinitely more educational value for him because it penetrated his personality slowly.

So, once again, we see that Technique allows us to progress quantitatively to the level of culture spoken of, but at the same time interdicts us from making any progress in depth. In the circumstances, is it really possible to speak of "culture" at all? All technical progress exacts a price. We cannot believe that Technique brings us nothing; but we must not think that what it brings it brings free of charge.

2. THE PROBLEMS POSED BY TECHNICAL PROGRESS

The second aspect of the ambiguity of technical progress concerns the following point: When Technique evolves, it does so by solving a certain number of problems, and by raising others.

The further we advance into the technological society, the more convinced we become that, in any sphere whatever, there are nothing but technical problems. We conceive all problems in their technical aspect, and think that solutions to them can only appear by means of further perfecting techniques. In a certain sense, we are right; it is true that Technique permits us to solve the majority of the problems we encounter. But we are compelled to note (perhaps not often enough) that each technical evolution raises new problems, and that, as a consequence, there is never *one* technique which solves *one* problem. The technological movement is more complicated; one technique solves one problem, but at the same time creates others.

Let us take some simple examples of this fact. We are well acquainted with the details of the gravest sociological problem faced by the nineteenth century, i.e., that of the proletariat, a problem which we are only now in process of solving (with difficulty). The phenomenon of the proletariat is not to be considered a simple one, and Marx himself did not describe it as "merely" the exploitation of the workers by certain wicked capitalists. His explanation of the "proletarian condition" was very much more profound; he demonstrated that the proletariat was a result of the division and the mechanization of labor. He expressly states that "it is necessary to pass through the stage represented by the proletariat." For Marx, therefore, the problem is not, say, a moral one, with "bad guys exploiting good guys." Marx never puts the problem in this way; he always poses it as lying outside good or bad moral qualities, external to value judgments, and on the level of fact. And the fact is the fact of the division of labor, and of the machine, giving rise to a society in which exploitation is inevitable, i.e., drawing off surplus values. The phenomenon of the proletariat is therefore, even in the Marxian analysis, the result of technical progress. The machine and the division of labor allowed, from the economic point of view, an extraordinary expansion, but, at the same time, and as a result of the same movement, posed the social problem which it has taken a whole century to resolve.

Let us consider in the same way the extension of the above problem as it appears in the questions which will eventually but certainly be posed by the so-called "automation." Again, automation is not just another simple economic fact; indeed, we are gradually coming to realize that it will entail difficulties which, from our present point of view, can only be characterized as insurmountable. *First* of all, automation implies a production of goods in a relatively constant series of types. This means that when production has been automated, it is no longer possible to vary types, so that an unavoidable condition of immobilism with regard to production must ensue. An automated production line, considered in its full context of operation, is so expensive that amortization must occur over terms so long that the exclusive production of certain types of goods without any possibility of modification must be a consequence. *But,* up to the present, no commercial market of the capitalist world is suited to the absorption of the production of an unchanging line of goods. No presently existing Western economic organization, *on the commercial plane,* is prepared to find an answer to automated production.

Another difficulty of automation is the fact that it will result in a massive diminution of the necessary labor force. The simplistic reaction to this problem will clearly be to hold that the solution is easy. It is not necessary to cut down on the number of the workers but only to diminish the number of daily working hours of each. This solution is quite clearly impossible for a very simple reason. Automation cannot be applied to any arbitrarily selected industry or production, and this for reasons which are basic and not due to the temporary exigencies of, say, the money market. Certain kinds of production can and will be automated; certain others cannot and will never be automated. Consequently, it is not possible to cut down working hours over the working class as a whole. There are industrial sectors in which the workers would conceivably work one hour per day, whereas in others the workers would have to continue working a normal day of eight hours. Hence, as a result of automation, there will be extended sectors of the economy emptied of manpower, while other sectors will continue on the normal standard.

Diebold estimates that in the single year 1955–1956, in the United States, automation reduced the total number of working hours by seven per cent. In the automated plants of the Ford Motor Company there was a reduction of personnel by 25 per cent; and in 1957, in industrial branches in which automation gained most (in particular in the manufacture of electric bulbs and in the very highly automated chemical industry), it was possible to dispense with the services of 800,000 workers. In other words, automation does not result in labor saving favorable to the workers, but is expressed through unemployment and employment disequilibration.

It might be alleged that the situation described is true of capitalist countries but cannot be identical in socialist. This statement is not exact; in socialist countries the problem likewise is posed, primarily because of socialist egalitarianism. The problem is the same for the Soviet Union, for example, where automation is commencing, as for the United States. There will be specialized workers in some industries who will be freed from the necessity to work in one way or another, while in other branches of industry the eight-hour day will have to remain in force, a situation clearly unacceptable to the egalitarian theories of socialism.

A *second* problem is bound to arise in connection with the *retraining* of the "liberated" workers for jobs in new industrial sectors in which there is a shortage of manpower. But, such retraining more often than not presents enormous difficulties, since the disemployed worker is generally semi-skilled (or unskilled) and a completely new apprenticeship is implied of such a nature as to steer him toward other branches of industry.

A *third* difficulty occasioned by automation is the problem of *wages*. The wage problem produced by automation has, up till now, not been solved. How is it possible to fix a wage scale for automated industrial plants? It cannot be done on the piecework plan—machines do all the work. It cannot be done on the basis of time put in on the job. If it is desired to reduce unemployment by reducing the work day to, say, two or three hours, a given worker would only be employed for a very short period each day. Should such a worker, then, be paid according to a wage schedule which pays him for two hours of work at the equivalent of a worker who must work eight? The injustice of such a procedure is clear. How, then, should wages be calculated in an automated industry? One is forced to the admission that the relation between wages and productivity, on the one hand, and between wages and job time, on the other, *must* disappear. Wages will be calculated only as a function of the purchasing power given to the worker (with a view to maximum consumption) by dividing the total production value by the total number of workers. Such a method is really the only one feasible. Since 1950, in Russia, it has actually been tried twice. But the results were unsatisfactory, and it very soon became necessary to return to the system of hourly wages, since, in the present state of affairs, the necessary calculations prove unfeasible. But then the difficulties mentioned above (inherent in calculating either according to job-time or according to production) return, and, at the moment, wage calculation in automated industries is completely shrouded in uncertainties.

Still another problem is presented by the fact that modern economic crises most often result from a "distortion" between the different economic sectors, more exactly, from unequal growth of the different sectors. Here, automation must prove to be an economic factor much to be feared: There will not only be disparity of economic growth between the automated and the non-automated industrial sectors, but still more between industry and agriculture. *Either* capitalist countries must look forward to an increase of crises due to automation, *or* they must adopt planning aimed at rectifying the distortions (and planning by authoritarian measures, as in the Soviet Union). At the present time, even the Soviet planners find that their planning is insufficient to meet the problems of automation, since it is not "flexible" enough, on the one hand, and not "extensive" enough to re-equilibrate the out-of-phase sectors, on the other.

Here, then, are a number of problems (and there are a great many others) with which we must expect to be confronted by the fact of automation, all of which furnish us with examples of our thesis that Technique raises, in proportion to its progress, problems of greater and greater difficulty.

Let me indicate one final example of this, i.e., the problem of overpopulation, resulting from the application of medical and prophylactic health techniques, the final result of which is the suppression of infant mortality and the prolongation of human life. The phenomenon of overpopulation, in its turn, produces the tragic phenomenon of underconsumption. A century hence, all of us *without exception* will be menaced by a general underconsumption which will afflict the whole human race, *if* the expansion of the world's population increases. Here we are confronted by a problem clearly provoked by certain techniques, certain *positive techniques*.

The common factor of all these examples is that technical progress raises whole complexes of problems which we are in no position to solve. Examples of such problems are literally innumerable.

3. THE EVIL EFFECTS OF TECHNIQUE ARE INSEPARABLE FROM THE GOOD

An idea frequently to be encountered in superficial inquiries concerning Technique is the following: "At bottom, everything depends on the way Technique is employed; mankind has only to use Technique for the good and avoid using it for the bad." A common example of this notion is the usual recommendation to employ techniques for the beneficent purposes of peace and eschew them for the maleficent purposes of war. All then will go well.

Our thesis is that technical progress contains simultaneously the good *and* the bad. Consider automation, the problem which we have just been discussing. It is indisputable that technological unemployment is the result of mechanical progress. It cannot be otherwise. All mechanical progress necessarily entails a saving of labor and, consequently, a necessary technological unemployment. Here we have an ill-omened effect indissolubly connected with one which is in itself beneficial. The progress of mechanization necessarily entails unemployment. The technological unemployment so produced can be resolved by either of two means, which are the only two means economically or politically possible, viz., spreading it out either in *space* or in *time*.

A capitalist economist holds that the solution to unemployment is "that technological unemployment ultimately dies out of itself." This means that the workers who have been "freed" (the optimistic formula for unemployment) because of technical advances, will ultimately find jobs, either by directing themselves toward industries with manpower shortages or through the fact that new inventions will produce new opportunities of employment and new vocations. The standard example cited in defense of this thesis is that of the vocational opportunities connected with the invention of the automobile. Admittedly, this technological device did suppress a certain number of vocations, but it brought innumerable others into being with the final result that a vast number of persons are now employed by the servicing required by this industry. Hence, the machine in question has actually created employment.

All of this is indeed true. It is nevertheless a terribly heartless view of the situation, because it neglects to mention the *interim* period. It is all very well to say that the worker rendered jobless will, *with the lapse of a certain time*, again find employment . . . and that, after he has been reclassified, unemployment will die out. But, humanly speaking, what is the situation of the unemployed worker in the interim? Here the problem of spreading out unemployment in time is posed.

In the Soviet Union, unemployment of a technological nature (which not only exists but springs from the same sources) is spread out in space. By this I mean that when, in one place new machines are applied and workers "liberated" the affected workers will, without having to wait very long, receive a work-card which tells them in effect: "Two thousand kilometers from here a job has been assigned to you; you are hereby directed to remove yourself to such and such a factory." In one way, such a procedure seems a little less inhuman; but, in another way, it seems just as inhuman as the time procedure of the capitalists, since no account is taken of one's attachments to family, friends, locality, and so on. The human being is only a pawn to be moved about. It is hard to tell, between the capitalist and the socialist ways of handling the problem, which solution presents the worse indecencies.

A further example of the inseparable mingling of good and bad effects is furnished by the noteworthy study of the American sociological historian, J. U. Nef, concerning "industry and war." Nef shows how industrialism, i.e., the development of industry taken as a whole, necessarily prods industrialized societies in the direction of war. His analysis has nothing to do with the inner essence of industrialism; the phenomena described by him lie purely at the level of the human being.

First, industrialism gives an increasing population the means to live. It is a law sociologically irrefutable that, the denser the population, the greater the number of wars. This phenomenon is, of course, well known as a *practical* matter to all sociologists, but only Nef has studied it carefully.

Second, industrialism creates the media of the press, transmission of information, and transport, and finally the means of making war, all of which make it more and more difficult and even almost impossible to distinguish between the aggressor and the aggressed. At the present, no one knows (and perhaps no one can know) which side has commenced hostilities, a fact not solely due to armaments, but also to facility of transport. The extraordinary rapidity of transport allows an aggression to be launched within 24 hours, or even less, without anyone being able to foresee it. Here, the influence of the press is extremely important, since the press function is to confuse and addle the facts so that no one is able to gain any correct intelligence of them.

Finally, Nef indicates that the new means of destruction created by industrialism have greatly reduced the trouble, the difficulties, and the anguish implied in the act of killing people. A bombardier or artillerist has no feeling at all of killing anyone; he is in fact able to reach the conclusion that he has killed someone only with the aid of a syllogism. In hand-to-hand combat all the tiresome difficulties of conscience about the evil of murder keep obtruding themselves. In such ways, then, positive elements of industry result essentially (by very complex expedients) in favoring war and even in provoking it, even if no one has the *intention* of using Technique "badly."

Let us consider, as a final example of the relation between good effects and bad effects, the press and information.

It seems to be a simple matter, for example, to distinguish between information and propaganda. But, closer study of the problem reveals that it is practically impossible to make such a distinction. Considering but a few elements of the situation, the problem of information is today no longer that of the necessity of transmitting *honest* information—everybody agrees on this point. On the moral level it is a commonplace that we ought to transmit true information. I merely inquire, "How do we get it?" To remain on the *moral* level is simply not to understand the situation. The *concrete* situation, to take but a single example, is something like the following: Over the wires and into the offices of the Associated Press pass daily up to 300,000 words of world news, approximately equal to an enormous volume of 1000 pages. From this mass of words, it is necessary for the Associated Press, in competition with all the other world agencies, to choose, cut, and re-expedite as quickly as possible, perhaps a twentieth part of the whole to its subscribers. How is it possible to select from such a flood just what should be retained, what is true, what is possibly false, etc.? The editors have no criteria, they are at the mercy of whatever comes in, and (even when they judge in good faith and knowledge) they must essentially judge subjectively. Then again, even if the editor had only true news, how should he assign it a coefficient of importance? To do so is his business, and here the stereotypes of the editor are true enough: The Catholic editor will deem the news of the latest Vatican Council of great significance, information which has not the slightest importance to the Communist editor. What we have to do with here is not a question of bad faith, but of a difference of perspective on the world. The result is that we never know, even under the most favorable circumstances, if a given piece of information is subjective. And we must always bear in mind that this information, whatever it is, has been worked over by at least four or five different pairs of hands.

My reasons for maintaining that good effects are inseparable from bad are now, I trust, clear. And, as communications improve, the freer will be the flow of the news and the more available to all agencies concerned. These factors will play an ever greater role, making the difficulties of editing proportionately more difficult, and the chance of selecting absurd rather than sound news ever greater.

4. ALL TECHNICAL PROGRESS CONTAINS UNFORESEEABLE EFFECTS

The final aspect of the ambiguity of technical progress resides in the following state of affairs: When scientists carry out their researches in one or another discipline and hit upon new technical means, they generally see clearly in what sphere the new technique will be applicable. Certain results are expected and gotten. *But*, there are always secondary effects which had not been anticipated, which in the primary stage of the technical progress in question could not *in principle* have been anticipated. This unpredictability arises from the fact that predictability implies complete possibility of experimenting in *every* sphere, an inconceivable state of affairs.

The most elementary example is furnished by drugs. You have a cold in the head; you take an aspirin. The headache disappears, but aspirin has other actions besides doing away with headaches. In the beginning we were totally oblivious of these side effects; but, I should imagine, by now everyone has read articles warning against the use of aspirin because of its possible dangerous effects, say, on the blood picture. Grave hemorrhages have appeared in people who habitually took two or three aspirins daily. Yet aspirin was thought the perfect remedy a scant ten years ago— on the ground that no side effects were to be feared. Now, such effects begin to appear even in what was, and is, probably the most harmless of all drugs.

Another spectacular example is that of DDT, a chemical which in 1945 was thought to be a prodigiously successful means for the destruction of all kinds of vermin and insects. One of the most admirable things about DDT was that it was said to be completely innocuous toward human beings. DDT was sprinkled over the whole surface of the globe. Then, by accident, it was discovered that in certain areas veal cattle were wasting away and dying. Research revealed that DDT in oily solution causes anemia. Cattle had been dusted with DDT in order to get rid of insects; they had subsequently licked themselves clean and ingested the DDT. The chemical in question passed into their milk and by this route found its way into oily solution, i.e., in the milk fat. Calves suckled by such cows died of anemia, and it is needless to add that the same milk was ingested by human infants. Identical problems are potentially raised by *all* chemicals consumed by animals or men. Recall the recent example of thalidomide.

This is an example of the so-called secondary effects, effects which are essentially unpredictable and only revealed after the technique in question has been applied on a grand scale, i.e., when it is no longer possible to retrace one's steps.

Another interesting example is furnished by the psycho-sociological studies of the particular psychology of big city dwellers, where, once more, we are confronted with the effect of the technical environment on the human being. One of the principal elements of big city life is the feeling of isolation, loneliness, absence of human contacts, etc. One of the leading ideas of Le Corbusier in his *Maison des Hommes* was the admission that "big city dwellers do not know one another." "Let us create," said Le Corbusier, "great blocks of dwellings where people will meet one another as they did in the village, with everything (grocer, baker, butcher) included in the block so that people will get to know one another and a community will come into being. . . ." The result of Le Corbusier's creation was exactly the opposite of what had been planned; problems of loneliness and isolation in such blocks of dwellings proved to be much more tragic than in the normal and traditional city.

Then, it was held (and this is the penultimate word in city planning) that it was necessary to rediscover human groupings *on a human scale*, not on the scale of a block with, say, 5000 separate dwelling units. In the works and writings of sociologists and of city planners of perhaps seven or eight years ago we read: "At bottom, the only ones who understood what a city was were the people of the Middle Ages, who knew how to create a true city corresponding to the demands of a genuine city-planning technique, i.e., a human community centered about a small square surrounded by small houses, toward which converged the (straight) city streets, etc. . . ." The new city planners in keeping with these theories, applied them to the suburbs of Chicago, and in particular, to the well known "village" of Park Forest. There, it was thought, was to be found the distinctively human formula, one which really allows the human being his full scope. But, the most recent sociological and psychological analyses show this model community to represent nothing less than a new and unexpected difficulty. This time, people are traumatized because they are perpetually under the eyes and under the surveillance of their neighbors. The affected group is indeed much reduced in size; but no one dares to budge, because everybody knows just what everybody else is up to, a frightfully constricting situation, to say the least. It is clear that, even with the best intentions and with the application of hypermodern and profound research in psychology and sociology, we only succeed in coming to results in every case which could not possibly have been anticipated.

I shall give one last example of these unforeseeable effects, this time from agriculture, viz., the massive cultivation of certain plants like corn and cotton. The cultivation of these plants in the "new countries" seems to represent undeniable progress. The deforestation of land too heavily forested is a felicitous operation, profitable from every point of view, and consequently, represents technical progress. But, it could not have been anticipated that corn and cotton are plants which not only impoverish the soil, but even annihilate it by the twofold action of removing certain natural elements and destroying the relation between the humus and the soil particles. Both these last are destroyed by the roots of cotton and corn to the degree that, after 30 or 40 years of cultivation of these agricultural products, the soil is transformed into a veritable dust bowl. A strong wind need only to pass over it to reduce it to bare rock.

The phenomenon is world wide, and is to be encountered in the United States, Brazil, and Russia, among others. It is a bone of contention between Khrushchev and certain Soviet agricultural specialists. Khrushchev essentially emphasizes the cultivation of corn, as is well known; but many Soviet specialists insist that this emphasis is a very dangerous one. It allows a very rapid economic progress for, say, 20 years, only to be followed by a destruction of hitherto fertile lands which may last for centuries.

The inquiries of Castro and Vogt have shown that, at the present, in certain regions 20 per cent of cultivated land is threatened with destruction in this way. If this factor is considered in connection with that of population growth, a very considerable difficulty seems to lurk in the offing. If arable land continues to diminish in extent beyond possibility of recovery, our chances of survival diminish correspondingly. Here we have an example of typical and unpredictable secondary effects, effects which in corn and cotton agriculture do not reveal themselves except after 30 years of experience. It is again impossible, therefore, to say whether technical progress is in essence good or bad.

We are launched into a world of an astonishing degree of complexity; at every step we let loose new problems and raise new difficulties. We succeed progressively in solving these difficulties, but only in such a way that when one has been resolved we are confronted by another. Such is the progress of technology in our society. All I have been able to do is to give a few fragmentary examples. What would be necessary in order to comprehend the problem in its entirety is a systematic and detailed study of all these points.

EDGAR ANSEL MOWRER

E. A. Mowrer, a prominent foreign correspondent and political analyst, was born in 1913 and attended the Universities of Michigan and Chicago and the Sorbonne. He covered World War I in France for the Chicago Daily News, *and remained in Europe as head of the* News *bureau in Berlin. His uncompromising stories of the rise of the Nazi regime forced his departure from Germany and won him the 1932 Pulitzer Prize for Journalism. After stints in China, Japan, France, and England, he became during World War II Deputy Director of the U. S. Office of Facts and Figures (later the Office of War Information) and traveled widely in Asia and Europe. Among his books are* Immortal Italy *(1922),* Germany Puts Back the Clock *(1932),* The Dragon Awakes: A Report from China *(1938),* Challenge and Decision *(1950), and* An End to Make-Believe *(1961). The present essay first appeared in the* Saturday Review, *December 8, 1956.*

SAWDUST, SEAWEED, AND SYNTHETICS

A great-grandfather of mine left Central Illinois as "too darned civilized" when he failed to sight a deer on his own birthday. Another close relative finds my house in the New Hampshire woods "too lonely," although the nearest neighbor is less than a quarter of a mile away! Even under ideal conditions there are always some people who will think the world is too crowded. In a scientific sense, however, it is important to ask: How many people are too many?

To begin with, any humane or logical blueprint of an optimum earth must allow for varying degrees of human density, from the 137 people per acre in Manhattan (87,680 per square mile) to the utter emptiness of Antarctica.

The earth's present density (forty-two per square mile of land) still permits almost everybody able to travel to find somewhat the sort of environment that means the most. But not for long—not at the present rate of human increase. Java suffers from no less than 1,000 souls per square mile. There a drive through the so-called countryside resembles, for the number of people encountered, the U.S. seacoast between Miami Beach and Fort Lauderdale, Florida—an unending suburb! And the eastern seaboard of the United States, taken as a single area, already counts 180 to the square mile, over three times the national average.

Thanks to her readiness to accept the Lord's living bounty our country is confounding the population "experts" of the Twenties and Thirties who dolefully predicted a stationary or diminishing American population. In fact, a great change has come over American society. The average young American woman, according to Betsy Talbot Blackwell, editor of *Mademoiselle*, "follows the current trend of marrying in her late teens or early twenties, and raising as many children as the good Lord gives her." The American people have increased no less than 31 million in the past twenty years. Two and eight-tenths millions joined the throng in 1955, and each successive sunrise (as of October 1956) sees 7,200 more citizens than the previous dawn.

Certainly these child-eager American young women, taken together, seem to have reversed what demographers thought was a one-way street, namely, the so-called Demographic Transition. This was the breakthrough from an original situation as a high birth-rate, high death-rate country to a low birth-rate, low death-rate country. It was thought to occur whenever a population reached a certain standard of living. Instead, an American birth-rate that from 1935 to 1945 was about 20 per 1,000 has since the end of World War II stayed around 25 per 1,000. The United States is setting a new pattern: middle birth-rate with low death-rate. As a result future estimates have been drastically revised upward. One demographer predicts a U.S. population of 193,400,000 for 1975 and no less than 320 million for the year 2000! Although population forecasting is obviously more of an art than a science present calculations might well turn out to be correct. For the American reversal of the prewar trend, if it continues, is something new—a rising living standard provoking more rather than less conception.

Anyhow, for two-thirds of the world's population births are still running close to the physiological maximum. Costa Rica (1952) chalked up no less a birth-rate than 54.6 per 1,000 inhabitants. India is another example. India's population, thanks to a high death-rate, remained virtually stable for two or three thousand years prior to 1850—and the country was well fed and prosperous. Since the British cut the death-rate the number of Indians has zoomed skyward with no promise of relief. Ceylon's population is growing by 3 per cent a year! Before Perry Japan had a stable population. Since that gentleman "opened" it the Japanese have multiplied like weeds. Under American occupation after World War II they grew almost visibly—and still do. Some have calculated that the world's people will by the year 2106 have reached 20 billion.

Nature's explosive fecundity is as awesome as the power of the atom. A well-fed amoeba will double in an hour. Given adequate food and favorable circumstances it could by the sixth day have produced enough amoebas to exceed the weight of the entire earth! One type of plant louse breeds so quickly that if all its progeny survived the lice would in ten generations weigh as much as 500 million stout men (Huxley). If every codfish egg became adult and reproduced, within six years the Atlantic Ocean would be a solid mass of cod. Certain protozoa might, theoretically, fill *all known space* in a few years.

Human beings cannot quite keep up but some try hard. The Hutterites of the USA and Canada have increased by some nineteen times in the last seventy years. At the present rate they would in 250 years more equal the present population of the United States. The original 6,000 French settlers of Canada have multiplied no less than 700 times in a little over 300 years. Let present death rates sink further—as seems likely if mankind avoids a major atomic war—and there seem no *a priori* limits on the number of people except those of available food and other primary resources.

Already the vehemence of our growth threatens with extinction many other forms of organic life. A contemporary zoologist, N. J. Berrill, believes that the earth produces roughly the same amount of life at all times. It follows that when one organic element, in this case the human race, starts roaring its expansive way across the earth's surface other elements fade and die out. Hence, the present growing "prevalence of people" must—Berrill holds—seem to all other life *"like a cancer whose strange cells multiply without restraint, ruthlessly demanding the nourishment that all the body has need of."* And he concludes that sooner or later the body (or the community) is starved of support and perishes.

As a whole Americans are still barely aware of any problem. Our tradition is one of limitless spaces to be filled, limitless resources to be developed. Businessmen are purring over the flood of new customers. Even trained economists look upon the torrent of new babies primarily in terms of the ever-expanding market. The spectacle of suburbs mushrooming out over once pastoral landscapes around our cities may at some point cause a reconsideration. But in proportion to other countries ours is still only moderately populated. As against less than one acre of cultivated land per person in most parts of the earth, our own ratio, though down to just over two acres per head, is still sufficient to flood the country with unconsumed food which the Government lets rot rather than sell, give, or throw away. Botanist Karl Sax states that even "with present agricultural techniques, the United States and Canada could provide ample food for a population of 200 million and a subsistence diet for nearly 1 billion." So Americans need not yet fear hunger. Not so a country like India. There—according to chemist Harrison Brown—nine-tenths of the *total labor* is already devoted to obtaining food. Unless the birth rate falls sharply no improvement seems conceivable.

Such rapid human increase has started a first-class controversy among experts, both recognized and self-proclaimed. Obviously, unlimited reproduction must *at some point*—unless offset by a growing death rate—lead to starvation. The dispute is about the location of that point.

Viewers-with-alarm (who go back to the Church father Tertullian) see the limit as fairly close at hand. And anyhow, even if we do not soon run out of food we are—they believe—rapidly using up many other essential resources (including cheap water) whose exhaustion or decline would shortly force us back into a purely agricultural condition. On the other hand, specialists of equal prestige regard natural growth as a sign of laudable virility which will correct itself before it becomes dangerous.

The argument—with the specialists so divided—is as confusing as all-important. Nonetheless, if a layman may presume, it seems largely irrelevant to the real question. The demographers are mostly overlooking the essential point. This is not what is the earth's *maximum*, but what is its *optimum* population? *At what density are human beings most able to live the Good Life?* If by stepping up the fertility of our women we can provide more favorable surroundings for their children, well and good. If, on the other hand, further urbanization and suburbanization will prevent the fullest individual development of which people are capable then it is time to slow down.

It is surprising how few population students seem to have centered their investigation upon this point. Even the promising title "Ideal Size for Our Population" (*New York Times* Magazine, May 1, 1955), by the sociologist Kingsley Davis, is deceptive. Mr. Davis at one point writes bravely:

"Some (person) will, as I do, see certain disadvantages in an ever larger number of people—disadvantages which do not concern tangibles such as food and housing but rather the intangible but nonetheless treasured aspects of life." But then he spoils the effect: "These may seem *trivial* considerations and *in a way they are*." (My italics.)

Personal freedom, nature, beauty, privacy, solitude, variety, savor— trivial? Surely Mr. Davis would admit that all are essential components of valid human living even at the present dubious level.

It is, or should be, perfectly obvious that the greater the crowding, the larger the number of people in proportion to diminishing natural resources, the more the authorities will be obliged to curtail their liberties, not because they are necessarily opposed to freedom but because they must do so if living is to be made endurable for any of them. The result could well be the hive, or world-wide welfare state, which looks after the material needs of all its citizens while strictly controlling their actions; in short, a kind of benevolent "Nineteen Eighty-four" where Big Brother is looking at each person just about every minute.

Now the drive for freedom, we know, is not only anchored in the freeman's soul, it is a part of his biological nature. The reaction against constraint is one of the earliest and deepest to appear in higher animals. It will hardly disappear in man, or if it does seems bound to reappear later. Constraint and an overdense population are inseparable.

What of that close relationship between man and the rest of nature which crowding is already tending to distort? How far can mankind lose contact with both the organic substratum and the macrocosmic framework of his life and prosper spiritually?

Many individuals have little or no desire for natural surroundings. Nature—except human nature—leaves them unmoved. Some have nonetheless been greatly creative.

Yet how many more human creators have felt just the other way! Poets of all times and places, most painters and sculptors, the majority of great writers, many abstract thinkers, the greatest scientists have avowed an intimate need of nature. In some of them the thirst for natural things, for the full sky, landscapes, trees, flowers, wild animals, the tang of the autumn wind, the tumbling seas and tranquil lakes, has been an obsession. They have truly fed upon nature in all its aspects. The implication is clear that severed from nature man's imagination and inquiring mind would diminish, perhaps wither utterly.

How long could a rashly multiplying mankind continue to find enough beauty? So far in history people seem to have derived beauty chiefly from two things—nature, primitive or cultivated, and the nature-inspired products of man's own mind and hands. Where would they seek it if a growing population should cover most of the earth with utilitarian devices —and desecrate the remainder in the process?

To be sure, modern expressionistic, abstract, and functional art claims to supply the thirsting soul with all that previous generations got from *natural* content, *natural* expression, and *natural* ornament. Architects not only justify their banal (not to say primitive) designs but glorify them on the theory that "function determines form" and that a successfully embodied "function" has a beauty of its own superior to the "illustrative" or "ornamental" designs of the past.

To what extent are these claims fulfilled? Opinions differ widely. Where the evidence is still inconclusive one can but express a personal conviction. I literally grew up in a generation of writers and artists frantically striving to free themselves from naturalistic form and conscious meaning. And I conclude that wherever and whenever man no longer has a full natural environment on which to feed his sense of beauty he will succumb to dreariness. Think of today's slums and slagheaps, garbage dumps, and polluted rivers. Consider our ruined landscapes, commercially exploited U.S. highways, all the monotonous Levittowns. How avoid the conclusion that too many people and sufficient beauty—natural or man-made—seem incompatible?

What of the diminishing privacy that accompanies crowding? Privacy is freedom from observation, disturbance, and interference, whether with thoughts, emotions, or acts. It is privately that people receive their most powerful and original impulses. But who—today—wants privacy? Certainly not the "integration-minded" American teachers who rate pupil conformity and popularity above ability to learn or express. Not those millions who instinctively flock together like sparrows when there is plenty of room elsewhere.

Perhaps the need for privacy begins only with individuals of a certain kind. And perhaps even among them only those understand its value who have seen what life without it can become—the awful promiscuity of the boat-dwellers on the Pearl River at Canton, China; or crowded Calcutta on a summer night during the monsoon; or Russian workers packed four families in a room and unable to open the window lest they freeze! Even without these sights many Americans who passed some time in crowded military camps in wartime learned how essential some privacy can become to happiness. Certainly without it the creative portion of mankind would find it more difficult to achieve that concentration essential to maximum mental creativity.

Solitude is something else. One can—with sufficient will power—find solitude in a crowd, in a suburban rose garden, or indoors in a great city, windows closed and doors barred. Some great minds have done so. But surely that solitude is best where the possibility of being alone is coupled with privacy, silence, and the exciting quality of remoteness which only untouched nature seems to possess. Certain supreme beauties move one more the further away from cities they lie—the empty starlit sky, the glint of moonlight on a lake, towering mountains. Clearly for the few drawn to contemplation and the search for truth, who are the teachers of the race, a world with no remaining wilderness would be poor indeed.

Needs differ, even among animals—as any dog-lover can testify. Any good society must provide for varying preferences—for crowd-warmth as well as for freedom, nature, natural beauty, privacy, and solitude. So, if we say that an optimum population for this planet is one that can most fully enjoy the *savor* of life we have to admit that savor is hard to define. It includes all sorts of things—freedom, nature, beauty, spaciousness, the sense of adventure—and a certain smacking of the lips. It can even (at least for me) be *symbolized* by the type of available food.

It is here that the demographers reveal their appalling inhumanity. Solemnly they calculate the amount of nourishment necessary to fill ever more billions of bellies. Looking for the maximum nourishment obtainable, some are already counting on wood pulp and algae. Through tens of millions of acres of forests or algae "farms" in the sea and floating islands whose inhabitants would cut down their physical activities so as to need a minimum of calories, the earth—they reason—might conceivably nourish no less than 200 billion creatures—though whether they could any longer at that point be called human I cannot say. Some masterminds go further. A British physicist, J. D. Bernal, has suggested solving the food problem by synthesizing an edible something from coal, limestone, and air. (This has, I believe, been done and I would wish Communists like Bernal no worse than having to live on it.) On such a basis, zoologist Berrill acidly comments, there might develop "a population so universally dense that there would be sitting room only." Yet if maximum multiplication is a man's aim (or fate) here is a promising approach.

It inspires a less promising conclusion: Raising as many children as the good Lord sends may—short of catastrophe—at some point require everyone to live upon *sawdust, seaweed,* and/or *synthetics.* Provided one cared to live at all. Personally I should not. Suffering we can stand if we must. But not the tedium of a savorless existence.

Sir Charles Darwin insists that man, like any other organism, will regularly reproduce right up to the starvation limit. Some people have always been hungry. Some are hungry today. Some always will be hungry. Nothing that man does can change it. Perhaps not. But if man's will cannot limit the size of his family how can Sir Charles know that his statement is anything but a conditioned reflex, empty of either truth or falsehood? Determinism anywhere makes argument useless. Besides, other distinguished specialists believe that mankind can control its numbers if it puts its mind to it.

One other objection to limiting population deserves more consideration. It runs that by limiting the number of human beings we would actually worsen the race by limiting the occurrence of superior men and women. If—one may reason—"teachers of the human race" occur in anything like a regular proportion, then the more people, the more outstanding individuals on earth at any time and the faster civilization will grow.

What little we know about the frequency of greatness does not sustain this view. Observed evidence is all the other way. Athens, Alexandria, Florence, Cordova, medieval Paris—these seem to have brought forth genius in all fields far more thickly than modern New York or London, not to speak of Canton or Calcutta. Renaissance Italy, Germany, France, Britain, and the Low Countries, Persia at one period—with relatively few inhabitants—appear to have been proportionately richer in high-quality individuals than today's teeming supernations. A serious investigation of population density and human quality might well indicate an optimum size to cities as well as an optimum human density. Such an investigation would be difficult. And maintaining the optimum, once it was found, even harder. After all, in our own times two countries, Ireland and Sweden, have kept their numbers under control with admirable results.

One ingenious way to control population has been stated by an inhabitant of Lin Yutang's imaginary island of Thainos: "Very simple. We have a system of proportionate taxation. The larger the family the higher the tax. That stops it, all right."

Difficult to enact and enforce? Perhaps. But compare it with an alternative remedy currently proposed. Dr. Fritz Zwicky suggests that those who find the earth too crowded simply bomb large pieces out of frigid planets like Jupiter, Saturn, and Neptune, create out of the material salvaged a hundred new planets with climates and motions like the earth's, and go live on them. He even offers, given ten years and enough money, to build an interplanetary ship. Which is more utopian: to call upon people to limit the number of their offspring or to rearrange the Solar System?

Until the advent of nuclear weapons it could be argued that no Great Power, however desirous of promoting the quality rather than the quantity of its citizens, dare do so lest it be militarily overwhelmed by a conceivably inferior but more numerous enemy. But the H-bombs seem to have become the "equalizers" of nations much as the six-shooter was that of individuals. Certainly they have made it unlikely that man can surmount the next half-century without a holocaust that would solve the population problem for some time unless he establishes some sort of supernational authority. On this account the threat of multiplication to where "the earth is covered with a writhing mass of human beings much as a dead cow is covered with a writhing mass of maggots" is presumably just a poetic nightmare. Yet the dilemma of some not-too-distant future is real enough—an increasingly dreary, shrinking life for ever more people, or an ever nobler, broader life for a limited number. There is no escape. So maybe the average American young woman had better start helping God to keep human quality up by some limitation on human numbers.

E. B. WHITE

Elwyn Brooks White, born in 1899, was graduated from Cornell in 1921 and joined the staff of The New Yorker *in 1926. He regularly wrote its "Notes and Comment" section until 1938. His sensitive, humorous char-*

acter and his witty yet natural and exact literary style, along with the congenial talents of James Thurber and a few others, were largely responsible for the extraordinary reputation of New Yorker *writing at that time. He contributed a monthly column, entitled "One Man's Meat," to* Harper's *from 1938 to 1943 and resumed writing for* The New Yorker *on a free-lance basis in 1945. Since 1937 he has taken periodic refuge in a Maine farm, which he manages and writes about with enthusiasm. He has published two excellent children's books,* Stuart Little *(1945) and* Charlotte's Web *(1952), two volumes of poetry, collections of his magazine pieces, and other books. Among the best known are* Is Sex Necessary?, *written with James Thurber (1929);* One Man's Meat *(1942);* The Wild Flag *(1946); and* The Elements of Style *(1959), a reverent re-editing of the textbook of his former teacher William Strunk, Jr. The story we present below, taken from* The Second Tree From the Corner *(1954), was first published in* The New Yorker *in February, 1950.*

THE MORNING OF THE DAY
THEY DID IT

My purpose is to tell how it happened and to set down a few impressions of that morning while it is fresh in memory. I was in a plane that was in radio communication with the men on the platform. To put the matter briefly, what was intended as a military expedient turned suddenly into a holocaust. The explanation was plain enough to me, for, like millions of others, I was listening to the conversation between the two men and was instantly aware of the quick shift it took. That part is clear. What is not so clear is how I myself survived, but I am beginning to understand that, too. I shall not burden the reader with an explanation, however, as the facts are tedious and implausible. I am now in good health and fair spirits, among friendly people on an inferior planet, at a very great distance from the sun. Even the move from one planet to another has not relieved me of the nagging curse that besets writing men—the feeling that they must produce some sort of record of their times.

The thing happened shortly before twelve noon. I came out of my house on East Harding Boulevard at quarter of eight that morning, swinging my newspaper and feeling pretty good. The March day was mild and springlike, the warmth and the smells doubly welcome after the rotten weather we'd been having. A gentle wind met me on the Boulevard, frisked me, and went on. A man in a leather cap was loading bedsprings into a van in front of No. 220. I remember that as I walked along I worked my tongue around the roof of my mouth, trying to dislodge a prune skin. (These details have no significance; why write them down?)

A few blocks from home there was a Contakt plane station and I hurried in, caught the 8:10 plane, and was soon aloft. I always hated a jet-assist takeoff right after breakfast, but it was one of the discomforts that went with my job. At ten thousand feet our small plane made contact with the big one, we passengers were transferred, and the big ship went on up to fifty thousand, which was the height television planes flew at. I was a script writer for one of the programs. My tour of duty was supposed to be eight hours.

I should probably explain here that at the period of which I am writing, the last days of the planet earth, telecasting was done from planes circling the stratosphere. This eliminated the coaxial cable, a form of relay that had given endless trouble. Coaxials worked well enough for a while, but eventually they were abandoned, largely because of the extraordinary depredations of earwigs. These insects had developed an alarming resistance to bugspray and were out of control most of the time. Earwigs increased in size and in numbers, and the forceps at the end of their abdomen developed so that they could cut through a steel shell. They seemed to go unerringly for coaxials. Whether the signals carried by the cables had anything to do with it I don't know, but the bugs fed on these things and were enormously stimulated. Not only did they feast on the cables, causing the cables to disintegrate, but they laid eggs in them in unimaginable quantities, and as the eggs hatched the television images suffered greatly, there was more and more flickering on the screen, more and more eyestrain and nervous tension among audiences, and of course a further debasement of taste and intellectual life in general. Finally the coaxials were given up, and after much experimenting by Westinghouse and the Glenn Martin people a satisfactory substitute was found in the high-flying planes. A few of these planes, spotted around the country, handled the whole television load nicely. Known as Strato-video planes, they were equipped with studios; many programs originated in the air and were transmitted directly, others were beamed to the aircraft from ground stations and then relayed. The planes flew continuously, twenty-four hours a day, were refuelled in air, and dropped down to ten thousand feet every eight hours to meet the Contakt planes and take on new shifts of workers.

I remember that as I walked to my desk in the Stratoship that morning, the nine-o'clock news had just ended and a program called "Author, Please!" was going on, featuring Melonie Babson, a woman who had written a best-seller on the theme of euthanasia, called "Peace of Body." The program was sponsored by a dress-shield company.

I remember, too, that a young doctor had come aboard the plane with the rest of us. He was a newcomer, a fellow named Cathcart, slated to be the physician attached to the ship. He had introduced himself to me in the Contakt plane, had asked the date of my Tri-D shot, and had noted it down in his book. (I shall explain about these shots presently.) This doctor certainly had a brief life in our midst. He had hardly been introduced around and shown his office when our control room got a radio call asking if there was a doctor in the stratosphere above Earth-point F-plus-6, and requesting medical assistance at the scene of an accident.

F-plus-6 was almost directly below us, so Dr. Cathcart felt he ought to respond, and our control man gave the word and asked for particulars and instructions. It seems there had been a low-altitude collision above F-plus-6 involving two small planes and killing three people. One plane was a Diaheliper, belonging to an aerial diaper service that flew diapers to rural homes by helicopter. The other was one of the familiar government-owned sprayplanes that worked at low altitudes over croplands, truck gardens, and commercial orchards, delivering a heavy mist of the deadly Tri-D solution, the pesticide that had revolutionized agriculture, eliminated the bee from nature, and given us fruits and vegetables of undreamed-of perfection but very high toxicity.

The two planes had tangled and fallen onto the observation tower of a whooping-crane sanctuary, scattering diapers over an area of half a mile and releasing a stream of Tri-D. Cathcart got his medical kit, put on his parachute, and paused a moment to adjust his pressurizer, preparatory to bailing out. Knowing that he wouldn't be back for a while, he asked if anybody around the shop was due for a Tri-D shot that morning, and it turned out that Bill Foley was. So the Doctor told Foley to come along, and explained that he would give him his injection on the way down. Bill threw me a quick look of mock anguish, and started climbing into his gear. This must have been six or seven minutes past nine.

It seems strange that I should feel obliged to explain Tri-D shots. They were a commonplace at this time—as much a part of a person's life as his toothbrush. The correct name for them was Anti-Tri-D, but people soon shortened the name. They were simply injections that everyone had to receive at regular twenty-one-day intervals, to counteract the lethal effect of food, and the notable thing about them was the great importance of the twenty-one-day period. To miss one's Tri-D shot by as much as a couple of hours might mean serious consequences, even death. Almost every day there were deaths reported in the papers from failure to get the injection at the proper time. The whole business was something like insulin control in diabetes. You can easily imagine the work it entailed for doctors in the United States, keeping the entire population protected against death by poisoning.

As Dr. Cathcart and Bill eased themselves out of the plane through the chute exit, I paused briefly and listened to Miss Babson, our author of the day.

"It is a grand privilege," she was saying, "to appear before the television audience this morning and face this distinguished battery of critics, including my old sparring partner, Ralph Armstrong, of the *Herald Tribune*. I suppose after Mr. Armstrong finishes with me I will be a pretty good candidate for euthanasia myself. Ha. But seriously, ladies and gentlemen, I feel that a good book is its own defense."

The authoress had achieved a state of exaltation already. I knew that her book, which she truly believed to be great, had been suggested to her by an agent over a luncheon table and had been written largely by somebody else, whom the publisher had had to bring in to salvage the thing. The final result was a run-of-the-can piece of rubbish easily outselling its nearest competitor.

Miss Babson continued, her exaltation stained with cuteness:

"I have heard my novel criticized on the ground that the theme of euthanasia is too daring, and even that it is anti-Catholic. Well, I can remember, way back in the dark ages, when a lot of things that are accepted as commonplace today were considered daring or absurd. My own father can recall the days when dairy cows were actually bred by natural methods. The farmers of those times felt that the artificial-breeding program developed by our marvellous experiment stations was highfalutin nonsense. Well, we all know what has happened to the dairy industry, with many of our best milch cows giving milk continuously right around the clock, in a steady stream. True, the cows do have to be propped up and held in position in special stanchions and fed intravenously, but I always say it isn't the hubbub that counts, it's the butterfat. And I doubt if even Mr. Armstrong here would want to return to the days when a cow just gave a bucket of milk and then stopped to rest."

Tiring of the literary life, I walked away and looked out a window. Below, near the layer of cumulus, the two chutes were visible. With the help of binoculars I could see Bill manfully trying to slip his chute over next to the Doc, and could see Cathcart fumbling for his needle. Our telecandid man was at another window, filming the thing for the next newscast, as it was a new wrinkle in the Tri-D world to have somebody getting his shot while parachuting.

I had a few chores to do before our program came on, at eleven-five. "Town Meeting of the Upper Air" was the name of it. "Town Meeting" was an unrehearsed show, but I was supposed to brief the guests, distribute copies of whatever prepared scripts there were, explain the cuing, and make everybody happy generally. The program we were readying that morning had had heavy advance billing, and there was tremendous interest in it everywhere, not so much because of the topic ("Will the fear of retaliation stop aggression?") or even the cast of characters, which included Major General Artemus T. Recoil, but because of an incidental stunt we were planning to pull off. We had arranged a radio hookup with the space platform, a gadget the Army had succeeded in establishing six hundred miles up, in the regions of the sky beyond the pull of gravity. The Army, after many years of experimenting with rockets, had not only got the platform established but had sent two fellows there in a Spaceship, and also a liberal supply of the New Weapon.

The whole civilized world had read about this achievement, which swung the balance of power so heavily in our favor, and everyone was aware that the damned platform was wandering around in its own orbit at a dizzy distance from the earth and not subject to gravitational pull. Every kid in America had become an astrophysicist overnight and talked knowingly of exhaust velocities, synergy curves, and Keplerian ellipses. Every subway rider knew that the two men on the platform were breathing oxygen thrown off from big squash vines that they had taken along. The *Reader's Digest* had added to the fun by translating and condensing several German treatises on rockets and space travel, including the great *Wege zur Raumschiffahrt*. But to date, because of security regulations and technical difficulties, there had been no radio-television hookup. Finally we got clearance from Washington, and General Recoil agreed to interview the officers on the platform as part of the "Town Meeting" program. This was big stuff—to hear directly from the Space Platform for Checking Aggression, known pretty generally as the SPCA.

I was keyed up about it myself, but I remember that all that morning in the plane I felt disaffected, and wished I were not a stratovideo man. There were often days like that in the air. The plane, with its queer cargo and its cheap goings on, would suddenly seem unaccountably remote from the world of things I admired. In a physical sense we were never very remote: the plane circled steadily in a fixed circle of about ten miles diameter, and I was never far from my own home on East Harding Boulevard. I could talk to Ann and the children, if I wished, by radio-phone.

In many respects mine was a good job. It paid two hundred and twenty-five dollars a week, of which two hundred and ten was withheld. I should have felt well satisfied. Almost everything in the way of social benefits was provided by the government—medical care, hospitalization, education for the children, accident insurance, fire and theft, old-age retirement, Tri-D shots, vacation expense, amusement and recreation, welfare and well-being, Christmas and good will, rainy-day resource, staples and supplies, beverages and special occasions, babysitzfund—it had all been worked out. Any man who kept careful account of his pin money could get along all right, and I guess I should have been happy. Ann never complained much, except about one thing. She found that no matter how we saved and planned, we never could afford to buy flowers. One day, when she was a bit lathered up over household problems, she screamed, "God damn it, I'd rather live dangerously and have one dozen yellow freesias!" It seemed to prey on her mind.

Anyway, this was one of those oppressive days in the air for me.

Something about the plane's undeviating course irritated me; the circle we flew seemed a monstrous excursion to nowhere. The engine noise (we flew at subsonic speed) was an unrelieved whine. Usually I didn't notice the engines, but today the ship sounded in my ears every minute, reminding me of a radiotherapy chamber, and there was always the palpable impact of vulgar miracles—the very nature of television—that made me itchy and fretful.

Appearing with General Recoil on "Town Meeting of the Upper Air" were to be Mrs. Florence Gill, president of the Women's Auxiliary of the Sons of Original Matrons; Amory Buxton, head of the Economics and Withholding Council of the United Nations; and a young man named Tollip, representing one of the small, ineffectual groups that advocated world federation. I rounded up this stable of intellects in the reception room, went over the procedure with them, gave the General a drink (which seemed to be what was on his mind), and then ducked out to catch the ten-o'clock news and to have a smoke.

I found Pete Everhardt in the control room. He looked bushed. "Quite a morning, Nuncle," he said. Pete not only had to keep his signal clean on the nine-o'clock show (Melonie Babson was a speaker who liked to range all over the place when she talked) but he had to keep kicking the ball around with the two Army officers on the space platform, for fear he would lose them just as they were due to go on. And on top of that he felt obliged to stay in touch with Dr. Cathcart down below, as a matter of courtesy, and also to pick up incidental stuff for subsequent newscasts.

I sat down and lit a cigarette. In a few moments the day's authoress wound up her remarks and the news started, with the big, tense face of Ed Peterson on the screen dishing it out. Ed was well equipped by nature for newscasting; he had the accents of destiny. When he spread the news, it penetrated in depth. Each event not only seemed fraught with meaning, it seemed fraught with Ed. When he said "I predict . . ." you felt the full flow of his pipeline to God.

To the best of my recollection the ten-o'clock newscast on this awful morning went as follows:

(Announcer) "Good morning. Tepky's Hormone-Enriched Dental Floss brings you Ed Peterson and the news."

(Ed) "Flash! Three persons were killed and two others seriously injured a few minutes ago at Earthpoint F-plus-6 when a government sprayplane collided with a helicopter of the Diaheliper Company. Both pilots were thrown clear. They are at this moment being treated by a doctor released by parachute from Stratovideo Ship 3, from which I am now speaking. The sprayplane crashed into the observation tower of a whooping-crane sanctuary, releasing a deadly mist of Tri-D and instantly killing three wardens who were lounging there watching the love dance of the cranes. Diapers were scattered widely over the area, and these sterile garments proved invaluable to Dr. Herbert L. Cathcart in bandaging the wounds of the injured pilots, Roy T. Bliss and Homer Schenck. [Here followed a newsreel shot showing Cathcart winding a diaper around the head of one of the victims.] You are now at the scene of the disaster," droned Ed. "This is the first time in the history of television that an infant's napkin has appeared in the role of emergency bandage. Another first for American Tel. & Vid.!

"Washington! A Senate committee, with new facts at its disposal, will reopen the investigation to establish the blame for Pearl Harbor.

"Chicago! Two members of the Department of Sanitation were removed from the payroll today for refusal to take the loyalty oath. Both are members of New Brooms, one of the four hundred thousand organizations on the Attorney General's subversive list.

"Hollywood! It's a boy at the Roscoe Pews. Stay tuned to this channel for a closeup of the Caesarean section during the eleven-o'clock roundup!

"New York! Flash! The Pulitzer Prize in editorial writing has been awarded to Frederick A. Mildly, of the New York *Times,* for his nostalgic editorial 'The Old Pumphandle.'

"Flash! Donations to the Atlantic Community Chest now stand at a little over seven hundred billion dollars. Thanks for a wonderful job of giving—I mean that from my heart.

"New York! The vexing question of whether Greek athletes will be allowed to take part in next year's Olympic Games still deadlocks the Security Council. In a stormy session yesterday the Russian delegate argued that the presence of Greek athletes at the games would be a threat to world peace. Most of the session was devoted to a discussion of whether the question was a procedural matter or a matter of substance.

"Flash! Radio contact with the two United States Army officers on the Space Platform for Checking Aggression, known to millions of listeners as the SPCA, has definitely been established, despite rumors to the contrary. The television audience will hear their voices in a little more than one hour from this very moment. You will *not* see their faces. Stay tuned! This is history, ladies and gentlemen—the first time a human voice freed from the pull of gravity has been heard on earth. The spacemen will be interviewed by Major General Artemus T. Recoil on the well-loved program 'Town Meeting of the Upper Air.'

"I predict: that because of SPCA and the Army's Operation Space, the whole course of human destiny will be abruptly changed, and that the age-old vision of peace is now on the way to becoming a reality."

Ed finished and went into his commercial, which consisted of digging a piece of beef gristle out of his teeth with dental floss.

I rubbed out my cigarette and walked back toward my cell. In the studio next ours, "The Bee" was on the air, and I paused for a while to watch. "The Bee" was a program sponsored by the Larry Cross

Pollination Company, aimed principally at big orchardists and growers
—or rather at their wives. It was an interminable mystery-thriller sort
of thing, with a character called the Bee, who always wore a green hood
with two long black feelers. Standing there in the aisle of the plane,
looking into the glass-enclosed studio, I could see the Bee about to
strangle a red-haired girl in slinky pajamas. This was America's pollination hour, an old standby, answer to the housewife's dream. The Larry
Cross outfit was immensely rich. I think they probably handled better
than eighty per cent of all fertilization in the country. Bees, as I have
said, had become extinct, thanks to the massive doses of chemicals, and
of course this had at first posed a serious agricultural problem, as vast
areas were without natural pollination. The answer came when the Larry
Cross firm was organized, with the slogan "We Carry the Torch for
Nature." The business mushroomed, and branch offices sprang up all
over the nation. During blossom time, field crews of highly trained men
fanned out and pollinized everything by hand—a huge job and an arduous
one. The only honey in the United States was synthetic—a blend of
mineral oil and papaya juice. Ann hated it with a morbid passion.

When I reached my studio I found everybody getting ready for the
warmup. The Town Crier, in his fusty costume, stood holding his bell
by the clapper, while the makeup man touched up his face for him.
Mrs. Gill, the S.O.M. representative, sat gazing contemptuously at young
Tollip. I had riffled through her script earlier, curious to find out what
kind of punch she was going to throw. It was about what I expected.
Her last paragraph contained the suggestion that all persons who advocated a revision of the Charter of the United Nations be automatically
deprived of their citizenship. "If these well-meaning but misguided
persons," ran the script, "with their utopian plans for selling this nation
down the river are so anxious to acquire world citizenship, I say let's
make it easy for them—let's take away the citizenship they've already
got and see how they like it. As a lineal descendant of one of the Sons
of Original Matrons, I am sick and tired of these cuckoo notions of one
world, which come dangerously close to simple treachery. We've enough
to do right here at home without . . ."

And so on. In my mind's ear I could already hear the moderator's
salutary and impartial voice saying, "Thank you, Mrs. Florence Gill."

At five past eleven, the Crier rang his bell. "Hear ye! See ye! Town
Meetin' today! Listen to both sides and make up your own minds!"
Then George Cahill, the moderator, started the ball rolling.

I glanced at Tollip. He looked as though his stomach were filling
up with gas. As the program got under way, my own stomach began
to inflate, too, the way it often did a few hours after breakfast. I remember very little of the early minutes of that morning's Town Meeting.
I recall that the U.N. man spoke first, then Mrs. Gill, then Tollip (who
looked perfectly awful). Finally the moderator introduced General Re-

coil, whose stomach enjoyed the steadying effects of whiskey and who spoke in a loud, slow, confident voice, turning frequently to smile down on the three other guests.

"We in the Army," began the General, "don't pretend that we know all the answers to these brave and wonderful questions. It is not the Army's business to know whether aggression is going to occur or not. Our business is to put on a good show if it *does* occur. The Army is content to leave to the United Nations and to idealists like Mr. Tollip the troublesome details of political progress. I certainly don't know, ladies and gentlemen, whether the fear of retaliation is going to prevent aggression, but I *do* know that there is no moss growing on we of Operation Space. As for myself, I guess I am what you might call a retaliatin' fool. [Laughter in the upper air.] Our enemy is well aware that we are now in a most unusual position to retaliate. That knowledge on the part of our enemy is, in my humble opinion, a deterrent to aggression. If I didn't believe that, I'd shed this uniform and get into a really well-paid line of work, like professional baseball."

Will this plane never quit circling? (I thought). Will the words never quit going round and round? Is there no end to this noisy carrousel of indigestible ideas? Will no one ever catch the brass ring?

"But essentially," continued the General, "our job is not to deal with the theoretical world of Mr. Tollip, who suggests that we merge in some vast superstate with every Tom, Dick, and Harry, no matter what their color or race or how underprivileged they are, thus pulling down our standard of living to the level of the lowest common denominator. Our job is not to deal with the diplomatic world of Mr. Buxton, who hopes to find a peaceful solution around a conference table. No, the Army must face the world as it is. We know the enemy is strong. In our dumb way, we think it is just horse sense for us to be stronger. And I'm proud, believe me, ladies and gentlemen, proud to be at one end of the interplanetary conversation that is about to take place on this very, *very* historic morning. The achievement of the United States Army in establishing the space platform—which is literally a man-made planet—is unparalleled in military history. We have led the way into space. We have given Old Lady Gravity the slip. We have got there, and we have got there fustest with the mostest. [Applause.]

"I can state without qualification that the New Weapon, in the capable hands of the men stationed on our platform, brings the *en*tire globe under our dominion. We can pinpoint any spot, anywhere, and sprinkle it with our particular brand of thunder. Mr. Moderator, I'm ready for this interview if the boys out there in space are ready."

Everyone suspected that there might be a slipup in the proceedings at this point, that the mechanical difficulties might prove insuperable. I glanced at the studio clock. The red sweep hand was within a few jumps of eleven-thirty—the General had managed his timing all right.

Cahill's face was tenser than I had ever seen it before. Because of the advance buildup, a collapse at this moment would put him in a nasty hole, even for an old experienced m.c. But at exactly eleven-thirty the interview started, smooth as silk. Cahill picked it up from the General.

"And now, watchers of television everywhere, you will hear a conversation between Major General Artemus T. Recoil, who pioneered Operation Space, and two United States Army officers on the platform —Major James Obblington, formerly of Brooklyn, New York, now of Space, and Lieutenant Noble Trett, formerly of Sioux City, Iowa, now of Space. Go ahead, General Recoil!"

"Come in, Space!" said the General, his tonsils struggling in whiskey's undertow, his eyes bearing down hard on the script. "Can you hear me, Major Obblington and Lieutenant Trett?"

"I hear you," said a voice. "This is Trett." The voice, as I remember it, astonished me because of a certain laconic quality that I had not expected. I believe it astonished everyone. Trett's voice was cool, and he sounded as though he were right in the studio.

"Lieutenant Trett," continued the General, "tell the listeners here on earth, tell us, in your position far out there in free space, do you feel the pull of gravity?"

"No, sir, I don't," answered Trett. In spite of the "sir," Trett sounded curiously listless, almost insubordinate.

"Yet you are perfectly comfortable, sitting there on the platform, with the whole of earth spread out before you like a vast target?"

"Sure I'm comfortable."

The General waited a second, as though expecting amplification, but it failed to come. "Well, ah, how's the weather up there?" he asked heartily.

"There isn't any," said Trett.

"No weather? No weather in space? That's very interesting."

"The hell it is," said Trett. "It's God-damn dull. This place is a dump. Worse than some of the islands in the Pacific."

"Well, I suppose it must get on your nerves a bit. That's all part of the game. Tell us, Lieutenant, what's it like to be actually a part of the solar system, with your own private orbit?"

"It's all right, except I'd a damn sight rather get drunk," said Trett.

I looked at Cahill. He was swallowing his spit. General Recoil took a new hold on his script.

"And you say you don't feel the pull of gravity, not even a little?"

"I just told you I didn't feel any pull," said Trett. His voice now had a surly quality.

"Well, ah," continued the General, who was beginning to tremble, "can you describe, briefly, for the television audience—" But it was at this point that Trett, on the platform, seemed to lose interest in talking with General Recoil and started chinning with Major Obblington, his sidekick in space. At first the three voices clashed and blurred, but the General, on a signal from the moderator, quit talking, and the conversation that ensued between Trett and Obblington was audible and clear. Millions of listeners must have heard the dialogue.

"Hey, Obie," said Trett, "you want to know something else I don't feel the pull of, besides gravity?"

"What?" asked his companion.

"Conscience," said Trett cheerfully. "I don't feel my conscience pulling me around."

"Neither do I," said Obblington. "I ought to feel some pulls but I don't."

"I also don't feel the pull of duty."

"Check," said Obblington.

"And what is even more fantastic, I don't feel the pull of dames."

Cahill made a sign to the General. Stunned and confused by the turn things had taken, Recoil tried to pick up the interview and get it back on the track. "Lieutenant Trett," he commanded, "you will limit your remarks to the—"

Cahill waved him quiet. The next voice was the Major's.

"Jesus, now that you mention it, I don't feel the pull of dames, either! Hey, Lieutenant—you suppose gravity has anything to do with sex?"

"God damn if *I* know," replied Trett. "I know I don't *weigh* anything, and when you don't weigh anything, you don't seem to *want* anything."

The studio by this time was paralyzed with attention. The General's face was swollen, his mouth was half open, and he struggled for speech that wouldn't come.

Then Trett's cool, even voice again: "See that continent down there, Obie? That's where old Fatso Recoil lives. You feel drawn toward that continent in any special way?"

"Naa," said Obblington.

"You feel like doing a little shooting, Obie?"

"You're rootin' tootin' I feel like shootin'."

"Then what are we waiting for?"

I am, of course, reconstructing this conversation from memory. I am trying to report it faithfully. When Trett said the words "Then what are we waiting for?" I quit listening and dashed for the phones in the corridor. As I was leaving the studio, I turned for a split second and looked back. The General had partially recovered his power of speech. He was mumbling something to Cahill. I caught the words "phone" and "Defense Department."

The corridor was already jammed. I had only one idea in my head— to speak to Ann. Pete Everhardt pushed past me. He said crisply, "This is it." I nodded. Then I glanced out of a window. High in the east a crazy ribbon of light was spreading upward. Lower down, in a terrible parabola, another streak began burning through. The first blast was felt only slightly in the plane. It must have been at a great distance. It was followed immediately by two more. I saw a piece of wing break up, saw one of the starboard engines shake itself loose from its fastenings and fall. Near the phone booths, the Bee, still in costume, fumbled awkwardly for a parachute. In the crush one of his feelers brushed my face. I never managed to reach a phone. All sorts of things flashed through my mind. I saw Ann and the children, their heads in diapers. I saw again the man in the leather cap, loading bedsprings. I heard again Pete's words, "This is it," only I seemed to hear them in translation: "Until the whole wide world to nothingness do sink." (How durable the poets are!) As I say, I never managed the phone call. My last memory of the morning is of myriads of bright points of destruction where the Weapon was arriving, each pyre in the characteristic shape of an artichoke. Then a great gash, and the plane tumbling. Then I lost consciousness.

I cannot say how many minutes or hours after that the earth finally broke up. I do not know. There is, of course, a mild irony in the fact that it was the United States that was responsible. Insofar as it can be said of any country that it had human attributes, the United States was well-meaning. Of that I am convinced. Even I, at this date and at this distance, cannot forget my country's great heart and matchless ingenuity. I can't in honesty say that I believe we were wrong to send the men to the platform —it's just that in any matter involving love, or high explosives, one can never foresee all the factors. Certainly I can't say with any assurance that Tollip's theory was right; it seems hardly likely that anyone who suffered so from stomach gas could have been on the right track. I did feel sympathetic toward some of his ideas, perhaps because I suffered from flatulence myself. Anyway, it was inevitable that it should have been the United States that developed the space platform and the new weapon that made the H-bomb obsolete. It was inevitable that what happened, at last, was conceived in good will.

Those times—those last days of earth! I think about them a lot. A sort of creeping ineptitude had set in. Almost everything in life seemed wrong to me, somehow, as though we were all hustling down a blind alley. Many of my friends seemed mentally confused, emotionally unstable, and I have an idea I seemed the same to them. In the big cities, horns blew before the light changed, and it was clear that motorists no longer had the capacity to endure the restrictions they had placed on their own behavior. When the birds became extinct (all but the whooping crane), I was reasonably sure that human beings were on the way out, too. The cranes survived only because of their dance—which showmen were quick to exploit. (Every sanctuary had its television transmitter, and the love dance became a more popular spectacle than heavyweight prizefighting.) Birds had always been the symbol of freedom. As soon as I realized that they were gone, I felt that the significance had gone from my own affairs. (I was a cranky man, though—I must remember that, too—and am not trying here to suggest anything beyond a rather strong personal sadness at all this.)

Those last days! There were so many religions in conflict, each ready to save the world with its own dogma, each perfectly intolerant of the other. Every day seemed a mere skirmish in the long holy war. It was a time of debauch and conversion. Every week the national picture magazines, as though atoning for past excesses, hid their cheesecake carefully away among four-color reproductions of the saints. Television was the universal peepshow—in homes, schools, churches, bars, stores, everywhere. Children early formed the habit of gaining all their images at second hand, by looking at a screen; they grew up believing that anything perceived directly was vaguely fraudulent. Only what had been touched with electronics was valid and real. I think the decline in the importance of direct images dated from the year television managed to catch an eclipse of the moon. After that, nobody ever looked at the sky, and it was as though the moon had joined the shabby company of buskers. There was really never a moment when a child, or even a man, felt free to look away from the television screen—for fear he might miss the one clue that would explain everything.

In many respects I like the planet I'm on. The people here have no urgencies, no capacity for sustained endeavor, but merely tackle things by fits and starts, leaving undone whatever fails to hold their interest, and so, by witlessness and improvidence, escape many of the errors of accomplishment. I like the apples here better than those on earth. They are often wormy, but with a most wonderful flavor. There is a saying here: "Even a very lazy man can eat around a worm."

But I would be lying if I said I didn't miss that other life, I loved it so.

The Function of Art

Citizens have been telling artists what to do at least since Plato's day (see above, p. 205), and artists have responded variously, sometimes with a sublime incoherence but occasionally with that resonant authority that is theirs alone. The fact that more than half of the essays in this section are by artists—one painter and four writers—gives the artists more than their usual share of representation in the debate on the function of art. The rest is given over to the philosopher, the social theorist, and the editor, each of whom perpetuates Plato's function in his own way. What all have in common, however, is the conviction that art is important. Mrs. Langer's magisterial essay stresses the role of art in the rendering of imagination and feeling, of subjective reality. Matisse, the painter, with deceptively artless simplicity, writes "notes" on painting that imply an aesthetic related to Mrs. Langer's. The Marxist critic Ernst Fischer finds in art the link between the limited life of the individual and a richer, more communal existence, and he attempts to define the special "function of art in a class society at war within itself." The Editors of *Life* take a position in part surprisingly close to Fischer's, issuing a call for art—in this case the novel— as an expression of the central character of our culture and our aspirations. Camus and Orwell justify the art that has political purpose. De Quincey distinguishes didactic purpose from emotive; Pater, likewise an English essayist of the nineteenth century, gives what is widely taken to be the classical expression of "the love of art for art's sake."

SUSANNE K. LANGER

THE CULTURAL IMPORTANCE
OF ART

Originally a lecture delivered at Syracuse University, this essay was first published in Aesthetic Form and Education, *ed. M. F. Andrews (1958). It later appeared as Chapter 5 in Mrs. Langer's* Philosophical Sketches *(1962), and it is this text which we reprint below. For information about the author and her writings, see page 59.*

•

Every culture develops some kind of art as surely as it develops language. Some primitive cultures have no real mythology or religion, but all have some art—dance, song, design (sometimes only on tools or on the human body). Dance, above all, seems to be the oldest elaborated art.

The ancient ubiquitous character of art contrasts sharply with the prevalent idea that art is a luxury product of civilization, a cultural frill, a piece of social veneer.

It fits better with the conviction held by most artists, that art is the epitome of human life, the truest record of insight and feeling, and that the strongest military or economic society without art is poor in comparison with the most primitive tribe of savage painters, dancers, or idol carvers. Wherever a society has really achieved culture (in the ethnological sense, not the popular sense of "social form") it has begotten art, not late in its career, but at the very inception of it.

Art is, indeed, the spearhead of human development, social and individual. The vulgarization of art is the surest symptom of ethnic decline. The growth of a new art or even a great and radically new style always bespeaks a young and vigorous mind, whether collective or single.

What sort of thing is art, that it should play such a leading role in human development? It is not an intellectual pursuit, but is necessary to intellectual life; it is not religion, but grows up with religion, serves it, and in large measure determines it.

We cannot enter here on a long discussion of what has been claimed as the essence of art, the true nature of art, or its defining function; in a single lecture dealing with one aspect of art, namely its cultural influence, I can only give you by way of preamble my own definition of art, with categorical brevity. This does not mean that I set up this definition in a categorical spirit, but only that we have no time to debate it; so you are asked to accept it as an assumption underlying these reflections.

Art, in the sense here intended—that is, the generic term subsuming painting, sculpture, architecture, music, dance, literature, drama, and film—may be defined as the practice of creating perceptible forms expressive of human feeling. I say "perceptible" rather than "sensuous" forms because some works of art are given to imagination rather than to the outward senses. A novel, for instance, usually is read silently with the eye, but is not made for vision, as a painting is; and though sound plays a vital part in poetry, words even in poetry are not essentially sonorous structures like music. Dance requires to be seen, but its appeal is to deeper centers of sensation. The difference between dance and mobile sculpture makes this immediately apparent. But all works of art are purely perceptible forms that seem to embody some sort of feeling.

"Feeling" as I am using it here covers much more than it does in the technical vocabulary of psychology, where it denotes only pleasure and displeasure, or even in the shifting limits of ordinary discourse, where it sometimes means sensation (as when one says a paralyzed limb has no feeling in it), sometimes sensibility (as we speak of hurting someone's feelings), sometimes emotion (e.g., as a situation is said to harrow your feelings, or to evoke tender feeling), or a directed emotional attitude (we say we feel strongly *about* something), or even our general mental or physical condition, feeling well or ill, blue, or a bit above ourselves. As I use the word, in defining art as the creation of perceptible forms expressive of human feeling, it takes in all those meanings; it applies to everything that may be felt.

Another word in the definition that might be questioned is "creation." I think it is justified, not pretentious, as perhaps it sounds, but that issue is slightly beside the point here; so let us shelve it. If anyone prefers to speak of the "making" or "construction" of expressive forms, that will do here just as well.

What does have to be understood is the meaning of "form," and more particularly "expressive form"; for that involves the very nature of art and therefore the question of its cultural importance.

The word "form" has several current uses; most of them have some relation to the sense in which I am using it here, though a few, such as "a form to be filled in for tax purposes" or "a mere matter of form," are fairly remote, being quite specialized. Since we are speaking of art, it might be good to point out that the meaning of stylistic pattern—"the sonata form," "the sonnet form"—is not the one I am assuming here.

I am using the word in a simpler sense, which it has when you say, on a foggy night, that you see dimly moving forms in the mist; one of them emerges clearly, and is the form of a man. The trees are gigantic forms; the rills of rain trace sinuous forms on the windowpane. The rills are not fixed things; they are forms of motion. When you watch gnats weaving in the air, or flocks of birds wheeling overhead, you see dynamic forms —forms made by motion.

It is in this sense of an apparition given to our perception that a work of art is a form. It may be a permanent form like a building or a vase or a picture, or a transient, dynamic form like a melody or a dance, or even a form given to imagination, like the passage of purely imaginary, apparent events that constitutes a literary work. But it is always a perceptible, self-identical whole; like a natural being, it has a character of organic unity, self-sufficiency, individual reality. And it is thus, as an appearance, that a work of art is good or bad or perhaps only rather poor—as an appearance, not as a comment on things beyond it in the world, or as a reminder of them.

This, then, is what I mean by "form"; but what is meant by calling such forms "expressive of human feeling"? How do apparitions "express" anything—feeling or anything else? First of all, let us ask just what is meant here by "express," what sort of "expression" we are talking about.

The word "expression" has two principal meanings. In one sense it means self-expression—giving vent to our feelings. In this sense it refers to a symptom of what we feel. Self-expression is a spontaneous reaction to an actual, present situation, an event, the company we are in, things people say, or what the weather does to us; it bespeaks the physical and mental state we are in and the emotions that stir us.

In another sense, however, "expression" means the presentation of an idea, usually by the proper and apt use of words. But a device for present-ing an idea is what we call a symbol, not a symptom. Thus a word is a symbol, and so is a meaningful combination of words.

A sentence, which is a special combination of words, expresses the idea of some state of affairs, real or imagined. Sentences are complicated sym-bols. Language will formulate new ideas as well as communicate old ones, so that all people know a lot of things that they have merely heard or read about. Symbolic expression, therefore, extends our knowledge be-yond the scope of our actual experience.

If an idea is clearly conveyed by means of symbols we say it is well expressed. A person may work for a long time to give his statement the best possible form, to find the exact words for what he means to say, and to carry his account or his argument most directly from one point to an-other. But a discourse so worked out is certainly not a spontaneous reac-tion. Giving expression to an idea is obviously a different thing from giving expression to feelings. You do not say of a man in a rage that his anger is well expressed. The symptoms just are what they are; there is no critical standard for symptoms. If, on the other hand, the angry man tries to tell you·what he is fuming about, he will have to collect himself, curtail his emotional expression, and find words to express his ideas. For to tell a story coherently involves "expression" in quite a different sense: this sort of expression is not "self-expression," but may be called "conceptual expression."

Language, of course, is our prime instrument of conceptual expression. The things we can say are in effect the things we can think. Words are the terms of our thinking as well as the terms in which we present our thoughts, because they present the objects of thought to the thinker himself. Before language communicates ideas, it gives them form, makes them clear, and in fact makes them what they are. Whatever has a name is an object for thought. Without words, sense experience is only a flow of impressions, as subjective as our feelings; words make it objective, and carve it up into *things* and *facts* that we can note, remember, and think about. Language gives outward experience its form, and makes it definite and clear.

There is, however, an important part of reality that is quite inaccessible to the formative influence of language: that is the realm of so-called "inner experience," the life of feeling and emotion. The reason why language is so powerless here is not, as many people suppose, that feeling and emotion are irrational; on the contrary, they seem irrational because language does not help to make them conceivable, and most people cannot conceive anything without the logical scaffolding of words. The unfitness of language to convey subjective experience is a somewhat technical subject, easier for logicians to understand than for artists; but the gist of it is that the form of language does not reflect the natural form of feeling, so that we cannot shape any extensive concepts of feeling with the help of ordinary, discursive language. Therefore the words whereby we refer to feeling only name very general kinds of inner experience—excitement, calm, joy, sorrow, love, hate, and so on. But there is no language to describe just how one joy differs, sometimes radically, from another. The real nature of feeling is something language as such—as discursive symbolism —cannot render.

For this reason, the phenomena of feeling and emotion are usually treated by philosophers as irrational. The only pattern discursive thought can find in them is the pattern of outward events that occasion them. There are different degrees of fear, but they are thought of as so many degrees of the same simple feeling.

But human feeling is a fabric, not a vague mass. It has an intricate dynamic pattern, possible combinations and new emergent phenomena. It is a pattern of organically interdependent and interdetermined tensions and resolutions, a pattern of almost infinitely complex activation and cadence. To it belongs the whole gamut of our sensibility—the sense of straining thought, all mental attitude and motor set. Those are the deeper reaches that underlie the surface waves of our emotion, and make human life a life of feeling instead of an unconscious metabolic existence interrupted by feelings.

It is, I think, this dynamic pattern that finds its formal expression in the arts. The expressiveness of art is like that of a symbol, not that of an emotional symptom; it is as a formulation of feeling for our conception that a work of art is properly said to be expressive. It may serve somebody's need of self-expression besides, but that is not what makes it good or bad art. In a special sense one may call a work of art a symbol of feeling, for, like a symbol, it formulates our ideas of inward experience, as discourse formulates our ideas of things and facts in the outside world. A work of art differs from a genuine symbol—that is, a symbol in the full and usual sense—in that it does not point beyond itself to something else. Its relation to feeling is a rather special one that we cannot undertake to analyze here; in effect, the feeling it expresses appears to be directly given with it —as the sense of a true metaphor, or the value of a religious myth—and is not separable from its expression. We speak of the feeling *of*, or the feeling *in*, a work of art, not the feeling it means. And we speak truly; a work of art presents something like a direct vision of vitality, emotion, subjective reality.

The primary function of art is to objectify feeling so that we can contemplate and understand it. It is the formulation of so-called "inward experience," the "inner life," that is impossible to achieve by discursive thought, because its forms are incommensurable with the forms of language and all its derivatives (e.g., mathematics, symbolic logic). Art objectifies the sentience and desire, self-consciousness and world-consciousness, emotions and moods, that are generally regarded as irrational because words cannot give us clear ideas of them. But the premise tacitly assumed in such a judgment—namely, that anything language cannot express is formless and irrational—seems to me to be an error. I believe the life of feeling is not irrational; its logical forms are merely very different from the structures of discourse. But they are so much like the dynamic forms of art that art is their natural symbol. Through plastic works, music, fiction, dance, or dramatic forms we can conceive what vitality and emotion feel like.

This brings us, at last, to the question of the cultural importance of the arts. Why is art so apt to be the vanguard of cultural advance, as it was in Egypt, in Greece, in Christian Europe (think of Gregorian music and Gothic architecture), in Renaissance Italy—not to speculate about ancient cavemen, whose art is all that we know of them? One thinks of culture as economic increase, social organization, the gradual ascendancy of rational thinking and scientific control of nature over superstitious imagination and magical practices. But art is not practical; it is neither philosophy nor science; it is not religion, morality, or even social comment (as many drama critics take comedy to be). What does it contribute to culture that could be of major importance?

It merely presents forms—sometimes intangible forms—to imagination. Its direct appeal is to that faculty, or function, that Lord Bacon considered the chief stumbling block in the way of reason, and that enlightened writers like Stuart Chase never tire of condemning as the source of all nonsense and bizarre erroneous beliefs. And so it is; but it is also the source of all insight and true beliefs. Imagination is probably the oldest mental trait that is typically human—older than discursive reason; it is probably the common source of dream, reason, religion, and all true general observation. It is this primitive human power—imagination—that engenders the arts and is in turn directly affected by their products.

Somewhere at the animalian starting line of human evolution lie the beginnings of that supreme instrument of the mind—language. We think of it as a device for communication among the members of a society. But communication is only one, and perhaps not even the first, of its functions. The first thing it does is to break up what William James called the "blooming, buzzing confusion" of sense perception into units and groups, events and chains of events—things and relations, causes and effects. All these patterns are imposed on our experience by language. We think, as we speak, in terms of objects and their relations.

But the process of breaking up our sense experience in this way, making reality conceivable, memorable, sometimes even predictable, is a process of imagination. Primitive conception is imagination. Language and imagination grow up together in a reciprocal tutelage.

What discursive symbolism—language in its literal use—does for our awareness of things about us and our own relation to them, the arts do for our awareness of subjective reality, feeling and emotion; they give form to inward experiences and thus make them conceivable. The only way we can really envisage vital movement, the stirring and growth and passage of emotion, and ultimately the whole direct sense of human life, is in artistic terms. A musical person thinks of emotions musically. They cannot be discursively talked about above a very general level. But they may nonetheless be known—objectively set forth, publicly known—and there is nothing necessarily confused or formless about emotions.

As soon as the natural forms of subjective experience are abstracted to the point of symbolic presentation, we can use those forms to imagine feeling and understand its nature. Self-knowledge, insight into all phases of life and mind, springs from artistic imagination. That is the cognitive value of the arts.

But their influence on human life goes deeper than the intellectual level. As language actually gives form to our sense experience, grouping our impressions around those things which have names, and fitting sensations to the qualities that have adjectival names, and so on, the arts we live with

—our picture books and stories and the music we hear—actually form our emotive experience. Every generation has its styles of feeling. One age shudders and blushes and faints, another swaggers, still another is godlike in a universal indifference. These styles in actual emotion are not insincere. They are largely unconscious—determined by many social causes, but *shaped* by artists, usually popular artists of the screen, the jukebox, the shop window, and the picture magazine. (That, rather than incitement to crime, is my objection to the comics.) Irwin Edman remarks in one of his books that our emotions are largely Shakespeare's poetry.

This influence of art on life gives us an indication of why a period of efflorescence in the arts is apt to lead a cultural advance: it formulates a new way of feeling, and that is the beginning of a cultural age. It suggests another matter for reflection, too—that a wide neglect of artistic education is a neglect in the education of feeling. Most people are so imbued with the idea that feeling is a formless, total organic excitement in men as in animals that the idea of educating feeling, developing its scope and quality, seems odd to them, if not absurd. It is really, I think, at the very heart of personal education.

There is one other function of the arts that benefits not so much the advance of culture as its stabilization—an influence on individual lives. This function is the converse and complement of the objectification of feeling, the driving force of creation in art: it is the education of vision that we receive in seeing, hearing, reading works of art—the development of the artist's eye, that assimilates ordinary sights (or sounds, motions, or events) to inward vision, and lends expressiveness and emotional import to the world. Wherever art takes a motif from actuality—a flowering branch, a bit of landscape, a historic event, or a personal memory, any model or theme from life—it transforms it into a piece of imagination, and imbues its image with artistic vitality. The result is an impregnation of ordinary reality with the significance of created form. This is the subjectification of nature that makes reality itself a symbol of life and feeling.

The arts objectify subjective reality, and subjectify outward experience of nature. Art education is the education of feeling, and a society that neglects it gives itself up to formless emotion. Bad art is corruption of feeling. This is a large factor in the irrationalism which dictators and demagogues exploit.

HENRI MATISSE

One of the most notable twentieth-century painters, Matisse was born in France in 1869. He first studied under Adolphe Bougereau, whom he found too academic; he then studied under Gustave Moreau, spending a great deal of time copying paintings of old masters at the Louvre. When he discovered the impressionists, he changed radically, joined the new school, and became one of its most memorable representatives. His first successful original painting, "Dinner Table," was exhibited in 1897, and in the next years Matisse painted a whole series of what have since been called masterpieces. He has also done some sculpting, worked with lithographs and etchings, illustrated many books, and designed two ballet sets—one for Diaghilev. In 1943 he left Paris for Vence, a small village in the hills behind Nice; he continued to paint and also designed the chapel of the Rosary for the Dominican nuns there. Matisse died in Nice in 1954 at the age of 85. "Notes of a Painter" was originally published in La Grande Revue, *Paris, on December 25, 1908. We have taken our text from the English translation, by Margaret Scolari Barr, which was published first in* Henri-Matisse *(The Museum of Modern Art, 1931) and later in* Matisse: His Art and His Public, *by Alfred H. Barr, Jr. (1951). We have omitted the paragraph headings added by the editor.*

NOTES OF A PAINTER

A painter who addresses the public not in order to present his works but to reveal some of his ideas on the art of painting exposes himself to several dangers. In the first place, I know that some people like to think of painting as dependent upon literature and therefore like to see in it not general ideas suited to pictorial art, but rather specifically literary ideas. I fear, therefore, that the painter who risks himself in the field of the literary man may be regarded with disapproval; in any case, I myself am fully convinced that the best explanation an artist can give of his aims and ability is afforded by his work.

However, such painters as Signac, Desvallières, Denis, Blanche, Guérin, Bernard etc. have written on such matters in various periodicals. In my turn I shall endeavor to make clear my pictorial intentions and aspirations without worrying about the writing.

One of the dangers which appears to me immediately is that of contradicting myself. I feel very strongly the bond between my old works and my recent ones. But I do not think the way I thought yesterday. My fundamental thoughts have not changed but have evolved and my modes of expression have followed my thoughts. I do not repudiate any of my paintings but I would not paint one of them in the same way had I to do it again. My destination is always the same but I work out a different route to get there.

If I mention the name of this or that artist it will be to point out how our manners differ so that it may seem that I do not appreciate his work. Thus I may be accused of injustice towards painters whose efforts and aims I best understand, or whose accomplishments I most appreciate. I shall use them as examples not to establish my superiority over them but to show clearly through what they have done, what I am attempting to do.

What I am after, above all, is expression. Sometimes it has been conceded that I have a certain technical ability but that, my ambition being limited, I am unable to proceed beyond a purely visual satisfaction such as can be procured from the mere sight of a picture. But the purpose of a painter must not be conceived as separate from his pictorial means, and these pictorial means must be the more complete (I do not mean complicated) the deeper is his thought. I am unable to distinguish between the feeling I have for life and my way of expressing it.

Expression to my way of thinking does not consist of the passion mirrored upon a human face or betrayed by a violent gesture. The whole arrangement of my picture is expressive. The place occupied by figures or objects, the empty spaces around them, the proportions, everything plays a part. Composition is the art of arranging in a decorative manner the various elements at the painter's disposal for the expression of his feelings. In a picture every part will be visible and will play the rôle conferred upon it, be it principal or secondary. All that is not useful in the picture is detrimental. A work of art must be harmonious in its entirety; for superfluous details would, in the mind of the beholder, encroach upon the essential elements.

Composition, the aim of which is expression, alters itself according to the surface to be covered. If I take a sheet of paper of given dimensions I will jot down a drawing which will have a necessary relation to its format—I would not repeat this drawing on another sheet of different dimensions, for instance on a rectangular sheet if the first one happened to be square. And if I had to repeat it on a sheet of the same shape but ten times larger I would not limit myself to enlarging it: a drawing must have a power of expansion which can bring to life the space which surrounds it. An artist who wants to transpose a composition onto a larger canvas must conceive it over again in order to preserve its expression; he must alter its character and not just fill in the squares into which he has divided his canvas.

Both harmonies and dissonances of color can produce very pleasurable effects. Often when I settle down to work I begin by noting my immediate and superficial color sensations. Some years ago this first result was often enough for me—but today if I were satisfied with this my picture would remain incomplete. I would have put down the passing sensations of a moment; they would not completely define my feelings and the next day I might not recognize what they meant. I want to reach that state of condensation of sensations which constitutes a picture. Perhaps I might be satisfied momentarily with a work finished at one sitting but I would soon get bored looking at it; therefore, I prefer to continue working on it so that later I may recognize it as a work of my mind. There was a time when I never left my paintings hanging on the wall because they reminded me of moments of nervous excitement and I did not like to see them again when I was quiet. Nowadays I try to put serenity into my pictures and work at them until I feel that I have succeeded.

Supposing I want to paint the body of a woman: first of all I endow it with grace and charm but I know that something more than that is necessary. I try to condense the meaning of this body by drawing its essential lines. The charm will then become less apparent at first glance but in the long run it will begin to emanate from the new image. This image at the same time will be enriched by a wider meaning, a more comprehensively human one, while the charm, being less apparent, will not be its only characteristic. It will be merely one element in the general conception of the figure.

Charm, lightness, crispness—all these are passing sensations. I have a canvas on which the colors are still fresh and I begin work on it again. The colors will probably grow heavier—the freshness of the original tones will give way to greater solidity, an improvement to my mind, but less seductive to the eye.

The impressionist painters, Monet, Sisley especially, had delicate, vibrating sensations; as a result their canvases are all alike. The word "impressionism" perfectly characterizes their intentions for they register fleeting impressions. This term, however, cannot be used with reference to more recent painters who avoid the first impression and consider it deceptive. A rapid rendering of a landscape represents only one moment of its appearance. I prefer, by insisting upon its essentials, to discover its more enduring character and content, even at the risk of sacrificing some of its pleasing qualities.

Underneath this succession of moments which constitutes the superficial

existence of things animate and inanimate and which is continually ob-
scuring and transforming them, it is yet possible to search for a truer,
more essential character which the artist will seize so that he may give to
reality a more lasting interpretation. When we go into the XVII and
XVIII century sculpture rooms in the Louvre and look for instance at a
Puget, we realize that the expression is forced and exaggerated in a very
disquieting way. Then, again, if we go to the Luxembourg the attitude
in which the painters seize their models is always the one in which the
muscular development will be shown to greatest advantage. But movement
thus interpreted corresponds to nothing in nature and if we catch a
motion of this kind by a snapshot the image thus captured will remind
us of nothing that we have seen. Indication of motion has meaning for
us only if we do not isolate any one sensation of movement from the
preceding and from the following one.

There are two ways of expressing things; one is to show them crudely,
the other is to evoke them artistically. In abandoning the literal representation of movement it is possible to reach towards a higher ideal of beauty.
Look at an Egyptian statue: it looks rigid to us; however, we feel in it
the image of a body capable of movement and which despite its stiffness
is animated. The Greeks too are calm; a man hurling a discus will be
shown in the moment in which he gathers his strength before the effort
or else, if he is shown in the most violent and precarious position implied
by his action, the sculptor will have abridged and condensed it so that
balance is re-established, thereby suggesting a feeling of duration. Movement in itself is unstable and is not suited to something durable like a
statue unless the artist has consciously realized the entire action of which
he represents only a moment.

It is necessary for me to define the character of the object or of the
body that I wish to paint. In order to do this I study certain salient points
very carefully: if I put a black dot on a sheet of white paper the dot will
be visible no matter how far I stand away from it—it is a clear notation;
but beside this dot I place another one, and then a third. Already there is
confusion. In order that the first dot may maintain its value I must enlarge
it as I proceed putting other marks on the paper.

If upon a white canvas I jot down some sensations of blue, of green,
of red—every new brushstroke diminishes the importance of the preceding ones. Suppose I set out to paint an interior: I have before me a cupboard; it gives me a sensation of bright red—and I put down a red which
satisfies me; immediately a relation is established between this red and
the white of the canvas. If I put a green near the red, if I paint in a yellow
floor, there must still be between this green, this yellow and the white of
the canvas a relation that will be satisfactory to me. But these several tones
mutually weaken one another. It is necessary, therefore, that the various
elements that I use be so balanced that they do not destroy one another.
To do this I must organize my ideas; the relation between tones must be

so established that they will sustain one another. A new combination of colors will succeed the first one and will give more completely my interpretation. I am forced to transpose until finally my picture may seem completely changed when, after successive modifications, the red has succeeded the green as the dominant color. I cannot copy nature in a servile way, I must interpret nature and submit it to the spirit of the picture—when I have found the relationship of all the tones the result must be a living harmony of tones, a harmony not unlike that of a musical composition.

For me all is in the conception—I must have a clear vision of the whole composition from the very beginning. I could mention the name of a great sculptor who produces some admirable pieces but for him a composition is nothing but the grouping of fragments and the result is a confusion of expression. Look instead at one of Cézanne's pictures: all is so well arranged in them that no matter how many figures are represented and no matter at what distance you stand, you will be able always to distinguish each figure clearly and you will always know which limb belongs to which body. If in the picture there is order and clarity it means that this same order and clarity existed in the mind of the painter and that the painter was conscious of their necessity. Limbs may cross, may mingle, but still in the eyes of the beholder they will remain attached to the right body. All confusion will have disappeared.

The chief aim of color should be to serve expression as well as possible. I put down my colors without a preconceived plan. If at the first step and perhaps without my being conscious of it one tone has particularly pleased me, more often than not when the picture is finished I will notice that I have respected this tone while I have progressively altered and transformed the others. I discover the quality of colors in a purely instinctive way. To paint an autumn landscape I will not try to remember what colors suit this season, I will only be inspired by the sensation that the season gives me; the icy clearness of the sour blue sky will express the season just as well as the tonalities of the leaves. My sensation itself may vary, the autumn may be soft and warm like a protracted summer or quite cool with a cold sky and lemon yellow trees that give a chilly impression and announce winter.

My choice of colors does not rest on any scientific theory; it is based on observation, on feeling, on the very nature of each experience. Inspired by certain pages of Delacroix, Signac is preoccupied by complementary colors and the theoretical knowledge of them will lead him to use a certain tone in a certain place. I, on the other hand, merely try to find a color that will fit my sensation. There is an impelling proportion of tones that can induce me to change the shape of a figure or to transform my composition. Until I have achieved this proportion in all the parts of the composition I strive towards it and keep on working. Then a moment comes when every part has found its definite relationship and from then on it would be impossible for me to add a stroke to my picture without having to paint it all over again. As a matter of fact, I think that the theory of complementary colors is not absolute. In studying the paintings of artists whose knowledge of colors depends only upon instinct and sensibility and on a consistency of their sensations, it would be possible to define certain laws of color and so repudiate the limitations of the accepted color theory.

What interests me most is neither still life nor landscape but the human figure. It is through it that I best succeed in expressing the nearly religious feeling that I have towards life. I do not insist upon the details of the face. I do not care to repeat them with anatomical exactness. Though I happen to have an Italian model whose appearance at first suggests nothing but a purely animal existence yet I succeed in picking out among the lines of his face those which suggest that deep gravity which persists in every human being. A work of art must carry in itself its complete significance and impose it upon the beholder even before he can identify the subject matter. When I see the Giotto frescoes at Padua I do not trouble to recognize which scene of the life of Christ I have before me but I perceive instantly the sentiment which radiates from it and which is instinct in the composition in every line and color. The title will only serve to confirm my impression.

What I dream of is an art of balance, of purity and serenity devoid of troubling or depressing subject matter, an art which might be for every mental worker, be he business man or writer, like an appeasing influence, like a mental soother, something like a good armchair in which to rest from physical fatigue.

Often a discussion arises upon the value of different processes, and their relation to different temperaments. A distinction is made between artists who work directly from nature and those who work purely from their imagination. I think neither of these methods should be preferred to the exclusion of the other. Often both are used in turn by the same man; sometimes he needs tangible objects to provide him with sensations and thus excite his creative power; at other times when his pictorial sensations are already present in his mind he needs contact with reality before he can organize them into a picture. However, I think that one can judge of the vitality and power of an artist when after having received impressions from nature he is able to organize his sensations to return in the same mood on different days, voluntarily to continue receiving these impressions (whether nature appears the same or not); this power proves he is sufficiently master of himself to subject himself to discipline.

The simplest means are those which enable an artist to express himself best. If he fears the obvious he cannot avoid it by strange representations, bizarre drawing, eccentric color. His expression must derive inevitably from his temperament. He must sincerely believe that he has only painted what he has seen. I like Chardin's way of expressing it: "I put on color until it resembles (is a good likeness)," or Cézanne: "I want to secure a likeness," or Rodin: "Copy nature!" or Leonardo: "He who can copy can do (create)." Those who work in an affected style, deliberately turning their backs on nature, are in error—an artist must recognize that when he uses his reason his picture is an artifice and that when he paints he must feel that he is copying nature—and even when he consciously departs from nature he must do it with the conviction that it is only the better to interpret her.

Some will object perhaps that a painter should have some other outlook upon painting and that I have only uttered platitudes. To this I shall answer that there are no new truths. The rôle of the artist, like that of the scholar, consists in penetrating truths as well known to him as to others but which will take on for him a new aspect and so enable him to master them in their deepest significance. Thus if the aviators were to explain to us the researches which led to their leaving earth and rising in the air they would be merely confirming very elementary principles of physics neglected by less successful inventors.

An artist has always something to learn when he is given information about himself—and I am glad now to have learned which is my weak point. M. Peladan in the "Revue Hébdomadaire" reproaches a certain number of painters, amongst whom I think I should place myself, for calling themselves *"Fauves"* (wild beasts) and yet dressing like everyone else so that they are no more noticeable than the floor walkers in a department store. Does genius count for so little? In the same article this excellent writer pretends that I do not paint honestly and I feel that I should perhaps be annoyed though I admit that he restricts his statement by adding, "I mean honestly with respect to the Ideal and the Rules." The trouble is that he does not mention where these rules are—I am willing to admit that they exist but were it possible to learn them what sublime artists we would have!

Rules have no existence outside of individuals: otherwise Racine would be no greater genius than a good professor. Any of us can repeat a fine sentence but few can also penetrate the meaning. I have no doubt that from a study of the works of Raphael or Titian a more complete set of rules can be drawn than from the works of Manet or Renoir but the rules followed by Manet and Renoir were suited to their artistic temperaments and I happen to prefer the smallest of their paintings to all the work of those who have merely imitated the "Venus of Urbino" or the "Madonna of the Goldfinch." Such painters are of no value to anyone because, whether we want to or not, we belong to our time and we share in its opinions, preferences and delusions. All artists bear the imprint of their time but the great artists are those in which this stamp is most deeply impressed. Our epoch for instance is better represented by Courbet than by Flandrin, by Rodin better than by Fremiet. Whether we want to or not between our period and ourselves an indissoluble bond is established and M. Peladan himself cannot escape it. The aestheticians of the future may perhaps use his books as evidence if they get it in their heads to prove that no one of our time understood a thing about the art of Leonardo da Vinci.

ERNST FISCHER

Ernst Fischer was born in Austria in 1899. A member of the Social Democratic Party, he edited the Vienna Arbeiter Zeitung (Workers' Newspaper) from 1927 to 1934. That year he emigrated to Prague and became a member of the Communist party. He spent a number of years in Moscow where he was active in literary circles, and during World War II became a radio commentator. In 1945 he returned to Austria, became active in politics, and served from 1945 to 1959 as a member of Parliament in the National Assembly. He is the author of many political and literary works. The selection we print below is the opening chapter of his The Necessity of Art: A Marxist Approach, trans. Anna Bostock (1963), originally published as Von der Notwendigkeit der Kunst in 1959.

THE FUNCTION OF ART

'Poetry is indispensable—if I only knew what for.' With this charmingly paradoxical epigram Jean Cocteau has summed up the necessity of art—as well as its questionable role in the late bourgeois world.

The painter Mondrian spoke of the possible 'disappearance' of art. Reality would, he believed, increasingly displace the work of art, which was essentially a substitute for an equilibrium that reality lacked at present. 'Art will disappear as life gains more equilibrium.'

Art as a 'life substitute', art as a means of putting man in a state of equilibrium with the surrounding world—the idea contains a partial recognition of the nature of art and its necessity. And since a perpetual equilibrium between man and the surrounding world cannot be expected to exist even in the most highly developed society, the idea suggests, too, that art was not merely necessary in the past but will always remain so.

Yet is art really no more than a substitute? Does it not also express a deeper relationship between man and the world? Indeed, can the function of art be summed up at all in a single formula? Does it not have to satisfy many and various needs? And if, as we reflect upon the origins of art, we become aware of its initial function, has not that function also changed with the changing of society, and have not new functions come into being?

This book is an attempt to answer questions such as these, founded on the conviction that art has been, still is, and always will be necessary.

As a first step we must realize that we are inclined to take an astonishing phenomenon too much for granted. And it is certainly astonishing: countless millions read books, listen to music, watch the theatre, go to the cinema. Why? To say that they seek distraction, relaxation, entertainment, is to beg the question. Why is it distracting, relaxing, entertaining to sink oneself in someone else's life and problems, to identify oneself with a painting or a piece of music or with the characters in a novel, play, or film? Why do we respond to such 'unreality' as though it were reality intensified? What strange, mysterious entertainment is this? And if one answers that we want to escape from an unsatisfactory existence into a richer one, into experience without risk, then the next question arises: why is our own existence not enough? Why this desire to fulfil our un-fulfilled lives through other figures, other forms, to gaze from the dark-ness of an auditorium at a lighted stage where something that is only play can so utterly absorb us?

Evidently man wants to be more than just himself. He wants to be a *whole* man. He is not satisfied with being a separate individual; out of the partiality of his individual life he strives towards a 'fulness' that he senses and demands, towards a fulness of life of which individuality with all its limitations cheats him, towards a more comprehensible, a more just world, a world that *makes sense*. He rebels against having to consume himself within the confines of his own life, within the transient, chance limits of his own personality. He wants to refer to something that is more than 'I', something outside himself and yet essential to himself. He longs to absorb the surrounding world and make it his own; to extend his inquisitive, world-hungry 'I' in science and technology as far as the remotest constellations and as deep as the innermost secrets of the atom; to unite his limited 'I' in art with a communal existence; to make his individuality *social*.

If it were man's nature to be no more than an individual, this desire would be incomprehensible and senseless, for as an individual he would then *be* a whole: he would be all that he was capable of being. Man's desire to be increased and supplemented indicates that he is more than an individual. He feels that he can attain wholeness only if he takes possession of the experiences of others that might potentially be his own. Yet what a man apprehends as his potential includes everything that humanity as a whole is capable of. Art is the indispensable means for this merging of the individual with the whole. It reflects his infinite capacity for association, for sharing experiences and ideas.

And yet: is this definition of art as the means of becoming one with the whole of reality, as the individual's way to the world at large, as the expression of his desire to identify himself with what he is not, perhaps too romantic? Is it not rash to conclude, on the basis of our own near-hysterical sense of identification with the hero of a film or a novel, that this is the universal and original function of art? Does art not also contain the opposite of this 'Dionysian' losing of oneself? Does it not also contain the 'Apollonian' element of entertainment and satisfaction which consists precisely in the fact that the onlooker does *not* identify himself with what is represented but *gains distance* from it, overcomes the direct power of reality through its deliberate representation, and finds, in art, that happy freedom of which the burdens of everyday life deprive him? And is not the same duality—on the one hand the absorption in reality, on the other the excitement of controlling it—also evident in the way the artist himself works? For make no mistake about it, work for an artist is a highly conscious, rational process at the end of which the work of art emerges as mastered reality—not at all a state of intoxicated inspiration.

In order to be an artist it is necessary to seize, hold, and transform experience into memory, memory into expression, material into form. Emotion for an artist is not everything; he must also know his trade and enjoy it, understand all the rules, skills, forms, and conventions whereby nature —the shrew—can be tamed and subjected to the contract of art. The passion that consumes the dilettante *serves* the true artist: the artist is not mauled by the beast, he tames it.

Tension and dialectical contradiction are inherent in art; not only must art derive from an intense experience of reality, it must also be *constructed*, it must gain form through objectivity. The free play of art is the result of mastery. Aristotle, so often misunderstood, held that the function of drama was to purify the emotions, to overcome terror and pity, so that the spectator identifying himself with Orestes or Oedipus was liberated from that identification and lifted above the blind workings of fate. The ties of life are temporarily cast off, for art 'captivates' in a different way from reality, and this pleasant temporary captivity is precisely the nature of the 'entertainment', of that pleasure which is derived even from tragic works.

Bertolt Brecht said of this pleasure, this liberating quality of art:

> Our theatre must encourage the thrill of comprehension and train people in the pleasure of changing reality. Our audiences must not

only hear how Prometheus was set free, but also train themselves in the pleasure of freeing him. They must be taught to feel, in our theatre, all the satisfaction and enjoyment felt by the inventor and the discoverer, all the triumph felt by the liberator.

Brecht points out that in a society of class struggle, the 'immediate' effect of a work of art demanded by the ruling aesthetic is to suppress the social distinctions within the audience and thus, while the work is being enjoyed, create a collective not divided into classes but 'universally human'. On the other hand, the function of 'non-Aristotelian drama' which Brecht advocated was precisely to divide the audience by removing the conflict between feeling and reason which has come about in the capitalist world.

Both feeling and reason degenerated in the age of capitalism when that age was drawing towards its end, and entered into a bad, unproductive conflict with each other. But the rising new class and those who fight on its side are concerned with feeling and reason engaged in *productive* conflict. Our feelings impel us towards the maximum effort of reasoning, and our reason purifies our feelings.

In the alienated world in which we live, social reality must be presented in an arresting way, in a new light, through the 'alienation' of the subject and the characters. The work of art must grip the audience not through passive identification but through an appeal to reason which demands action and decision. The rules according to which human beings live together must be treated in the drama as 'temporary and imperfect' so as to make the spectator do something more productive than merely watch, stimulating him to think along with the play and finally to pass judgment: 'That's not the way to do it. This is very strange, almost unbelievable. This must stop.' And so the spectator, who is a working man or woman, will come to the theatre to

... enjoy, as entertainment, his own terrible and never-ending labours by which he is meant to support himself, and suffer the shock of his own incessant change. Here he may *produce himself* in the easiest fashion: for the easiest fashion of existence is in art.

Without claiming that Brecht's 'epic theatre' is the only possible kind of militant working-class drama, I quote Brecht's important theory as an illustration of the dialectic of art and of the way that the function of art changes in a changing world.

The *raison d'être* of art never stays entirely the same. The function of art in a class society at war within itself differs in many respects from its original function. But nevertheless, despite different social situations, there is something in art that expresses an unchanging truth. It is this that enables us, who live in the twentieth century, to be moved by prehistoric cave paintings or very ancient songs. Karl Marx described the epic as the art form of an undeveloped society,[1] and then added:

> But the difficulty is not in grasping the idea that Greek art and epos are bound up with certain forms of social development. It rather lies in understanding why they still constitute with us a source of aesthetic enjoyment and in certain respects prevail as the standard and model beyond attainment.

He then offered the following answer:

> Why should the social childhood of mankind, where it had obtained its most beautiful development, not exert an eternal charm as an age that will never return? There are ill-bred children and precocious children. Many of the ancient nations belong to the latter class. The Greeks were normal children. The charm their art has for us does not conflict with the primitive character of the social order from which it had sprung. It is rather the product of the latter, and is rather due to the fact that the unripe social conditions under which the art arose and under which alone it could appear can never return.

Today we may doubt whether, compared with other nations, the ancient Greeks were 'normal children'. Indeed, in another connexion Marx and Engels themselves drew attention to the problematic aspects of the Greek world with its contempt for work, its degradation of women, its eroticism reserved solely for courtesans and boys. And since then we have discovered a great deal more about the seamy side of Greek beauty, serenity, and harmony. Today our ideas of the ancient world coincide only in part with those of Winckelmann, Goethe, and Hegel. Archaeological, ethnological, and cultural discoveries no longer allow us to accept classical Greek art as belonging to our 'childhood'. On the contrary, we see in it something relatively late and mature, and in its perfection in the age of Pericles we detect hints of decadence and decline. Many works, once praised as 'classical', by the sculptors who followed the great Phidias, a large number of those heroes, athletes, discus throwers, and charioteers, strike us today as empty and meaningless compared with Egyptian or Mycenean works. But to go deeper into these matters would take us too far from the question Marx raised and the answer he supplied.

What matters is that Marx saw the time-conditioned art of an undeveloped social stage as a *moment of humanity*, and recognized that in this lay its power to act beyond the historical moment, to exercise an eternal fascination.

We may put it like this: all art is conditioned by time, and represents

---

[1] *A Contribution to the Critique of Political Economy*, Kegan Paul, Trench Trübner, 1904.

humanity in so far as it corresponds to the ideas and aspirations, the needs and hopes of a particular historical situation. But, at the same time, art goes beyond this limitation and, within the historical moment, also creates a moment of humanity, promising constant development. We should never underestimate the degree of continuity throughout the class struggle, despite periods of violent change and social upheaval. Like the world itself, the history of mankind is not only a contradictory discontinuum but also a continuum. Ancient, apparently long-forgotten things are preserved within us, continue to work upon us—often without our realizing it—and then, suddenly, they come to the surface and speak to us like the shadows in Hades whom Odysseus fed with his blood. In different periods, depending on the social situation and the needs of rising or declining classes, different things which have been latent or lost are brought again into the light of day, awakened to new life. And just as it was no coincidence that Lessing and Herder, in their revolt against the feudal and the courtly and all the contemporary false posturings with wig and alexandrine, discovered Shakespeare for the Germans, so it is no coincidence that, today, Western Europe in its denial of humanism and in the fetish-like character of its institutions reaches back to the fetishes of pre-history and constructs false myths to hide its real problems.

Different classes and social systems, while developing their own ethos, have contributed to the forming of a universal human ethos. The concept of freedom, though it always corresponds to the conditions and aims of a class or a social system, nevertheless tends to grow into an all-embracing idea. In the same way, constant features of mankind are captured even in time-conditioned art. In so far as Homer, Aeschylus, and Sophocles mirrored the simple conditions of a society based on slavery, they are time-bound and out of date. But in so far as, in that society, they discovered the greatness of man, gave artistic form to his conflicts and passions, and hinted at his infinite potentiality, they remain as modern as ever. Prometheus bringing fire to earth, Odysseus in his wanderings and his return, the fate of Tantalus and his children, all this has preserved its original power for us. Though we may regard the subject-matter of *Antigone*—a struggle for the right to give honourable burial to a blood relative—as archaic, though we may need historical commentaries in order to understand it, the figure of Antigone is as moving today as it ever was, and so long as there are human beings in the world they will be moved by her words: 'My nature is to join in love, not hate.' The more we come to know of long-forgotten works of art, the clearer become their common and continuous elements, despite their variety. Fragment joins fragment to make humanity.

We may conclude from a constantly growing wealth of evidence that art in its origins was *magic*, a magic aid towards mastering a real but unexplored world. Religion, science, and art were combined in a latent form—germinally as it were—in magic. This magic role of art has progressively given way to the role of illuminating social relationships, of enlightening men in societies becoming opaque, of helping men to recognize and change social reality. A highly complex society with its multiple relationships and social contradictions can no longer be represented in the manner of a myth. In such a society, which demands literal recognition and all-embracing consciousness, there is bound to be an overwhelming need to break through the rigid forms of earlier ages where the magic element still operated, and to arrive at more open forms—at the freedom, say, of the novel. Either of the two elements of art may predominate at a particular time, depending on the stage of society reached —sometimes the magically suggestive, at other times the rational and enlightening; sometimes dreamlike intuition, at other times the desire to sharpen perception. But whether art soothes or awakens, casts shadows or brings light, it is never merely a clinical description of reality. Its function is always to move the *whole* man, to enable the 'I' to identify itself with another's life, to make its own what it is not and yet is capable of being. Even a great didactic artist like Brecht does not act purely through reason and argument, but also through feeling and suggestion. He not only confronts the audience with a work of art, he also lets them 'get inside' it. He himself was aware of this, and pointed out that it was not a problem of absolute contrasts but of shifting stresses. 'In this way the emotionally suggestive or the purely rationally persuasive may predominate as a means of communication.'

True as it is that the essential function of art for a class destined to change the world is not that of *making magic* but of *enlightening* and *stimulating action*, it is equally true that a magical residue in art cannot be entirely eliminated, for without that minute residue of its original nature, art ceases to be art.

In all the forms of its development, in dignity and fun, persuasion and exaggeration, sense and nonsense, fantasy and reality, art always has a little to do with magic.

Art is necessary in order that man should be able to recognize and change the world. But art is also necessary by virtue of the magic inherent in it.

THE EDITORS OF *LIFE*

WANTED: AN AMERICAN NOVEL

The following editorial appeared in the September 12, 1955, issue of Life.

•

Sloan Wilson, a young writer whose first novel (*The Man in the Gray Flannel Suit*) is moving up best-seller lists, recently made a statement in defense of his book's happy ending which is worth repeating: "The world's treated me awfully well," he said, "and I guess it's crept into my work. . . . These are, we forget, pretty good times. Yet too many novelists are still writing as if we were back in the Depression years."

Wilson put his finger on a strange contradiction. Ours is the most powerful nation in the world. It has had a decade of unparalleled prosperity. It has gone further than any other society in the history of man toward creating a truly classless society. Yet it is still producing a literature which sounds sometimes as if it were written by an unemployed homosexual living in a packing-box shanty on the city dump while awaiting admission to the county poorhouse.

This is doubly strange because past American eras have produced art which faithfully mirrored their times; *The Great Gatsby* still speaks eloquently of Prohibition's frauds and deceits, *Main Street* of the high tide of provincial self-satisfaction, *The Grapes of Wrath* with a just anger for the unnecessary humiliations of Depression, while *Look Homeward, Angel* may well speak for a timeless America. But who speaks for America today? One might argue, with some plausibility, that the fearful indecisions of an atomic age keep a representative literature from being born, but when has life ever been secure? Atomic fear or not, the incredible accomplishments of our day are surely the raw stuff of saga.

Wilson's uneven book may be flimsy art but it is at least affirmative. Happily there are a few other signs of a trend away from degeneracy and negation. For example, Lionel Shapiro's *Sixth of June*, though it revolves about a triangle, is not resolved by adultery. Herman Wouk's *Marjorie Morningstar* is a mutiny, says *Time*, against "three decades of

U.S. fiction dominated by skeptical criticism, sexual emancipation, social protest and psychoanalytical sermonizing." Wouk's book even endorses premarital chastity. And there is visible in other work what Critic Maxwell Geismar calls "a return to the security of a religious universe."

A change is needed. Nobody wants Pollyanna literature. Poets have always had what Robert Frost admits is "a vested interest in human misery"; agony begets art. Maybe art mistrusts prosperity. But at least the breeches-busting Paul Bunyan of the U.S. today seems to deserve better literature than the papaya-smelly, overripe school of the Truman Capotes, or the obscenity-obsessed school of "new realism" exemplified by a parade of war novels which mostly read like the diary of a professional grievance collector with a dirty mind and total recall. James Gould Cozzens' *Guard of Honor* was one of the few military novels that rang true with dignity. In most of the others the enemy is not the one shooting at us but our own officers and Army.

Europeans are already prejudiced against America by savage animadversions in their own classics against our "vulgar" democracy ("If I had remained another day in that horrible . . . United States, where there is neither hope nor faith, nor charity," wrote Balzac, "I should have died without being sick"). Small wonder that our own self-depreciation helps them enlarge the evil image to that which France's Michel Mohrt describes in his new study of American novels: "a hypocritical society based on the power of money, racial prejudice, sexual taboos. Exile, alcohol, suicide seem the only escape." Such a onetime exile, Henry (*Tropic of Cancer*) Miller, puts it more savagely in the current *Chicago Review*. The American seen through the eyes of our leading writers, he asserts, is "a digit in machine-made formulas . . . he has neither face nor name but is shuffled about like the victim of a soulless society on an electronic chessboard operated by a dummy hidden in the cells of a publisher's diseased brain. . . ." The writing, he adds, "reeks of embalming fluid."

It is understandable that American groups which feel the most isolated should produce the most anguished writing, and that so much of it should come from the South. Its ante bellum slave society was in some ways similar to the feudal Russian system whose injustices and tensions produced a Dostoevski and a Tolstoi. William Faulkner has a patent kinship with Dostoevski and his preoccupation with guilt. But Faulkner, for all his enormous gifts, can be searched in vain for that quality of redemption, through love and brotherhood, which always shines amid Dostoevski's horrors. It shines also amid the worst havoc of Tolstoi's overturned world (Moscow, too, was burned, even if not by Sherman).

To find this redeeming quality of spiritual purpose today's reader must turn not to novels but to nonfiction like Russell Davenport's *The Dignity of Man* or to the British book, *The Conquest of Everest*. That conquest held a deeper meaning than the achievement. The European Hillary and the Asian Tenzing are a hopeful symbol for a wider brotherhood yet to be achieved. Their final triumph expresses the unquenchable reaching of man's soul for a truth higher than reality, for a good better than himself, the qualities which modern literature so often deny. In every healthy man there is a wisdom deeper than his conscious mind, reaching beyond memory to the primeval rivers, a yea-saying to the goodness and joy of life. This is what is most missing from our hothouse literature—the joy of life itself.

ALBERT CAMUS

WHAT CAN THE ARTIST DO IN THE WORLD OF TODAY?

At least two interviews with Camus have been translated into English under the title The Artist and His Time. *We present below a section of the 1953 interview printed in* The Myth of Sisyphus and Other Essays, *translated by Justin O'Brien (1955). For information about the author and his writings, see page 135.*

•

He is not asked either to write about co-operatives or, conversely, to lull to sleep in himself the sufferings endured by others throughout history. And since you have asked me to speak personally, I am going to do so as simply as I can. Considered as artists, we perhaps have no need to interfere in the affairs of the world. But considered as men, yes. The miner who is exploited or shot down, the slaves in the camps, those in the colonies, the legions of persecuted throughout the world—they need all those who can speak to communicate their silence and to keep in touch with them. I have not written, day after day, fighting articles and texts, I have not taken part in the common struggles because I desire the world to be covered with Greek statues and masterpieces. The man who has such a desire does exist in me. Except that he has something better to do in trying to instill life into the creatures of his imagination. But from my first articles to my latest book I have written so much, and perhaps too much, only because I cannot keep from being drawn toward every-day life, toward those, whoever they may be, who are humiliated and debased. They need to hope, and if all keep silent or if they are given a choice between two kinds of humiliation, they will be forever deprived of hope and we with them. It seems to me impossible to endure that idea, nor can he who cannot endure it lie down to sleep in his tower. Not through virtue, as you see, but through a sort of almost organic intoler-ance, which you feel or do not feel. Indeed, I see many who fail to feel it, but I cannot envy their sleep.

This does not mean, however, that we must sacrifice our artist's nature to some social preaching or other. I have said elsewhere why the artist was more than ever necessary. But if we intervene as men, that experience will have an effect upon our language. And if we are not artists in our language first of all, what sort of artists are we? Even if, militants in our lives, we speak in our works of deserts and of selfish love, the mere fact that our lives are militant causes a special tone of voice to people with men that desert and that love. I shall certainly not choose the moment when we are beginning to leave nihilism behind to stupidly deny the values of creation in favor of the values of humanity, or vice versa. In my mind neither one is ever separated from the other and I measure the greatness of an artist (Molière, Tolstoy, Melville) by the balance he managed to maintain between the two. Today, under the pressure of events, we are obliged to transport that tension into our lives likewise. This is why so many artists, bending under the burden, take refuge in the ivory tower or, conversely, in the social church. But as for me, I see in both choices a like act of resignation. We must simultaneously serve suffering and beauty. The long patience, the strength, the secret cunning such service calls for are the virtues that establish the very renascence we need.

One word more. This undertaking, I know, cannot be accomplished without dangers and bitterness. We must accept the dangers: the era of chairbound artists is over. But we must reject the bitterness. One of the temptations of the artist is to believe himself solitary, and in truth he hears this shouted at him with a certain base delight. But this is not true. He stands in the midst of all, in the same rank, neither higher nor lower, with all those who are working and struggling. His very vocation, in the face of oppression, is to open the prisons and to give a voice to the sorrows and joys of all. This is where art, against its enemies, justifies itself by proving precisely that it is no one's enemy. By itself art could probably not produce the renascence which implies justice and liberty. But without it, that renascence would be without forms and, consequently, would be nothing. Without culture, and the relative freedom it implies, society, even when perfect, is but a jungle. This is why any authentic creation is a gift to the future. (1953)

GEORGE ORWELL

WHY I WRITE

This essay is taken from Orwell's collection, Such, Such Were the Joys *(1953). For further information about the author and his writings, see page 74.*

•

From a very early age, perhaps the age of five or six, I knew that when I grew up I should be a writer. Between the ages of about seventeen and twenty-four I tried to abandon this idea, but I did so with the consciousness that I was outraging my true nature and that sooner or later I should have to settle down and write books.

I was the middle child of three, but there was a gap of five years on either side, and I barely saw my father before I was eight. For this and other reasons I was somewhat lonely, and I soon developed disagreeable mannerisms which made me unpopular throughout my schooldays. I had the lonely child's habit of making up stories and holding conversations with imaginary persons, and I think from the very start my literary ambitions were mixed up with the feeling of being isolated and undervalued. I knew that I had a facility with words and a power of facing unpleasant facts, and I felt that this created a sort of private world in which I could get my own back for my failure in everyday life. Nevertheless the volume of serious—*i.e.* seriously intended—writing which I produced all through my childhood and boyhood would not amount to half a dozen pages. I wrote my first poem at the age of four or five, my mother taking it down to dictation. I cannot remember anything about it except that it was about a tiger and the tiger had "chair-like teeth"— a good enough phrase, but I fancy the poem was a plagiarism of Blake's "Tiger, Tiger." At eleven, when the war of 1914–18 broke out, I wrote a patriotic poem which was printed in the local newspaper, as was another, two years later, on the death of Kitchener. From time to time, when I was a bit older, I wrote bad and usually unfinished "nature poems" in the Georgian style. I also, about twice, attempted a short story which was a ghastly failure. That was the total of the would-be serious work that I actually set down on paper during all those years.

However, throughout this time I did in a sense engage in literary activities. To begin with there was the made-to-order stuff which I produced quickly, easily and without much pleasure to myself. Apart from school work, I wrote *vers d'occasion*, semi-comic poems which I could turn out at what now seems to me astonishing speed—at fourteen I wrote a whole rhyming play, in imitation of Aristophanes, in about a week—and helped to edit school magazines, both printed and in manuscript. These magazines were the most pitiful burlesque stuff that you could imagine, and I took far less trouble with them than I now would with the cheapest journalism. But side by side with all this, for fifteen years or more, I was carrying out a literary exercise of a quite different kind: this was the making up of a continuous "story" about myself, a sort of diary existing only in the mind. I believe this is a common habit of children and adolescents. As a very small child I used to imagine that I was, say, Robin Hood, and picture myself as the hero of thrilling adventures, but quite soon my "story" ceased to be narcissistic in a crude way and became more and more a mere description of what I was doing and the things I saw. For minutes at a time this kind of thing would be running through my head: "He pushed the door open and entered the room. A yellow beam of sunlight, filtering through the muslin curtains, slanted on to the table, where a matchbox, half open, lay beside the inkpot. With his right hand in his pocket he moved across to the window. Down in the street a tortoiseshell cat was chasing a dead leaf," etc., etc. This habit continued till I was about twenty-five, right through my non-literary years. Although I had to search, and did search, for the right words, I seemed to be making this descriptive effort almost against my will, under a kind of compulsion from outside. The "story" must, I suppose, have reflected the styles of the various writers I admired at different ages, but so far as I remember it always had the same meticulous descriptive quality.

When I was about sixteen I suddenly discovered the joy of mere words, *i.e.* the sounds and associations of words. The lines from *Paradise Lost*—

> So hee with difficulty and labour hard
> Moved on: with difficulty and labour hee,

which do not now seem to me so very wonderful, sent shivers down my backbone; and the spelling "hee" for "he" was an added pleasure. As for the need to describe things, I knew all about it already. So it is clear what kind of books I wanted to write, in so far as I could be said to want to write books at that time. I wanted to write enormous naturalistic novels with unhappy endings, full of detailed descriptions and arresting similes, and also full of purple passages in which words were used partly for the sake of their sound. And in fact my first completed novel, *Burmese Days*, which I wrote when I was thirty but projected much earlier, is rather that kind of book.

I give all this background information because I do not think one can assess a writer's motives without knowing something of his early development. His subject matter will be determined by the age he lives in—at least this is true in tumultuous, revolutionary ages like our own—but before he ever begins to write he will have acquired an emotional attitude from which he will never completely escape. It is his job, no doubt, to discipline his temperament and avoid getting stuck at some immature stage, or in some perverse mood: but if he escapes from his early influences altogether, he will have killed his impulse to write. Putting aside the need to earn a living, I think there are four great motives for writing, at any rate for writing prose. They exist in different degrees in every writer, and in any one writer the proportions will vary from time to time, according to the atmosphere in which he is living. They are:

(1) Sheer egoism. Desire to seem clever, to be talked about, to be remembered after death, to get your own back on grownups who snubbed you in childhood, etc., etc. It is humbug to pretend that this is not a motive, and a strong one. Writers share this characteristic with scientists, artists, politicians, lawyers, soldiers, successful businessmen—in short, with the whole top crust of humanity. The great mass of human beings are not acutely selfish. After the age of about thirty they abandon individual ambition—in many cases, indeed, they almost abandon the sense of being individuals at all—and live chiefly for others, or are simply smothered under drudgery. But there is also the minority of gifted, wilful people who are determined to live their own lives to the end, and writers belong in this class. Serious writers, I should say, are on the whole more vain and self-centred than journalists, though less interested in money.

(2) Esthetic enthusiasm. Perception of beauty in the external world, or, on the other hand, in words and their right arrangement. Pleasure in the impact of one sound on another, in the firmness of good prose or the rhythm of a good story. Desire to share an experience which one feels is valuable and ought not to be missed. The esthetic motive is very feeble in a lot of writers, but even a pamphleteer or a writer of textbooks will have pet words and phrases which appeal to him for non-utilitarian reasons; or he may feel strongly about typography, width of margins, etc. Above the level of a railway guide, no book is quite free from esthetic considerations.

(3) Historical impulse. Desire to see things as they are, to find out true facts and store them up for the use of posterity.

(4) Political purpose—using the word "political" in the widest possible

sense. Desire to push the world in a certain direction, to alter other people's idea of the kind of society that they should strive after. Once again, no book is genuinely free from political bias. The opinion that art should have nothing to do with politics is itself a political attitude.

It can be seen how these various impulses must war against one another, and how they must fluctuate from person to person and from time to time. By nature—taking your "nature" to be the state you have attained when you are first adult—I am a person in whom the first three motives would outweigh the fourth. In a peaceful age I might have written ornate or merely descriptive books, and might have remained almost unaware of my political loyalties. As it is I have been forced into becoming a sort of pamphleteer. First I spent five years in an unsuitable profession (the Indian Imperial Police, in Burma), and then I underwent poverty and the sense of failure. This increased my natural hatred of authority and made me for the first time fully aware of the existence of the working classes, and the job in Burma had given me some understanding of the nature of imperialism: but these experiences were not enough to give me an accurate political orientation. Then came Hitler, the Spanish civil war, etc. By the end of 1935 I had still failed to reach a firm decision. I remember a little poem that I wrote at that date, expressing my dilemma:

> A happy vicar I might have been
> Two hundred years ago,
> To preach upon eternal doom
> And watch my walnuts grow;
>
> But born, alas, in an evil time,
> I missed that pleasant haven,
> For the hair has grown on my upper lip
> And the clergy are all clean-shaven.
>
> And later still the times were good,
> We were so easy to please,
> We rocked our troubled thoughts to sleep
> On the bosoms of the trees.
>
> All ignorant we dared to own
> The joys we now dissemble;
> The greenfinch on the apple bough
> Could make my enemies tremble.
>
> But girls' bellies and apricots,
> Roach in a shaded stream,
> Horses, ducks in flight at dawn,
> All these are a dream.
>
> It is forbidden to dream again;
> We maim our joys or hide them;

Horses are made of chromium steel
And little fat men shall ride them.

I am the worm who never turned,
The eunuch without a harem;
Between the priest and the commissar
I walk like Eugene Aram;

And the commissar is telling my fortune
While the radio plays,
But the priest has promised an Austin Seven,
For Duggie always pays.

I dreamed I dwelt in marble halls,
And woke to find it true;
I wasn't born for an age like this;
Was Smith? Was Jones? Were you?

The Spanish war and other events in 1936–7 turned the scale and thereafter I knew where I stood. Every line of serious work that I have written
since 1936 has been written, directly or indirectly, *against* totalitarianism and *for* democratic socialism, as I understand it. It seems to me nonsense, in a period like our own, to think that one can avoid writing of
such subjects. Everyone writes of them in one guise or another. It is simply a question of which side one takes and what approach one follows.
And the more one is conscious of one's political bias, the more chance
one has of acting politically without sacrificing one's esthetic and intellectual integrity.

What I have most wanted to do throughout the past ten years is to
make political writing into an art. My starting point is always a feeling
of partisanship, a sense of injustice. When I sit down to write a book, I
do not say to myself, "I am going to produce a work of art." I write it
because there is some lie that I want to expose, some fact to which I
want to draw attention, and my initial concern is to get a hearing. But
I could not do the work of writing a book, or even a long magazine
article, if it were not also an esthetic experience. Anyone who cares
to examine my work will see that even when it is downright propaganda
it contains much that a full-time politician would consider irrelevant.
I am not able, and I do not want, completely to abandon the world-view
that I acquired in childhood. So long as I remain alive and well I shall
continue to feel strongly about prose style, to love the surface of the
earth, and to take a pleasure in solid objects and scraps of useless information. It is no use trying to suppress that side of myself. The job is to
reconcile my ingrained likes and dislikes with the essentially public, non-
individual activities that this age forces on all of us.

It is not easy. It raises problems of construction and of language, and
it raises in a new way the problem of truthfulness. Let me give just

one example of the cruder kind of difficulty that arises. My book about the Spanish civil war, *Homage to Catalonia*, is, of course, a frankly political book, but in the main it is written with a certain detachment and regard for form. I did try very hard in it to tell the whole truth without violating my literary instincts. But among other things it contains a long chapter, full of newspaper quotations and the like, defending the Trotskyists who were accused of plotting with Franco. Clearly such a chapter, which after a year or two would lose its interest for any ordinary reader, must ruin the book. A critic whom I respect read me a lecture about it. "Why did you put in all that stuff?" he said. "You've turned what might have been a good book into journalism." What he said was true, but I could not have done otherwise. I happened to know, what very few people in England had been allowed to know, that innocent men were being falsely accused. If I had not been angry about that I should never have written the book.

In one form or another this problem comes up again. The problem of language is subtler and would take too long to discuss. I will only say that of late years I have tried to write less picturesquely and more exactly. In any case I find that by the time you have perfected any style of writing, you have always outgrown it. *Animal Farm* was the first book in which I tried, with full consciousness of what I was doing, to fuse political purpose and artistic purpose into one whole. I have not written a novel for seven years, but I hope to write another fairly soon. It is bound to be a failure, every book is a failure, but I do know with some clarity what kind of book I want to write.

Looking back through the last page or two, I see that I have made it appear as though my motives in writing were wholly public-spirited. I don't want to leave that as the final impression. All writers are vain, selfish and lazy, and at the very bottom of their motives there lies a mystery. Writing a book is a horrible, exhausting struggle, like a long bout of some painful illness. One would never undertake such a thing if one were not driven on by some demon whom one can neither resist nor understand. For all one knows that demon is simply the same instinct that makes a baby squall for attention. And yet it is also true that one can write nothing readable unless one constantly struggles to efface one's own personality. Good prose is like a window pane. I cannot say with certainty which of my motives are the strongest, but I know which of them deserve to be followed. And looking back through my work, I see that it is invariably where I lacked a *political* purpose that I wrote lifeless books and was betrayed into purple passages, sentences without meaning, decorative adjectives and humbug generally.

[1947]

THOMAS DE QUINCEY

❦

De Quincey (1785–1859) is most popularly known for his Confessions
of an English Opium-Eater *(1822), based on an addiction that had begun
with his taking opium for pain. He was, however, a very wide-ranging
writer on other subjects, and a good literary critic. He attended Oxford
University, became for a time closely associated with the poets Wordsworth and Coleridge, was a friend of the essayist Charles Lamb, and was
an important contributor to the leading literary periodicals of his time. It
is from a long review of* "The Works of Alexander Pope, Esquire. By
W. Roscoe, Esq." *in the August, 1848,* North British Review *that we take
the following passage, almost an essay in itself and traditionally given the
present title.*

THE LITERATURE OF KNOWLEDGE
AND THE LITERATURE OF POWER

What is it that we mean by *literature*? Popularly, and amongst the
thoughtless, it is held to include everything that is printed in a book.
Little logic is required to disturb *that* definition; the most thoughtless
person is easily made aware that in the idea of *literature* one essential
element is—some relation to a general and common interest of man,
so that what applies only to a local—or professional—or merely personal
interest, even though presenting itself in the shape of a book, will not
belong to literature. So far the definition is easily narrowed; and it is as
easily expanded. For not only is much that takes a station in books not
literature; but inversely, much that really *is* literature never reaches a
station in books. The weekly sermons of Christendom, that vast pulpit
literature which acts so extensively upon the popular mind—to warn,
to uphold, to renew, to comfort, to alarm, does not attain the sanctuary
of libraries in the ten thousandth part of its extent. The drama again,

as, for instance, the finest of Shakspere's plays in England, and all leading Athenian plays in the noontide of the Attic stage, operated as a literature on the public mind, and were (according to the strictest letter of that term) *published* through the audiences that witnessed[1] their representation some time before they were published as things to be read; and they were published in this scenical mode of publication with much more effect than they could have had as books, during ages of costly copying or of costly printing.

Books, therefore, do not suggest an idea co-extensive and interchangeable with the idea of literature; since much literature, scenic, forensic, or didactic, (as from lecturers and public orators,) may never come into books; and much that *does* come into books, may connect itself with no literary interest. But a far more important correction, applicable to the common vague idea of literature, is to be sought—not so much in a better definition of literature, as in a sharper distinction of the two functions which it fulfils. In that great social organ, which collectively we call literature, there may be distinguished two separate offices that may blend and often *do* so, but capable severally of a severe insulation, and naturally fitted for reciprocal repulsion. There is first the literature of *knowledge*, and secondly, the literature of *power*. The function of the first is—to *teach;* the function of the second is—to *move:* the first is a rudder, the second an oar or a sail. The first speaks to the *mere* discursive understanding; the second speaks ultimately it may happen to the higher understanding or reason, but always *through* affections of pleasure and sympathy. Remotely, it may travel towards an object seated in what Lord Bacon calls *dry* light; but proximately it does and must operate, else it ceases to be a literature of *power,* on and through that *humid* light which clothes itself in the mists and glittering *iris* of human passions, desires, and genial emotions. Men have so little reflected on the higher functions of literature, as to find it a paradox if one should describe it as a mean or subordinate purpose of books to give information. But this is a paradox only in the sense which makes it honourable to be paradoxical. Whenever we talk in ordinary language of seeking information or gaining knowledge, we understand the words as connected with something of absolute novelty. But it is the grandeur of all truth which *can* occupy a very high place in human interests, that it is never absolutely novel to the meanest of minds: it exists eternally by way of germ or latent principle in the lowest as in the highest, needing to be developed but never to be planted. To be capable of transplantation is the immediate criterion of a truth that ranges on a lower scale. Besides which, there is a rarer thing than truth, namely, *power* or deep sympathy

---

[1] Charles I., for example, when Prince of Wales, and many others in his father's court, gained their known familiarity with Shakspere—not through the original quartos, so slenderly diffused, nor through the first folio of 1623, but through the court representations of his chief dramas at Whitehall.

with truth. What is the effect, for instance, upon society—of children? By the pity, by the tenderness, and by the peculiar modes of admiration, which connect themselves with the helplessness, with the innocence, and with the simplicity of children, not only are the primal affections strengthened and continually renewed, but the qualities which are dearest in the sight of heaven—the frailty for instance, which appeals to forbearance, the innocence which symbolizes the heavenly, and the simplicity which is most alien from the worldly, are kept up in perpetual remembrance, and their ideals are continually refreshed. A purpose of the same nature is answered by the higher literature, viz. the literature of power. What do you learn from Paradise Lost? Nothing at all. What do you learn from a cookery-book? Something new, something that you did not know before, in every paragraph. But would you therefore put the wretched cookery-book on a higher level of estimation than the divine poem? What you owe to Milton is not any knowledge, of which a million separate items are still but a million of advancing steps on the same earthly level; what you owe—is *power*, that is, exercise and expansion to your own latent capacity of sympathy with the infinite, where every pulse and each separate influx is a step upwards—a step ascending as upon a Jacob's ladder from earth to mysterious altitudes above the earth. *All* the steps of knowledge, from first to last, carry you farther on the same plane, but could never raise you one foot above your ancient level of earth: whereas, the very *first* step in power is a flight —is an ascending into another element where earth is forgotten.

Were it not that human sensibilities are ventilated and continually called out into exercise by the great phenomena of infancy, or of real life as it moves through chance and change, or of literature as it recombines these elements in the mimicries of poetry, romance, &c., it is certain that, like any animal power or muscular energy falling into disuse, all such sensibilities would gradually droop and dwindle. It is in relation to these great *moral* capacities of man that the literature of power, as contra-distinguished from that of knowledge, lives and has its field of action. It is concerned with what is highest in man: for the Scriptures themselves never condescend to deal by suggestion or co-operation, with the mere discursive understanding: when speaking of man in his intellectual capa-city, the Scriptures speak not of the understanding, but of *"the under-standing heart,"*—making the heart, *i. e.*, the great *intuitive* (or non-dis-cursive) organ, to be the interchangeable formula for man in his highest state of capacity for the infinite. Tragedy, romance, fairy-tale, or epopee, all alike restore to man's mind the ideals of justice, of hope, of truth, of mercy, of retribution, which else, (left to the support of daily life in its realities,) would languish for want of sufficient illustration. What is meant for instance by *poetic justice?*—It does not mean a justice that differs by its object from the ordinary justice of human jurisprudence; for then it must be confessedly a very bad kind of justice; but it means a justice that differs from common forensic justice by the degree in which it *attains* its object, a justice that is more omnipotent over its own ends, as dealing—not with the refractory elements of earthly life—but with elements of its own creation, and with materials flexible to its own purest preconceptions. It is certain that, were it not for the literature of power, these ideals would often remain amongst us as mere arid notional forms; whereas, by the creative forces of man put forth in literature, they gain a vernal life of restoration, and germinate into vital activities. The commonest novel, by moving in alliance with human fears and hopes, with human instincts of wrong and right, sustains and quickens those affections. Calling them into action, it rescues them from torpor. And hence the pre-eminency over all authors that merely *teach,* of the meanest that *moves;* or that teaches, if at all, indirectly *by* moving. The very highest work that has ever existed in the literature of knowledge, is but a *provisional* work: a book upon trial and sufferance, and *quamdiu bene se gesserit.* Let its teaching be even partially revised, let it be but expanded, nay, even let its teaching be but placed in a better order, and instantly it is superseded. Whereas the feeblest works in the literature of power, surviving at all, survive as finished and unalterable amongst men. For instance, the *Principia* of Sir Isaac Newton was a book *militant* on earth from the first. In all stages of its progress it would have to fight for its existence: 1*st,* as regards absolute truth; 2*dly,* when that combat is over, as regards its form or mode of presenting the truth. And as soon as a La Place, or anybody else, builds higher upon the foundations laid by this book, effectually he throws it out of the sunshine into decay and darkness; by weapons won from this book he superannuates and destroys this book, so that soon the name of Newton remains, as a mere *nominis umbra,* but his book, as a living power, has transmigrated into other forms. Now, on the contrary, the Iliad, the Prometheus of Æschylus,—the Othello or King Lear,—the Hamlet or Macbeth,—and the Paradise Lost, are not militant but triumphant for ever as long as the languages exist in which they speak or can be taught to speak. They never *can* transmigrate into new incarnations. To reproduce *these* in new forms, or variations, even if in some things they should be improved, would be to plagiarize. A good steam-engine is properly superseded by a better. But one lovely pastoral valley is not superseded by another, nor a statue of Praxiteles by a statue of Michael Angelo. These things are not separated by imparity, but by disparity. They are not thought of as unequal under the same standard, but as differing in *kind,* and as equal under a different standard. Human works of immortal beauty and works of nature in one respect stand on the same footing: they never absolutely repeat each other: never approach so near as not to differ; and they differ not as better and worse, or simply by more and less: they differ by undecipherable and incommunicable differences, that cannot be caught by mimicries, nor be reflected in the mirror of copies, nor become ponderable in the scales of vulgar comparison.

Applying these principles to Pope, as a representative of fine literature in general, we would wish to remark the claim which he has, or which any equal writer has, to the attention and jealous winnowing of those critics in particular who watch over public morals. Clergymen, and all the organs of public criticism put in motion by clergymen, are more especially concerned in the just appreciation of such writers, if the two canons are remembered, which we have endeavoured to illustrate, viz., that all works in this class, as opposed to those in the literature of knowledge, 1st, work by far deeper agencies; and, 2dly, are more permanent; in the strictest sense they are κτηματα ἐς ἀει [possessions forever]: and what evil they do, or what good they do, is commensurate with the national language, sometimes long after the nation has departed. At this hour, 500 years since their creation, the tales of Chaucer,[2] never equalled on this earth for tenderness, and for life of picturesqueness, are read familiarly by many in the charming language of their natal day, and by others in the modernizations of Dryden, of Pope, and Wordsworth. At this hour, 1800 years since their creation, the Pagan tales of Ovid, never equalled on this earth for the gaiety of their movement and the capricious graces of their narrative, are read by all Christendom. This man's people and their monuments are dust: but *he* is alive: he has survived them, as he told us that he had it in his commission to do, by a thousand years; "and *shall* a thousand more."

All the literature of knowledge builds only ground-nests, that are swept away by floods, or confounded by the plough; but the literature of power builds nests in aerial altitudes of temples sacred from violation, or of forests inaccessible to fraud. *This* is a great prerogative of the *power* literature: and it is a greater which lies in the mode of its influence. The *knowledge* literature, like the fashion of this world, passeth away. An Encyclopædia is its abstract; and, in this respect, it may be taken for its speaking symbol—that, before one generation has passed, an Encyclopædia is superannuated; for it speaks through the dead memory and unimpassioned understanding, which have not the *rest* of higher faculties, but are continually enlarging and varying their phylacteries. But all literature, properly so called—literature κατ᾽ ἐξοχην [i.e., great literature], for the very same reason that it is so much more durable than the literature of knowledge, is (and by the very same proportion it is) more intense and electrically searching in its impressions. The directions in which the tragedy of this planet has trained our human feelings to play, and the combinations into which the poetry of this planet has thrown our human passions of love and hatred, of admiration and contempt, exercises

---

[2] The Canterbury Tales were not made public until 1380 or thereabouts: but the composition must have cost 30 or more years; not to mention that the work had probably been finished for some years before it was divulged.

a power bad or good over human life, that cannot be contemplated when seen stretching through many generations, without a sentiment allied to awe.[3] And of this let every one be assured—that he owes to the impassioned books which he has read, many a thousand more of emotions than he can consciously trace back to them. Dim by their origination, these emotions yet arise in him, and mould him through life like the forgotten incidents of childhood.

---

[3] The reason why the broad distinctions between the two literatures of power and knowledge so little fix the attention, lies in the fact, that a vast proportion of books—history, biography, travels, miscellaneous essays, &c., lying in a middle zone, confound these distinctions by interblending them. All that we call "amusement" or "entertainment," is a diluted form of the power belonging to passion, and also a mixed form; and where threads of direct *instruction* intermingle in the texture with these threads of *power*, this absorption of the duality into one representative *nuance* neutralises the separate perception of either. Fused into a *tertium quid*, or neutral state, they disappear to the popular eye as the repelling forces, which in fact they are.

WALTER PATER

Pater (1839–1894) spent most of his life as a student and Fellow at Oxford. His great reputation as an essayist and critic is partly based on the many articles on literature and art he published in the serious reviews of his time. A trip to Italy in 1865 sharpened his already great interest in the visual arts, and his resulting essays on renaissance subjects were collected and published in 1873 as Studies in the History of the Renaissance. The present essay is the book's "Conclusion," as it appeared in the third edition of this work (1888). It was printed with the following note: "This brief 'Conclusion' was omitted in the second edition of this book, as I conceived it might possibly mislead some of those young men into whose hands it might fall. On the whole, I have thought it best to reprint it here, with some slight changes which bring it closer to my original meaning. I have dealt more fully in Marius the Epicurean with the thoughts suggested by it." Marius the Epicurean is Pater's most famous longer work, a "philosophical romance" about the intellectual and spiritual life of a young Roman of the time of Marcus Aurelius. It is written in the rich, polished *style for which Pater is noted, and expounds in great detail the author's own philosophy of beauty.*

CONCLUSION FROM
THE RENAISSANCE

Λέγει που Ἡράκλειτος ὅτι πάντα χωρεῖ καὶ οὐδὲν μένει

[Heraclitus says somewhere that all things move and nothing stays]

To regard all things and principles of things as inconstant modes or fashions has more and more become the tendency of modern thought. Let us begin with that which is without—our physical life. Fix upon it in one of its more exquisite intervals, the moment, for instance, of delicious recoil from the flood of water in summer heat. What is the whole physical life in that moment but a combination of natural elements to which science gives their names? But these elements, phosphorus and lime and delicate fibres, are present not in the human body alone: we detect them in places most remote from it. Our physical life is a perpetual motion of them— the passage of the blood, the wasting and repairing of the lenses of the eye, the modification of the tissues of the brain by every ray of light and sound—processes which science reduces to simpler and more elementary forces. Like the elements of which we are composed, the action of these forces extends beyond us; it rusts iron and ripens corn. Far out on every side of us those elements are broadcast, driven by many forces; and birth and gesture and death and the springing of violets from the grave are but a few out of ten thousand resultant combinations. That clear, perpetual outline of face and limb is but an image of ours, under which we group them—a design in a web, the actual threads of which pass out beyond it. This at least of flamelike our life has, that it is but the concurrence, renewed from moment to moment, of forces parting sooner or later on their ways.

Or if we begin with the inward world of thought and feeling, the whirlpool is still more rapid, the flame more eager and devouring. There it is no longer the gradual darkening of the eye and fading of colour from the wall,—the movement of the shore-side, where the water flows down indeed, though in apparent rest,—but the race of the midstream, a drift of momentary acts of sight and passion and thought. At first sight experience seems to bury us under a flood of external objects, pressing upon us with a sharp and importunate reality, calling us out of ourselves in a thousand forms of action. But when reflexion begins to act upon those objects they are dissipated under its influence; the cohesive force seems suspended like a trick of magic; each object is loosed into a group of impressions—colour, odour, texture—in the mind of the observer. And if we continue to dwell in thought on this world, not of objects in the solidity with which language invests them, but of impressions unstable, flickering, inconsistent, which burn and are extinguished with our consciousness of them, it contracts still further; the whole scope of observation is dwarfed to the narrow chamber of the individual mind. Experience, already reduced to a swarm of impressions, is ringed round for each one of us by that thick wall of personality through which no real voice has ever pierced on its way to us, or from us to that which we can only conjecture to be without. Every one of those impressions is the impression of the individual in his isolation, each mind keeping as a solitary prisoner its own dream of a world. Analysis goes a step farther still, and assures us that those impressions of the individual mind to which, for each one of us, experience dwindles down, are in perpetual flight; that each of them is limited by time, and that as time is infinitely divisible, each of them is infinitely divisible also; all that is actual in it being a single moment, gone while we try to apprehend it, of which it may ever be more truly said that it has ceased to be than that it is. To such a tremulous wisp constantly reforming itself on the stream, to a single sharp impression, with a sense in it, a relic more or less fleeting, of such moments gone by, what is real in our life fines itself down. It is with this movement, with the passage and dissolution of impressions, images, sensations, that analysis leaves off—that continual vanishing away, that strange, perpetual weaving and unweaving of ourselves.

Philosophiren, says Novalis, *ist dephlegmatisiren vivificiren*. The service of philosophy, of speculative culture, towards the human spirit is to rouse, to startle it into sharp and eager observation. Every moment some form grows perfect in hand or face; some tone on the hills or the sea is choicer than the rest; some mood of passion or insight or intellectual excitement is irresistibly real and attractive for us,—for that moment only. Not the fruit of experience, but experience itself, is the end. A counted number of pulses only is given to us of a variegated, dramatic life. How may we see in them all that is to be seen in them by the finest senses? How shall we pass most swiftly from point to point, and be present always at the focus where the greatest number of vital forces unite in their purest energy?

To burn always with this hard, gemlike flame, to maintain this ecstasy, is success in life. In a sense it might even be said that our failure is to form habits: for, after all, habit is relative to a stereotyped world, and meantime it is only the roughness of the eye that makes any two persons, things, situations, seem alike. While all melts under our feet, we may well catch at any exquisite passion, or any contribution to knowledge that seems by a lifted horizon to set the spirit free for a moment, or any stirring of the senses, strange dyes, strange colours, and curious odours, or work of the artist's hands, or the face of one's friend. Not to discriminate every moment some passionate attitude in those about us, and in the brilliancy of their gifts some tragic dividing of forces on their ways, is, on this short day of frost and sun, to sleep before evening. With this sense of the splendour of our experience and of its awful brevity, gathering all we are into one desperate effort to see and touch, we shall hardly have time to make theories about the things we see and touch. What we have to do is to be for ever curiously testing new opinions and courting new impressions, never acquiescing in a facile orthodoxy of Comte, or of Hegel, or of our own. Philosophical theories or ideas, as points of view, instruments of criticism, may help us to gather up what might otherwise pass unregarded by us. "Philosophy is the microscope of thought." The theory or idea or system which requires of us the sacrifice of any part of this experience, in consideration of some interest into which we cannot enter, or some abstract theory we have not identified with ourselves, or what is only conventional, has no real claim upon us.

One of the most beautiful passages in the writings of Rousseau is that in the sixth book of the *Confessions*, where he describes the awakening in him of the literary sense. An undefinable taint of death had always clung about him, and now in early manhood he believed himself smitten by mortal disease. He asked himself how he might make as much as possible of the interval that remained; and he was not biassed by anything in his previous life when he decided that it must be by intellectual excitement, which he found just then in the clear, fresh writings of Voltaire. Well! we are all *condamnés*, as Victor Hugo says: we are all under sentence of death but with a sort of indefinite reprieve—*les hommes sont tous condamnés à mort avec des sursis indéfinis:* we have an interval, and then our place knows us no more. Some spend this interval in listlessness, some in high passions, the wisest, at least among "the children of this world," in art and song. For our one chance lies in expanding that interval, in getting as many pulsations as possible into the given time. Great passions may give us this quickened sense of life, ecstasy and sorrow of love, the various forms of enthusiastic activity, disinterested or otherwise, which come naturally to many of us. Only be sure it is passion—that it does yield you this fruit of a quickened, multiplied consciousness. Of this wisdom, the poetic passion, the desire of beauty, the love of art for art's sake, has most; for art comes to you professing frankly to give nothing but the highest quality to your moments as they pass, and simply for those moments' sake.

INDEX

RUTH BENEDICT was born in New York City in 1887. After receiving a B.A. degree from Vassar, she taught English in a girls' school and wrote and published some poetry under the name Anne Singleton. In 1914 she married Stanley R. Benedict, a biochemist. Five years later, at the age of thirty-two, Mrs. Benedict enrolled at Columbia, apparently because she wanted "busy work." Thus, almost by accident, she began the study of anthropology under Franz Boas, whom she later described as "the greatest of living anthropologists." She completed her doctorate in 1923 and immediately joined the faculty of Columbia, where she remained until her death in 1948. Mrs. Benedict's research, conducted on periodic field trips, made her a leading authority on the Indians of the American West. She has also been considered a pathfinder in her awareness of the relationship between anthropology and such other social sciences as psychology and sociology. Some books by Mrs. Benedict are *The Concept of Guardian Spirit in North America* (1923), *Patterns of Culture* (1934), *Zuñi Mythology* (1935), *Race: Science and Politics* (1940), and *The Chrysanthemum and the Sword* (1946).

WILLIAM FAULKNER (1897–1962) lived most of his life in Oxford, Mississippi. He left high school to work in his grandfather's bank, served as a pilot in the Royal Canadian Air Force during World War I, and enrolled at the University of Mississippi in the fall of 1919 but withdrew without taking a degree. Discouraged at trying to earn a living by writing, he took a job as night superintendent of a power plant in the summer of 1929. The publication of the novel *Sanctuary* the next year won him a popular following, financial security, and marked the turning point of his career, which culminated in his receiving the Nobel Prize for literature in 1949. From 1957 until his death in 1962 he was a writer in residence at the University of Virginia.

In *Sartoris* (1929), Faulkner first created Yoknapatawpha, a fictional Mississippi county which became the locale for a number of his best novels. His fiction is vividly memorable for its unique style and its dense, uncompromising portrayal of Southern life. Some of his best known books are *The Sound and the Fury* (1929); *As I Lay Dying* (1930); *Absalom, Absalom!* (1936); *Light in August* (1950); The Snopes Trilogy: *The Hamlet* (1940), *The Town* (1957), and *The Mansion* (1959); and *A Fable* (1954), for which he received the Pulitzer Prize.

MAX LERNER was born in Minsk, Russia, in 1902 and was brought to the United States in 1907. He received his B.A. from Yale in 1923 and studied law there. In 1927 he received the Ph.D. from the Brookings Graduate School of Economics and Government in Washington, D.C. He has taught at Sarah Lawrence, Harvard, and Williams, and is presently Professor of American Civilization at Brandeis University, where he has also served as Dean of the Graduate School. He has pursued a lively journalistic career between and during stints of teaching. He edited *The Nation* from 1936 to 1938, was a radio commentator and editor of *PM* from 1943 to 1948, columnist for the *New York Star* in 1948 and 1949, and since 1949 a world-wide syndicated columnist for the *New York Post*. Among his many books are *It Is Later Than You Think* (1938), *America as a Civilization* (1957), and *The Age of Overkill* (1962).

CHARLES MUSCATINE is Professor of English at the University of California at Berkeley, where he has taught since 1948. He received the Ph.D. from Yale University and has served as a Visiting Professor at Wesleyan University and the University of Washington. A distinguished medievalist, Professor Muscatine is the author of *Chaucer and the French Tradition* and *The Book of Geoffrey Chaucer* and has published widely in professional journals. He has been chairman of the Committee on Freshman English at Berkeley, and was co-author and editor of *Education at Berkeley*, the report of the faculty's Select Committee on Education.

MARLENE GRIFFITH received her B.A. from American International College in Springfield, Mass., and her M.A. from the University of California at Berkeley. Since 1959 she has taught Humanities and expository and creative writing at Western College for Women, at San Francisco State College, at Berkeley, and at Laney College, Oakland, where she is now a member of the Department of English. She has been a contributor to *College Composition and Communication*, *Twentieth Century Literature*, and *Modern Fiction Studies*.

A NOTE ON THE TYPE

The text of this book was set on the Linotype in Janson, a recutting made direct from type cast from matrices long thought to have been made by the Dutchman Anton Janson, who was a practicing type founder in Leipzig during the years 1668–87. However, it has been conclusively demonstrated that these types are actually the work of Nicholas Kis (1650–1702), a Hungarian, who most probably learned his trade from the master Dutch type founder Dirk Voskens. The type is an excellent example of the influential and sturdy Dutch types that prevailed in England up to the time William Caslon developed his own incomparable designs from these Dutch faces.

This book was composed by The Haddon Craftsmen, Inc., Scranton, Pa., printed and bound by Kingsport Press, Kingsport, Tennessee.